Gender and emotion

When is someone called emotional? Why is it generally accepted that women are emotional and men are not? What are the actual differences between men and women with regard to specific emotions? Under what circumstances are these differences most pronounced? How can we explain these alleged differences? In this book a distinguished international group of scholars seek to address these and other questions in an attempt to disentangle the complex and fascinating relationship between gender and emotion. Presenting a systematic overview of the most recent social psychological research in this field, the contributors combine empirical evidence and theoretical explanations to examine a wide range of emotions and emotional expressions and how they vary according to gender and context.

STUDIES IN EMOTION AND SOCIAL INTERACTION

Second Series

Series Editors

Keith Oatley
University of Toronto

Antony Manstead
University of Amsterdam

This series is jointly published by the Cambridge University Press and the Editions de la Maison des Sciences de l'Homme, as part of the joint publishing agreement established in 1977 between the Foundation de la Maison des Sciences de l'Homme and the Syndics of the Cambridge University Press.

Cette publication est publiée co-édition par Cambridge University Press et les Editions de la Maison des Sciences de l'Homme. Elle s'intègre dans le programme de co-édition établi en 1977 par la Fondation de la Maison des Sciences de l'Homme et les Syndics de Cambridge University Press.

Titles published in the Second Series

The Psychology of Facial Expression
0 521 496675 hardback and 0 521 587 964 paperback
Edited by James A. Russell and José Miguel Fernández-Dois

Emotions, the Social Bond, and Human Reality: Part/Whole Analysis
0 521 584914 hardback and 0 521 584547 paperback
Thomas J. Scheff

Intersubjective Communication and Emotion in Early Ontogeny
0 521 622573 hardback and 2 7351 07728 hardback (France only)
Edited by Stein Bråten

Emotion Across Languages and Cultures: Diversity and Universals
0 521 590426 hardback and 0 521 599717 paperback
Anna Wierzbicka

Gender and emotion:

Social psychological perspectives

Edited by
Agneta H. Fischer

CAMBRIDGE
UNIVERSITY PRESS

& Editions de la Maison des Sciences de l'Homme
Paris

PUBLISHED BY THE PRESS SYNDICATE OF THE UNIVERSITY OF CAMBRIDGE
The Pitt Building, Trumpington Street, Cambridge, United Kingdom
and
EDITIONS DE LA MAISON DES SCIENCES DE L'HOMME
54 Boulevard Raspail, 75270 Paris Cedex 06, France

CAMBRIDGE UNIVERSITY PRESS
The Edinburgh Building, Cambridge CB2 2RU, UK   http://www.cup.cam.ac.uk
40 West 20th Street, New York, NY 10011–4211, USA   http://www.cup.org
10 Stamford Road, Oakleigh, Melbourne 3166, Australia

First published 2000

Printed in the United Kingdom at the University Press, Cambridge

Typeset in 10/12 pt Palatino in QuarkXPress® [SE]

A catalogue record for this book is available from the British Library

Library of Congress cataloguing in Publication data

Gender and emotion: social psychological perspectives / [edited by]
Agneta H. Fischer.
     p.   cm. – (Studies in emotion and social interaction. Second
series)
   Includes bibliographical references and index.
   ISBN 0–521–63015–0 (hardback) – ISBN 0–521–63986–7 (paperback)
   1. Expression – Sex differences.   2. Emotions – Sex differences.
I. Fischer, Agneta, 1958–   .   II. Series.
BF591.G45   2000
155.3'3–dc21   00-29140   CIP

ISBN 0 521 63015 0 hardback
ISBN 0 521 63986 7 paperback

To Luca and Sandro

Contents

vii

Preface

I have never understood why women are thought to be "the emotional sex." As far back as I can remember I have encountered emotional men; indeed, I have met more emotional men than emotional women. My father could not control his nerves while watching our national sports heroes on television (which made watching hardly bearable); my uncle immediately got damp eyes on hearing the first note of the Dutch national anthem; a friend would lock himself in his room for days when angry; a teacher at school once got so furious that he dragged a pupil out of the class room and hung him up by his clothes on a coat-hook; one of the male managers at our institute was only able to prevent having a nervous breakdown by rigidly trying to exercise total control over his environment; and a male colleague's constant embarrassment in public situations forced him to avoid such settings altogether. I submit that these men are not simply exceptions that confirm the rule; nor are they just extraordinary cases who happened to be part of my personal environment. Emotional behavior on the part of men is simply not that uncommon.

I can hear you asking, "but what about the women?" Of course, I could easily add observations about the emotional behavior of women. However, my point is simply to demonstrate that the notion that women are considered to be the emotional sex, whereas men are not, is not self-evidently true. Stephanie Shields was one of the first authors to put this issue on the research agenda of psychologists. She argued that the statement that women are considered emotional and men rational "is recognized in everyday life as Natural Law; scientifically it remains untested" (Shields, 1987, p. 231). Since then, research on gender and emotions has expanded, investigating such questions as "When do people call someone 'emotional'?", "What are the reasons for the persistence of this dichotomy between emotional women and unemotional men?"; "What are the actual differences between men and women with respect to various specific emotions?"; "In which circumstances do these differences come to the fore?"; and "How can we explain the alleged differences in emotional reactions between men and women?"

In this book the authors address these and other questions, in an effort to disentangle the centuries-old, always fascinating, and often complex relationship between gender and emotions.

The aim of this book is to summarize existing knowledge and to stimulate current debate on gender and emotions in the social and psychological domain by presenting an overview of current research, by critically reviewing existing theoretical explanations and research questions, and by raising new issues and questions. The focus of the present volume is social psychological in its broadest sense, including developmental, cultural, and physiological approaches. The reason for adopting a disciplinary focus, rather than extending the volume to sociological, biological, or cultural anthropological perspectives, is not that the latter perspectives are regarded as unimportant, but rather that it seemed to me to be the right moment for a more specific focus, enabling authors to specify their knowledge and analyses at a particular level of analysis, namely that of social interaction.

I am very much indebted to the contributing authors, all of them acknowledged experts in the field, who have invested a great deal of effort to help make this book what I hoped it would be: a compelling, useful, and inspiring source of research and theorizing in the area of gender and emotions. I especially want to thank Kay Deaux who kindly agreed to serve as a referee and who wrote the final overview chapter. Two other authors also deserve special thanks: Jeroen Jansz and Tony Manstead. They have shared many emotions concerning this book with me, they have supported me in many ways, and they never have let me down.

I dedicate this book to my two sons, who in their daily displays of a vast array of emotions have triggered my curiosity and sharpened my observations.

Agneta H. Fischer
Amsterdam, January 1999

Contributors

Michele G. Alexander   University of Maine, USA
Leslie R. Brody   Boston University, USA
Janine P. Buckner   Emory University, Atlanta, USA
Jason D. Carter   Northeastern University, Boston, USA
Kay Deaux   City University New York, USA
Heidi L. Eyre   Simon Fraser University, Burnaby, British Columbia
Lisa Feldman Barrett   Boston College, USA
Tamara J. Ferguson   Utah State University, Logan, USA
Robyn Fivush   Emory University, Atlanta, USA
Agneta H. Fischer   University of Amsterdam, the Netherlands
Judy A. Hall   Northeastern University, Boston, USA
Marvin Hecht   Louisiana College, Pineville, USA
Terrence G. Horgan   Northeastern University, Boston, USA
Jeroen Jansz   Leiden University, the Netherlands
Ann M. Kring   Vanderbilt University, Nashville, USA
Marianne LaFrance   Yale University, New Haven, USA
Tracey E. Madden   Boston College, USA
Antony S. R. Manstead   University of Amsterdam, the Netherlands
Paula R. Pietromonaco   University of Massachusetts, Amherst, USA
Jan Scheirs   Tilburg University, The Netherlands
Stephanie A. Shields   Pennsylvania State University, USA
Ad Vingerhoets   Tilburg University, The Netherlands
Wendy Wood   Texas A&M University, USA.
Vanda L. Zammuner   University of Padova, Padova, Italy

PART I

Culture, gender, and emotional beliefs

1. Thinking about gender, thinking about theory: Gender and emotional experience

STEPHANIE A. SHIELDS

In 1996 the US Supreme Court ruled on a case concerning the Virginia Military Institute (VMI), a state-supported public college. The college had admitted only male students since its nineteenth-century founding, and was resisting pressure to become co-educational. A legal challenge to sex-segregation ensued, and the arguments made by the defendant's side are particularly pertinent to the study of emotion. The case was hotly debated and watched across the country, in part because the institution is very prestigious within the state of Virginia, and the networks of power in that state include many VMI alumni. The record of arguments to sustain publicly supported sex discrimination in access to study is replete with sex stereotypes, and a generous portion of those arguments hinge on generalizations about emotion. According to reports in the *Chronicle of Higher Education*, witnesses for Virginia testified in the lower courts that VMI "was not suitable for most women, because, compared with men, women are more emotional, less aggressive, suffer more from fear of failure, and cannot withstand stress as well" (Greenberger & Blake, 1996, p. A52). The sweeping generalizations about the emotions of women, evident in witness statements and *amicus curiae* briefs, are illustrated in the testimony of one educator who confidently concluded that "women are not capable of the ferocity requisite to make the program work, and they are also not capable of enduring without . . . psychological trauma" (Greenberger & Blake, 1996, p. A52). Fears of women's emotions running amok notwithstanding, the court ruled against VMI and in favor of the admission of women.[1]

This example drawn from contemporary life illustrates the significant role played by popular conceptions of differences between women's and men's emotional lives. The reiteration of stereotypes is, however, just the surface of what the VMI case reveals. At a deeper level this case reveals the prevailing Western conception of emotion as internal to the person, whether through "having emotion" as a felt experience or

3

"being emotional" as a disposition to feel (Parrott, 1995). The equation of emotion with feeling brings with it a set of presuppositions about the controllability, rationality, and expression of that feeling. And at a deeper level still, the VMI case illustrates an intimate connection between the complexities of beliefs about gender and emotion and the arrogation of those beliefs in the maintenance (and potentially the subversion) of structures of social power. The motif of gender and emotion, especially gender differences, prominent in popular culture, is also visible in the legal and social arrangements of contemporary US society. Indeed, beliefs about emotion are marshaled in the defense of the status quo whenever gender boundaries are threatened. In the VMI case, the stakes were clearly access to power through political and social networks within the state of Virginia.

The richness of the VMI example illustrates the directions in which the study of gender and emotion can develop within psychology. Over the past decade we have seen not only a dramatic increase in the study of emotion, but also a correspondingly increased interest in examining how gender and emotion may be linked. Much of this work, especially in US psychology, has approached the topic from the conventional and traditional framework of trait-based sex differences (as in, for example, framing the research question as one of "Which sex is more emotional?") or gender and psychopathologies that have some emotive component (as in the examination of sex differences in rates of depression). Some of the more innovative work has turned to the question of the relation between beliefs about emotion, especially gender stereotypes, and the "real" operation of emotion in human life. Study of stereotypes breaks with the trait-based tradition and in so doing, opens up new areas of questions for research. Such new areas may include, for example, mapping the complexity and conditions under which those stereotypes are operative in the acquisition and practice of gender-coded behavior (e.g., Fischer, 1993; Robinson, Johnson, & Shields, 1998; Shields, 1987). By "gender coded" I mean behavior or experience that is believed to be more typical, natural, or appropriate for one sex than the other.[2] Examination of gender stereotypes, however, is just the first step in advancing theory on gender and emotion. Psychology now needs to bring theoretical and methodological sophistication to a new level.

In this chapter I examine four promising themes for furthering study of the links between gender and emotion:

1 context as a framework for interpreting experience;
2 the salience of interpersonal relationships in accounts of emotion;
3 how interactional goals produce and maintain gender effects in emotion;
4 power as an explanatory variable.

Each of the themes can be discerned already in the sometimes method-ologically messy and often atheoretical earlier work on sex-related dif-ferences in emotion; each has been developed to some degree in the emerging literature that takes theory of gendered emotion seriously and centrally within a larger psychology of human emotion. My goal here is to move the discussion forward. I consider each theme particu-larly in terms of emotional experience. Research concerned with emo-tional experience is especially informative, not only because of the Western equation of emotion with felt experience, but because of the significance of gender coded beliefs about emotional experience in grounding people's understanding of their own and others' experi-enced emotion.

I must begin, however, with a set of caveats. My focus is on the psychology of emotion, where most of the work is based on US and European samples. While this can give us some clue as to cross-national trends, we must be very cautious before generalizing across cultures or historical times. My conclusions are thus limited to practices within contemporary Westernized post-industrial society. My second caveat concerns the limitations with which we can represent "contemporary Westernized post-industrial society." In nearly all of the research I draw on here, neither racial ethnicity nor class are theorized variables. Like many other areas of psychology, the presumptive "human adult" is white and, if adult, is more than likely a university student. The study of emotion is not unlike other areas of psychology in which a consider-ation of race, class, and ethnicity is honored in the breach, largely through apologetic paragraphs such as this one. Insertion of an apolo-getic note is not a solution. Focusing on gender while bracketing social class, racial ethnicity, and other within-gender differences, what Parlee (1995) calls "gender-with-brackets-on," acknowledges the issues raised, but in doing so sets them outside the "normal" course of inquiry (see also Yoder & Kahn, 1993; Wyche, 1998).

Mapping domains: Gender, emotion, and experience

Before turning to the four themes, it is helpful to map out briefly some pertinent trends in recent work on gender, emotion, and expe-rience.

Gender and emotion

The psychology of gender has evolved over the past 20 years from descriptive cataloging of "sex differences" (and similarities) to become an exciting area of inquiry (see, for example, Deaux & LaFrance, 1997).

Whereas theory of 20 years ago assumed gender to be simply a stable and trait-like component of identity, recent theorizing construes gender as an ongoing enactment. That is, gender is something that one practices (in nearly every sense of the word), rather than only what one inflexibly is. This new view of gender takes research beyond the descriptive ("How much do women and men differ?") by shifting the focus to variables that mediate when and how gender effects occur ("What drives the occurrence and magnitude of difference?"). The question that underlies this notion of gender as a practice, as a performance, is a question of how "gender" is accomplished and made to seem natural. With the focus on contextual variables that mediate when and how gender effects occur, research becomes concerned with a new set of questions: Under what conditions does gender matter? What is at stake in those situations?

An analogous shift in the study of emotion over the past two decades has particular resonance with the psychology of gender. Emotion, too, has come to be viewed as fundamentally a social process, a shift which brings with it a renewed focus on the contexts within which emotion occurs. The theme of emotion as a feature of relationships is especially evident in developmental psychology (e.g., Saarni, 1989). Joseph Campos notes that the new psychology of emotion is characterized by "postulation of a close interrelation between emotion and the goals and strivings of the person; its emphasis on emotional expressions as social signals; and the hypothesis that the physiology of emotion, far from involving only homeostasis and the internal milieu, can regulate and be regulated by, social processes" (Campos, 1994, p. 1). The move towards viewing emotion as essentially social has become as readily embraced by theorists who espouse an evolutionary perspective as by those who work from a social constructionist perspective (see, for example, Oatley & Jenkins, 1996, for summary of the range of current emotion theories).

One manifestation of the rediscovery of emotion as a social phenomenon is a new emphasis on the intersection of emotion and gender. The first indication that there was much to be gained by investigating this intersection were several reviews that aimed to make some sort of theoretical sense out of a literature that largely had grown out of atheoretical investigations of sex-related differences (Brody, 1985; Brody & Hall, 1993; LaFrance & Banaji, 1992; Manstead, 1992; Shields, 1991). These reviews set out to go beyond simply cataloging gender differences to examine gender effects within some sort of organizing theoretical or methodological framework: Manstead (1992) employs an individual differences approach to organize an evaluation of gender effects in emotional expressiveness, physiological response, and emotion concepts; La France and Banaji (1992) use methodological analysis as a basis for examining how self-presentation and self-verification account for gender effects in self-reports of emotion; Brody and Hall (1993) employ a developmental model of socialization to explain the acquisition of gender-stereotypic emotion behavior and attitudes. In my own work I examine how emotion values and language are central to the concepts of femininity and masculinity and, as such, to the acquisition and practice of gender-coded behavior (Shields, 1991; 1995).[3]

What is emotional "experience"?

A persistent question in the study of emotion concerns the properties of emotion that signal its distinctiveness as a state of consciousness; that is, what makes emotion a "vivid, unforgettable condition" experienced as uniquely different from nonemotive states (Duffy, 1941)? Theories of emotion consciousness (i.e., experienced emotion; "felt" emotion) are by no means in agreement on what constitutes the experiential component of emotion. For example, debate revolves around questions such as the extent to which emotion consciousness is a necessary or an integrated part of emotion processes, whether awareness is necessary to "experience," and which are the defining feature(s) of emotion consciousness (see, for example, Ekman & Davidson, 1994 for a sample of the range of points of view that prevail in Western emotions research). Even if the questions about emotion consciousness were, in fact, settled, measurement of the subjective side of emotion inevitably depends on a second-degree inference: emotional experience cannot be directly measured by the researcher, only inferred from the respondent's representation of her or his experience in language (or para-language or proto-language) or the embodiment of that experience in physiological or expressive activity. Fundamental questions of definition and function notwithstanding, a significant body of research has been concerned with mapping the preconditions, dimensions, and outcomes of emotional experience.

The representation of experience is both less and more than the emotion *qua* "experience." Because they are necessarily representations, indices of emotional "experience" are always inference based, for others and for the self. This is true whether the index is the respondent's verbal representation of experience in the form of numerical ratings of emotion labels (e.g., "How angry on a scale of 1 to 7?") or a self-generated narrative of felt emotion. Reported experience is not a direct read-out of feeling, but the outcome of a set of judgments (see for example, Solomon, 1993). Similarly, the investigator's assessment of the respondent's expressive behavior or physiological responses is constituted of judgments about the respondent's subjective experience and that which the investigator can see and measure. Keeping this fact in mind as a cautionary background helps analysis of reports about emotional experience in at least two important ways. First, we are reminded not to mistake the report of the experience for the experience itself. Explanatory models, for example, may explain the report, but can only provide representations, not explanations, of an experiential "essence." Second, being mindful that experience is not measured directly can actually facilitate a broader notion of what reports of experience can tell. Specifically, for example, these representations can be used to understand how individuals construct accounts of themselves through their emotional lives. Reports about emotional experience, because they are representations – self-representations or the investigator's inference from the research subject's self-representations – reveal the power of language to represent to oneself and to others what emotion is and what it means.

Building theories of gender-coded emotion

How can we best continue to move research on gender and emotion forward? Which questions or problem areas that have emerged from the reviews and growing empirical literature hold most promise for generating useful theory that connects the operation of gender and of emotion in everyday life? In the following section I consider four themes apparent in contemporary research on gender and emotion that I believe hold particular promise.

Context as a framework for interpreting experience

Reviews cited above all reveal that measurement context is linked to the kind and degree of sex-related differences that are observed in research. Rarely is context the direct object of study, and so effects are inferred from other constituents of the research such as demand characteristics, "nuisance" variables, or independent variables other than sex of research participants. Nevertheless, the effects of context – especially if considered across the range of work on a specific topic – exhibit distinct patterns. For example, one area that seems to be particularly affected by context is deployment of emotion knowledge, specifically, a discrepancy between emotion knowledge and emotion performance (Shields, 1995).

To move the discussion forward and answer questions about when and how context matters, we need to incorporate "context" into the explanatory structure itself. In other words, it is not sufficient simply to insert "context" into the standard gender differences paradigm by changing the question, "Who is more emotional?" to "Who is more emotional within context X?" Instead, context itself needs to become the focus of theorizing: Under what conditions does gender matter? What is at stake in those situations? To accomplish this also requires extending the notion of context to include a broader sense of the environment that individuals draw on to interpret and understand their own (or others') emotions. In this broader sense, context encompasses not only the immediate surroundings of the study (the independent variables), but the socio-structural context (historical, cultural, linguistic community) that frames the situation.

An extended example illustrates how a change in framing the question of context has an impact. Elsewhere I have proposed that ideas about emotion are significant for the individual in acquiring a gendered sense of self (Shields, 1995). I suggest that, whether explicitly represented in emotion stereotypes, or more subtly transmitted in other media, emotion standards define the core of "masculine" and "feminine." In their role of defining cultural representations of masculinity/femininity, gendered emotion standards mediate the individual's acquisition and maintenance of a gendered identity via the practice of gender coded emotional values and behavior. This proposal suggests that gender-coded emotion beliefs can actually shape individuals' interpretation of their own emotional experience under certain conditions. Robinson, Johnson, and Shields (1998) investigated the conditions under which people use gender stereotypes about emotion to make judgments about the emotions of themselves and others. They hypothesized that when people lack concrete information about emotion experience and behavior, that they rely on stereotypes as a kind of heuristic device to make inferences about what happened. In a first study participants either played or watched a competitive word game (actual game conditions) or imagined themselves playing or watching the game (hypothetical condition). Participants in the actual game conditions made judgments about emotion either immediately after they played the game or after a delay of one day (observers) or one week (players). Both self-reports of emotional experience and perceptions of the emotional displays of others showed an influence of gender stereotypes, in that reports and perceptions more closely matched stereotypes the more distant in time from the event. In a second study the investigators compared self-ratings with ratings of hypothetical others and found that participants who rated others were more likely to use gender stereotypes of emotion than were participants who rated themselves.

Other researchers have also reported a context-driven relationship between gender stereotypes of emotion and self-reports of experience. Feldman Barrett and her colleagues (Feldman Barrett & Morganstein,

1995; Feldman Barrett, Robin, Pietromonaco, & Eyssell, 1998) find that global, retrospective reports tend to match gender stereotypes, but on-line momentary self-descriptions do not. Feldman Barrett and Morganstein (1995), for example, gathered college students' self-ratings on scales assessing seven emotions (happiness, surprise, fear, anger, sadness, interest, and shame/guilt) three times each day over a 90 day period. The same participants also completed a set of widely available self-report scales designed to tap global self-evaluation of emotionality and negative emotion. Questionnaire responses that reflected global, retrospective report revealed that gender effects mirrored gender stereotypes for memory-based but not on-line responses. A second study in which participants' retrospective self-ratings were compared with daily ratings over a 60-day period yielded the same pattern of results. Feldman Barrett et al. (1998) employed a diary procedure to obtain college students' self-reports of the occurrence, felt intensity, and expression of a set of specific emotions in everyday dyadic social inter-actions. Most relevant here is their conclusion that whereas women and men did not differ in their average experience of specific emotions measured immediately after social interactions, differences did emerge on global ratings, with women reporting more intense experience and expression. Thus, in studies employing quite different designs and self-assessment instruments (Feldman Barrett & Morganstein, 1995; Feldman Barrett et al., 1998; Robinson et al., 1998) a pattern of empirical results converges with conclusions drawn in research reviews (e.g., La France & Banaji, 1992; Shields, 1991; 1995). These studies point to the way in which stereotypes can serve as a heuristic device if distinctive details have faded from memory or if questions pertain to global and fuzzy concepts like emotionality.

What guides selectivity in the application of stereotypes to represen-tations of one's self and others? Why do stereotypes sometimes fill in the gaps of memory or inform one's answer to a vague and general question? On-line gender differences in the reported experience of emo-tions, after all, are sometimes observed (e.g., Grossman & Wood, 1993). The presence of an audience is one feature of context that exerts a strong effect on the likelihood that people will describe themselves in gen-dered terms or otherwise behave in consonance with gender stereo-types (e.g., LaFrance, 1993; Berman, 1980). The demarcation between public and private contexts, however, is not always obvious. The ima-gined audience can exert an effect just as an audience that is physically present. Another feature of context that bears closer investigation is what sort of self-evaluative information is readily available. For example, I have proposed that when people do not have much immedi-ate information about experience, they may compare themselves to a gender-coded emotional standard to explain or label their response (Shields, 1995). As the evidence above suggests, self-evaluation is not a deliberate or self-conscious act, but is implicit in the question "What do *I* feel? What do *I* express?" where that "I" is gendered.

How context encourages reliance on a gender heuristic (or conversely, reliance on more individuated memory) for understanding one's own experienced emotion is a rich and promising area of study. A related set of questions addresses how gender coded beliefs are implicated in the meta-narratives of the individual's emotional life. One such meta-narrative pertains to the salience of interpersonal relationships in emotion accounts, the second theme that I consider.

Considering the salience of interpersonal relationships in accounts of emotion

Women and men (as well as girls and boys) are more similar than different in their beliefs about emotion (see also Zammuner, this volume). Among the few differences reported with some regularity is a pattern that suggests that men, unless prompted, are less likely to incorporate social-relational themes in their accounts of emotion, and further, they appear to be less interested in introducing talk about emotion in social interaction. When the interactional context calls for a consideration of emotion themes, however, gender differences are attenuated or disappear. For example, when asked to discuss family relations topics in same-sex pairs of friends, both the proportion and content of linguistic references to emotion are similar for women and men (Anderson, Michels, Starita, St. John, & Leaper, 1996). In less emotionally evocative situations, however, the literature suggests a greater willingness among women to discuss emotion directly. Reviewing the literature as well as citing her own research, Thomas (1996) concludes that even feelings of anger, an emotion stereotypically associated with males and masculinity, appear to be discussed more readily by women. Kuebli, Butler, and Fivush (1995) have also shown that girls' propensity to talk about emotion shows up early in childhood (see also Fivush & Buckner, this volume).

The co-occurrence of viewing emotion as part of a relationship and using emotion-related talk as a way to conduct relationships points to a significant link between emotion beliefs and the practice of being a social person. The apparent pattern of gender difference in interest in emotion talk further suggests that it may be fruitful to inquire as to how the practice of being an emotional person is congruous with practice as a gendered person. Crawford, Kippax, Onyx, Gault, and Benton (1992) explored this question using the technique of "memory-work" to examine the ways in which women construct their emotions. Through collective discussions of group members' individual memories of emotions on a specific theme, they searched for common elements and meanings, and then further distilled these commonalties into a sense of what their individual reflections meant for a more general understanding of women's emotional lives. They found good evidence of the "gendered-ness" of emotional interaction. For anger episodes, for example, they concluded that women are condemned as neurotic if they show uncontrolled anger, but they are also condemned for suppressing anger and are then labeled depressed. Crawford et al.'s work offers a convincing illustration of the inseparability of gender and emotion as aspects of the social self.

I would caution against concluding that women's incorporation of social–relational themes in their verbal representations of emotion occur because women "are" relational. To do so mistakes a description of the finding for an explanation of it. Further, as noted above, conclusions about the salience of the interpersonal meaning of emotion for girls and women are based almost exclusively on research with European-origin white Americans. Citing cross-national research, Cross and Madson (1997) posit that for certain cultural communities within the US, a relational self-concept, what they term "interdependent self-construal," may be equally descriptive of men and women. A model that predicts gender differences based on research with a more-or-less homogenous cultural group runs the risk of rashly defining a standard from which gender patterns of other racial ethnic, socioeconomic, or national groups are interpreted as "deviations."

If we do not wish to settle for an essentialist explanation, we still need to explain why the pattern occurs with regularity for some groups. An examination of motivation may be the key. Cross and Madson (1997), for example, hypothesize that self-construal frames one's understanding of the implications of emotion in that it moderates social interactions and alters the tone of relationships. As a consequence, expression of emotion may differ for individuals with differing self-construals as they pursue divergent goals in social situations. For example, the research literature shows consistently that girls and boys, women and men know the same things about emotion, yet equivalence of knowledge is not invariably reflected in similarity in the application of that knowledge. Saarni's work on children's acquisition and practice of display rules (culture-specific norms for when, how, and to whom to visibly express specific emotions) illustrates this knowledge-performance gap (Saarni, 1988; 1989). Her work has shown that, although girls and boys may be equally knowledgeable about affective display rules and the conditions for expressive dissembling, they differ in how likely they are to follow those rules in an actual social situation. Girls, especially older girls, are more likely to moderate their expression to be in line with the display rules for the situation.

Outline the role of interactional goals in producing and maintaining gender effects

Interactional goals encompass what the individual tactically or strategically aims to accomplish in the course of emotional relationships with others. A related concept, outcome expectancies, long used in research on children's aggressive behavior, has more recently been applied to emotion (von Salisch, 1996) and refers to the awareness, explicit or implicit, that consequences accrue to emotional exchange. Awareness that there are consequences, even when the range of those consequences is not explicitly known, influences the direction and outcome of the exchange. Both sexes are very knowledgeable about the social consequences, or lack thereof, for how they respond emotionally to others, and awareness of emotion's impact on the give-and-take of relationships is as evident in children as in adults (e.g., Josephs, 1993). Saarni (1989) has proposed that folk theories of emotion provide children with a set of expectations about how script-like sequences of emotion-provoking events unfold and what constitute the "appropriate" range of responses for expressing feelings and coping with emotion-evoking events. These outcome expectancies shape the individual's approach to emotion and come to focus her or his views of what is possible as well as what is desirable. Outcome expectancies thus underlie the achievement of emotional competence, that is, self-efficacy in the context of emotion-eliciting social transactions.

A consideration of interactional goals asks: What do people expect will happen to them if they do or do not experience (or express) emotion in particular ways at particular times? What is at stake for the individual? The empirical research here for the most part addresses explicit knowledge of the consequences of the outcomes of emotional exchanges. For example, emotion can be viewed both as a regulator of social relationships and as a constituent of them. Clark and her colleagues, for example, find that expressions of anger decrease observers' liking for the angry other, whereas expressions of happiness increase liking for that person (Clark, Pataki, & Carver, 1996).

Stoppard's research has most comprehensively mapped beliefs about the costs and benefits we believe accrue to displaying (or withholding display of) emotion (e.g., McWaid & Stoppard, 1994; Stoppard, 1993). For example, Stoppard and Gunn Gruchy (1993) examined gender-differentiated norms for expressing emotion. Among other observations, they found that women believe themselves required to express positive emotion toward others and expect negative social sanctions if they do not, whereas men expect no negative consequences for failure to express positive emotion. Clark (1996) also reports that the effects of expressing a specific emotion (happiness, sadness, or anger) on an observer's rating of the expressor's likability is, in part, a function of the sex of the expressor and of the observer. For example, expressing sadness appears to increase the perceived neediness and to decrease the perceived likability of the person expressing it, except in dyads in which a woman expresses sadness to a man.

The operation of interactional goals in everyday life is well illustrated in the literature on marital interaction. Christensen and Heavey (1990) have shown that a spouse's tactic of using withdrawal or demand in resolving conflict depends on the outcome she or he desires. Gottman and Levenson (e.g., 1988; 1992) have described marital relationships as having a particular gendered pattern to conflict management, with wives more likely to seek engagement, while husbands withdraw emotionally. Gottman suggests that this pattern becomes exaggerated as conflict escalates. He explains this pattern in terms of management of physiological arousal, but an alternate (or supplemental) explanation is based on the relative control of resources within the marriage. Reasoning that desire to maintain or change the *status quo* should influence whether one opposes or withdraws from discussion of problematic issues, Christensen and Heavey (1990) rated the interactions of married couples on topics for which one spouse wanted to change the other. They found that the goal of the partner, not the sex, determined whether withdrawal or demand characterized the individual's style. Wife demand/husband withdrawal occurred most often when the wife wanted to change the husband; when the husband wanted to change the wife, the demand/withdrawal pattern was reversed. The overall appearance of a consistent gender-related difference in strategy would be interpreted as an artifact of who is in a position to desire change and who benefits from maintenance of the *status quo*. Thomas' (1996) qualitative study of women's anger found that the most pervasive theme in women's descriptions of the precipitants of their anger was the role of power, or lack thereof, especially within work and family relationships (see also Denham & Bultemeier, 1993). One respondent quoted offers a perfect illustration of the demand strategy:

> "I felt like my weekends were spent cleaning the house while his weekends were spent playing, and I resented that . . Like I told him when I was angry, "You don't want to compare what you do and what I do because you'll lose, trust me. How many times do you do the laundry, and how many times do you fold and put up clothes, and cook the meals and run the kids?" He knows he doesn't do that. He knows I do most of it and he likes it that way and he wants to keep it that way" (Denham & Bultemeier, 1993, p. 61).

The point here is that a serious discrepancy in privilege sets up the conditions under which, once a woman feels some degree of entitlement to an altered situation, the experience of anger becomes a tool to bring about change. Initiating change requires an assertive stance, a stance that appears as a "demand" strategy. Emotional withdrawal or stonewalling may subserve physiological homeostasis, but it also is an efficacious strategy for maintaining a *status quo* situation that advantages oneself at the expense of one's spouse.

Power as an explanatory variable

As anthropologist Barbara Smuts observes, "Feminist theory focuses on issues of power: who has it, how they get it, how it is used, and what are its consequences" (Smuts, 1995, p. 2). Power is the capacity to get what one wants, to achieve one's own goals. The exercise of power is aimed at restoring, maintaining, or acquiring what one values. Where gender is concerned, what is at stake is the *status quo* of social arrangements that inequitably benefit one sex over the other. In defining "benefit," I would include achieving one's goals in the near term, but more important, the maintenance of social structures and practices that preserve power inequities.

I want to stress here that an analysis of power is not about *this* woman, *this* man, but about the broader sense of how the interconnections of gender and emotion can be agents of social change or serve the *status quo*. Fischer's analysis of powerful and powerless emotions offers a good illustration of how gendered emotion subserves institutional structures of gender inequities. Fischer (1993) finds, for example, that emotions for which greater female expressivity seems to be the rule, such as sadness, anxiety, and fear, can be regarded as "powerless" in the sense that the situation is experienced as one that one is powerless to change. Stereotypically masculine emotions such as anger, pride, and contempt, on the other hand, reflect an attempt to gain or regain control over the situation. She also reports an association between the powerful–powerless axis and women's and men's understanding of specific emotion labels (Fischer, 1995).

Here I summarize two ways in which the concept of power can usefully be interrogated. The first examines the power in naming emotion; the second, the display of emotion as an exercise of power.

The power of naming. As prevalent as emotional exchange is in interpersonal interaction – both reading others' emotional display, and monitoring one's own emotional display – verbal identification of emotions is a rarity in ordinary conversation. A number of investigators have reported that emotion labels appear with very low frequency in ordinary conversation (Anderson & Leaper, 1996; Shields & MacDowell, 1987: Shimanoff, 1985), even when people are specifically asked to describe their reactions to emotion-evoking events (Fischer, 1995; Haviland & Goldston, 1992). That emotion labels constitute such a small proportion of ordinary talk indicates that they are not used simply to offer a verbal commentary or an additional channel for affective information that is conveyed through expression, vocal tone and contour, or context.

Labeling experience or behavior as "emotion" is not a value-neutral act, but implies questions about the emotional person's intensity and legitimacy of feeling, and capacity for self-control (Shields & MacDowell, 1987). Naming emotion is a value-laden act, whether the label is generic "emotional" or a specific emotion (e.g., "angry" versus "bitchy"). The conventional approach to the psychology of emotion tends to treat constructs such as "emotion," "emotionality," and "inexpressivity" as (relatively) nonproblematic concepts that reference tangible things, treating these as foundational constructs. When the concept of "emotion" is problematized and itself becomes the object of study, we begin to ask how the concept is invested with substance by science, popular culture, and interpersonal relationships. Extending the analysis to gender and emotion, we ask questions such as "What does it mean to say someone is 'emotional'?" and "Who decides what is or is not 'emotional' behavior?" and "Who has the power to label, and to make that label 'stick'?"

The authority to name emotion confers power. Interrogation of the circumstances in which emotion and emotionality are named illustrates the key role that entitlement plays in exercising rights to emotion. Shields and Crowley (1996), for example, gave college-student participants brief scenarios that described an emotion-evoking event and manipulated both protagonist gender and the description of protagonist's response as "emotional" or as a specific emotion (happy, sad, angry). For both male and female protagonists, a response described as emotional was rated as more intense, less controlled, and less appropriate than responses described by a specific emotion label. Open-ended responses, however, showed that respondents adapted the meaning of emotion terms to fit gender stereotypes. For example, in the scenario, "Karen (Brian) was emotional when she (he) found out that her (his) car had been stolen," respondents judged "emotional" differently for Brian and Karen. Not only did they attribute the cause of her reaction more to her personality than to the situation, respondents imagined her reaction would be overblown and hysterical. One respondent, for example, described her probable reaction this way: "Karen's car got ripped off and she flipped!! Started screaming and crying no one could calm her down." On the other hand, Brian's behavior, when identified as emotional, was downplayed, rationalized, or described as what any ordinary person might do in that situation: "I just imagined any average reaction (i.e., my own) if I found out that my car was stolen. I just imagined that he probably worked pretty hard for his car, and that he had taken care of it, so of course it would be upsetting." Instead of making counterstereotypic attributions, our participants maintained their stereotypic beliefs by changing the meaning of the emotional response to be consistent with gender expectations.

Emotion display as the exercise of power. Status is not by itself power, but it offers the opportunity for exercise of power that is immediately visible. Lower status positions exert power, too – the stereotype of the tyrant petty bureaucrat or power-wielding secretary are as well known in real life as they are in cartoons and jokes. Examination of how status intersects with gender (or racial ethnicity, class, etc.) can help us sort out and eventually theorize some of the gender-related findings that occur with regularity across measurement modalities and contexts. Brody, Lovas and Hay (1995) found that both men and women reported feeling more anger towards a woman who was presented in an enviable position (e.g., getting a free airline ticket) than toward a man in an identical enviable position. These findings were interpreted as consistent with violation of expectancy theories. By virtue of the lower status accorded by gender, the woman who wins is seen as less deserving of good fortune and hence more appropriate as a target of anger. When status is made more explicit, however, the implied status of gender has an attenuated effect. Maybury (1997) examined the influence of sex and status of protagonist and anger type on observer judgments of anger displays. College students read scenarios that described the protagonist responding with either physical or verbal anger toward a co-worker of higher, equivalent, or lower status after that co-worker had committed a significant work-related error. Whereas sex of protagonist had few effects, the effect of protagonist status was substantial. High status protagonists' anger displays were judged as more appropriate, favorable, and situationally motivated than those of low and moderate status protagonists. They were also rated as less likely to be fired for their anger display. One unique feature of this study is that status was explicitly stated. Maybury believes it is this feature that accounts for the powerful status effect and absence of sex-of-protagonist effects. When explicit status information is available (job position relative to the other), observers do not attend to implicit status information (such as sex of the protagonist or target) which under more ambiguous circumstances would be used to determine the actor's status.

These paper-and-pencil studies of emotion language offer a compelling case to get serious about power (see also Hall, this volume;

LaFrance & Hecht, this volume, for further discussion on the role of power). By including analysis of power explicitly in research, we have an opportunity to move beyond questions about gender and emotion within the delimited contexts on which the field has focused thus far. By foregrounding power, we can develop accounts of the reciprocal relationship between gender and emotion that assess that relationship's place in creating and maintaining gender inequity. And not least, it would further the creation of a socially responsible social psychology of gender and emotion.

A final word

> There is perhaps no field aspiring to be scientific where flagrant personal bias, logic martyred in the cause of supporting a prejudice, unfounded assertions, and even sentimental rot and drivel have run riot to such an extent as here. (Psychologist Helen Thompson Woolley (1910))

Over 20 years ago I cited Woolley's observations on the state of sex differences research to illustrate the sorry state of thinking about the psychology of women in the early twentieth century (Shields, 1975). Although psychology has grown more sophisticated in the sorts of questions that are asked about women, men, and gender, we have yet to see the psychology of emotions effectively move beyond a differences approach to questions of gender and emotion. The conceptual shortcomings of the differences framework have been amply discussed and documented by feminist researchers in psychology and other disciplines (e.g., Bacchi, 1990; Crawford, 1995; Hare-Mustin & Marecek, 1990). To answer questions about gender and emotion we first need to recognize that focusing on the gender differences themselves is not particularly informative: finding a gender difference neither explains how the difference got there nor what maintains it. There are, of course, differences in the way that women and men, as groups, approach emotion and understand and express their own experience; however, to focus *only* on identification of differences (or similarities) is unnecessarily limiting. The case of VMI shows the power of stereotypes and folk accounts of gendered emotion in the social, political, and legal maneuverings of everyday life. We do not need a psychology of gendered emotion that, because it fails to move beyond a simple "differences" model, inadvertently reproduces folk notions and stereotypes. We do need psychology's research and theory to provide an understanding of gendered emotion in all its complexity – complexity in the individual's experience and in the social arrangements that gendered emotion subserves.

To advance our understanding of the dynamic complexity of the relation between gender and emotion our questions must work toward greater theoretical sophistication: Under what conditions are differences manifested (attenuated)? What drives those conditions to exert their influence? To create models of the dynamics requires a different strategy, one that addresses directly the conditions that can attenuate or exaggerate the occurrence of behavioral differences between women and men. These conditions may be local and situated in the relationship in which the emotion occurs, or structural in the role relationships played out against a backdrop of sociocultural beliefs about emotion.

I must also insert here the obligatory discussion of "real" differences. There is inevitably a point at which certain readers cry "what about biology!?" Their cry may be accusatory ("but what are the *real* differences?") or simply reflect a desire to press on to the next question of theory ("but *how* do we connect the social realm with the wiring?"). Let me address the former group first. What are the real differences? First, "real" differences (and similarities) encompass both the "givens" of evolutionary and individual heredity as well as the "givens" of enculturation, individual history, and behavioral context. Second, preoccupation with distal speculative evolutionary conditions may make interesting discussion, but it does not address the immediate and, to my mind, more pressing question of what maintains these behaviors and what about context or personality or interpersonal dynamics causes them to be exaggerated or attenuated. Biology continues today to be privileged in North American psychology's emotions research. That is, much of psychology begins with the foundational assumption that nature necessarily precedes and supersedes nurture (Shields, 1990).

In this chapter I have attempted to move the discussion about gender and emotion beyond the discussion of differences, not only to advance theory on gender and emotion, but also to set the stage for a more sophisticated discussion of the intersections of gender and emotion with racial ethnicity, historical period, culture, and social class. I was able only partially to achieve the latter aim and it is clear that if progress is to be made on this front, these variables must be placed at the center, not the periphery, of the inquiry. Without greater attentiveness to the ways in which social identity other than gender (or in addition to gender) may play a role in the individual's experience of emotion and representations of that experience, we risk mistaking effects that are representative of one segment of society for effects representative of all women and men. Further, we may mistakenly conclude that a gender difference exists when what we have observed is attributable to variables other than gender (Unger, 1996).

When the connection between gender and emotion is made explicit, each is transformed in the course of being viewed from a previously unexplored perspective. For emotion, the new perspective shows that representations of emotion (emotion language; beliefs about emotion) must be incorporated into psychological models of how people use emotion information. For gender, the new perspective raises questions about how emotion beliefs and behavior play a role in the formation and performance of gendered identity. How does emotion, whether construed as experience, as a label for behavior, or as a medium of interpersonal interaction, assume such a significant role in who we define ourselves to be as girls and women, boys and men? This question, which turns our attention to the question of identity, will foster the next generation of research on gender and emotion.

Acknowledgments

I would like to express my thanks to Cathy Guttentag for her research assistance and comments on earlier drafts, and to Agneta Fischer for her insightful editorial suggestions.

Notes

1 The *Chronicle of Higher Education* reports that the first class including female cadets at VMI finished their first year (March 27, 1998, p. A8). The year started with 460 first year cadets, 30 of whom were women. The first months at VMI are arduous, including torment of the first-year "rats" by upperclassmen and concluding with "Breakout": a mass climb up a muddy 20-foot hill in frosty early spring weather. Seventy-seven percent of the women and 84% of the men who began the first year made it to the end.
2 Here I will bracket the question of who determines typical, natural, or appropriate for whom.
3 My own theoretical orientation is most closely aligned with social constructionist perspectives, especially in my focus on the creation of gender through relationships and in the course of social interaction. This position shifts research even further in the direction of an examination of contextual effects and problematizing foundational constructs. As Rachel Hare-Mustin and Jeanne Marecek note, "Whereas positivism asks what are the facts, constructivism asks what are the assumptions; whereas positivism asks what are the answers, constructivism asks what are the questions" (Hare-Mustin & Marecek, 1994, p. 52).

References

Anderson, K. J. & Leaper, C. (1996, March). *The social construction of emotion and gender between friends.* Paper presented at the Society for Research on Adolescence, Boston, MA.
Anderson, K. J., Michels, J., Starita, M., St. John, M. & Leaper, C. (1996, March). *Emotion talk in same-and mixed-gender friendships: Forms and function of expression.* Paper presented at the Society for Research on Adolescence, Boston, MA.
Bacchi, C. L. (1990). *Same difference: Feminism and sexual difference.* St. Leonards, Australia: Allen & Unwin.

Berman, P. W. (1980). Are women more responsive than men to the young? A review of developmental and situational variables. *Psychological Bulletin, 88*, 668–695.

Brody, L. R. (1985). Gender differences in emotional development: A review of theories and research. *Journal of Personality, 53*, 102–149.

Brody, L. R. & Hall, J. A. (1993). Gender and emotion. In M. Lewis & J. Haviland (Eds.), *Handbook of emotions* (pp. 447–461). New York, NY: Guilford.

Brody, L. R., Lovas, G. S., & Hay, D. H. (1995). Sex differences in anger and fear as a function of situational context. *Sex Roles, 32*, 47–78.

Campos, J. (1994). The new functionalism in emotion. *SRCD Newsletter*, Spring, 1, 7, 9–14.

Christensen, A. & Heavey, C. L. (1990). Gender and social structure in the demand/withdrawal pattern of marital conflict. *Journal of Personality and Social Psychology, 59*, 73–81.

Clark, M. S. (August, 1996). *What role might gender play in strategic self-presentation of emotion?* Paper presented at the International Society for Research on Emotions, Toronto, Canada.

Clark, M. S., Pataki, S. P., & Carver, V. H. (1996). Some thoughts and findings on self-presentation of emotions in relationships. In G. J. O. Fletcher & J. Fitness (Eds.), *Knowledge structures in close relationships: A social psychological approach* (pp. 247–274). Mahwah, NJ: Lawrence Erlbaum.

Crawford, J., Kippax, S., Onyx, J., Gault, U., & Benton, P. (1992). *Emotion and gender: Constructing meaning from memory.* London: Sage.

Crawford, M. (1995). *Talking difference: On gender and language.* Thousand Oaks, CA: Sage.

Cross, S. E. & Madson, L. (1997). Models of the self: Self-construals and gender. *Psychological Bulletin, 122*, 5–37.

Deaux, K. & LaFrance, M. (1997). Gender. In D. T. Gilbert, S. T. Fiske, & G. Lindzey (Eds.), *Handbook of social psychology* (pp. 788–827). Boston, MA: McGraw-Hill.

Denham, G. & Bultemeier, K. (1993). Anger: Targets and triggers. In S. P. Thomas (Ed.), *Women and anger* (pp. 68–90). New York, NY: Springer.

Duffy, E. (1941). An explanation of "emotional" phenomena without the use of the concept "emotion." *Journal of General Psychology, 25*, 283–293.

Ekman, P. & Davidson, R. J. (1994). *The nature of emotion: Fundamental questions.* New York, NY: Oxford University Press.

Feldman Barrett, L. & Morganstein, M. (1995, August). *Sex differences in the experience of emotion: Retrospective versus momentary ratings of emotion.* Paper presented at the annual conference of the American Psychological Association, New York.

Feldman Barrett, L., Robin, L., Pietromonaco, P. R., & Eyssell, K. M. (1998). Are women the "more emotional" sex? Evidence from emotional experiences in social context. *Cognition and Emotion, 12*, 555–579.

Fischer, A. H. (1993). Sex differences in emotionality: Fact or stereotype. *Feminism and Psychology, 3*, 303–318.

Fischer, A. H. (1995). Emotion concepts as a function of gender. In J. A. Russell, J. M. Fernández-Dols, A. S. R. Manstead, & J. C. Wellenkamp (Eds.), *Everyday concepts of emotion: An introduction to the psychology, anthropology, and linguistics of emotion* (pp. 457–474). Dordrecht, The Netherlands: Kluwer.

Gottman, J. M., & Levenson, R. W. (1988). The social psychophysiology of marriage. In P. Noller & M. A. Fitzpatrick (Eds.), *Perspectives on marital interaction* (pp. 182–200). San Diego, CA: College Hill Press.

Gottman, J. M. & Levenson, R. W. (1992). Marital processes predictive of later dissolution: Behavior, physiology and health. *Journal of Personality and Social Psychology, 63,* 221–223.

Greenberger, M. D. & Blake, D. L. (1996, July 5). The VMI decision: Shattering sexual stereotypes. *The Chronicle of Higher Education.*

Grossman, M. & Wood, W. (1993). Sex differences in intensity of emotional experience: A social role interpretation. *Journal of Personality and Social Psychology, 65,* 1010–1022.

Hare-Mustin, R. T. & Marecek, J. (1994). On making a difference. *Making a difference: Psychology and the construction of gender.* New Haven, CT: Yale University Press.

Haviland, J. M. & Goldston, R. B. (1992). Emotion and narrative: The agony and the ecstasy. In K. T. Strongman (Ed.), *International Review of Studies on Emotion* (Vol. 2, pp. 219–246). New York, NY: Wiley.

Josephs, I. E. (1993). *The regulation of emotional expression in preschool children.* New York, NY: Waxmann Münster.

Kuebli, J., Butler, S., & Fivush, R. (1995). Mother-child talk about past emotions: Relations of maternal language and child gender over time. *Cognition and Emotion, 9,* 265–283.

LaFrance, M. (June 1993). *Towards a reconsideration of the gender-emotion relationship.* Paper presented at the meeting of the American Psychological Society, Chicago, IL.

LaFrance, M. & Banaji, M. (1992). Towards a reconsideration of the gender-emotion relationship. In M. Clark (Ed.), *Emotion and Social Behavior: Review of personality and social psychology* (Vol. 14, pp. 178–201). Newbury Park, CA: Sage.

Manstead, A. S. R. (1992). Gender differences in emotion. In M. A. Gale & M. W. Eysenck (Eds.), *Handbook of individual differences: Biological perspectives* (pp. 355–387). Chichester, England: Wiley.

Maybury, K. K. (1997). *The influence of status and sex on observer judgements of anger displays.* Unpublished doctoral dissertation, University of California, Davis.

McWaid, E. C. & Stoppard, J. M. (1994). Gender and reactions to anger expression. *Psychologie Canadienne, 35,* 65.

Oatley, K., & Jenkins, J. M. (1996). *Understanding emotions.* Toronto, Canada: Blackwell.

Parlee, M. B. (1995) [book review]. *Feminism and Psychology, 5,* 375–381.

Parrott, W. G. (1995). The heart and the head: Everyday conceptions of being emotional. In J. A. Russell, J. M. Fernández-Dols, A. S. R. Manstead, & J. C. Wellenkamp (Eds.), *Everyday conceptions of emotions* (pp. 73–84). Dordecht, The Netherlands: Kluwer.

Robinson, M. D., Johnson, J. T., & Shields, S. A. (1998). The gender heuristic and the data base: Factors affecting the perception of gender-related differences in the experience and display of emotions. *Basic and Applied Social Psychology, 20,* 206–219.

Saarni, C. (1988). Children's understanding of the interpersonal consequences of dissemblance of nonverbal emotional-expressive behavior. *Journal of Nonverbal Behavior, 12,* 275–294.

Saarni, C. (1989). Children's understanding of strategic control of emotional expression in social transactions. In C. Saarni & P. L. Harris (Eds.), *Children's understanding of emotion* (pp. 181–208). Cambridge University Press.

Shields, S. A. (1975). Functionalism, Darwinism, and the psychology of women: A study in social myth. *American Psychologist, 30*, 739–754.

Shields, S. A. (1987). Women, men, and the dilemma of emotion. In P. Shaver & C. Hendrick (Eds.), *Sex and gender: Review of personality and social psychology* (Vol. 7, pp. 229–250). Beverly Hills: Sage.

Shields, S. A. (1990). Conceptualizing the biology-culture relationship in emotion: An analogy with gender. *Cognition and Emotion, 4*, 359–374.

Shields, S. A. (1991). Gender in the psychology of emotion: A selective research review. In K. T. Strongman (Ed.), *International review of studies on emotion* (Vol. 1, pp. 227–245). New York, NY: Wiley.

Shields, S. A. (1995). The role of emotion beliefs and values in gender development. In N. Eisenberg (Ed.), *Review of personality and social psychology* (Vol. 15, pp. 212–232). Thousand Oaks, CA: Sage.

Shields, S. A. & Crowley, J. C. (1996). Appropriating questionnaires and rating scales for a feminist psychology: A multi-method approach to gender and emotion. In S. Wilkinson (Ed.), *Feminist social psychologies* (pp. 218–232). Philadelphia, PA: Open University Press.

Shields, S. A. & MacDowell, K. A. (1987). "Appropriate" emotion in politics: Judgments of a televised debate. *Journal of Communication, 37*, 78–89.

Shimanoff, S. B. (1995). Expressing emotions in words: Verbal patterns of interaction. *Journal of Communication, 35*, 16–31.

Smuts, B. (1995). The evolutionary origins of patriarchy. *Human Nature, 6*, 1–32.

Solomon, R. C. (1993). *The passions: Emotions and the meaning of life.* Indianapolis, IN: Hackett.

Stoppard, J. M. (1993, June). *Beyond gender stereotypes: Putting the gender-emotion relationship into context.* Paper presented at the meeting of the American Psychological Society, Chicago, IL.

Stoppard, J. M. & Gunn Gruchy, C. D. (1993). Gender, context, and expression of positive emotion. *Personality and Social Psychology Bulletin, 19*, 143–150.

Thomas, S. P. (1996). Women's anger: Causes, manifestations, and correlates. In C. D. Spielberger, I. G. Sarason, J. M. T. Brebner, E. Greenglass, P. Laungani, & A. M. O'Roark (Eds.), *Stress and emotion: Anxiety, anger, and curiosity* (Vol. 15, pp. 53–74). Philadelphia, PA: Taylor & Francis.

Unger, R. K. (1996). Using the master's tools: Epistemology and empiricism. In S. Wilkinson (Ed.), *Feminist social psychologies: International perspectives* (pp. 165–181). Philadelphia, PA: Open University Press.

von Salisch, M. (August, 1996). *What boys and girls expect when they express their anger towards a friend.* Paper presented at the International Society for Research on Emotions, Toronto, Canada.

Woolley, H. T. (1910). Psychological literature: A review of the recent literature on the psychology of sex. *Psychological Bulletin, 7*, 335–342.

Wyche, K. F. (1998). On reading "Bias in Psychology": The more things change, the more they stay the same. *Feminism and Psychology, 8*, 90–93.

Yoder, J. D. & Kahn, A. S. (1993). Working toward an inclusive psychology of women. *American Psychologist, 48*, 844–850.

2. The socialization of gender differences in emotional expression: Display rules, infant temperament, and differentiation

LESLIE R. BRODY

The socialization of gender differences in emotional expression is a complex process, and has some surprising, even counter-intuitive aspects. For example, I will present data to show that even when parents socialize their sons and daughters in the same ways, such as with equal levels of nurturance, their sons and daughters may respond with different patterns of emotional expression. In this chapter, I will focus my discussion of emotion socialization on three areas: the role played by cultural display rules and imitation; the impact of gender differences in infant temperament and language development on socialization; and the sometimes surprising influence of processes of differentiation between mothers' and children's emotional expressiveness. I will theorize that each of these processes plays an important role in the eventual divergence of emotional expression for the two sexes, and will present new data addressing processes of differentiation in the emotional expression of mothers and their children.

Although I acknowledge that biological differences between infant males and females play a role in shaping their emotional development, I argue that the subsequent emergence of gender differences in emotional expressiveness is heavily influenced by cultural values and attitudes concerning gender roles. Cultural values influence caretakers to respond to biological gender differences in particular ways. Perhaps the most provocative part of my argument is that socializing the two sexes to express different emotions serves to maintain a bifurcation of gender roles, and to maintain the power and status differences between women and men. Although the research I will review is based primarily on samples from Western cultures, my argument takes into consideration that cultural differences may exist in many aspects of emotional expression (see Brody, 1997, 1999).

Display rules and imitation

Much research shows that gender differences in emotional expressiveness are socialized in accordance with display rules, prescriptive social norms that dictate how, when and where emotions can be expressed by males and females in any particular culture (see Underwood, Coie & Herbsman, 1992). The content of display rules generally conforms to the gender stereotypes that each individual culture holds about emotional expressivity, such as boys should not cry, or girls should not be aggressive.

Display rules are implicitly assumed and learned within social interactions, and their non-obvious nature may be one reason that inter-cultural communication and adaptation is sometimes so difficult. When studying display rules, researchers have relied on several sources of indirect data in the absence of explicit evidence, for example, comparisons between emotions expressed in private versus public settings (Soussignon & Schaal, 1996), or between inner emotional experiences versus outward emotional expressions (Underwood et al., 1992).

Various types of evidence have indicated that different emotional expressions are acceptable for the two sexes in American and many European cultures. The expression of sadness, depression, fear, and dysphoric self-conscious emotions such as shame and embarrassment are viewed as "unmanly," and men who display such emotions are not only evaluated more negatively than females (Siegel & Alloy, 1990), but are also less likely to be comforted than are women (Barbee, Cunningham, Winstead, Derlega, Bulley, Yaneeklov, & Druen, 1993). In contrast, the expression of anger and aggression are seen as acceptable for men, but not for women. More specifically, aggressive boys are judged to be more likable and socially competent than non-aggressive boys (Hart, DeWolf & Burts, 1993; Serbin, Marchessault, McAffer, Peters, & Schwartzmann, 1993). In contrast, aggressive girls are judged to be less likable than non-aggressive girls, and aggressive girls tend to have a wide variety of problems in peer relationships (Crick, 1997). Even in adulthood, women anticipate more negative social consequences for expressing aggression than men do (Eagly & Steffen, 1986; Lerner, 1980; Shields & Koster, 1989), and are especially concerned that the expression of anger and aggression will disrupt their social relationships (Davis, LaRosa, & Foshee, 1992; Frost & Averill, 1982).

The expression of any emotion which threatens to hurt or impair a social relationship, such as pride in the face of winning a competition, or lack of guilt or remorse in the face of a social wrongdoing, tends to be unacceptable for women in Western cultures. And conversely, emotions which facilitate social relationships, such as warmth, support, and cheerfulness, are prescribed as appropriate for women (Hochschild, 1983). For example, adolescent girls training to be cheerleaders are taught to look happy even when they are uncomfortable or disappointed (Eder & Parker, 1987). In fact, the very word "cheerleader," a female role, implies trying to bring cheer, or happiness to others in a supportive, non-competitive role. Women are also expected to express pride and cheerfulness in the face of others' accomplishments and victories (e.g., Graham et al., 1981).

Conformity to display rules sets in relatively early in development. For example, by school age, girls appear to be more skillful than boys at changing their facial expressions to foster social relationships. Several studies have shown that preschool and early school-aged girls express fewer negative emotions (including facial expressions and behaviors) when receiving an unattractive gift than boys do (Cole, 1986; Davis, 1995). In one study, first- and third-grade girls did better than boys when asked to "trick" an experimenter into believing that they actually liked a disappointing gift. Even when motivated to hide their negative feelings by the promise of a prize, the boys did not, or perhaps could not, suppress their negative expressions (Davis, 1995). Girls also inhibit their negative emotional displays more in the presence of an examiner than when alone, again suggesting that social approval is a motivation for their deceptive emotional expressiveness (Davis, 1995; Soussignon & Schaal, 1996).

Peers and socialization

The display rules I have outlined above are transmitted and reinforced by both adults' and children's peer groups. Within peer groups, children attend to, prefer, and imitate sex-role stereotypic behaviors more than non-sex-role stereotypic behaviors (Perry & Bussey, 1979). Children probably also imitate their peers' sex-role stereotypic emotions rather than non-sex role stereotypic emotions, although very little data has been collected as to how children imitate the emotions expressed by their peers.[1]

Peers have been found to reinforce and maintain conformity to display rules through processes such as social acceptance and popularity, or alternatively, rejection and teasing. Observational research has shown that boys who conform to masculine display rules are viewed as "cool," which partially involves being defensive about revealing feelings over possible rejection and vulnerability. Popular boys also act "tough" and aggressive, challenge adult authority, and boast and brag about their sometimes rule-violating exploits. Boys and girls who are less popular with their peers tend to violate the display rules for their own sex. Boys who are low in popularity are those who are seen as vulnerable or weak, who cry easily, or who are the most frequently hurt or defeated in athletic games, the so-called "sissies" (Adler, Kless, & Adler, 1992). Similarly, Dodge, Coie, Pettit, and Price (1990) showed that more popular males were those who were rated low on sadness by their peers.

In contrast, popular and well-liked girls are observed to be those who are able to express themselves verbally, to understand group dynamics, to be less aggressive, and to be interested in social relationships, especially with boys (Adler, Kless, & Adler, 1992; Chung & Asher, 1996; Crick, 1997; Serbin et al., 1993).

Young children seem to be aware that they are required to regulate their emotional expressiveness in front of their peers, anticipating rejection, ridicule, or reprimands if they do not conform to display rules (Saarni, 1988; Zeman & Garber, 1996). However, the expectations that the two sexes have about peers' reactions may follow different developmental pathways. For example, pre-adolescent and adolescent girls actually preferred showing their real feelings to peers than to parents, whereas same-aged boys were split evenly between preferring to show their feelings to adults and peers (Saarni, 1988). Moreover, Underwood et al. (1992) found that girls reported that they would mask sadness and anger less as they approached adolescence, whereas boys reported that they would mask expressions of anger and sadness more as they got older, perhaps in an effort to appear to be "cool."

Socialization by parents

Parents are motivated to raise children who are well liked and socially acceptable (Ruddick, 1982), and socializing their children to conform to display rules (perhaps even unconsciously) is one way to maximize the likelihood of reaching those goals. In accordance with display rules, parents of both preschoolers and young school aged children differentially emphasize the expression of sadness and fear to their daughters but not to their sons, and anger to their sons but not to their daughters (Fivush, 1989; 1993; Greif, Alvarez, & Ullmann, 1981; Zahn Waxler, Ridgeway, Denham, Usher, & Cole, 1993). This has been found to be characteristic of parent–child interactions when parents are asked to create stories for their children using wordless illustrations (Greif et al., 1981), when parents and children reconstruct memories for actual events which occurred in their lives (Fivush, 1989, 1993), and when parents discuss pictures of facial expressions with their children (Zahn-Waxler et al., 1993).

Block (1973, 1984) found that across 5 different American and European cultures, with children ranging in age from 3 to 20 across a

wide range of ethnic and socioeconomic backgrounds, parents emphasized the control of emotional expression (often without specifying particular emotions) for their sons and the control of aggression for their
daughters. For example, mothers of boys endorsed "I teach my child to
control his feelings at all times,"[2] whereas mothers of girls did not. Both
mothers and fathers said they would express affection by holding,
kissing, and hugging their girls more than their boys, and both would
encourage their daughters to talk about their troubles more than they
would their sons. Also consistent with the display rule that females
should display cheerfulness are studies which have shown that mothers
smile more at their infant daughters than their sons, as well as engage
in more positive interactions with daughters than with sons (Malatesta
Culver, Tesman, & Shepherd, 1989; Malatesta & Haviland, 1982; Parnell,
1991).

In addition to parents and peers, other socialization influences, such
as the media, teachers, and schools, also socialize emotional expression
in accordance with gender-stereotypic display rules and provide children with gender-stereotypic models that they imitate (see Brody, 1999).

Display rules and cultural values

Display rules ensure that existing cultural values surrounding gender
roles are maintained, including the power and status imbalances
between the two sexes (Brody, 1999). For example, when males and
females interact, females are more apt to let their weaknesses show than
are males, and are therefore at a disadvantage in terms of power and
control. The emotions women are encouraged to express (warmth,
cheerfulness, vulnerability) as well as those they are discouraged from
expressing (aggression and anger) also maximize the possibility that
they will successfully fulfill their designated social roles as child and
family caretakers (see Brody, 1997, 1999). The emotions men are discouraged from expressing (sadness, vulnerability, depression) as well as
those they are encouraged to express (anger in the form of aggression)
ensure that they will successfully complete their roles as competitive
providers with an emphasis on individual achievement, higher power
and status. Fischer and Manstead (see ch. 4, this volume) explore the
hypothesis that men in individualistic cultures suppress their emotions
so as not to appear weak or powerless.

If the argument that display rules serve to maintain cultural values is
correct, then different cultures with varying degrees of power imbalances between the two sexes should have dissimilar display rules that
correspond to their culturally mandated gender roles. Such cross-cultural evidence has not been systematically collected. However, we do

have another form of convincing evidence which shows that the display rules for each sex have shifted at different historical time periods in accordance with cultural values concerning gender roles. For example, a provocative study showed that the rules for emotional expressiveness advocated by popular magazines changed as gender roles for women became transformed (Cancian & Gordon, 1988). In the early part of the century, popular magazines advised traditional kinds of emotional expressiveness for women, including the ideas of self-sacrifice, avoiding conflict and minimizing anger. Expressing these emotions was adaptive for women's roles as family caretakers, whereas the expression of anger was adaptive for men's roles in the workplace (Stearns, 1988). In more recent times, magazines promote a different message. The open communication of negative and positive feelings for women, including anger, is now viewed as appropriate, and signals a more autonomous role for women. In brief, the needs of the culture and how social relationships are managed at any point in time are related to the quality of existing display rules for each sex.

Gender differences in infant temperament and language abilities

I have previously argued that subtle differences in infant male and female language development, activity and arousal levels, and sociability may drive parents to interact differently with their sons and daughters (Brody, 1993; Brody & Hall, 1993; Brody, 1999). The differing qualities of these parent–child interactions may lead the development of sons' and daughters' emotional expressiveness along different developmental pathways. Although space does not permit me to thoroughly review the evidence for early gender differences in each of these domains (see Brody, 1999, for a more detailed exposition), I will give a brief overview of each area. Gender differences in each of the infant characteristics I will discuss are undoubtedly shaped by a complex interaction between social and biological processes, with emerging evidence especially indicating that activity levels and empathy (a form of sociability) have modest heritability, based on comparisons of these characteristics in identical and fraternal twins (Zahn-Waxler, Robinson, & Emde, 1992b; Saudino, Plomin, & DeFries, 1996; Saudino & Eaton, 1991).

As measured by both objective and subjective ratings, boys consistently have higher activity levels than do girls (Eaton & Ennis, 1986). Higher arousal on the part of male infants has also been documented. For example, 6-month-old sons evidence more negativity, fussiness, and twisting and turning away from their mothers than do daughters when mothers are instructed to stop smiling at them (Weinberg, Tronick,

Cohn, & Olson, in press). Research also shows that the rates at which mismatched mother–infant emotional states (for example, mother is happy while baby is sad) are repaired and changed to matching states are slower for mother–son than for mother–daughter dyads. Sons' disregulation may make it harder to repair negative social relationships, and may increase the rate of interactive response errors that occur when relating to infants (Weinberg et al., in press). Moreover, girls also regulate some social behaviors, such as taking turns, at earlier ages than do boys and are better able to inhibit inappropriate behaviors (Kochanska, Murray, Jacques, Koenig, & Vandegeest, 1996).

In the realm of empathy and sociability, 1-year-old girls have been found to react with more empathy and distress than do their same age male counterparts when experimenters pretend to hurt themselves (Sigman & Kasari, 1994; Zahn Waxler, Radke-Yarrow, Wagner, & Chapman, 1992a; Zahn-Waxler et al., 1992b). At 6, 9, and 12 months, girls initiate more social interactions than do boys, even though mothers' behaviors toward their sons and daughters do not differ (Gunnar & Donahue, 1980). Girls also respond more to their mothers when their mothers speak to them than boys do (Clarke-Stewart, 1973; Gunnar & Donahue, 1980; Klein & Durfee, 1978). Moreover, infant girls engage in social referencing more than boys do, using cues in their mother's and stranger's faces and voices to guide their behavior. For example, when their mothers display fear, girls stay away from a toy, while boys do not (Rosen, Adamson, & Bakeman, 1992). Eight- to 30-month old girls also look at an experimenter's face more than boys do when a small moving robot toy enters the room (Sigman & Kasari, 1994).

In the realm of language, girls learn expressive language earlier than boys do (Schachter, Shore, Hodapp, Chalfin, & Bundy, 1978), having better and earlier language skills than males do, including more extensive and earlier vocabularies, reading abilities, and word fluency (Huttenlocher, Haight, Bryk, Seltzer, & Lyons, 1991; Iaccino, 1993).

These differing characteristics of boys and girls evoke different parental reactions. In an effort to constrain their sons' activity levels and help them to regulate their emotional arousal, parents might encourage boys to minimize their emotional expressivity. Research has shown that sons are taught to control their feelings, while daughters are taught to experience them fully (e.g. Fivush, 1993, and ch. 11, this volume). Fathers also emphasize explanations and understanding events for their sons, even when the task is not set up to be about feelings (Bronstein, 1988). These patterns of interaction may lead to a more analytical, abstract way of expressing feelings by sons than by daughters.

Interacting with language-oriented and sociable infant girls may induce parents to express positive emotions to their daughters, especially using language (see Brody, 1999). Perhaps in response to their daughters' language abilities, mothers use a greater variety of emotion words when talking to their preschool daughters than to their preschool sons (Fivush, 1989, 1993; Dunn, Bretherton, & Munn, 1987; Zahn-Waxler et al., 1993), as do fathers (Schell & Gleason, 1989). By 24 months, girls produce more emotion words than do boys (Dunn et al., 1987).

Another consequence of differing sociability/activity levels of sons and daughters is that mothers may feel they need to exaggerate their facial displays of emotion more to sons than to daughters. Exaggerated facial expressions would provide clear signals to sons, helping them to regulate their social interactions as well as to modulate their active behaviors. One compelling study did indicate that mothers exaggerated the facial expressions of fear they displayed to their sons in contrast to those they displayed to their daughters when confronted with novel toys (Rosen et al., 1992). Ironically, the mothers' fear faces, which were stronger for their sons, affected their sons' behavior less than it did their daughters'. Mothers may have tried to exaggerate and emphasize facial expressions of fear in order to get their bold and somewhat socially unresponsive sons to pay more attention to the warnings conveyed in their facial messages. It is certainly possible that the long-term consequences of seeing exaggerated facial expressions is that sons may never learn how to read subtle emotional signals in others, as daughters would be forced to do.

It is important to note here that parents' socialization processes are influenced not only by children's temperaments, but also by many characteristics of the family system, including the parents' own temperaments, the quality of the marital relationship, cultural and socioeconomic background, the particular gender constellation of children in a family, and values and attitudes concerning gender roles (Brody, 1999). For example, parents' gender role stereotypes about males and females may affect their reactions to their infants' temperament, such as data showing that parents are more accepting of shy behaviors in their daughters than in their sons (Radke-Yarrow, Richters, & Wilson, 1988; Stevenson-Hinde, 1988).

In summary, parental socialization influences may be partially driven by characteristics of the infant boys and girls themselves, as well as by cultural values that dictate the acceptability of those characteristics for each sex. Higher activity and arousal levels on the part of sons, and higher sociability and expressive language abilities on the part of daughters may shift the nature of parent–child interactions in particular directions.

Differentiating a gender role identity

A differentiation model of gender identity formation suggests that both males and females differentiate their own emotional expressiveness from what they perceive the opposite sex's emotional expressiveness to be (Fast, 1984). In other words, if females (either peers or adults) express sadness, to be a "real" boy means not to express sadness. If males hit, to be a "real" girl means not to hit. Early pressures to consolidate a gender role identity for boys are complicated by the fact that fathers are generally unavailable to their children, spending with them ⅕ to ⅓ of the time that mothers do (Lamb & Oppenheim, 1989). Without an available role model, boys cannot imitate their father's emotional expressiveness, but rather, are theorized to develop a masculine gender identity by becoming different from their mothers in emotional expressiveness. They attempt to express emotions in accordance with culturally stereotypic models of masculinity, a process termed "positional identification" (cf. Chodorow, 1978). In the case of emotional expressiveness, this would involve the minimization of emotional expression, especially in a social context in which expressing intense emotions is considered to be "feminine" and the minimization of emotional expression is considered to be "masculine" (Fast, 1984; Chodorow, 1978).

In contrast, girls do not need to develop a gender identity which is different from that of their mothers. They are theorized to identify with and model their mother's emotional expressiveness as females, learning to express a wide range of emotions in close relationships with their mothers (Chodorow, 1978). But what girls do need to do, particularly during adolescence, is to develop a sense of self that is different from that of their mothers. Particularly in adolescence, females are theorized to have difficulties in separating from their mothers and in developing their own identities (Blos, 1962). They may learn to use the expression of negative emotions, especially hostility and distress, as a way of communicating differentiation or autonomy needs from their mothers (Chodorow, 1978; Brody, 1996, 1999). This would be especially true in a Western context, where the development of adolescent autonomy is adaptive for both males and females.

Description of family study of emotional expressiveness

In a sample of 95 families, I explored processes of differentiation in the emotional expressiveness of children and families. The primary hypothesis in this study was that sons' emotional expressiveness would be positively related to that of their fathers, but would be inversely related to that of their mothers in both valence (whether positive versus negative emotions were expressed) and intensity. Daughters' emotional expressiveness was hypothesized to be positively related to their mothers in terms of its relative valence and intensity. It was also hypothesized that sons and daughters with mothers who had difficulty with differentiation themselves (that is, who were more restrictive or less individuated from their children, thereby imposing their own feelings onto those of their children), would have children who expressed intense negative emotions as a way of communicating their needs for separation.

The sample consisted of parents (29 to 63 years old) who had been married or living together for at least three years. There were 51 families with a participating daughter (X_{age} = 9.32 years, s.d. = 2.12), and 44 with a participating son (M_{age} = 9.53, s.d. = 2.32). (However, only 46 fathers of daughters participated in the study and only 38 fathers of sons.) There was no significant age difference for boys and girls. The median socioeconomic status for the families was middle-level administrator (Hollingshead & Redlich, 1958), and parents' education averaged 2 years of college. The sample was primarily Caucasian and included various ethnic and religious groups, including American-Irish, -Italian, -Portuguese, -Jewish, -Catholic, -Hindu, and -Protestant.

In order to explore differentiation processes between parents and their children, mothers and fathers independently completed the Block Child Rearing Practices Report (CRPR; Block, 1965), yielding measures of maternal and paternal nurturance/warmth (alpha = .82), maternal and paternal restrictiveness (alpha = .69), and a measure of maternal individuation from the child (alpha = .56). Items from each scale are shown in table 2.1. The nurturance and restrictiveness scales came from previous research (DeKovic, Janssens, & Gerris, 1991), whereas the individuation scale was developed for the present study.

To measure emotional expressivity, both children and parents were independently administered the Children's and the Adults' Emotional Story Tests (CEST and EST: Brody, Lovas & Hay, 1995). These measures depict various situations which evoke a variety of emotions, including fear, warmth, anger, and hurt (see table 2.1). Half of the stories in each task had female story characters and half had male story characters. Participants were asked to rate the intensity with which they would experience four emotions toward both male and female story characters: scared, angry, hurt, and warm, on a 0 to 3 scale for children and a 0 to 5 scale for adults. For each emotion, the average intensity was computed across all stories.

Children's emotional expressiveness was also measured with a projective storytelling measure, the revised Tasks for Emotional Development (TED-R; Brody & Hay, 1991). Children were given 3 pictures of individuals with no facial features: one of a same sexed person

Table 2.1. *Sample items from measures*

The Block Child Rearing Practices Report	
Nurturance	"I hug my child."
	"I joke and play with my child."
	"I make sure my child knows that I appreciate what he/she tries or accomplishes."
Restrictiveness	"I try to keep my child away from children or families who have different ideas or values from our own."
	"I teach my child to keep control of his/her feelings at all times."
Individuation	"I like some time to myself, away from my child."
	"I wish my child didn't grow up so fast."
Emotional Story Test CEST (children's version)	
Fear	"You're sitting in your room and suddenly you see someone looking in your window."
Anger	"Someone takes your chocolate-chip cookie away without asking you."
Emotional Story Test EST (adult's version)	
Fear	"You're walking to your car at night and suddenly you see a stranger approaching you."
Anger	"You ask someone to turn down loud music which is bothering you and they refuse to do so."

looking in a mirror; one of two same sexed people looking at each other; and one of two opposite sexed people looking at each other. Children were asked to write a story about the story characters, including what they were feeling and thinking. The types of story characters children wrote about were coded, including mothers, fathers, or no family members, in order to explore and test theories about how children's emotional expressiveness was related to their sense of being connected to their family members (Brody, Wise & Monuteaux, 1997; Brody, 1999). Including parents as story characters was assumed to be a measure of children's identification with them, since the pictures children were asked to write about did not depict images of their parents or other adults. The types of emotions that children wrote about were also coded, including the positive or negative emotional tone of the story (3-point scale: negative, neutral, and positive), and the frequencies with which children mentioned positive emotions (such as liking), and negative emotions (such as angry or sad). Story tone was averaged across the three stories, controlling for the total word count used by each participant, and the frequencies of each type of emotion and story character were summed across the three stories, again controlling for the total word count.

Table 2.2. *Means and standard deviations for mothers' and fathers'*
nurturance and restrictiveness

	Nurturance		Restrictiveness	
	M	SD	M	SD
Mothers				
Sons	6.29	.54	3.57	.81
Daughters	6.20	.48	3.42	.85
Fathers				
Sons	5.34	1.07	3.86	.84
Daughters	5.79	.49	3.78	.78

Results: Sex differences in child rearing and parent emotions

Means and standard deviations for parents' child rearing styles are displayed in table 2.2. Two-way ANOVAs (parent sex × children's sex) and subsequent post hoc Newman Keuls analyses using the Block CRPR indicated that fathers reported being more nurturing toward daughters than toward sons, $F(1,88) = 6.67, p < .01$. Mothers reported themselves to be equally nurturing toward daughters and toward sons, but more nurturing toward both sexes than were fathers, $F(1,88) = 63.40, p < .001$. The higher nurturance of fathers toward daughters is consistent with display rules about encouraging the expression of affection and warmth in daughters, as well as with the observations discussed above that daughters may be more sociable than are young sons, perhaps eliciting their fathers' nurturance more than sons do. Although there were no parent sex × child sex interactions for restrictiveness, fathers also reported being more restrictive toward both daughters and sons than did mothers, $F(1,87) = 6.34, p < 02$.

As displayed in table 2.3, mothers reported more hurt, $F(1,89) = 6.54$, $p < .01$; more anger, $F(1,89) = 3.20, p < .05$, and more fear than did fathers, $F(1,89) = 21.65, p < .001$. Women's higher expressions of anger are not in accordance with stereotypic display rules for women, but are in accordance with previous literature showing that women report more intense anger to hypothetical stories than men (see Brody, 1997). Because Pearson-r correlations indicated that expressions of fear, hurt, and anger were significantly related to each other in both mothers and fathers, factor scores for the expression of negative emotions were created for mothers and fathers using principal components factor analyses of fear, hurt and anger on the EST. For mothers, this negative emotions factor (accounting for 65% of the variance) was not significantly

Table 2.3. *Gender differences in parents' and children's emotions*[a]

	Males		Females	
	M	SD	M	SD
Children				
CEST-Fear	.43	.26	.55	.23
Parents				
Anger	−.05	.34	.05	.39
Hurt	−.07	.48	.09	.25
Fear	−.10	.26	.08	.32

Note:
[a] Based on scores corrected for word count

related to warmth/respect ($r = -.01$, n.s.). For fathers, the negative emotions factor (accounting for 51% of the variance) was significantly positively related to warmth/respect ($r = .34$, $p < .001$), suggesting that fathers who are emotionally expressive are expressive of both positive and negative emotions, unlike their wives.

Using Pearson-r correlations, fathers' and mothers' emotions were found to relate significantly to their child rearing styles. Mothers who were more restrictive expressed more fear ($r = .22$, $p < .05$) and more hurt ($r = .23$, $p < .02$) than did mothers who were less restrictive. Mothers who were less individuated also tended to express more fear ($r = .16$, $p < .10$), and more anger ($r = .17$, $p < .10$). This supports previous work (Parker, 1983) that restrictive and intrusive mothers' child-rearing style may be related to high levels of fear, anxiety, or hostility.

Both mothers and fathers who were more nurturing on the Block CRPR responded to stories on the EST by expressing more warmth/respect than did parents who were less nurturing (fathers: $r = .30$, $p = .01$; mothers $r = .20$, $p < .05$). Because parental nurturance and the intensity of parental expressions of warmth were significantly correlated, these two variables were averaged to form two composite scores, one for mothers and one for fathers, which will hereafter be referred to as maternal or paternal warmth.

Sex differences in children's emotions

Sex differences in the emotions children reported to the CEST, and the TED-R are displayed in table 2.3. As consistent with previous work showing more intense expressions of fear and vulnerability by females rather than males, two-tailed t-tests indicated that girls reported more fear to the CEST than did boys, $t(118) = 2.48$, $p = .01$). There were no gender differences on the TED-R, either in types of emotions or in the types of story characters that boys and girls included in their stories.

Further, the two sexes showed differing patterns of emotional expressiveness. When a principal components factor analysis was conducted on the intensity of warmth, anger, hurt, and fear expressed by daughters on the CEST, their 4 emotions loaded on a single factor which accounted for 64% of the variance. Warmth loaded negatively (-.52), while anger (.88), hurt (.90) , and fear (.82) loaded positively. In other words, for girls, expressing negative feelings was inversely related to expressing positive feelings. This is consistent with the idea that for girls, the expression of positive and negative feelings are not independent: girls may use positive feelings to mask negative feelings, or may find it difficult to express both positive and negative feelings in their reactions to situations. In contrast, for boys, positive and negative feelings were independent factors. The likelihood of expressing warmth loaded on a separate factor, accounting for 27% of the variance, from the likelihood of expressing the negative emotions of anger (factor loading $= .85$), fear (factor loading $= .85$), and hurt (factor loading $= .87$), accounting for 56% of the variance.

Relationships between mothers' characteristics and sons' emotions

The results of the partial correlations (controlling for children's age) testing the relationship between maternal emotion, maternal child rearing variables and children's emotional expressiveness are displayed in table 2.4. The results indicated that the intensity with which sons and mothers expressed warmth was inversely related. Boys whose mothers scored highly on expressing intense warmth/nurturance reported less intense warmth and less intense negative emotions, in contrast to other boys. And, counter-intuitively, mothers who reported more intense negative emotions had sons who tended to score highly on expressing warmth.

What is especially interesting is that boys who reported less warmth on the CEST were also significantly less likely to place their mothers in their projective TED-R stories ($r = -.32, p < .01$). This suggests that sons who expressed less warmth relative to other sons were those who identified less with, were more differentiated from, or were more independent of their mothers.

The results also supported the idea that sons may express intense negative emotions as a way of communicating needs for distance from mothers. Alternatively, perhaps mothers become more restrictive and less individuated when their sons express more intense negative emotions. As shown in table 2.4, mothers who reported themselves to be less

Table 2.4. *Partial correlations between mothers' child rearing and emotions and children's emotions*

| | Mothers' emotions and child rearing style | | | | | | | |
| | Warmth/Nurturance | | Negative emotions | | Restrictiveness | | Individuation[a] | |
Children's emotions	Girls	Boys	Girls	Boys	Girls	Boys	Girls	Boys
Negative emotions (CEST Fact. 1)-Boys		$-.39^{**}$		.01		$-.01$		$.28^{*}$
Warmth (CEST Fact. 2)-Boys		$-.30^{*}$		$.26^{T}$		.04		.14
High negative/low positive intensity (CEST Fact. 1 - Girls)	$.27^{*}$		.21		.03		$.23^{T}$	
Negative tone (TED-R)	$-.04$	.10	$-.02$	$-.08$	$-.08$	$.25^{T}$	$-.03$	$.30^{*}$
Positive frequency (TED-R)	.14	.03	.16	.12	.07	$-.20$	.00	$-.09$
Negative frequency (TED-R)	$-.26^{*}$	.10	$-.08$	$-.20$	$-.05$	.22	$-.22$	.17
Mothers as characters	$-.10$	.22	$-.08$	$-.32^{*}$	$-.08$	$-.33^{*}$	$-.13$	$-.32^{*}$
Fathers as characters	.15	$-.13$	$-.12$	.10	.00	$.28^{T}$	$-.01$	.15
No family members in stories	$.35^{*}$	.05	.20	.20	$-.09$	.20	$-.18$	$.43^{**}$

Notes:
[a] Higher scores represent mothers who report themselves to be more merged with their children.
$* p < .05$; $** p < .01$; $^{T} p < .10$

individuated from their sons or more restrictive in their child rearing had sons who expressed *more intense* negative emotions or a more negative story tone. And in turn, sons with more negative story tone on the TED-R tended to be less likely to place their mothers in their stories ($r = -.25$, $p < .10$). Sons were also less likely to place mothers in their stories when their mothers reported themselves to be more restrictive, less individuated, and when their mothers expressed more intense negative emotions in comparison to other mothers (see table 2.4).

Since mothers who reported a lack of individuation or high restrictiveness also expressed increased intensity of negative emotions, it may be that children of less individuated or highly restrictive mothers are simply imitating their mothers' negative emotional expressiveness. In order to explore this idea, the relative contributions of mothers' child-rearing style versus their emotional expressiveness to the intensity of their sons' negative emotions was compared in 2 sets of stepwise multiple regression analyses. These analyses indicated that when mothers' child rearing style was entered following her negative emotions, the change in R^2 was significant (change in R^2 for individuation: predicting to sons' negative affect tone = .09, $p < .05$; predicting to sons' negative intensity = .07, $p < .06$; change in R^2 for restrictiveness predicting to sons' negative affect tone = .08, $p < .06$). The change in R^2 was never significant when mothers' emotions were entered following her individuation or following her restrictiveness. In other words, sons' negative emotions were significantly related to their mothers' lack of individuation and her high levels of restrictiveness, not to the negative emotions she reported.

Relationships between mothers' characteristics and daughters' emotions

As displayed in table 2.4, partial correlations revealed that there were discrepancies between how the intensity and frequency of daughters' negative emotions related to mothers' warmth. Daughters with mothers high on warmth displayed *increased intensity* of negative feelings on the CEST while at the same time expressing *less frequent* negative emotions on the TED-R. How do we make sense of this seeming contradiction? It may be that daughters of warm and nurturing mothers internalize a sense of well being and actually experience less frequent negative feelings than do other daughters, thereby expressing them less frequently. However, when they do express negative feelings, they may feel comfortable expressing them intensely because their nurturing mothers respond non-punitively to intense affect. This argument would be consistent with the object relations perspective that nurturing and close mothers foster positive emotions in their daughters (thus accounting for their daughters' less frequent expression of negative emotions) and also foster comfort with the expression of a wide range of intense affects (Sandler & Sandler, 1986). Although an object relations model may explain why daughters who are nurtured are more comfortable expressing intense negative feelings, it does less well explaining why such daughters would express less intense positive feelings. As displayed in table 2.4, girls with nurturing mothers minimized the intensity of positive feelings they displayed on the CEST, in contrast to girls with less nurturing mothers.

Alternatively, the finding that high levels of maternal warmth are related to increased negative emotional intensity and decreased positive intensity on the part of daughters can also be interpreted as a way daughters differentiate from their nurturing mothers (see Brody, 1996). This differentiation hypothesis is also supported by the finding that girls were less likely to write about family members in their stories when their mothers were nurturing (see table 2.4). They were also less likely to write about family members when they themselves expressed more intense negative emotions on the CEST ($r = .42, p < .001$).

Unlike boys, girls did not show a clear pattern of expressing intense or frequent negative emotions in relation to mothers who were restrictive or more merged with them. Only one trend emerged: daughters of mothers who reported being less individuated from them tended to express more intense negative feelings on the CEST. Multiple regression analyses conducted to assess the relative contributions of mothers' emotions as compared to mothers' individuation to daughters' negative emotional expressiveness on the CEST showed insignificant results. Neither maternal variable (individuation or negative emotions) related strongly enough to daughter's expressiveness to show significant R^2 changes following the entry of the other variable.

Relationships between fathers' characteristics and children's emotions

As displayed in table 2.5, there were few significant relationships between fathers' emotional expressiveness, fathers' child rearing, and children's emotional expressiveness, especially for girls. There were a few suggestions that boys' emotional expressiveness tended to relate positively to that of their fathers, with fathers who scored more highly on the expression of negative emotions having sons who tended to express more intense negative emotions on the CEST and more frequent negative emotions on the TED-R. These sons, however, also tended to express more frequent positive emotions on the TED-R. As tended to be true of restrictive mothers, fathers who were restrictive had sons who expressed a higher frequency of negative affect words on the TED-R than did other sons. Finally, in relation to higher paternal nurturance,

Table 2.5. *Partial correlations between fathers' child rearing and emotions and children's emotions*

	Fathers' emotions and child rearing style					
	Warmth/Nurturance		Negative emotions		Restrictive	
Children's emotions	Girls	Boys	Girls	Boys	Girls	Boys
Negative emotions (CEST Fact. 1)-Boys		−.20		.27^T		.23
Warmth (CEST Fact. 2)-Boys		.17		−.10		−.01
High Negative/Low Positive Intensity (CEST Fact. 1 – Girls)	−.13		−.05		.14	
Negative Tone (TED-R)	−.26^T	.04	−.04	.22	−.14	.00
Positive Frequency (TED-R)	.01	−.03	.01	.27^T	.05	.06
Negative Frequency (TED-R)	−.17	.10	.19	.28^T	.06	.32*
Mothers as Characters	.19	.09	.26^T	.10	.01	.23
Fathers as Characters	.14	.03	.05	.15	−.11	.00
No family members in stories	−.15	−.08	−.09	.01	.10	.22

Notes:
* $p<.05$; ** $p<.01$;^{T} $p<.10$

girls' stories were less negative in emotional tone, indicating that paternal nurturance may foster positive feelings in girls. Differentiating from fathers may be less salient for girls at this developmental stage than differentiating from mothers. On the other hand, when fathers expressed more intense negative emotions, girls tended to be more likely to put mothers in their stories as characters (see table 2.5), suggesting that girls may distance from fathers who express negative emotions, or that fathers may become more expressive of negative emotions in the face of close mother–daughter relationships.

In summary, these complex findings can be summarized as follows. Mothers' child-rearing style and quality of emotional expressiveness were more clearly related to their children's emotional expressiveness, especially their sons, than was fathers'. Even though mothers did not differ in the extent to which they reported themselves to be nurturing, restrictive, or merged toward their daughters versus their sons, there were gender differences in the patterns of relationships between mothers' child-rearing characteristics and their sons' and daughters' expressed emotions. Mothers who were more restrictive or more merged with their children had sons who tended to express more intense negative emotions relative to other children. Sons of these mothers were also less likely to incorporate their mothers in stories they wrote, suggesting attempts to establish distance from their mothers. The extent to which mothers were individuated or restrictive contributed more to the variance in their sons' negative emotional expressiveness than did the mothers' own negative emotional expressiveness. Daughters' expression of negative emotions was not significantly related to the restrictiveness of their mothers. As similar to boys, there was one trend for daughters to express more intense emotions when their mothers were less individuated from them. These data indicate that separation pressures may relate more to boys' than to girls' emotional expressivity at this developmental stage.

Both boys and girls also showed some evidence that they expressed emotions which were negatively related in intensity to the intensity of the emotions that their mothers expressed, with boys showing clearer evidence than girls. Mothers who expressed more intense warmth and nurturance than other mothers had sons who expressed less intense warmth and less intense negative emotions than other boys. Further, mothers who expressed relatively more intense negative emotions had sons who tended to express more intense warmth. Girls whose mothers expressed warmth and nurturance expressed less intense positive and more intense negative emotions, but also less frequent negative emotions relative to other girls.

Although it is possible that differentiation from the opposite sex may be an inherent part of gender identity formation (regardless of cultural values), the fact that differentiation occurs specifically in the area of emotional expressiveness is probably due to cultural stereotypes concerning differences between the emotional expressiveness of the two sexes. In other words, boys could become different from their mothers in myriad ways: by wearing blue shirts instead of pink, by eating with chopsticks instead of forks (or vice versa), or by walking backward instead of forward. The ways in which boys actually do become different from their mothers (by minimizing their emotions, or by expressing different emotions from those of their mothers) are those that are reinforced by the culture as being gender-linked.

It is also possible that sons' style of emotional expressiveness may drive their mothers to respond to them in particular ways. Sons who minimize their expression of emotion may induce mothers to be nurturing toward them. This may be true if we speculate that mothers are more comfortable nurturing sons who conform to stereotypic masculine display rules. Similarly, sons who cut off from their mothers (as suggested by not placing them as characters in their stories) or who express intense negative emotions may have mothers who respond by becoming more restrictive and more merged in their identification with their sons.

Overview

I have argued that the socialization of gender differences in emotional expression is complex. I have reviewed three different, yet interacting areas involved in the socialization process: display rules and imitation; gender-differentiated parent–child interactions, which may be driven by gender differences in infant temperament; and processes of differentiation between the emotional expressions of children and their parents. All of these processes are shaped by cultural values concerning gender roles, and take place within a cultural context in which females have lower power and status relative to males. Socializing emotional expressiveness differently for the two sexes maintains culturally mandated gender roles, including power and status imbalances.

Notes

1 Although there have been many studies of similarities in parent–child emotional expressiveness, few have focused on imitation *per se* (see Halberstadt, 1991).

2 The item "I sometimes tease and make fun of my child" was also endorsed more by fathers of boys in two samples than by fathers of girls. The item "I feel it is good for a child to play competitive games" was endorsed more for boys than for girls by both mothers and fathers.

References

Adler, P. A., Kless, S. J., & Adler, P. (1992). Socialization to gender roles: Popularity among elementary school boys and girls. *Sociology of Education*, 65, 169–187.

Barbee, A, Cunningham, M., Winstead, B., Derlega, V., Bulley, M, Yaneeklov, P., & Druen, P. (1993). Effects of gender role expectations on the social support process. *Journal of Social Issues*, 49, 175–190.

Block, J. H. (1965). The child-rearing practices report, Berkeley: Institute of Human Development, University of California, unpublished manuscript.

Block, J. (1973). Conceptions of sex role: Some cross cultural and longitudinal perspectives. *American Psychologist*, 28, 512–526.

Block, J. (1984). *Sex Role Identity and Ego Development*. San Francisco: Jossey Bass.

Blos, P. (1962). *On Adolescence: A Psychoanalytic Interpretation*. New York: The Free Press of Glencoe.

Brody, L. R. (1993). On understanding gender differences in the expression of emotion: Gender roles, socialization and language. In S. Ablon, D. Brown, E. Khantzian, & J. Mack (Eds.), *Human feelings: Explorations in affect development and meaning* (pp. 89–121). Hillsdale, NJ: Analytic Press.

Brody, L. R. (1996). Gender, emotional expressiveness and parent–child boundaries. In R. Kavanaugh, B. Zimmerberg-Glick, & S. Fein (Eds.), *Emotion: Interdisciplinary perspectives* (pp. 139–170). Mahwah, NJ: Lawrence Erlbaum.

Brody, L. R. (1997). Beyond stereotypes: gender and emotion. *Journal of Social Issues*, 53, 369–394.

Brody, L. R. (1999). *Gender, emotion and the family*. Cambridge, MA: Harvard University Press.

Brody, L. R., & Hay, D. (1991). A projective measure of self esteem based on the TED: An alternative to self-report measures. Presented at the Biennial Meeting of the Society for Research in Child Development, April 1991, Seattle, WA.

Brody, L. R., & Hall, J. (1993). Gender and emotion, In M. Lewis & J. Haviland (Eds.), *Handbook of emotions* (pp. 447–460). New York: Guilford Press.

Brody, L. R., Lovas, G., & Hay, D. (1995). Sex differences in anger and fear as a function of situational context. *Sex Roles*, 32, 47–78.

Brody, L., Wise, D., & Monuteaux, D. (1997). *Children's emotional story themes, gender, and parenting styles*. Poster presented at the Biennial Meeting of the Society for Research in Child Development, Washington, D.C.

Bronstein, P. (1988). Father child interaction: implications for gender role socialization. In Bronstein, P., & Cowan, C. P. (Eds.), *Fatherhood today: Men's changing role in the family* (pp.107–124). New York: Wiley.

Cancian, F. M., & Gordon, S. L. (1988). Changing emotion norms in marraige: Love and anger in US women's magazines since 1900. *Gender and Society*, 2, 308–342.

Chodorow, N. (1978). *The reproduction of mothering*. Berkeley: University of California Press.

Chung, T., & Asher, S. R. (1996). Children's goals and strategies in peer conflict situations. *Merrill-Palmer Quarterly, 42,* 125–147.

Clarke-Stewart, K. (1973). Interactions between mothers and their young children: characteristics and consequences. *Monographs of the Society for Research in Child Development, 38,* 6–7, Serial No. 153.

Cole, P. (1986). Children's spontaneous control of facial expression. *Child Development, 57,* 1309–1321.

Crick, N. (1997). Engagement in gender normative versus nonnormative forms of aggression: links to social-psychological adjustment. *Developmental Psychology, 33,* 610–617.

Davis, M., LaRosa, P., & Foshee, D. (1992). Emotion work in supervisor-subordinate relations: Gender differences in the perception of angry displays. *Sex Roles, 26,* 513–531.

Davis, T. L. (1995). Gender differences in masking negative emotions: Ability or motivation? *Developmental Psychology, 31,* 660–667.

DeKovic, M., Janssens, J., & Gerris, J. (1991). Factor structure and construct validity of the Block Child Rearing Practices Reports (CRPR). *Psychological Assessment, 2,* 182–187.

Dodge, K., Coie, J., Pettit, G., & Price, J. (1990). Peer status and aggression in boys' groups: Developmental and contextual analyses. *Child Development, 61,* 1289–1309.

Dunn, J., Bretherton, I., & Munn, P. (1987). Conversations about feeling states between mothers and their children. *Developmental Psychology, 23,* 132–139.

Eagly, A. H., & Steffen, V. (1986). Gender and aggressive behavior: a meta-analytic review of the social psychological literature. *Psychological Bulletin, 100,* 309–330.

Eaton, W., & Ennis, L. (1986). Sex differences in human motor activity level. *Psychological Bulletin, 100,* 19–28.

Eder, D., & Parker, S. (1987). The cultural production and reproduction of gender: The effect of extracurricular activities on peer group culture. *Sociology of Education, 60,* 200–213.

Fast, I. (1984). *Gender identity: A differentiation model.* New York: Analytic Press.

Fivush, R. (1989). Exploring sex differences in the emotional content of mother–child conversations about the past. *Sex Roles, 20,* 675–691.

Fivush, R. (1993). Emotional content of parent–child conversations about the past. In D. A. Nelson (Ed.), *Memory and affect in development: Minnesota symposia on child psychology* (pp. 39–78). Hillsdale, NJ: Lawrence Erlbaum.

Frost, W., & Averill, J. (1982). Differences between men and women in the everyday experience of anger. In J. Averill, *Anger and aggression: An essay on emotion* (pp. 281–316). New York: Springer-Verlag.

Graham, J., Gentry, K., & Green, J. (1981). The self presentational nature of emotional expression: Some evidence. *Personality and Social Psychology Bulletin, 7,* 467–474.

Greif, E., Alvarez, M., & Ulman, K. (1981). *Recognizing emotions in other people: Sex differences in socialization.* Presented at the Biennial meeting of the Society for Research in Child Development, Boston, MA.

Gunnar, M., & Donahue, M. (1980). Sex differences in social responsiveness between six months and twelve months. *Child Development, 51,* 262–265.

Halberstadt, A. (1991). Socialization of expressiveness: Family influences in particular and a model in general. In R. S. Feldman & B. Rimé (Eds.), *Fundamentals in nonverbal behavior* (pp. 106–160). Cambridge University Press.

Hart, C. H., DeWolf, M., & Burts, D. (1993). Parental disciplinary strategies and preschoolers' play behavior in playground settings In C. H. Hart (Ed.), *Children in Playgrounds* (pp. 271–313). Albany, NY: SUNY Press.

Hochschild, A. (1983). *The managed heart: Commercialization of human feeling.* Berkeley: University of California Press.

Hollingshead, A., & Redlich, F. (1958). *Social class and mental illness: A community study.* New York: Wiley.

Huttenlocher, J., Haight, W., Bryk, A., Seltzer, M., & Lyons, T. (1991). Early vocabulary growth: Relation to language input and gender. *Developmental Psychology, 27,* 236–248.

Iaccino, J. (1993). *Left brain right brain differences: Inquiries, evidence and new approaches.* Hillsdale, NJ: Lawrence Erlbaum.

Klein, R., & Durfee, J. (1978). Effects of sex and birth order on infant social behavior. *Infant Behavior and Development, 1,* 106–117.

Kochanska, G., Murray, K., Jacques, T., Koenig, A., & Vandegeest, K. (1996). Inhibitory control in young children and its role in emerging internalization. *Child Development, 67,* 490–507.

Lamb, M., & Oppenheim, D. (1989). Fatherhood and father–child relationships. In S. Cath, A. Gurwitt, & L. Gunsberg (Eds.), *Fathers and their families* (pp. 11–16). Hillsdale, NJ: The Analytic Press.

Lerner, H. (1980). Internal prohibitions against female anger. *American Journal of Psychoanalysis, 40,* 137–148.

Malatesta, C., Culver, C., Tesman, J., & Shepard, B. (1989). The development of emotion expression during the first two years of life. *Monographs of the Society for Research in Child Development, 50,* 1–2, Serial No. 219.

Malatesta, C., & Haviland, J. (1982). Learning display rules. *Child Development, 53,* 991–1003.

Parker, G. (1983). *Parental overprotection: A risk factor in psychosocial development.* New York: Grune & Stratton.

Parnell, K. (1991). Toddler interaction in relation to mother and peers. Unpublished doctoral dissertation, Boston University.

Perry, D., & Bussey, K. (1979). The social learning theory of sex differences: Imitation is alive and well. *Journal of Personality and Social Psychology, 37,* 1699–1712.

Radke-Yarrow, M., Richters, J., & Wilson, W. E. (1988). Child development in a network of relationships. In R. Hinde, & J. Stevenson-Hinde (Eds.), *Relationships within families: Mutual influences* (pp. 48–67). Oxford: Clarendon Press.

Rosen, W. D., Adamson, L. B., & Bakeman, R. (1992). An experimental investigation of infant social referencing: Mothers' messages and gender differences. *Developmental Psychology, 28,* 1172–1178.

Ruddick, S. (1982). Maternal thinking. In B. Thorne, & M. Yalom (Eds), *Rethinking the family* (pp. 76–94). New York: Longman.

Saarni, C. (1988). Children's understanding of the interpersonal consequences of dissemblance of nonverbal emotional expressive behavior. *Journal of Nonverbal Behavior, 12,* 275–294.

Sandler, J., & Sandler, A.M. (1986). On the development of object relationships and affects. In P. Buckley (Ed.), *Essential papers on object relations* (pp. 272–292). New York University Press.

Saudino, K., & Eaton, W. (1991). Continuity and change in objectively assessed temperament: A longitudinal twin study of activity level. *Child Development, 62,* 1167–1174.

Saudino, K.J., Plomin, R., & Defries, J. (1996). Tester-rated temperament at 14, 20, and 24 months: Environmental change and genetic continuity. *British Journal of Developmental Psychology, 14,* 129–144.

Schachter, F., Shore, E., Hodapp, R. Chalfin, S., & Bundy, C. (1978). Do girls talk earlier? Mean length of utterance in toddlers. *Developmental Psychology, 14,* 388–392.

Schell, A., & Gleason, J. B. (1989, December). *Gender differences in the acquisition of the vocabulary of emotion.* Presented at the Annual meeting of the American Association of Applied Linguistics, Washington D.C.

Serbin, L., Marchessault, K., McAffer, V., Peters, P., & Schwartzman, A. (1993). Patterns of social behavior on the playground in 9 to 11 year girls and boys: Relation to teacher perceptions and to peer ratings of aggression, withdrawal, and likability. In C. Hart (Ed.), *Children on playgrounds: Research perspectives and applications* (pp. 162–183). Albany: SUNY Press.

Shields, S., & Koster, B. (1989). Emotional stereotyping of parents in child rearing manuals, 1915–1980. *Social Psychology Quarterly, 52,* 44–55

Siegel, S., & Alloy, L. (1990). Interpersonal perceptions and consequences of depressive-significant other relationships: A naturalistic study of college roommates. *Journal of Abnormal Psychology, 99,* 361–373

Sigman, M., & Kasari, C. (June, 1994). Social referencing, shared attention, and empathy in infants. Paper presented at the International conference on infant studies, Paris France.

Soussignon, R., & Schaal, B. (1996). Children's facial responsiveness to odors: Influences of hedonic valence of odor, gender, age, and social presence. *Developmental Psychology 32,* 367–379.

Stearns, C. (1988). "Lord help me walk humbly": Anger and sadness in England and America, 1570–1750. In C. Stearns, & P. Stearns (Eds.), *Emotion and Social Change* (pp. 39–68). New York: Holmes and Meier.

Stevenson-Hinde, J. 1988. Individuals in relationships. In R. A. Hinde & J. Stevenson-Hinde (Eds.), *Relationships within families: Mutual influences* (pp. 68–82). Oxford: Clarendon Press.

Underwood, M., Coie, J., & Herbsman, C. (1992). Display rules for anger and aggression in school-age children. *Child Development, 63,* 366–380.

Weinberg, K., Tronick, E. Z., Cohn, J. F., & Olson, K. L. (in press). Gender differences in emotional expressivity and self-regulation during early infancy. *Developmental Psychology.*

Zahn-Waxler, C., Ridgeway, D., Denham, S., Usher, B., & Cole, P. (1993). Pictures of infants' emotions: A task for assessing mothers' and young children's verbal communications about affect. In R. Emde, J. Osofsky, & P. Butterfield (Eds.), *The IFEEL pictures: A new instrument for interpreting emotions.* Clinical infant reports series of the ZERO TO THREE/National Center for Clinical Infant Programs (pp. 217–236). International Universities Press, Inc, Madison, CT.

Zahn-Waxler, C., Radke-Yarrow, M., Wagner, E., & Chapman, M. (1992a). Development of concern for others. *Developmental Psychology, 28,* 126–136.

Zahn-Waxler, C., Robinson, J., & Emde, R. (1992b). The development of empathy in twins. *Developmental Psychology, 28,* 1038–1047.

Zeman, J. & Garber, J. (1996). Display rules for anger, sadness, and pain: It depends on who is watching. *Child Development, 67,* 957–973.

3. Men's and women's lay theories of emotion

VANDA L. ZAMMUNER

The function and contents of lay theories of emotion

What we believe about the social world, how we conceptualize it, and how we feel towards it, contributes to shape how we deal with it. In turn, the information that results from our transactions with the social world serves to construct, modify, enlarge, or update our knowledge (e.g., Nisbett & Ross, 1980; Fiske & Taylor, 1991). The focus of this chapter is people's lay theories of emotion, specifically in relation to gender roles and identities. A lay theory can be defined as a more or less coherent, rich, and structured set of beliefs in relation to a given domain or object of our social world, ourselves included. The richness of a lay theory is expected to be related to the culturally based subjective salience of the object it focuses upon (Mesquita & Frijda, 1992), a hypothesis that has been verified in relation to other kinds of knowledge schemata, such as the self-concept (e.g., Fiske & Taylor, 1991). Lay theories of emotion are likely to be salient as well as extensive, because emotional experiences pervade our entire life, both directly and indirectly. The occasions to learn about emotions are countless. We learn from our own experiences, from others' reaction to them, from observing others experience emotions, or from emotional stories as told in novels or movies. Moreover, we are motivated to become emotionally competent, because, as most of us discover quite early in life, emotional incompetence is likely to result in social rejection, loneliness, or greater stress (e.g., Saarni, 1990).

Lay theories may include different types of emotion beliefs. *Aspecific emotion beliefs* focus on aspects of the superordinate category, such as, what conditions are likely to trigger an emotion in general (e.g., "You get emotional if an event is important to you"), or what it means to feel it (e.g., "It is difficult to conceal an intense emotion"). *Specific emotion beliefs* instead describe specific members of the category, such as, what kind of experience anger is (e.g., "Anger is typically an intense, but short-lasting emotion"). Finally, beliefs may be either *context-free*, that is, general descriptions that hold independently of a specific emotion

48

transaction, or *context-bound* (e.g., "At work you need to control your anger," or "It might be useful to let your partner know that you are angry with him"). In general these beliefs are expected to be congruent with culturally based norms about the meaning, adequacy, and legitimacy of emotions (see also Camras & Allison, 1989; Conway & Bekerian, 1987; Fehr & Russell, 1984; Shaver, Schwartz, Kirson, & O'Connor, 1987).

When individuals interpret, judge, or predict an emotional transaction, the gender of the protagonist may be crucial for the contents of lay theories on emotion. In most cultures gender is associated with descriptive and prescriptive norms about almost every aspect of a person's life, emotional experiences included. To borrow a term from Levy (1984), we may argue that social categorization based on biological sex is "hypercognized." According to gender norms, women are expected to be nurturant, caring for others, interested in interpersonal relationships, in other words, to fulfill social roles that require a communal, expressive, and somewhat passive orientation. This orientation to a great extent presupposes emotionality. Men instead are expected to be active agents who give priority to impersonal goals and are capable of mastering their world, that is, to fulfill instrumental, agentic roles that require rationality (see, for instance, Brody & Hall, 1993; Deaux, 1985; Fabes & Martin, 1991; Wood, Christensen, Hebl, & Rothgerber, 1997). In sum, gender role profiles imply different ways of dealing with the world, and the dichotomy emotionality–rationality is at their very core. We may therefore expect lay theories to include emotion beliefs that are gendered according to this dichotomy.

Note, however, that "emotionality" is an ambiguous concept, because it may refer to quite different beliefs about the nature, significance, causes, and consequences of emotional experiences. If women are expected to be more emotional than men, does this mean that, in comparison with men, they have more intense emotions, longer-lasting emotions, more frequent emotions, emotions that occur in a larger variety of contexts, or in reaction to stimuli of lesser magnitude? Does "emotionality" imply greater competence in emotion-related behaviors, such as expressing one's emotions and understanding others, or does it instead imply emotional incompetence?

We also need to consider how gender prescriptions in emotion beliefs are related to the *rationality norm*, originally formulated by Greek philosophers about two millennia ago, yet its "truth" has been stressed to date (e.g. Calhoun & Solomon, 1984; Ruozzi, 1994). This rationality norm stems from a conceptual opposition between two essential faculties of human beings, that is, reason and emotion, mind and heart. On the one hand, emotions are acknowledged as intrinsic to human nature in its transactions with the world; on the other hand, they are conceived as bad, irrational forces that bias people's appraisals, choices and behaviors. People, both men and women, should therefore appraise the world and act in/upon it according to their reason rather than their emotions. Given the long-standing salience of the rationality norm in Western culture, we might expect it to play a prominent role in people's lay theories of emotion.

In sum, lay theories of emotion are expected to contain both ungendered and gendered beliefs. The latter are at least partially based on the fact that gender roles imply that men and women encounter, with a different frequency, events of a different nature (e.g., impersonal versus interpersonal) that are associated with different emotional demands and consequences for men and women (see Deaux, 1984; Fischer, 1993; LaFrance & Banaji, 1992; Rosario, Shinn, March, & Huckabee, 1988; Shields, 1991; Wharton & Erickson 1993; Wood et al. 1997). We thus need to ask when gender plays a crucial role in lay theories, as well as how gender is related to the rationality norm, and to what extent this norm colors or overrides gendered beliefs. We may expect people to invoke gendered beliefs mostly at the contextual level, namely when specific features of emotional transactions raise a concern more relevant for men rather than for women (or vice versa). Ungendered beliefs on the other hand are expected to play a prominent role either if gender is simply not salient, or when it is less salient than other variables.

The present chapter addresses these issues in terms of two questions. First, to what extent, and in relation to which aspects of emotion, do lay theories of emotion comprise beliefs that are coherent with gendered norms? Second, do male and female "theorists" hold similar or dissimilar ([un]gendered) beliefs? In the next sections, I will address these questions by reporting various studies on lay theories of emotion, collected from Italian subjects.

Studies of lay theories about the nature and adequacy of emotion

General aims and method

Lay theories were investigated in two types of questionnaire studies that will be referred to as *open-answer* and *closed-answer* studies. Subjects, female and male university students at various faculties in Northern Italy, judged either one event (in six parallel open-answer studies) or several events (in a closed-answer study). The event was typical of a specific emotion type, namely Jealousy, Envy, Sadness, Pride, Joy, and (in the open-answer studies only) Anger. Events were described in a vignette format, as a personal narrative, for example:

Table 3.1. *Events prototypical of six emotion types*

Emotion	Event label	Event gist
Jealousy	Kiss	P sees his/her partner kiss someone else
	Flirt	P sees his/her partner flirt with someone else, in a public situation
Envy	Equal skill	P's colleague, as capable as P, tells P that s/he has just been promoted to a higher position
	Greater skill	P's colleague, more capable, tells P that s/he has just been promoted to a higher position
Anger	Break-up	P's relationship breaks up: P is unjustly accused of "unfaithfulness"
	Holiday	P's planned holiday cancelled because friend F changes his/her mind
Sadness	Grandfather	P's grandfather, with whom P grew up, dies
	Dog	P's dog dies
Pride	Job	P is selected for an important job among many applicants
	Partner	P is congratulated by friends for his/her new partner
Joy	Lottery	P wins a big amount of money on a lottery
	Trip	P spends a pleasant day with friends at the seaside

Note:
P is the event protagonist, the person who experiences the event

"Paul and I are both employed by a local newspaper; we work on different issues, but both manage to be quite successful because of our writing style. The other day, while I was working at a column, Paul was called by the director. About an hour later he came back to our office and told me that he had been promoted chief-editor." The events within each emotion type differed in terms of their expected subjective salience, nature, and adequacy of the reactions they elicited (see table 3.1; for details and results, see Zammuner, 1994, 1995a–c, 1996a–b, 1998a–d; Zammuner & Frijda, 1994; Zammuner & Massai, 1998; Zammuner & Seminati, 1996).

In each study, subjects answered several questions, such as "What are the emotional reactions to this event?", "What is the intensity of the emotion?", "To what degree does this emotion induce conflict and uncertainty in the experiencer?", "Does one share this emotion with others?". Subjects were asked to make both "typical" and "adequate"

Table 3.2. *Examples of (partial) answers given by subjects in the open-answer studies*

"Typical" Reactions	
1 Jealousy (KISS)	After the *anger* [E] and the *jealousy* [E] perhaps one feels *indifference* [E], which is surely just a way to overcome the crisis.
2 Jealousy (FLIRT)	After I saw it [the partner's flirt], I would feel *cold* towards him [E] and I would *take on an attitude of behavioral rigidity* [B] until I would be able to *get an explanation of the fact from him* [B]; *with the girl I would be detached* [B, E] but *I would not avoid her* [B], moreover *I would not hide from others my annoyance* [B, E] [B] and my *embarrassment* ' [E].
3 Jealousy (FLIRT)	Initially the protagonist would feel a diffuse sensation of *interior pain* [E], then she would *try and understand if she has misinterpreted the situation* [C]. If she cannot explain to herself her husband's behavior she would feel *insecure* [E] and feel a *sense of inferiority* [E]. Afterwards, she would try to react [to the situation] by *attempting, by means of verbal but mainly of nonverbal behaviors, to make her husband feel the same sensation by her getting close to another man* ' [B].
"Adequate" Reactions	
1 Jealousy (KISS)	I think the best is to *go away* [B] and later *ask him for explanations* [B] [about the event] *without making a scene* [B].
2 Jealousy (FLIRT)	*Interfere in the conversation between the two of them* [B] in order to make her pay attention to him [the protagonist] and to *make her understand that he is jealous* [E].
3 Sadness (GRANDFATHER)	After a first moment of *discomfort* [E], she *helps her parents organize the funeral* [B] . . .

Note:
Concepts expressed in each answer, here italicized, were coded as: E: Emotion; B: Behavior; C: Cognition. The judged emotion type and event type are shown in the left column (see table 3.1).

attributions. Typical or descriptive beliefs were measured by asking people to describe how *in general* the protagonist of the described event would react. Next, participants were asked which reaction would be most adequate. This question was assumed to tap subjects' normative beliefs. The protagonists' sex either matched subjects' sex (in all the open-answer studies, and for half of the closed-answer subjects), or was of the opposite sex (for half of the closed-answer subjects).

In the open-answer studies, subjects were asked two questions: (a) "How would the protagonist in this vignette react?", and (b) "What reactions would be adequate in this situation, in order to face it in the best way?". In the closed-answer study, subjects answered four check-list questions twice, first in relation to 'typical' reactions, and then in relation to "adequate" ones. In the open-answer studies answers were coded in four major categories:

1. *Emotions*: verbal labels that specify emotions
2. *Cognitions*: thoughts, appraisals, and action tendencies the protagonist might experience in response to the event
3. *Behaviors*: actual actions of the protagonist
4. *Physiological, visceral and expressive reactions*, such as fainting, blushing, feeling paralyzed, crying, and smiling.

In the closed-answer study, subjects could choose as many options as they wished from this list (see also the section on the closed-answer study, and table 3.4). Answers to these questions, in both formats, were expected to provide information on the contents of subjects' lay theories.

The open-answer studies: Typical emotional reactions attributed by men and women to same-sex event protagonists

The main results concerning men's and women's (N total = 1176[1]) lay theories of emotion elicited by events prototypical of six emotion types are summarized in table 3.3. Table 3.2 shows examples of actual answers. To facilitate comparison across emotion types, as well as across open- and closed-answer studies, the (large number of) categories that were originally developed to code subjects' answers were *recoded* into the answer categories used in the closed-answer study. Each meaningful answer segment was coded into an appropriate category using mostly a data-driven content analysis method. Within each emotion type, subjects' statements and labels were initially used to form categories. Most categories were later grouped together on the basis of their conceptual similarity (for examples of answers and coding categories see Zammuner 1995a-c, 1994). Inter-rater coding agreement was, on the average, above 0.75. All categories were then coded as instances of one of the 4 macro-categories. Frequencies of each micro- and macro-category were computed, within each emotion type and for each level of the independent variables. The influence of the independent variables was analyzed by subjecting micro-category raw frequencies to the Correspondence analysis factorial method (Lebart, Morineau & Fenelon, 1982). The richness of lay theories was assessed by recoding individual answers into binary scores and submitting them to analyses of variance.

I will first report the general trends as regards both the richness and the contents of subjects' theories, as these trends provide a necessary background in evaluating the size and nature of gendered beliefs (see table 3.2 for examples). On average, subjects mentioned about three typical reactions in answer to the question what reactions the protagonist in this vignette would typically have. Negative emotion types, especially sadness, jealousy, and envy events, elicited more answers than positive ones (Mean = 3.1, *vs.* 2.7). The answers referred to various emotion components (see also the examples in table 3.2). This is in line with previously reported studies on emotion-specific knowledge structures (e.g., Shaver et al., 1987; Frijda, Kuipers, & ter Schure, 1989).

On average, Emotions was the most frequently mentioned category, whereas Physiological, visceral, and expressive reactions were the least frequent. The frequency of Cognitions and Behaviors varied according to the valence and nature of the events (see table 3.3). The number of answers also varied significantly according to the specific event, both across and within emotion types. For instance, more answers were supplied for Sadness than for Anger events (for other results about event differences, see Zammuner, 1988a, 1988b). Another example of the fact that answers varied with type of emotion is that *controlling the expression of one's own emotions, trying to control one's own emotional reaction itself,* and *having difficulties in controlling one's emotional reaction* are most frequently mentioned when the experience is negatively valenced, whereas *sincerely showing one's own emotions* and *talking about one's emotions* usually characterize positively valenced events (see table 3.3).

Gender differences

Women generally supplied more answers than did men (on average 3.2 answers, *vs.* 2.7), both for positive and negative emotion types. This difference is due the fact that women expressed a greater number of answers that referred to the categories Emotions, Behaviors, and Physiological, visceral and expressive reactions (see table 3.3). As regards the number of answers that were coded as Cognitions, men's answers outnumbered women's for Joy, Pride and Anger, whereas the reverse pattern was obtained for Jealousy and Envy. All in all, women appear to have richer emotion theories than men, reflecting the gender-congruent norm of women's greater emotionality, at least if we take the norm to mean that women have greater emotional expertise, possibly because they learn to be more sensitive towards their own and others' emotions.

Factorial analyses, performed on the original categories in which subjects' answers were coded, as well as on the recoded data shown in table 3.3, confirmed that beliefs varied substantially as a function of event and emotion type. For example, two factors, the first differentiating positive from negative emotion types, the second distinguishing Sadness from Jealousy, Anger, and Envy, explained about 70% of the variance. Subjects' sex significantly influenced beliefs only to a small extent: in the original data, subjects' sex explained roughly between 5% and 20% of the variance. These findings suggest that overall lay theories are ungendered:[2] men and women attribute similar reactions to male and female protagonists. However, subjects also expressed gendered beliefs, both gender-congruent and gender-incongruent.

Gender congruency and incongruency of emotion lay theories

Women on average more often mentioned *anxiety*, *insecurity*, and *sadness*. They also more often mentioned the positively toned emotions *joy* and *gladness* – the latter only when the event focused on interpersonal relationships, such as spending a day with friends, or getting their "approval" of one's new romantic partner. Incongruent with gender norms was men's greater mention of *anxiety* in relation to Anger events, and of *joy* when an equally capable colleague was promoted, and of *gladness* when the event implied a focus on the self, as in getting a job. Further, *anger*, a stereotypically male emotion, was always listed more frequently by women than by men. Counter-stereotypical was also the result that neither *jealousy* nor *envy* were mentioned more frequently by women than by men.

As regards Behaviors, women mentioned *talking about*, and *showing one's emotions* either somewhat more frequently than men (for instance, when winning money in a lottery, or getting a new job), or with similar frequency (Partner event). Subjects' belief that women express their emotions more than do men is also reflected in the finding that women mentioned more often expressive reactions such as crying and smiling. Men on the other hand mentioned the behaviors *showing*, and *talking about one's emotions* somewhat more often than did women, but only in situations in which emotional expressions implying powerlessness are legitimate for both sexes, for example in reaction to the Kiss event, in which the protagonist faces a serious threat to his romantic relationship.

Table 3.3. Percentages[a] and means[b] of Emotions, Cognitions, Behaviors, and Physiological, visceral, and expressive reactions attributed by women (F) and men (M) to same-sex event protagonists (open-answer studies)

Emotion type	Joy		Pride		Sadness		Jealousy		Envy		Anger		All	
Subject/protagonist	F	M	F	M	F	M	F	M	F	M	F	M	F	M
N subjects	120	120	107	88	120	120	173	128	60	60	40	40	6620	556
N concepts	2.90	2.49	2.73	2.49	3.66	3.25	3.40	2.65	3.31	2.75	3.17	2.20	33.19	2.70
Emotions	2.02	1.70	1.61	1.53	1.77	1.55	1.53	1.18	2.17	1.93	1.97	1.35	1.77	1.52
Anger	—	—	—	—	28	21	50	33	48	32	75	53	29	19
Disappointment	—	—	12	16	9	7	23	23	8	13	37	25	9	8
Surprise	18	12	69	53	—	—	21	21	15	23	15	15	15	15
Joy	112	96	51	50	—	—	—	—	—	—	—	—	37	34
Gladness	27	25	28	34	—	—	—	—	—	—	—	—	14	13
Insecurity	9	6	—	—	15	11	21	13	—	—	7	10	13	10
Anxiety	20	14	—	—	112	110	10	7	12	12	5	12	11	9
Sadness	5	6	—	—	10	5	13	4	37	15	57	20	33	29
Resignation	—	—	—	—	—	—	—	—	—	—	—	—	1	1
Jealousy/envy	—	—	—	—	—	—	11	15	57	50	—	—	9	9
Cognitions	0.32	0.35	0.33	0.38	1.06	1.07	0.45	0.37	0.48	0.32	0.27	0.40	0.51	0.51
Control oneself	—	—	2	5	3	1	9	5	23	15	5	5	6	4
Rationalize	—	3	—	—	4	8	—	—	2	2	—	—	1	3
Reflect	18	22	31	33	7	17	20	17	18	12	10	22	18	20
Difficulty with control	12	6	—	—	76	59	16	15	—	2	—	—	21	18
Behaviors	0.44	0.36	0.48	0.41	0.39	0.33	1.24	1.06	0.67	0.50	0.72	0.45	0.70	0.54
Control expression	4	2	—	3	6	3	34	35	60	30	12	2	17	13
Intervene	26	22	—	11	16	13	47	41	2	12	35	17	20	17
Talk about emotions	11	12	30	15	8	12	16	13	—	—	17	7	17	13
Show emotions	11	12	18	11	—	—	1	3	—	—	—	—	5	5

Isolate oneself	—	—	—	—	9	5	—	—	—	7	17	2	2
Leave situation	—	—	—	—	—	—	21	12	—	—	—	5	3
Physiological visceral, and expressive reactions	*0.15*	*0.07*	*0.31*	*0.17*	*0.43*	*0.30*	*0.19*	*0.05*	*0.00*	*0.20*	*0.00*	*0.23*	*0.12*

Notes:

[a] The percentages listed may be higher than 100, because subjects often mentioned more than one concept, and concepts of a similar nature have been grouped together (e.g., "well-being," "serene," and "joy") within a single category. Means will be shown in italic. The table does not report the frequency with which subjects supplied concepts that were originally categorized as «Other» due to their heterogeneity and low frequency of mention. The categories here listed are *not* the original categories that, within each emotion type, were used to code subjects' answers.

Gender-congruent beliefs were also found in relation to *Cognitions*. Men mentioned somewhat more often attempts to *rationalize* the event, and to *reflect* on it, whereas women more often mentioned *having difficulty in controlling their reactions to the event* (e.g., "not being able to remain calm," "feeling confused"), a response that suggests a difficulty in mastering one's own emotions. However, women mentioned cognitive *attempts at emotional control* either as frequently as men did, or more frequently, in the case of Envy and Jealousy. Further, *intervening* in/on the situation, a behavior that suggests an agentic orientation, was mentioned more often by men when events were positive, but by women when they were negative. These latter results seem to be more inconsistent with gender stereotypical norms. However, overall the *type of cognitive beliefs* men and women hold is gender-congruent.

To create a more precise measure of gender-(in)congruency, each individual answer was recoded according to whether it was *gender-congruent* or *gender-incongruent* (neutral statements were coded as well; see Zammuner, 1998a). The coding schema, on the basis of which answers were categorized as stereotypical male or female, was developed on the basis of existing research literature. For example, anger, physically aggressive behaviors, instrumental coping, and emotional control were defined as stereotypical male reactions, whereas intra-punitive emotions, crying, and other expressions of emotion were coded as stereotypical female reactions (e.g., Brody & Hall, 1993; Cross & Madson, 1997; Eagly & Wood, 1991; Fabes & Martin, 1991; Fischer, 1993; LaFrance & Banaji, 1992; Leaper, 1995; Heise & Calhan, 1995; Ricciardelli & Williams, 1995; Shields, 1991; Whissell, 1996). Within and across each macro-category gender-congruency scores were then summed and transformed into proportions. Within emotion types[3] scores were submitted to analyses of variance within and across categories.

The results (for details, see Zammuner, 1998a) showed that in reaction to Jealousy, Envy, and Pride men's and women's lay theories typically included a similar percentage of gender-congruent and incongruent beliefs. For Sadness and Joy, instead, women expressed beliefs congruent with their own gender profile more frequently than did men, whereas men more frequently expressed gender-incongruent beliefs than did women. In other words, in the case of Sadness and Joy, women stick more to the female gender profile than when judging other emotion types, whereas men more often "cross-over" and adhere to the opposite gender profile. The observed difference therefore implies a "theoretical convergence" of male and female reactions in that both sexes express a female-congruent emotion profile. This result can be accounted for by the fact that the emotional experience elicited by Sadness and Joy events is overall quite legitimate for both men and women. To illustrate, when someone dies sadness or numbness are normal, and it is perfectly appropriate to show them. By reporting that one would typically be sad, or cry, women express beliefs congruent with their own gender profile, whereas men express gender-incongruent beliefs.

These overall trends can be further specified by considering the extent to which subjects hold stereotypical beliefs in relation to the specific emotion components (except for beliefs about Physiological, visceral and expressive reactions, as they were both very infrequent, and heterogeneous). As regards Emotions, women expressed gender-congruent beliefs more frequently than men, for all emotion types except for Pride. Gender-incongruent beliefs were usually mentioned more frequently by men, Pride again being the exception, because the sexes did not differ. With respect to Cognitions, men listed more often gender-congruent beliefs in reaction to Jealousy and Pride events, and women in reaction to Sadness. The sexes did not differ in the type of Cognitions they assumed typical in the case of Envy and Joy. Gender-congruent beliefs concerning typical Behavior were listed more often by men for Jealousy and Envy, but by women for Joy; gender-incongruent beliefs on Jealousy showed the opposite trend. Men's gender-incongruent beliefs concerning Pride were more frequent than women's, whereas no gender differences were observed for Envy and Joy. Sadness, finally, did not elicit any gender difference in stereotypical or counter-stereotypical beliefs concerning typical behaviors. These analyses confirmed that the frequency of gender-congruent and gender-incongruent beliefs significantly varied as a function of emotion type: Joy elicited the least gender-congruent lay theories, Sadness the most.

In sum, the results obtained in the open-answer studies show that young adults generally possess rich lay theories about typical emotional reactions to events, and conceptualize emotional reactions in terms of various components. Overall men and women hold similar theories, and the majority of their emotion beliefs is ungendered. However, gendered beliefs, both gender-congruent and gender-incongruent, were also reported. As I argued earlier on, gender-incongruent beliefs can be explained by a "cross-over" process. Women are likely to invoke gender-congruent (rather than incongruent) reaction profiles when feelings are involved, and to "cross over" when cognitions or behaviors are involved. Men, in contrast, are much more likely to "cross-over" when feelings, rather than cognitions or behaviors, are concerned. When subjects "cross-over," they appropriate reactions that stereotypically define the opposite sex, thereby enriching one's own sex's repertoire of available reactions. However, the extent to which men's and women's beliefs are gender-(in)congruent, as well as the types of beliefs they report, is very much influenced by relevant emotion- and context-specific features.

The closed-answer study: Typical emotional reactions attributed by men and women to same-sex and cross-sex event protagonists

Open-answer studies tell us how people conceptualize emotions in their own terms, rather than by choosing a predefined answer from a list. However, the flexibility of this format also constitutes its limit. Open answers might be biased by incomplete or slanted memory search (e.g., due to little motivation to comply with the task, unavailability in memory of the sought information, or low subjective relevance of this information), and by the extent to which subjects are able to verbalize their thoughts (e.g., Fowler, 1995; Zammuner, 1998e).

The method used in the closed-answer study allowed us to verify the results obtained in the open-answer studies. Because subjects were asked to report typical reactions both for same-sex and for other-sex persons, it also allowed us to specify to what extent theories about opposite-sex event protagonists resemble those about same-sex protagonists. Subjects (N = 184) answered 4 checklist questions, one for each of the 4 macro-categories. Each answer category included various reactions, constructed on the basis of results obtained in the open-answer studies. For example, *joy* included happiness, euphoria, pride, and cheerfulness; *anxiety* included fear, anguish, dread. Each subject judged 5 events, one for each of the mentioned emotion types, Anger excluded (see table 3.1). Within each sex (N = 92), subjects made either same-sex or cross-sex attributions.

The results (see table 3.4) showed that subjects' answers on average comprised about 6 reactions, which is twice as many answers as had been reported by subjects in the open-answer studies (see table 3.3). However, although the closed-answer format influenced the quantity of reported beliefs, it generally did not affect the contents of the beliefs. Lay theories were in fact quite similar in their contents, and proportionally in their richness, to those reported by subjects in the open-answer studies. One noticeable exception is the much higher frequency with which subjects in this study attributed reactions of the Physiological, visceral, and expressive reactions category to the event protagonist. The fact that subjects are much more likely to mention Physiological reactions in a recognition (closed-answer) rather than in a production task (open-answer), might be interpreted as showing that these reactions are typically not very salient elements in the conceptualization of emotional experiences.

Gender differences and gender stereotyping

On average, men and women expressed similar emotion beliefs in same- and cross-sex attributions (for details, see Zammuner, 1988c). However, we also found some gender-congruent beliefs. Men more frequently listed reactions that imply regulation attempts, such as *cognitive control of one's reactions, reflecting on the event,* and *controlling the behavioral expression of emotions,* than did women. Women on the other hand more frequently listed *insecurity, sadness, disappointment, difficulty in facing the event, showing one's emotions, leaving the situation,* and various Physiological, visceral, and expressive changes. Male protagonists were attributed slightly more frequently *anger* and *surprise,* generally more cognitive reactions, and more *controlling the expression of emotions,* and *intervening* in the situation, compared to female protagonists. Female protagonists on the other hand were attributed more often than males most emotions, especially *envy,* and *talking about,* and *showing one's own emotions, isolating oneself,* and, most conspicuously, *difficulty in facing the event,* a reaction that was defined in the questionnaire as including "feeling confused," "not being able to keep calm," "being incredulous toward the event," or "bewildered by it." The only gender-incongruent results were that *insecurity* and *anxiety* were more frequently listed for male than for female protagonists, and the fact that women listed more often than men *anger* and *intervening in the situation.*

In a few cases an interaction between subjects' and protagonists' sex was observed too. Women more than men characterized males as likely to both *leave the situation* and *intervene in it,* whereas men more than women attributed to males both *cognitive* and *behavioral control* reactions. Note, however, that men attributed these reactions more often than did women to female protagonists as well. In other words, men's emphasis on control reflects an *own-gender congruent bias,* that is, the tendency to attribute to the other sex reactions that are stereotypical for one's own sex. An own-gender congruent bias was evident in women's attributions too in that women more often mentioned emotions, *talking about emotions with others,* and the powerless tendency of *abandoning the field,* than did men for both male and female protagonists. The bias did not apply for all beliefs, however – for instance, women attributed *anger* to females more often than did men.

In sum, (a) men and women hold similar rather than dissimilar theories about typical emotional reactions; (b) subjects' theories overall are ungendered, similar to the results obtained in the open-answer studies; (c) when men's and women's beliefs are gendered (rather than ungendered), they are influenced both by gender-congruent norms, and by an *own-gender* congruent bias; (d) the core of gendered beliefs seems to be defined by the control–non-control, or rationality–emotionality dichotomy: most typical of males is the wish or attempt to control emotional experiences and their expression, most typical of females is a felt difficulty in rationally coping with the event; (e) women's lay theories are somewhat richer than men's. However, the fact that this sex difference is proportionally much smaller in the closed-answer format than in the open-answer format leads us to hypothesize that motivational factors, rather than competence, play an important role in defining the richness of subjects' lay theories on emotions (see also Zammuner, 1998c).

Men's and women's normative beliefs about emotional reactions

As I argued previously, people's descriptive lay theories may sometimes be in conflict with their prescriptive beliefs. In particular, the attribution of emotionality to women is in conflict with the "rationality norm" that prescribes that people interact with the world according to their reason. The presence of conflicts between normative and descriptive lay theories can be assessed by analysing discrepancies between "adequate" emotional reactions, the normative beliefs, and "typical" reactions, the descriptive beliefs (the latter might be hypothesized to reflect immediate, natural, or relatively unchecked emotional reactions). Because results from closed-answer studies have a more standardized format, and thus are more easily reported and interpreted than the open-answer results, I will only discuss the "adequate" beliefs that subjects reported in the closed-answer study. Adequate beliefs were operationalized by asking subjects to answer 4 checklist questions identical to those from which they had selected "typical" reactions.

The results showed that Physiological, visceral, and expressive reactions, all negatively valenced emotions (e.g., *anger, disappointment, jealousy*), and the helpless, non-agentic behaviors *isolating oneself* and *leaving the situation* were less frequent than they had been as "typical" reactions (see table 3.4). In other words, they were judged to be inadequate. Instead, positively valenced emotions, *talking about felt emotions* and *showing them, cognitively controlling oneself, rationalizing the event*, and *reflecting on it*, were on average more frequently listed than they had been as "typical" reactions. Overall, the results showed that subjects clearly distinguished "adequate" reactions from "typical" ones (significant multivariate Discrepancy effects were obtained for all emotion types, and in relation to most emotion components). This differentiation is in line with the rationality norm: an adequate way of reacting to an emotion event is less emotional and more rational than typically is the case. This suggests that subjects believe that emotions ought to be regulated.

Did men and women differ in what they considered as adequate reactions for their own versus the opposite sex, especially in the extent to which they endorsed the rationality norm? Overall, the answer is negative: normative beliefs were even more egalitarian than descriptive beliefs (similar results were obtained in the open-answer studies; see Zammuner, 1988a). However, there was also evidence of gendered beliefs, because the frequency and nature of gendered beliefs was a function of whether subjects made same-sex or cross-sex attributions. For example, *anger, disappointment, surprise, minimizing the event's seriousness,* and *leaving the situation* were characterized as male reactions more frequently than as female reactions only in cross-sex attributions by women. In other words, more women than men judged these emotions and behaviors as appropriate for males than for females. Further, *joy, controlling the expression of emotions, talking about,* and *showing emotions* differed in same-sex attributions more than they did in cross-sex ones. For example, men thought *control* to be an adequate reaction for other men, but less so for women, whereas women thought *talking about emotions* more appropriate for women than it was for men.

The most interesting result as regards gendered beliefs, however, is the fact that they often implied a violation of stereotypical gender-norms, especially for male protagonists. Both sexes more frequently mentioned Physiological, visceral, and expressive reactions, *sadness, cognitive difficulty in facing events,* and both the powerless behaviors of *isolating oneself* and *leaving the situation,* as more adequate reactions for males than for females. *Control of emotion expression* was the only gender-congruent behavior that was judged appropriate for males more often than for females. Furthermore, both sexes judged *rationalizing the event* (more often attributed to males as a "typical" reaction), *reflecting on it,* and *intervening* in the situation (women had judged this as a "typical" male reaction) more often as adequate reactions for females than for males (*showing emotions* was the only gender-congruent adequate reaction for women).

In sum, on the whole subjects believe that rationalizing and controlling emotions are more adequate ways of reacting to emotion-inducing events than being and/or acting in an emotional way. However, irrationality (that is, emotionality, non-control) seems to be excused more for men than for women. Women are in fact expected to be sensitive and thoughtful about how they emotionally react to events, whereas men are particularly supposed to be more "in control," and less emotional than they "typically" are.

Table 3.4. Mean and percentages of "typical" and "adequate" reactions to an emotional event attributed by male and female subjects (M = 92; F = 92) to male (m) and female (f) protagonists (closed-answer study)[a]

Reactions	Typical				Adequate			
	F f	M m	F m	M f	M m	F m	F f	M f
Subjects								
Event protagonists[b]								
N subjects	460	460	460	460	460	460	460	460
Mean N answers	6.30	6.19	6.43	6.30	6.01	6.04	5.95	5.94
Emotions	2.24	2.17	2.34	2.23	1.92	2.02	1.93	1.87
Anger	18	19	20	15	9	15	11	10
Disappointment	18	15	17	15	9	11	9	8
Surprise	26	25	28	24	23	26	24	20
Joy	39	40	45	46	40	43	44	42
Gladness	29	30	30	30	37	37	36	37
Insecurity	13	11	14	10	8	8	8	7
Anxiety	10	10	11	9	8	7	7	8
Sadness	30	28	30	29	26	26	23	23
Resignation	10	11	11	12	15	16	17	16
Jealousy/Envy	30	28	28	31	17	13	13	16
Cognitions	1.27	1.33	1.24	1.32	1.46	1.40	1.46	1.52
Control oneself	31	38	31	37	47	42	42	47
Rationalize event	18	22	21	19	35	36	44	43
Reflect on the event	33	36	33	35	47	46	50	51
Minimize (Other)	6	9	8	7	6	7	5	4
Difficulty in facing event	40	29	31	34	11	10	5	7
Behaviors	1.41	1.38	1.48	1.45	1.38	1.39	1.40	1.37
Control emotional expression	27	33	29	32	33	30	26	30
Intervene to modify situation	9	7	13	8	6	5	8	8
Talk about emotions	34	35	35	38	44	47	49	46

Show emotions	46	43	45	45	52	46	48	50
Isolating oneself	11	10	10	12	1	3	3	1
Leave situation (Other)	14	10	15	11	3	4	5	2
Physiological, visceral, and expressive reactions	*1.37*	*1.30*	*1.38*	*1.29*	*1.15*	*1.22*	*1.22*	*1.17*

Notes:

[a] The mean number of concepts supplied for the entire category is reported in italics.

[b] The reported number of subjects is spurious, as in reality each subject judged 5 events in total, one for each emotion type, within a repeated measure design.

Conclusion

The results obtained in the two sets of studies reported here help us to gain a better understanding of how subjects in our studies conceptualize emotions. To summarize briefly, the results showed that young adults have articulate lay theories of emotion(s) that include beliefs that specify the nature of the emotional experience in terms of several components – such as, feelings, cognitions, behaviors, physiological and expressive changes, and regulation processes. Lay theories also specify how variations in emotion types or emotional events are associated with variations in the components, as regards the duration and intensity of the emotional experience, the need to regulate it, and so forth. In other words, lay models include both aspecific emotion knowledge about the superordinate category "emotion," and emotion specific context-bound knowledge, that is, beliefs about contextually defined instances of the category.

In contrast to results generally derived from studies on stereotypes, male and female participants in these studies generally did not differ in the richness of their emotion knowledge, or in its actual contents. In other words, Italian men and women have similar lay theories that are largely composed of ungendered beliefs. This applied to both their descriptive and prescriptive beliefs. It is still an open question whether this egalitarian nature of subjects' beliefs is due to the specific population (and culture) that was studied, to the historical moment, to the method employed in the reported studies, or to yet other factors.

Gendered beliefs, however, occurred at a context-specific level, though more or less occasionally, and usually to a small extent. These gendered beliefs were often congruent with gender-norms; for example, *cognitive emotion-control* was more often attributed to men than to women, whereas a *difficulty in emotionally facing events* was attributed more often to women than to men. Subjects also held gender-incongruent beliefs. When beliefs were about "typical" reactions, gender-incongruency often reflected an own-gender bias, that is, the tendency to attribute to both male and female protagonists those reactions that stereotypically characterize one's own sex. For example, men attributed *cognitive emotion-control* to females more often than did women, and women more often attributed *insecurity* to males than did men. When "adequate" reactions were at stake, gender-incongruent beliefs mostly reflected one of the following two processes: (a) adhesion to the "rationality" norm, implying that both sexes more often selected "rational" than "emotional" reactions; (b) "gender cross-over," that is, the endorsement of reactions stereotypical for the opposite sex.

From a more general viewpoint, the results just reported suggest, I believe, that gender differences and similarities in lay theories can be discussed more meaningfully if we do not disregard the fact that emotional transactions are conceptualized according to both emotion specific and emotion aspecific beliefs, and according to beliefs that are to a great extent context-bound. In other words, we need to measure gendered beliefs by relying on theoretical approaches that take into account the structural and conceptual complexity of lay theories about emotions, especially the impact of contextual variations. Last but not least, the validity of the results and conclusions obtained in any given study needs to be assessed taking into account what population was tested, and with what method (e.g., question format; kind of experimental stimuli, answer categories, instructions, etc., offered to subjects) because these aspects crucially influence the comparability of measures across studies, and therefore the extent to which we can reach a real understanding of the issues at stake.

Acknowledgments

The data presented in this chapter were collected and analyzed with the help of several people, mostly women students in psychology, whose cooperation I very much appreciated, including B. Scandroglio, L. Pellighelli, S. Sermi, L. Seminati, V. Massai, A. Lo Manto, M. G. Maffei, P. Albiero, R. Marando, S. Girola, E. Capoferri, V. Camerone, R. Riello, S. Arduino, A. Sussan, and C. Galli. Several of the studies here reported, and the preliminary work for this chapter, were partially supported by CNR grants (94.04147.CT08, 95.01860.CT08, 96.05178.CT08, and by a short mobility scholarship in 1996), and by MURST 40% grants (in the years 1994, 1995, 1996).

Notes

1 For "economy" reasons, the results reported in this chapter do not include data about all the Anger and Envy events.
2 Similar results were obtained in cross-cultural replications of the open-answer studies (Carrera Levillain, Zammuner, & Sanchez Colodron, 1994; Zammuner & Fischer, 1995; Zammuner, Arduino, & Fischer, 1996; Zammuner, Lo Manto, & Maffei, 1996), in self-attributions (Zammuner, 1995a), and in self-reports of Jealousy events (Zammuner & Pellinghelli, 1994).
3 Anger excluded, as the data were at the time not available.

References

Brody, L. R., & Hall, J. A. (1993). Gender and emotion. In M. Lewis and J. M. Haviland (Eds.), *Handbook of emotions* (pp. 447–460). New York: Guilford Press.
Calhoun, C., & Solomon, R. C. (Eds.) (1984). *What is an emotion? Classic readings in philosophical psychology.* New York: Oxford University Press.

Camras, L. A., & Allison, K. (1989). Children's and adults' beliefs about emotion elicitation. *Motivation and Emotion, 13,* 53–70.

Carrera Levillain P., Zammuner, V. L., & Sanchez Colodron, M. (1994). Somos sinceros al comunicar nuestras emociones a los demas? El caso de los celos y la tristeza. *Revista de Psicologia Social, 9,* 151–163.

Conway A. M., & Bekerian A. D. (1987). Situational knowledge and emotions. *Cognition and Emotion, 1,* 145–191.

Cross, S. E., & Madson, L. (1997). Models of the self: Self-construals and gender. *Psychological Bulletin, 122,* 5–37.

Deaux, K. (1985). Sex and gender. *Annual Review of Psychology, 36,* 49–81.

Deaux, K. (1984). From individual differences to social categories: Analysis of a decade's research on gender. *American Psychologist, 39,* 105–116.

Eagly, A. H., & Wood, W. (1991). Explaining sex differences in social behavior: A meta-analytic perspective. *Personality and Social Psychology Bulletin, 17,* 306–315.

Fabes, R. A., & Martin, C. L. (1991). Gender and age stereotypes of emotionality. *Personality and Social Psychology Bulletin, 17,* 532–540.

Fehr, B., & Russell, J. A. (1984). Concept of emotion viewed from a prototype perspective. *Journal of Experimental Psychology: General, 113,* 464–486.

Fischer, A. H. (1993). Sex differences in emotionality: fact or stereotype? *Feminism and Psychology, 3,* 303–318.

Fiske, S. T., & Taylor, S. E. (1991). *Social Cognition.* New York: McGraw-Hill.

Fowler, F. J. Jr. (1995). *Improving survey questions. Design and evaluation.* London: Sage.

Frijda, N. H., Kuipers, P., & ter Schure, L. (1989). Relations among emotion, appraisal and action tendency. *Journal of Personality and Social Psychology, 57,* 212–228.

Heise, D. R., & Calhan, C. (1995). Emotion norms in interpersonal events. *Social Psychology Quarterly, 58,* 223–240.

LaFrance, M., & Banaji, M. (1992). Towards a reconsideration of the gender–emotion relationship. In M. Clark (Ed.), *Emotion and Social Behavior: Review of Personality and Social Psychology* (Vol. 14, pp. 178–201). Newbury Park, CA: Sage.

Leaper, C. (1995). The use of Masculine and Feminine to describe women's and men's behavior. *The Journal of Social Psychology, 135,* 359–369.

Lebart, L., Morineau, A., & Fenelon, J. P. (1982). *Traitement des données statistiques.* Paris: Dunod.

Levy, R. (1984). The emotions in comparative perspective. In K. R. Scherer, & P. Ekman (Eds.), *Approaches to emotion* (pp. 397–412). Hillsdale, N.J.: Erlbaum.

Mesquita, B., & Frijda, N. H. (1992). Cultural variations in emotions: A review. *Psychological Bulletin, 112,* 179–204.

Nisbett, R. E., & Ross, L. (1980). *Human inference: strategies and shortcomings of social judgement.* Englewood Cliffs, N.J.: Prentice Hall.

Ricciardelli, L. A., & Williams, R. J. (1995). Desirable and undesirable gender traits in three behavioral domains. *Sex Roles, 33,* 637–657.

Rosario, M., Shinn, M., March, H., & Huckabee, C. B. (1988). Gender differences in coping and social supports: Testing socialization and role constraint theories. *Journal of Community Psychology, 16,* 55–69.

Ruozzi, G. (Ed.) (1994). *Scrittori italiani di aforismi. Vol. 1: I classici* (Italian Aphorism Writers. Vol. 1: The Classics). Milano: Mondadori.

Saarni, C. (1990). Emotional competence: How emotions and relationships become integrated. In R. Thompson (Ed.), *Socioemotional Development. Nebraska Symposium on Motivation, 1988* (Vol. 36, pp. 115–182). Lincoln, NE: University of Nebraska Press.

Shaver, P., Schwartz, J., Kirson, D., & O'Connor, C. (1987). Emotion knowedge: further exploration of a prototype approach. *Journal of Personality and Social Psychology, 52,* 1061–1086.

Shields, S. A. (1991). Gender in the psychology of emotion: a selective research review. In K. T. Strongman (Ed.), *International Review of Studies on Emotion* (pp. 227–247). New York: Wiley.

Wharton, A. S., & Erickson, R. J. (1993). Managing emotions on the job and at home: Understanding the consequences of multiple emotional roles. *Academy of Management Review, 18,* 457–486.

Whissell, C. M. (1996). Predicting the size and direction of sex differences in measures of emotion and personality. *Genetic, Social, and General Psychology Monographs, 1,* 255–284.

Wood, W., Christensen, P. N., Hebl, M. R., & Rothgerber, H. (1997). Conformity to sex-typed norms, affect, and the self-concept. *Journal of Personality and Social Psychology, 73,* 523–535.

Zammuner, V. L. (1994). Discrepancies between felt and communicated emotions. In N. H. Frijda (Ed.), *Proceedings of the VIII Conference of the International Society for Research on Emotion* (pp. 57–61). Storrs, CT: ISRE Publications.

Zammuner, V. L. (1995a). Naive Theories of Emotional Experience: Jealousy. In J. A. Russell, J. M. Fernàndez-Dols, A. S. R. Manstead & J. C. Wellenkamp (Eds.), *Everyday Conceptions of Emotion: An Introduction to the Psychology, Anthropology and Linguistics of Emotion* (pp. 435–456). Dordrecht: Kluwer.

Zammuner, V. L. (1995b, September). *Naive theories of emotion: Why people might be uncertain or in conflict about felt emotions.* Paper presented at the EASP Small Group Meeting on "The narrative organization of social representations," Budapest, Hungary.

Zammuner, V. L. (1995c). Teorie ingenue: L'esperienza emotiva di tristezza. (Naive theories: The emotional experience of sadness). In G. Bellelli (Ed.), *Sapere e sentire. L'emozionalità nella vita quotidiana* (pp. 257–280). Liguori: Napoli.

Zammuner, V. L. (1996a). Felt emotions, and verbally communicated emotions: The case of pride. *European Journal of Social Psychology, 26,* 233–245.

Zammuner, V. L. (1996b, July). Joy, pride, envy, jealousy, and sadness: are they "sincerely" shared? Paper presented at the meeting of the Experimental Association of European Social Psychology, Gmünden, Austria.

Zammuner, V. L. (1998a). *Gioia, tristezza, invidia, gelosia e orgoglio: Reazioni "immediate" e "adeguate" nelle teorie ingenue* (Joy, sadness, envy, jealousy, and pride: "Immediate" and "adequate" reactions in lay theories). Paper presented at the National Conference of the Experimental Psychology Section of the Italian Association of Psychology, Firenze, Italy.

Zammuner, V. L. (1998b). *La rabbia: L'esperienza emotiva, e la sua condivisione* (Anger: The emotional experience, and its sharing). Paper presented at *the National Conference of the Social Psychology Section of the Italian Association of Psychology,* Firenze, Italy.

Zammuner, V. L. (1998c). *Emozioni e loro rappresentazione concettuale: Differenze di "conoscenza" e di valutazione tra maschi e femmine* (Emotions and their conceptual representation: Male-Female differences in their "knowledge" and evaluation). Paper presented at the National Conference of the Experimental Psychology Section of the Italian Association of Psychology, Firenze, Italy.

Zammuner, V. L. (1998d). Lay theories of pride, joy, sadness, jealousy and envy. In Fischer, A. H. (Ed.), *Proceedings of the Xth Conference of the International Society for Research on Emotion* (pp. 345–350). Amsterdam: Faculty of Psychology.

Zammuner, V. L. (1998e). *Tecniche dell'intervista e del questionario* (Questionnaire and interview techniques). Bologna: Il Mulino.

Zammuner, V. L., Arduino, L., & Fischer, A. H. (1996). *Gelosia e tristezza: teorie ingenue nella cultura olandese* (Jealousy and sadness: Naive theories in the Dutch culture). Paper presented at the National Conference of the Experimental Psychology Section of the Italian Association of Psychology, Capri, Italy.

Zammuner, V. L., & Fischer, A. H. (1995). The social regulation of emotions in jealousy situations. *Journal of Cross-Cultural Psychology, 26*, 189–208.

Zammuner, V. L., & Frijda, N. H. (1994). Felt and communicated emotions: Sadness and jealousy. *Cognition and emotion, 8*, 37–53.

Zammuner, V. L., Lo Manto, A., & Maffei, M. G. (1996). *Gelosia e tristezza, e loro condivisione verbale: Sud vs. Nord* (Jealousy and sadness, and their verbal sharing: South *vs.* North Italy). Paper presented at the National Conference of the Experimental Psychology Section of the Italian Association of Psychology, Capri, Italy.

Zammuner, V. L., & Massai, V. (1998). Eteroattribuzioni di gioia: antecedenti tipici, ed emozioni provate e condivise (Eteroattributions of joy: typical antecedents, and felt and communicated emotions). *Revista de Psicologia Social, 13*, 25–44.

Zammuner, V. L., & Pellinghelli, L. (1994, September). *Il vissuto emotivo di gelosia e la sua valutazione* (The emotional experience of jealousy and its subjective evaluation). Paper presented at the XIII Congress of the Basic Research Division of the Italian Society of Psychology, Padova, Italy.

Zammuner, V. L., & Seminati, L. (1996). Invidia: l'esperienza emotiva e la sua condivisione a livello verbale (Envy: the emotional experience and its verbal sharing). *Giornale Italiano di Psicologia, 23*, 493–515.

4. The relation between gender and emotions in different cultures

AGNETA H. FISCHER AND ANTONY S. R. MANSTEAD

The Western dichotomy

Western cultures share the stereotypical belief that women are more emotional than men. This stereotype has long featured in Western philosophy, where a binary opposition between emotion and reason has been closely associated with the opposition between masculinity and femininity (Lloyd, 1984; Shields, 1984). The stereotype of the "emotional woman" and the "rational man" was fueled by the increase of sex segregation in the public and private realms which went hand in hand with the industrialization of Western societies from the middle of the nineteenth century onwards. Women were seen as the keepers of the heart. Their strong intuitions and sensitivities to the needs of others made them especially suited to the task of raising children and providing both children and husbands with affectionate and secure relationships within the home (Rosenberg, 1982)

The current stereotype still holds that emotionality, and particularly emotional expressiveness, is the core of the differences between the sexes (Ashmore, Del Boca, & Wohlers, 1986; Broverman, Vogel, Broverman, Clarkson, & Rosenkrantz, 1972; Fabes & Martin, 1991; Williams & Best, 1982, 1997). Femininity and female roles are associated with the ability to experience, express, and communicate emotions to others, and to empathize with others' feelings, whereas masculinity and male roles are defined as the ability to suppress and control one's emotions. If, however, degree of emotionality results from specific gender roles, we would expect it to vary with the extent to which gender roles are differentiated in a country (cf. Williams & Best, 1990). The focus of this chapter is on the cross-cultural generalizability of this dichotomy between female emotionality and male rationality.

When we first began to investigate the relationship between gender and culture in relation to emotions, we were surprised to find that there are very few studies in which this issue has been the central focus of the research. Most research investigating gender differences in emotions has used Western respondents (for reviews see Brody & Hall, 1993;

Fischer, 1993; Manstead, 1992). In the present chapter we review the handful of studies in which interactions between gender and culture have been investigated. We supplement these studies by reporting a secondary analysis of the "ISEAR database," one of the largest available datasets on cultural variations in emotion. This database arises from a large cross-national study of emotion antecedents and reactions, the "ISEAR study," conducted by Klaus Scherer and his colleagues (see Scherer, 1988; Scherer, 1997; Scherer & Wallbott, 1994; Wallbott & Scherer, 1988). We use this database to analyze the influence of different cultural variables that seemed to us to be likely to be relevant to gender differences in emotions. It will become clear to the reader that research on gender, culture and emotion is still in its infancy. As a result, our hypotheses have a more than usually speculative flavor, and the conclusions drawn should be regarded as provisional.

Gendered emotions in Western and non-Western countries

As noted above, most studies investigating the relation between gender and emotions have been conducted in Western countries. A general conclusion to be drawn from such studies is that women do indeed seem to respond more emotionally; although this is not true of all types of emotional response, or of all circumstances, or of all types of emotional stimuli (see also Brody, 1997). Differences between the sexes are larger for expressions, as compared to experiences (LaFrance & Banaji, 1992): women are especially likely to show their emotions to a greater extent than men do. Further, women seem to be more prone to experience and express prosocial emotions (e.g., empathy, joy, enthusiasm) and emotions that imply powerlessness or vulnerability, such as fear, sadness, or shame, than men (Brody & Hall, 1993; Fischer, 1993). These latter emotions are thought to pose a threat to Western conceptions of masculinity, because they make one appear weak, helpless, and out of control. In contrast, powerful emotions (e.g., anger, pride, contempt) appear to be more in keeping with the masculine role in Western culture, because they may help to confirm or enhance one's power or status (Fischer & Jansz, 1995). Despite such nuances, we can conclude on the basis of this research that when differences between the sexes are found with respect to emotion, women tend overall to display emotions more overtly and intensely than do men.

This notion that the display or inhibition of emotionality is a characteristic gender difference in Western culture raises the question of whether the same distinction is to be found in other cultures. As noted above, there is to date a dearth of research evidence on this issue. One relevant study is the International Study of Adult Crying (ISAC), a large cross-cultural project conducted by Vingerhoets and colleagues (Vingerhoets & Becht, 1996), in which data from 30 countries from all over the world were collected. Respondents completed questionnaires in which they had to report (among other things) their tendency to cry in a variety of situations (total crying score), their estimated crying frequency ("how often did you cry in the last four weeks?") and their general crying proneness ("how easily do you cry?"; 10–point scale, ranging from 1 "with difficulty" to 10 "very easily"). Overall women scored higher than men on all three measures. However, there was also some cultural variation in the extent to which the sexes differed. Gender differences in total crying were greatest in the Netherlands, Israel, Greece, Finland, Brazil, Austria, Sweden, and Poland; the smallest differences were found in Peru, Nigeria, India, Kenya, Jamaica, and Ghana. Gender differences in estimated crying frequency were largest in the Netherlands, Switzerland, Turkey, Chile, Lithuania, Spain, and Poland; and smallest in Nigeria, Austria, Kenya, Jamaica, and China. Gender differences in general crying proneness showed a similar picture. Although there are some exceptions, the general trend in these ISAC data is for gender differences in crying to be smaller in non-Western countries than in Western countries.

A similar general trend has been observed in studies in which the emotional reactions of Asian respondents were compared with those of American respondents. For example, Frymier, Klopf, and Ishii (1990) compared American and Japanese responses to the affect orientation scale. Although there was a significant difference between men and women in the American sample, no gender differences were observed in the Japanese sample. Copeland, Hwang, and Brody (1996) examined emotional expressiveness in different groups of students: American students with European ancestry; American students with Asian ancestry; and international students coming from Asia. They found a general tendency for women in all cultural groups to report more intense positive and negative emotions (as assessed by the Affect Intensity Measure) than men; however, in response to emotion-eliciting stories, women´s tendency to report more shame, fear and nervousness was far more evident in the American-European group than in the other cultural groups. Comparable results were reported with respect to positive emotions by Zahn-Waxler, Friedman, Cole, Mizuta, and Hiruma (1996), who studied the emotional reactions of Japanese and American children to hypothetical interpersonal dilemmas. They found interactions between culture and gender in the case of positive expressions. Within the American sample girls enacted more prosocial behavior in reaction to conflict dilemmas (e.g., nighttime fears, personal injury, theft, moral conflict) than boys did. Prosocial behavior was defined here as attempting to relieve another person's distress or to fix something (e.g., bring a "hurt doll" to the doctor). There was no comparable sex difference in the Japanese sample, and no interactions between culture and gender were found in relation to the other emotional and behavioral variables (see also Alexander & Wood, this volume, for comparable findings).

The number of studies reviewed here is small, but they nevertheless provide a reasonably consistent body of evidence suggesting that gender differences in emotion are more pronounced in Western countries than in non-Western countries. This raises the issue of how such findings can be explained. Western and non-Western countries can be distinguished on a variety of dimensions – political, cultural, social, economic – each of which may play a role in the way in which gender is shaped through emotions. In the studies reviewed above, theoretical explanations were not explicitly tested and the ad hoc explanations provided by the researchers were speculative in nature. Below we elaborate two hypotheses, and we go on to test these hypotheses using the ISEAR database.

Emotions as an extension of gender roles and gender role ideologies

We propose that there are two rather global, but distinct hypotheses that can be made with respect to the relation between culture and gender differences in emotions. The first is based upon Social Role Theory (e.g., Eagly, 1987) and assumes that a culture's sex-specific division of labor and associated sex-role ideology are important determinants of the contents of masculinity and femininity, and thereby influence emotional experiences and expression. According to Social Role Theory, a society's division of labor is the main source of sex-differentiated behavior, because roles not only shape one's skills, but also one's self, behavior, and emotions. There is evidence from countries all over the world that there are common features in male and female roles, partly as a consequence of the biological origin of the division of labor between the sexes. Women not only bear and breastfeed their children, they are also the primary caretakers of their children. Men, on the other hand, more often have the provider role and spend more time on outdoor activities (e.g., Munroe & Munroe, 1994).

In addition to the different tasks associated with these divergent gender roles, there are also differences in the amount of status assigned to these roles. Generalizing, female roles have lower status, women more often have a subordinate position and more often lack power. Thus, there are two features of female roles, caring for others and a lack of status and power, that may explain some of the gender differences that have been found in research on emotions. Caring requires emotional commitment, sensitivity to others, and the ability to help others cope with negative feelings. The experience and expression of prosocial emotions can therefore be considered to be a function of this female role. In addition, low social status may often be a sign of powerlessness and vulnerability and thus may give rise to what we earlier referred to as "powerless emotions," namely fear, sadness, and shame.

However, there is also variation between countries in the extent to which male and female roles overlap, in other words in the extent to which women participate in a country's labor force and hold positions of power. Generally, industrialized countries in Western Europe and North America have a higher degree of participation of women in the labor force than non-industrialized countries. If women's participation in the labor force is high, this implies a larger degree of overlap in sex roles, as compared to countries where women are for the large part homemakers. Based on the arguments of Social Role Theory, it would follow that the more traditional the division of labor between the sexes, the larger will be the gender gap in emotional reactions. Although this hypothesis conflicts with the findings of previous studies reviewed above, we will test this hypothesis using a larger database than the ones examined in previous studies.

There are several ways in which the differentiation of sex roles can be operationalized. First, we can consider the visible and tangible roles played by men and women in a particular society. The United Nations Development Program has developed an index, the Gender Empowerment Measure (GEM) that reflects the extent to which women actively participate in economic and political life. The GEM is computed on the basis of the following measures: percentage of seats in parliament held by women, percentage of administrators and managers, percentage of professional and technical workers who are female, and women's share of earned income in the country in question. GEM scores are relatively low in most African, Asian and South American countries, which are characterized by a traditional division of labor between the sexes. In countries with high GEM scores, namely most Western European countries, the USA, Australia, and New Zealand, women actively participate in public life, and men play some role in domestic tasks. Thus, female and male roles exhibit more overlap and differences in status and power are smaller, and/or less overt.

The division of labor in any given culture is generally accompanied by a particular sex-role ideology. Sex-role ideologies provide rationales for the division of labor between the sexes and refer to normative beliefs about the roles of men and women and about how the sexes should relate to one and another. However, an objectively more egalitarian position of women in a particular country is not necessarily accompanied by a modern sex-role ideology. Such a discrepancy can arise because of deeply rooted cultural values with respect to ideals of masculinity and femininity which then lag behind changes in the economic, political, and social status of women in a given country. These values may have their origin in religious beliefs, in family values, or in the social and political ideologies of a particular country. They form the basis of men and women's sex roles at a psychological level, rather than the roles they actually perform in society. Because these psychologically represented roles may have an influence on how the sexes respond emotionally that is different from that of the actual division of labor between the sexes, we decided to use a second cultural measure in order to tap values relating to masculinity and femininity.

Hofstede's (1991) masculinity–femininity dimension seemed to be an appropriate candidate, because he regards masculinity–femininity (M–F) not as a measure of actual or visible roles, but rather of the emotional roles played by men and women (Hofstede, 1998). In his well-known study of IBM employees, these values were derived from the importance ratings given to 14 work goals, some of which were labeled as masculine (e.g., the possibility of earning a lot of money, being recognized for one's achievements, the possibility of making a career, having challenges), and others as feminine (having a good working relationship with your superior, good collaboration with colleagues, a pleasant environment in which to live, emphasis on the quality of life). Countries scoring high on masculine values emphasize the differentiation between male and female roles. Men should be concerned with ego-enhancement: assertive, tough, and oriented towards material success. Women, in contrast, are supposed to be modest and tender, or ego-effacing. On the other hand, if men and women are both thought to be modest, tender, and oriented towards the quality of life, the culture in question scores higher on feminine values (Hofstede, 1980, 1991, 1998). Hofstede found that respondents in Japan, some central European countries (Austria, Italy and Switzerland), some Caribbean and South American countries (Colombia, Jamaica, Mexico, Venezuela), and some Asian countries (Philippines) endorsed masculine values most strongly. By contrast, respondents in some Northern European countries (Denmark, the Netherlands, Norway, Sweden) and in some South American countries (Chile, Guatemala) endorsed feminine values.

In sum, the assumption that the traditionally *feminine sex role* (whether actual or psychological), in which caring for others, subordination, and lack of power are primary features, is the source of women's greater emotionality leads one to expect that gender differences in emotion would be larger in cultures with a traditional division of labor and in cultures where the differentiation between sex roles is empha-sized. In other words, there are grounds for expecting an interaction between these cultural dimensions and gender with respect to emotion: countries with a low GEM score and more masculine values are expected to show larger gender differences in emotion, as compared to those with a high GEM score and more feminine values.

Cultural display rules for emotion

An alternative hypothesis concerning the relation between culture and gender differences in emotion focuses on prevailing cultural norms and rules relating to emotion. A distinction is often made between rules that apply to the elicitation and experience of emotions in response to par-ticular situations (constitutive rules or feeling rules) and rules that apply to the expression or display of these emotions (Ekman & Friesen, 1971; Hochschild, 1983; Levy, 1984). We assume that cultures differ not only in the contents of such display rules, but also in the strength in which these rules are applied. For example, the well-known study reported by Ekman and Friesen (Ekman, 1972; Friesen, 1972) suggests that in Japanese culture there is a display rule that prescribes that neg-ative feelings such as disgust should not be expressed in public settings, whereas such a rule does not apply (or at least applies to a lesser extent) in American culture. The presumed existence of an Asian display rule prescribing that negative faces should be masked in public is consistent with evidence from other studies (e.g., Triandis, 1989) and with anthro-pological characterizations of Japanese and other Asian cultures (e.g., Boesch, 1994; Lonner & Malpass, 1994). Other examples of cultural display rules are the suppression of public displays of anger among the Inuit (Briggs, 1970), or the taboo on expressions of sadness in Tahitian culture (Levy, 1984).

One explanation for cultural differences in the prevalence and strength of cultural display rules is to be found in the extent to which a culture adheres to collectivistic versus individualistic values (Hofstede, 1984). In an individualistic society ties between individuals are loose, and strong emphasis is placed on autonomy and independence; in col-lectivistic societies, on the other hand, individuals have lifelong and strong bonds with a social group (see Kim, Triandis, Kagitçibasi, Choi, & Yoon, 1994, for an overview of current research on individualism–col-lectivism [I–C]). Most studies support the following general description of the I–C dimension. In individualistic cultures there is a focus on autonomy, self-reliance, and individual expression, and relatively less emphasis on collective codes regarding how to behave or how to inter-pret situations. The expression of individuals' emotions is considered to be appropriate, whether positive or negative, as long as these feelings are authentic and an expression of a individual's inner thoughts or motives. The cultural rule that guides emotional behavior is therefore essentially individualistic and can be summarized as "be your self." In more collectivistic cultures, on the other hand, more emphasis is placed on an individual's relationship with the group. A person's behavior is therefore determined less by individual motives or beliefs than by collective codes and norms (see Triandis, 1989). These collective codes are based upon the emphasis placed on respect for others, and the importance of the context (e.g., the hierarchy within the group) as a guiding principle in one's conduct.

It is worth noting that the individualism–collectivism dimension has been found to be independent of gender differences in self-construal (Kashima, Kim, Gelfand, Yamaguchi, Choi, & Yuki, 1995). This implies that, irrespective of the division of labor between the sexes, cultural display rules regarding emotional behavior are similar for men and women. In other words, cultural norms override gender role norms in more collectivistic cultures. As a consequence, smaller gender differences in emotion should be found in collectivistic cultures. In other words, we predict that the difference between females and males is greater in individualistic than in collectivistic cultures.

Empirical evidence

The ISEAR database.[1]

The ISEAR database derives from questionnaire studies conducted in 37 countries on 5 continents. The participants were 2,917 university students, 1,301 male and 1,616 female (see Scherer & Wallbott, 1994, for a more detailed description of the samples). The questionnaires consisted of a general instruction and 7 two-page sections, one for each of 7 emotions: joy, fear, sadness, anger, disgust, shame and guilt. Participants first had to freely describe an incident in which they last experienced the emotion in question. Next, they answered a number of closed questions. The responses that will be analyzed in the present context concern the *intensity* of the emotion ("how intense was your emotion?"; responses were made on a 5-point scale, ranging from "not very" to "very"), the *duration* of the emotion ("how long did the emotion last?"; responses were made on a 4-point scale, from "a few minutes" to "a day or more"), and *nonverbal expressions* (laughing/smiling, crying/sobbing, screaming/yelling, abrupt bodily movements, moving against people/aggression, moving towards people/things, withdrawing from people/things, and other expressive reactions).

To investigate whether the ISEAR database provides any support for the theoretical arguments presented above, we first added GEM, M–F, and I–C scores to the ISEAR database. For 4 countries in the database, no GEM scores are reported in the United Nations dataset. These countries were simply excluded from the analyses in which GEM served as a factor. M–F and I–C scores were added in the form of the mean masculinity and individualism index scores reported by Hofstede (1991) for each country. Twenty-seven of the 37 countries represented in the ISEAR database were included in Hofstede's research. For the 10 countries not specifically named by Hofstede, the following solutions were adopted. First, old "Eastern bloc" countries (Bulgaria and Poland) were allocated the mean scores for the one former Eastern bloc country included in his research, namely former Yugoslavia. Second, African countries were allocated Hofstede masculinity or individualism scores (which are given by Hofstede only in terms of South Africa, East Africa, and West Africa) by assuming that Botswana, Malawi, Nigeria, and Zambia are for present purposes "West Africa," and Zimbabwe is for present purposes "South Africa." Honduras was allocated the same scores as those reported by Hofstede for El Salvador, and Lebanon was allocated the Hofstede individualism and masculinity–femininity scores for "Arab countries." Finally, China was allocated the scores reported by Hofstede for Taiwan. The GEM scores, individualism scores, and the masculinity scores used for each of the 37 countries are shown in table 4.1. For analysis purposes these scores were then divided at the median (GEM median = .48; individualism median = 38; masculinity median = 46) to create a group of "low GEM" versus "high GEM," "low individualism" versus "high individualism", and "low masculinity" versus "high masculinity" countries. Countries with scores falling at the median were classified as low in order to equate the numbers of participants in the low and high groups as far as possible.

We then computed a series of multivariate analyses using gender and the 3 cultural measures as factors and the 7 emotions as dependent variables. More specifically, we entered the three sets of dependent variables (intensity, duration, and expression) for each of the 7 emotions included in the ISEAR study into multivariate analyses of variance (one for each set of dependent measures), using as the factors sex of respondent and level of GEM (low versus high), masculinity (low versus high), or individualism (low versus high). Separate MANOVAs were conducted for intensity, duration and nonverbal expression of emotions. In the interests of conserving space and of maximizing reader-friendliness, we report only the multivariate main effects and interactions, and the univariate interaction effects.

Table 4.1. *Mean gender empowerment measure, Masculinity–Femininity index, and Individualism–Collectivism index scores of the 37 countries in the ISEAR sample*

Country	Total N	N males	N females	GEM score[a]	M–F score[b]	I–C score[c]
Australia	117	37	80	.664	61	90
Austria	69	28	41	.686	79	54
Botswana	79	54	25	.475	46	20
Brazil	58	16	42	.374	49	38
Bulgaria	73	31	42	.462	21	27
Chile	65	32	33	.416	28	23
China	79	48	31	.483	45	20
Costa Rica	58	29	29	.503	21	15
El Salvador	40	11	29	.480	40	19
Finland	76	25	51	.725	21	63
France	63	10	53	.489	43	71
Germany	117	45	72	.694	66	67
Greece	66	34	32	.438	57	35
Guatemala	44	21	23	.479	37	6
Honduras	55	10	45		40	19
Hong Kong	80	43	37		57	25
India	68	36	32	.228	56	48
Israel	43	15	28	.484	47	54
Italy	98	50	48	.521	70	76
Japan	214	97	114	.472	95	46
Lebanon	51	15	36		53	38
Malawi	75	38	37	.256	46	20
Mexico	139	64	75	.474	69	30
Netherlands	69	24	45	.689	14	80
New Zealand	60	22	38	.725	58	79
Nigeria	77	50	27		46	20
Norway	36	22	14	.790	8	69
Poland	87	43	44	.494	21	27
Portugal	88	21	67	.547	31	27
Spain	78	39	39	.617	42	51
Sweden	84	37	47	.790	5	71
Switzerland	80	22	58	.654	70	68
USA	69	40	29	.675	62	91
Venezuela	73	28	45	.414	73	12
Yugoslavia	80	40	40	.475	21	27
Zambia	110	72	38	.304	46	20
Zimbabwe	99	52	47	.428	63	65

Notes:
[a] Higher GEM scores reflect a higher degree of participation of women in political and economic life.
[b] Higher M–F scores reflect a higher degree of Masculinity.
[c] Higher I–C scores reflect a higher degree of Individualism.

Table 4.2. *Intensity of emotional experience as a function of GEM and sex*

	Low GEM			High GEM		
Emotion	Male (N = 674)	Female (N = 688)	M–F difference	Male (N = 509)	Female (N = 783)	M–F difference
Joy	3.10	3.17	.07	3.00	3.20	.20
Fear	3.05	3.07	.02	2.97	3.23	.26
Anger	3.06	2.97	−.09	3.00	3.03	.03
Sadness	3.21	3.27	.06	2.97	3.23	.26
Disgust	2.67	2.65	−.02	2.65	2.81	.16
Shame	2.62	2.57	−.05	2.51	2.63	.12
Guilt	2.63	2.57	−.05	2.50	2.62	.12
Overall difference			.36			1.15

Intensity

GEM

Analysis of the intensity scores for the 7 emotions revealed significant multivariate main effects for sex, F (7, 2644) $= 7.29$, $p < .0001$, and GEM, F (7, 2644) $= 4.30$, $p < .0001$. The main effect of sex was not significant for anger, shame or guilt, but women experienced more intense joy, fear, sadness, and disgust than men did. The GEM main effect was significant for sadness and disgust only. More importantly, there was also a significant multivariate interaction between sex and GEM, $F(7, 2644) = 3.31$, $p < .01$. Univariate analyses showed that this interaction effect was significant for six emotions and marginally significant for the seventh: joy, $F(1, 2650) = 3.89$, $p < .05$, fear, $F(1, 2650) = 11.77$, $p < .001$, anger, $F(1, 2650) = 3.45$, $p < .07$, sadness, $F(1, 2650) = 9.67$, $p < .01$, disgust, $F(1, 2650) = 5.93$, $p < .05$, shame, $F(1, 2650) = 5.51$, $p < .05$, and guilt $F(1, 2650) = 6.20$, $p < .05$. Inspection of the means (see table 4.2) shows that this interaction reflects the fact that difference between male and female means is smaller in countries with a lower GEM score.

Masculinity

The multivariate main effects of both masculinity, $F(7, 2907) = 2.80$, $p < .01$, and sex, $F(7, 2907) = 7.13$, $p < .001$, were significant. The multivariate interaction was not significant, $F(7, 2907) = 1.36$, ns. The masculinity

Table 4.3. *Intensity of emotional experience as a function of masculinity and sex*

Emotion	Low masculinity			High masculinity		
	Male (N=709)	Female (N=806)	M–F difference	Male (N=592)	Female (N=810)	M–F difference
Joy	3.10	3.19	.09	3.02	3.18	.16
Fear	3.02	3.20	.18	3.00	3.11	.11
Anger	3.05	2.99	−.06	2.98	2.99	.01
Sadness	3.16	3.26	.10	3.05	3.24	.19
Disgust	2.73	2.76	.03	2.58	2.67	.09
Shame	2.64	2.62	−.02	2.49	2.60	.11
Guilt	2.63	2.63	.00	2.50	2.59	.09
Overall difference			.48			.76

main effect was significant for sadness, disgust, shame, and guilt. In each case, the mean score for the low masculinity countries was higher than that of the high masculinity countries (see table 4.3). The univariate sex main effects were significant for joy, fear and sadness; in each case, the female mean is higher than the male mean.

Individualism

Analysis of the intensity scores for the 7 emotions revealed significant multivariate main effects for individualism, $F(7, 2907) = 6.00$, $p < .001$, and sex, $F(7, 2907) = 7.23$, $p < .001$, and also a significant multivariate interaction between these two factors, $F(7, 2907) = 2.75$, $p < .01$. In univariate terms, the individualism main effect was significant for joy, sadness, disgust and guilt. In each case, the mean reported intensity was higher in collectivistic countries than it was in individualistic countries. The sex main effect was significant for joy, fear and sadness, women reporting higher intensities of these emotions than men did. The interaction between individualism and sex was significant in the case of joy, $F(1, 2913) = 10.18$, $p < .001$, disgust, $F(1, 2913) = 4.658$, $p < .05$, shame, $F(1, 2913) = 3.85$, $p < 05$, and guilt, $F(1, 2913) = 4.96$, $p < .05$; it was also marginally significant in the case of sadness, $F(1, 2913) = 3.23$, $p < .08$. As can be seen in table 4.4, the gender difference in intensity is greater in individualistic than in collectivistic countries.

Table 4.4. *Intensity of emotional experience as a function of individualism and sex*

Emotion	Low individualism			High individualism		
	Male (N=701)	Female (N=777)	M–F difference	Male (N=600)	Female (N=839)	M–F difference
Joy	3.15	3.19	.04	2.96	3.19	.25
Fear	2.99	3.14	.15	3.03	3.16	.13
Anger	3.02	2.97	−.05	3.02	3.02	.00
Sadness	3.18	3.27	.09	3.04	3.24	.20
Disgust	2.66	2.64	−.02	2.66	2.79	.13
Shame	2.63	2.60	−.03	2.51	2.61	.10
Guilt	2.66	2.62	−.04	2.46	2.57	.09
Overall difference			.42			.90

In sum, gender differences in the intensity of emotional experiences appear to be affected by the division of sex roles and by the endorsement of individualistic versus collectivistic values in a particular country. Gender differences were greater in countries with a high Gender Empowerment Measure and in countries with relatively high individualistic values.

Duration

GEM

The main effects of both GEM, $F(7, 2644) = 23.52$, $p < .0001$, and sex, $F(7,2644) = 7611$, $p < .0001$, were significant. The GEM main effect was significant for all emotions, and reflected the fact that emotions were reported as lasting longer, on average, by respondents in low GEM countries. The sex main effect was significant for all emotions, except for shame, and shows that women reported their emotions as lasting longer than men did. The multivariate interaction between GEM and sex was only marginally significant, $F(7, 2644) = 1.83$, $p < .08$. Univariate analyses revealed that this interaction was significant for shame $F(1,2650) = 9.15$, $p < .01$, and was marginally significant in the case of fear, $F(1,2650) = 3.03$, $p < .09$, and anger, $F(1,2650) = 3.26$, $p < .08$. In each case, the gender difference was greater in high GEM countries than in low GEM countries.

Table 4.5. *Duration of emotional experience as a function of GEM and sex*

Emotion	Low GEM			High GEM		
	Male (N = 674)	Female (N = 688)	M-F difference	Male (N = 509)	Female (N = 783)	M-F difference
Joy	3.46	3.52	.06	3.09	3.24	.13
Fear	2.64	2.66	.02	2.20	2.39	.19
Anger	2.83	2.99	.16	2.45	2.78	.33
Sadness	3.59	3.69	.10	3.44	3.60	.16
Disgust	2.63	2.71	.09	2.28	2.42	.14
Shame	2.80	2.62	−.18	2.43	2.53	.10
Guilt	3.11	3.17	.06	2.98	3.10	.12
Overall difference			.67			1.27

Table 4.6. *Duration of emotional experience as a function of masculinity and sex*

Emotion	Low masculinity			High masculinity		
	Male (N = 709)	Female (N = 806)	M–F difference	Male (N = 592)	Female (N = 810)	M–F difference
Joy	3.39	3.40	.01	3.23	3.37	.14
Fear	2.53	2.67	.14	2.43	2.44	.01
Anger	2.64	2.78	.14	2.72	2.95	.23
Sadness	3.60	3.65	.05	3.48	3.64	.16
Disgust	2.51	2.53	.02	2.45	2.58	.13
Shame	2.77	2.61	−.16	2.50	2.58	.08
Guilt	3.09	3.14	.05	2.98	3.12	.14
Overall difference			.57			.89

Masculinity

The main effects of both masculinity, $F(7, 2907) = 7.31$, $p < .001$, and sex, $F(7, 2907) = 5.19$, $p < .001$, were significant, as was the multivariate interaction, $F(7, 2907) = 2.41$, $p < .02$. In univariate terms, the masculinity main effect was significant for joy, fear, anger, sadness and shame. In the cases of joy, fear, sadness, and shame, low masculinity countries reported longer durations than did high masculinity countries; for anger, the reverse was true (see table 4.6). The sex main effect was significant for all emotions except shame and disgust. The univariate interaction was significant in the case of shame, $F(1, 2913) = 7.45$, $p < .01$, and marginally significant for joy, $F(1, 2913) = 3.28$, $p < .08$, and sadness, $F(1, 2913) = 3.76$, $p < .06$. As can be seen in table 4.6, in low masculinity countries males reported equal or somewhat longer durations than did females, whereas in high masculinity countries the reverse was true.

Individualism

There were significant multivariate main effects of individualism, $F(7, 2907) = 15.54$, $p < .001$, and sex, $F(7, 2907) = 5.77$, $p < .001$; however, the multivariate interaction was not significant, $F < 1$. The individualism main effect was significant for all 7 emotions. In every case, the mean reported duration of the emotion was greater in collectivistic countries than in individualistic countries. The sex main effect was significant for all emotions, except disgust and shame. In every case, the mean duration of the reported emotion was greater for women than for men (see table 4.7).

In sum, both GEM and masculinity influenced the reports of duration of emotional experience. Again, gender differences were generally smaller in countries with a low GEM score and in countries with more feminine values. The gender difference in duration did not vary as a function of individualism.

Nonverbal expression

GEM

The main effects of both GEM, $F(7, 2644) = 4.54$, $p < .0001$, and sex, $F(7, 2644) = 8.43$, $p < .0001$, were significant. The GEM main effect was significant for joy, anger and sadness. Nonverbal expression of these emotions was greater in high GEM countries than in low GEM countries. The sex main effect was significant for all emotions, with women scoring higher than men. The multivariate interaction between GEM

Table 4.7. *Duration of emotional experience as a function of individualism and sex*

Emotion	Low individualism			High individualism		
	Male (N=701)	Female (N=777)	M–F difference	Male (N=600)	Female (N=839)	M–F difference
Joy	3.42	3.50	.08	3.20	3.28	.08
Fear	2.62	2.77	.15	2.33	2.35	.02
Anger	2.72	2.90	.18	2.62	2.83	.21
Sadness	3.61	3.70	.09	3.47	3.59	.12
Disgust	2.54	2.65	.11	2.41	2.46	.05
Shame	2.75	2.63	−.12	2.53	2.56	.03
Guilt	3.11	3.20	.09	2.96	3.06	.10
Overall difference			.81			.61

Table 4.8. *Expression of emotion as a function of GEM and sex*

Emotion	Low GEM			High GEM		
	Male (N=674)	Female (N=688)	M–F difference	Male (N=508)	Female (N=783)	M–F difference
Joy	1.36	1.48	.12	1.43	1.67	.24
Fear	.91	1.01	.10	.88	1.11	.23
Anger	1.20	1.36	.16	1.36	1.56	.20
Sadness	1.15	1.32	.17	1.17	1.50	.33
Disgust	.85	.96	.11	.83	1.03	.20
Shame	.88	.96	.08	.88	.97	.09
Guilt	.78	.79	.01	.69	.92	.23[b]
Overall difference			.75			1.52

and sex was only marginally significant, $F(7, 2644) = 1.95$, $p < .06$. Univariate analyses showed that this interaction was significant for guilt, $F(1, 2650) = 9.11$, $p < .01$, and marginally significant in the case of fear, $F(1, 2650) = 2.84$, $p < .10$, and sadness, $F(1, 2650) = 3.67$, $p < .06$. For all three emotions, the gender difference was greater in high GEM countries than in low GEM countries.

Table 4.9. *Expression of emotion as a function of masculinity and sex*

Emotion	Low masculinity			High masculinity		
	Male (N = 709)	Female (N = 806)	M–F difference	Male (N = 592)	Female (N = 810)	M–F difference
Joy	1.34	1.50	.16	1.46	1.65	.19
Fear	.87	1.07	.20	.93	1.05	.12
Anger	1.29	1.43	.14	1.28	1.48	.20
Sadness	1.17	1.36	.19	1.19	1.46	.27
Disgust	.85	.98	.13	.84	1.06	.22
Shame	.90	.96	.06	.90	.98	.08
Guilt	.78	.84	.06	.71	.89	.18
Overall difference			.94			1.26

Masculinity

The multivariate main effects of masculinity, $F(7, 2907) = 2.59$, $p < .05$, and sex, $F(7, 2907) = 8.71$, $p < .0001$, were both significant. In univariate terms, the main effect of masculinity was only significant for joy. As shown in table 4.9, expressions of joy were higher in high masculinity than in low masculinity countries. The univariate main effects of sex paralleled those found in the individualism analysis reported above. The multivariate interaction was not significant, $F(7, 2907) = 1.10$, ns.

Individualism

Analysis of the expression data revealed multivariate main effects for individualism, $F(7, 2907) = 3.23$, $p < .01$, and sex, $F(7, 2907) = 8.87$, $p < .001$. The multivariate interaction between these two factors was also significant, $F(7, 2907) = 3.21$, $p < .01$. The main effect for individualism was significant for joy and anger, and marginally significant for guilt. Joy and anger tended to be expressed to a greater extent in individualistic countries than in collectivistic countries, whereas for guilt there was a reverse tendency. In each case, however, the effect of individualism interacted strongly with sex of respondent. The sex main effect was significant for all emotions. In each case, women reported expressing their emotions to a greater extent than did men. The interaction between individualism and sex was significant for the following emotions: joy, $F(1, 2913) = 6.44$, $p < .05$, sadness, $F(1, 2913) = 19.11$, $p < .001$, and guilt, $F(1, 2913) = 3.97$, $p < .05$. In each case, the difference between women and men was greater in individualistic countries than in collectivistic countries (see Table 4.10).

Table 4.10. *Expression of emotion as a function of individualism and sex*

| Emotion | Low individualism | | | High individualism | | |
	Male (N = 701)	Female (N = 777)	M–F difference	Male (N = 600)	Female (N = 839)	M–F difference
Joy	1.39	1.48	.09	1.39	1.66	.27
Fear	.91	1.03	.12	.88	1.09	.21
Anger	1.26	1.38	.12	1.31	1.53	.22
Sadness	1.24	1.32	.08	1.10	1.51	.41
Disgust	.86	1.01	.15	.82	1.03	.21
Shame	.92	.97	.05	.87	.96	.09
Guilt	.81	.86	.05	.68	.87	.19
Overall difference			.66			1.60

In sum, gender differences in nonverbal expression of emotions were moderated by both GEM and individualism. Gender differences were larger in countries with a high GEM score and in countries with more individualistic values.

Discussion and conclusion

The analyses of the ISEAR database yielded findings that replicate those of earlier studies. First, we found the anticipated effects of sex of respondent with respect to all three aspects of emotion (intensity, duration, and expression), showing that women in all countries reported more intense emotions, and of a longer duration, and that they also expressed their emotions more overtly. We also found significant effects for all three cultural factors, such that respondents in countries with less traditional sex roles (high GEM), with less traditional sex-role ideologies (low masculinity), and with a prevalence of individualistic values (high individualism) generally reported stronger emotional reactions. More importantly, however, these effects were qualified by significant interactions between gender and culture, albeit not for all 3 cultural measures, or for all 7 emotions. All the observed interactions were nevertheless of a similar nature: gender differences in emotional response were larger in less traditional, individualistic countries than in more traditional, collectivistic countries (see also Brody, 1997).

These findings imply that our first hypothesis, namely that emotional differences between the sexes are due primarily to a differentiation of gender roles, must be rejected. Although GEM appeared to be the most important moderator of differences between male and female emotional reactions, in that it interacted significantly with gender for all 3 measures of emotional response, the pattern of means was precisely reverse of what we predicted. The same pattern was found for sex-role ideology, as operationalized by Hofstede's masculinity–femininity measure, although it is interesting to note that M–F was less predictive in this regard than was the measure of actual division of sex roles (GEM). Masculinity and gender only interacted significantly in the case of duration of emotion. It is also worth noting that GEM and the masculinity factor were essentially uncorrelated with each other ($r = .03$). As argued earlier, this lack of relationship between a measure of actual division of labor between the sexes and sex-role ideology may be due to the fact that the psychological representation of gender roles lags behind the actual division of labor. However, if this were the case we would expect stronger and more consistent interaction effects between gender and masculinity than between gender and GEM, on the grounds that the way in which sex roles are represented psychologically should have a stronger influence on other psychological variables (such as emotional reactions) than should a more objective measure of gender empowerment. An alternative explanation, of course, is that Hofstede's masculinity–femininity index is not a good measure of the sex-role ideology that prevails in a particular country.

The second hypothesis, concerning the prevalence of gender-aspecific display rules, was generally supported. Degree of endorsement of individualistic values interacted significantly with gender both for intensity and for expression of emotions, indicating that gender differences in individualistic countries are generally larger than in collectivistic countries. However, if we consider the fact that countries with more modern sex-role division generally are characterized by more individualistic values, which is reflected in a rank order correlation between GEM and individualism of .62, we may have an explanation for why we did not find support for our hypothesis based on Social Role Theory. The fact that gender-role division and the endorsement of individualistic values are not independent of each other suggests that the extent to which the roles performed by women and men in a given culture are the same or different is related to the degree to which that culture endorses collectivistic values, and thereby to the presence of collective, gender aspecific emotion rules.

The nature of the gender-by-culture interaction can serve to illustrate our argument. With respect to intensity of the experience, for example, we found that male experience of fear in individualistic cultures is less intense, relative to males and females in collectivistic cultures, as well as to females in individualistic cultures. The same pattern is apparent for the intensity of joy, sadness, shame, and guilt experiences. The pattern relating to intensity of disgust experiences, by contrast, shows that females in individualistic cultures experience this emotion more intensely than do females or males in collectivistic cultures, or males in individualistic cultures. A similar pattern is evident for some of the significant interactions between gender and culture with respect to duration of the emotion and emotional expression. For sadness and disgust, it is the individualistic females who score higher than the other three groups; whereas for fear, shame, and guilt, it is the individualistic males who score lower than the other three groups.

Our contention is that males who grow up in individualistic societies are encouraged in the course of sex-role socialization to learn to avoid situations that could give rise to emotions that pose a threat to their status as independent males who are (or should be) in control of the situation. This would explain why men in individualistic countries are especially likely to report lower intensities of sadness, shame and guilt, since these can be considered to be emotions that display powerlessness or a lack of control, and therefore a threat to Western conceptions of masculinity (Fischer & Jansz, 1995; see also Jansz, this volume). Despite the supposedly more liberal sex roles that tend to prevail in individualistic cultures, women learn that it is more admissible or even expected for them to be "overcome" by emotions. Women who grow up in individualistic cultures not only learn that it is acceptable to be overcome by emotional experiences. They also learn that they are expected by others to express these emotions, especially positive ones (see Stoppard & Gunn Gruchy, 1993), whereas males in these cultures learn that if they do experience powerless emotions, no premium attaches to expressing them. Thus the regulative rules that prevail in individualistic cultures are generally ones that lead women to value emotional expressiveness. In contrast, the constitutive rules that prevail in individualistic cultures are ones that generally lead men to define situations that could make them appear vulnerable as ones that either do not touch their concerns or do not exceed their coping resources.

Moreover, the less traditional division of sex roles in individualistic societies may even lead to a stronger emphasis of specific psychological differences between men and women. According to Markus and Kitayama (1991) the cultural task of the individual in an individualistic culture is to seek out, achieve, and maintain independence from others. However, the full accomplishment of these cultural tasks would threaten one of the bases of social life, namely the nuclear family. One way in which a culture can achieve a satisfactory balance between the competing demands of achieving and maintaining independence from others, on the one hand, and maintaining the integrity of the basic unit of social existence, on the other, is to create some degree of psychological task differentiation. In the same way that social groups have "task leaders" and "socio-emotional leaders" (Bales & Slater, 1955), it can be argued that individualistic cultures have created specialists in the achievement and maintenance of independence (i.e., males), and specialists in the achievement and maintenance of social relations (i.e., females). The fact that males learn to regulate their lives in such a way that emotions are experienced less intensely means that females have to compensate for this lack of emotionality in social life by being more overtly expressive. The need for a gendered role differentiation arises less strongly in collectivistic cultures. According to Markus and Kitayama (1991), the cultural task of the individual in a collectivistic culture is to adjust to significant others and to maintain interdependence with these others: thus there is no need for males to be socialized so that they experience emotions as little as possible, and there is therefore no need for females to compensate for the relative absence of emotion in one half of the population.

According to this analysis, greater individualism in a culture should be associated with diminished experience of emotion by males in that culture, and with enhanced expression of emotion by females. Whether or not this admittedly quite speculative account for the pattern of findings reported above and in previous research is tenable can only be assessed by conducting further research that is designed to test these predictions more directly. We began this chapter with what we referred to as the "Western dichotomy." As we have seen in the remainder of the chapter, it may be no accident that the association of independence with manhood and emotionality with womanhood is something that is more readily found in "Western," individualistic cultures than in their collectivistic counterparts.

Acknowledgments

We thank Leslie Brody and Harald Wallbott for their helpful comments of on a previous version of this chapter. We also are grateful to Wendy Wood for suggesting that we should consider using data from the United Nations Development Project (1996), available on internet at http://www.undp.org/hdro.

Notes

1. Data from this ISEAR project are part of a larger cross-cultural data bank, which is supported by the Maison des Sciences de l'Homme (Paris, France),

the Thyssen Foundation (Germany), and the Société Académique de l'Université de Genève (Switzerland). The data-bank consortium consists of Agneta Fischer (University of Amsterdam), Pierre Philippot (University of Louvain at Louvain-la-Neuve), and Harald Wallbott (University of Salzburg). The data of ISEAR project are available on internet: http://www.psy.uva.nl/DCE. People who are interested in the data bank should contact Agneta Fischer (e-mail: sp_fischer@macmail.psy.uva.nl).

References

Ashmore, R. D., Del Boca, F. K., & Wohlers, A. J. (1986). Gender stereotypes. In R. D. Ashmore & F. K. Del Boca (Eds.), *The social psychology of female-male relations* (pp. 69–120). Orlando, FL: Academic Press.

Bales, R. F., & Slater, P. E. (1955). Role differentiation in small decision-making groups. In T. Parsons & R. F. Bales (Eds.), *Family, socialization, and interaction process* (pp. 259–306). Glencoe, IL: Free Press.

Boesch, E. E. (1994). First experiences in Thailand. In W. J. Lonner & R. S. Malpass (Eds.), *Psychology and culture* (pp. 47–52). Needham Heights, MA: Allyn & Bacon.

Briggs, J. L. (1970). *Never in anger: Portrait of an Eskimo family.* Cambridge, MA: Harvard University Press.

Brody, L. R. (1997). Gender and emotion: Beyond stereotypes. *Journal of Social Issues, 53,* 369–394.

Brody, L. R., & Hall, J. (1993). Gender and emotion. In M. Lewis & J. Haviland (Eds.), *Handbook of emotions* (pp. 447–461). New York: Guilford Press.

Broverman, I. K., Vogel, S. R., Broverman, D. M., Clarkson, F. E., & Rosenkrantz, P. S. (1972). Sex-role stereotypes: A current appraisal. *Journal of Social Issues, 28,* 59–78.

Copeland, A. P., Hwang, H. , & Brody, L. R. (1996). Asian-American adolescents: Caught between cultures? Poster presented at the Society for Research in Adolescence, Boston, MA.

Eagly, A. H. (1987). *Sex differences in social behavior: A social-role interpretation.* Hillsdale, NJ: Erlbaum.

Ekman, P. (1972). Universals and cultural differences in facial expression of emotion. In J. Cole (Ed.), *Nebraska Symposium on Motivation* (Vol. 19, pp. 207–283). Lincoln, NE: University of Nebraska Press.

Ekman, P., & Friesen, W. V. (1971). Constants across cultures in the face and emotion. *Journal of Personality and Social Psychology, 58,* 342–353.

Fabes, R. A., & Martin, C. L. (1991). Gender and age stereotypes of emotionality. *Personality and Social Psychology Bulletin, 17,* 532–540.

Fischer, A. H. (1993). Sex differences in emotionality: Fact or stereotype? *Feminism and Psychology, 3,* 303–318.

Fischer, A. H., & Jansz, J. (1995). Reconciling emotions with Western personhood. *Journal for the Theory of Social Behavior, 25,* 59–81.

Friesen, W. V. (1972). Cultural differences in facial expressions in a social situation: An experimental test of the concept of display rules. Unpublished doctoral dissertation, University of California, San Francisco.

Frymier, A. B., Klopf, D. W., & Ishii, S. (1990). Japanese and Americans compared on the affect orientation construct. *Psychological Reports, 66,* 985–986.

Hochschild, A. (1983). *The managed heart.* Berkeley, CA: University of California Press.

Hofstede, G. (1980). *Culture's consequences: International differences in work-related values*. Beverley Hills, CA: Sage.

Hofstede, G. (1991). *Cultures and organizations: Software of the mind*. London: McGraw-Hill.

Hofstede, G. (1998). *Masculinity and femininity. The taboo dimension of national cultures*. Thousand Oaks, CA: Sage.

Kashima, Y., Yamaguchi, S., Kim, U., Gelfand, M. J., Choi, S., & Yuki, M. (1995). Culture, gender, and self: A perspective from individualism–collectivism research. *Journal of Personality and Social Psychology, 69*, 925–937.

Kim, U., Triandis, H. C., Kagitçibasi, C., Choi, S., & Yoon, G. (Eds.) (1994). *Individualism and collectivism. Theory, methods and applications*. Thousand Oaks, CA: Sage.

LaFrance, M., & Banaji, M. (1992). Toward a reconsideration of the gender-emotion relationship. In M. S. Clark (Ed.), *Review of Personality and Social Psychology: Emotions and Social Behavior* (Vol. 14, pp. 178–202). Newbury Park, CA: Sage.

Levy, R. I. (1984). Emotion, knowing and culture. In R. A. Schweder & R. A. Levine (Eds.), *Culture Theory: Issues on mind, self and emotion* (pp. 214–237). Cambridge University Press.

Lloyd, G. (1984). *The man of reason: "Male" and "female" in Western philosophy*. London: Methuen.

Lonner, W. J., & Malpass, R. S. (Eds.) (1994). *Psychology and culture*. Needham Heights, MA: Allyn & Bacon.

Manstead, A. S. R. (1992). Gender differences in emotion. M. A. Gale & M. W. Eysenck (Eds.), *Handbook of individual differences: Biological perspectives* (pp. 355–389). Chichester: Wiley.

Markus, H. R., & Kitayama, S. (1991). Culture and the self: Implications for cognition, emotion and motivation. *Psychological Review, 98*, 224–253.

Munroe, R. H., & Munroe, R. L. (1994). Behavior across cultures: Results from observational studies. In W. J. Lonner & R. S. Malpass (Eds.), *Psychology and culture* (pp. 107–111). Needham Heights, MA: Allyn & Bacon.

Rosenberg, R. (1982). *Beyond separate spheres*. New Haven, CT: Yale University Press.

Scherer, K. R. (Ed.) (1988). *Facets of emotion*. Hillsdale, NJ: Erlbaum.

Scherer, K. R. (1997). Profiles of emotion-antecedent appraisal: Testing theoretical predictions across cultures. *Cognition and Emotion, 11*, 113–150.

Scherer, K. R., Wallbott, H. G., Matsumoto, D., & Kudoh, T. (1988). Emotional experience in cultural context: A comparison between Europe, Japan and the United States. In K. R. Scherer (Ed.), *Facets of emotion* (pp. 5–31). Hillsdale, NJ: Erlbaum.

Scherer, K. R., & Wallbott, H. G. (1994). Evidence for universality and cultural variation of differential emotion response patterning. *Journal of Personality and Social Psychology, 66*, 310–328.

Shields, S. A. (1984). 'To pet, coddle and do for'. Caretaking and the concept of maternal instinct. In M. Lewin (Ed.), *In the shadow of the past: Psychology portrays the sexes* (pp. 256–274). New York: Columbia University Press.

Stoppard, J. M., & Gunn Gruchy, C. D. (1993). Gender, context, and expression of positive emotion. *Personality and Social Psychology Bulletin, 19*, 143–150.

Triandis, H. C. (1989). The self and social behavior in different cultural contexts. *Psychological Review, 96*, 506–520.

Vingerhoets, A., & Becht, M. (1996). The ISAC study: Some preliminary findings. Paper presented at the International Study on Adult Crying Symposium, Tilburg, the Netherlands.

Wallbott, H. G., & Scherer, K. R. (1988). How universal and specific is emotional experience? Evidence form 27 countries and five continents. In K. R. Scherer (Ed.), *Facets of emotion* (pp. 31–57). Hillsdale, NJ: Erlbaum.

Williams, J. E., & Best, D. L. (1982). *Measuring sex stereotypes: A multi-nation study.* Newbury Park, CA: Sage.

Williams, J. E., & Best, D. L. (1990). *Sex and psyche: Gender and self viewed cross-culturally.* Newbury Park, CA: Sage.

Williams, J. E., & Best, D. L. (1997). Sex, gender, and culture. In J. W. Berry, M. H. Segall, & C. Kagitçibasi (Eds.), *Handbook of Cross-cultural Psychology. Vol. 3: Social behavior and applications* (pp. 163–213). Boston, MA: Allyn & Bacon.

Zahn-Waxler, C., Friedman, R. J., Cole, P. M., Mizuta, I., & Hiruma, N. (1996). Japanese and United States preschool children's responses to conflict and distress. *Child Development, 67*, 2462–2477.

PART II

Emotion expression and communication

5. Gender differences in nonverbal communication of emotion

JUDITH A. HALL, JASON D. CARTER, AND
TERRENCE G. HORGAN

There is a large accumulation of research on gender differences in non-verbal communication. By nonverbal communication we mean specific behaviors such as smiling or gazing, as well as accuracy in nonverbal communication. Summaries of these gender differences are available (Hall, 1978, 1984, 1987; LaFrance & Hecht, this volume; Vrugt & Kerkstra, 1984). The present chapter is also concerned with gender and nonverbal communication, but differs from earlier treatments in that we discuss a selected group of nonverbal behaviors with specific interest in analyzing the role of *emotion* in understanding the gender differences.

Before beginning, it is important to make several points. First, non-verbal behavior does not necessarily signify emotion. Some examples will easily make this point. Smiles can serve the function of "listener responses" that signal comprehension and cue the other person to keep speaking (Brunner, 1979). Gaze is used to help coordinate the intricate process of turn-taking in conversation (Cappella, 1985). Hand move-ments aid in the process of speech encoding (Krauss, Chen, & Chawla, 1996). These are but a few examples of non-emotional meanings and functions of nonverbal cues.

Second, even when nonverbal cues *do* indicate emotion, it is often dif-ficult to identify what emotion is being felt. Nonverbal cues do not have fixed, dictionary-like meanings. So, a smile might convey either joy or anxiety, looking at someone might signify hostility or fascination, and so forth. Although someday we might understand the relations among contextual factors, motivational states, and specific muscle configura-tions well enough to permit a confident identification of which particu-lar emotions are being conveyed by which nonverbal behaviors, in our present state of knowledge we are often unable to do so.

Finally, even if nonverbal behavior is conveying emotional informa-tion, and even if we can identify which emotion is being conveyed, there is often great ambiguity about the authenticity of the display. People have considerable control over their nonverbal behavior (particularly facial expressions) and can therefore put on false expressions, intensify the expression of their true feelings, mask their true emotion with a neutral expression, and so forth. The issue of intentionality and authenticity is particularly relevant in the case of facial expressions such as smiling (see, for example, Buck, 1991; Chovil, 1991; Fernández-Dols & Ruiz-Belda, 1995; Fridlund, 1991; Frank, Ekman, & Friesen, 1993; Kraut & Johnston, 1979). Such ambiguities make some issues in the interpretation of gender differences particularly difficult.

These ambiguities provide serious obstacles to reaching firm conclusions about the relations among nonverbal behavior, emotions, and gender. Nevertheless, we undertake to examine these relations in hopes that a small amount of theoretical progress will result. We consider smiling, expressiveness/expression accuracy, and decoding (judgment) accuracy. These three categories of behavior have been well examined with respect to gender, and they show relatively large gender differences (Eagly, 1995; Hall, 1998). The word "relatively" is important here. In absolute terms psychological gender differences tend to be rather small. However, the nonverbal differences are larger than many other psychological gender differences (including cognitive skills, attitudes, personality, and other social behaviors) (Hall, 1998).

For smiling, expressiveness/expression accuracy, and decoding accuracy, we will first present a summary of gender differences, especially as they relate to emotion. We will then present a theoretical model that attempts to capture the rich diversity of possible explanatory factors for these gender differences, again with special attention to the role that emotion might be playing. Our model emphasizes *proximal* factors, that is, factors that are the more immediate precursors of smiling, such as motives that are aroused in a particular social situation or characteristics of that situation.

We recognize that a complete model would include more distal factors, which themselves could be grouped into *distal biological influences* and *distal environmental influences*. Some authors have argued for a likely biological influence on nonverbal gender differences (Andersen, 1998; Graham & Ickes, 1997). We concur that biological adaptation has surely played a role in shaping the human behavioral repertoire. Because many of the "problems" our progenitors faced were social in nature, it is indeed likely that socially important needs, motives, and emotions were favored by selection pressures. Examples would be the need to belong (Baumeister & Leary, 1995), the need to understand others (Stevens & Fiske, 1995), and the capacity for specific emotions such as guilt and gratitude (Leakey & Lewin, 1978). The ability to convey and interpret nonverbal information would have been adaptive to humans too (Darwin, 1872/1965; Fridlund, 1994).

To us other points remain less obvious, however. First, it is not necessary to posit that differences between males' and females' nonverbal behaviors and skills have evolved biologically; the observed differences could have come about through *cultural* learning and adaptation following from reproductive differences (e.g., the fact that for most of human history, lactation required that women stay near infants). Second, it seems likely that our biology prepares us to *learn about* or perhaps to be *pre-attuned* to nonverbal information, rather than providing us with innate knowledge of specific cue meanings and rules of usage (in contrast to Andersen, 1998, who in arguing that women's superior social skills are innate, implied both innate knowledge and motivation). Thus, a discussion of the evolutionary basis of nonverbal gender differences must identify what, exactly, has evolved differently – is it capacities, motives, knowledge, values, or what? It is our own view that although nonverbal behavior is biologically driven, the gender differences are likely to be experience dependent.

Distal *environmental* influences on gender differences include both what type of learning environment is provided to males versus females and what type of learning environment males and females are attracted to (see Brody & Hall, in press). Different social-learning environments would provide different experiences which in turn could lead to different repertoires of social behavior and social skills. For example, role expectations, folk wisdom, and stereotypes about females and males influence how each is socialized in society (Eagly, 1987). Mothers may talk more about emotions and display more varied facial expressions around their daughters than their sons (Kuebli, Butler, & Fivush, 1995; Malatesta, Culver, Tesman, & Shepard, 1989) because they believe females are more expressive or need to be more expressive than males. A more emotionally expressive, emotionally responsive, and emotionally differentiated environment in childhood could lead to more opportunities for nonverbal skill development in females, as well as to more motivation to display gender-appropriate behavior.

Smiling: Overview of gender differences

Hall's (1984) meta-analysis of male versus female social smiling used as its index of effect size the point-biserial correlation (r) between gender and smiling, with gender coded so that positive values indicated more female smiling and negative values indicated more male smiling. This same index of effect size is used in the present chapter. For 15 studies of adolescent and older samples, the average effect was $r = .30$ (Hall, 1984). In an updating of this review undertaken for the present chapter, an average effect of $r = .33$ was found for an additional 15 studies (the citations are available from the first author).

In the much larger quantitative review of LaFrance and Hecht (this volume), the average effect for social smiling was $r = .20$, a smaller value that may be due to LaFrance and Hecht entering unknown effect sizes as zero; in fact, when unknown effect sizes were included as zero in the earlier review, the average effect size was also .20 (Hall, 1984). In spite of this discrepancy, and acknowledging that there are numerous moderating influences (Hall & Halberstadt, 1986; LaFrance & Hecht, this volume), there is no contesting that the preponderance of research finds that women smile more than men do in social interaction.

Explanations for women's smiling

Because of the kinds of ambiguities discussed at the outset of this chapter, and because gender is obviously not under experimental control, it is extremely difficult to know what explains the gender difference in smiling (or any other nonverbal behavior), and, in particular, whether the difference is related to emotion. This problem is compounded by the typical form of research in which nonverbal behavior is examined in a gross quantitative way, for example by counting how many smiles occurred. Such methods permit only superficial conclusions about emotion since they pool expressions that might have diverse meanings.

While gender-role norms are the most commonly cited possible explanation for the smiling difference (as well as other nonverbal differences) (e.g., Henley, 1977; LaFrance & Hecht, this volume), a more comprehensive picture must include other proximal causes besides role conformity. The theoretical model we describe here is preliminary, and moreover we can present it in detail only for smiling, since that is what we are discussing first. When we discuss the other nonverbal behaviors, we will use the smiling model as the prototype, noting some of the differences that may pertain.

Figure 5.1 reveals that rather than trying to model the male–female *difference*, we consider female smiling by itself. We do this because the factors that increase women's smiling may not work simply in reverse for men. Later we will identify paths and/or factors that might be different for men. At the theoretical level, at least, treating the sexes separately provides some clarity over an analysis of differences (e.g., effect sizes in a meta-analysis), since differences by definition obscure the actual performance levels of men and women (for further discussion of this problem, see Hall, 1987).

As the title of figure 5.1 indicates, we believe the factors influencing women's smiling are affective, cognitive, and motivational. Although the figure does not show it, we assume there are influences *among* these

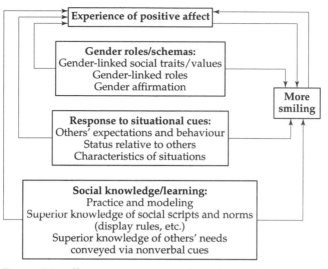

Figure 5.1 Affective, cognitive, and motivational factors in women's smiling

factors; for example, there could be an arrow from "gender-linked values" to "superior knowledge of social scripts and norms" because of the possibility that such values may promote skill development. We leave off these arrows for the sake of readability.

At the top of the list of possible explanatory factors is *positive affect*, under which we would include happiness and its variants such as pleasure, joy, contentment, enjoyment, and fun. The arrow going to increased smiling shows that, consistent with the "read-out" function of nonverbal behavior (Buck, 1984), more positive affect increases smiling. (At this point it is necessary to insert the cautionary "other things being equal." Obviously other factors could dampen this relationship, for example self-presentational goals that might suppress smiling; Friedman & Miller-Herringer, 1991.)

The arrow that goes from smiling back to positive affect is an extremely important feature of this model. It acknowledges the role of facial feedback in intensifying positive affect (e.g., Strack, Martin, & Stepper, 1988). Thus, *regardless of what factor or factors produced the smiling*, once smiling occurs it is likely to have a feedback effect on positive affect, which in turn could produce more smiling.

The following factor, called *gender roles/schemas*, encompasses a wide range of interrelated elements. By "gender-linked social values" we mean prosocial values and traits that are correlated with gender, for example interpersonal trust (Johnson-George & Swap, 1982), interpersonal orientation (Swap & Rubin, 1983), experience with intimacy (Reis,

Senchak, & Solomon, 1985), and positive attitudes toward other people and relationships (e.g., Filsinger, 1981; Matlin & Gawron, 1979; Warr, 1971). It can reasonably be suggested that one manifestation of these values and traits is smiling; for example, a person who is higher on interpersonal trust might smile because they wish to show others that they are trusted.

Note that feedback is present here too, not from smiling to positive affect as was the case above, but *from gender-linked social values to positive affect*. Such feedback can be predicted because holding and acting on positively valued traits is rewarding (Wood, Christensen, Hebl, & Rothgerber, 1997).

By "gender-linked roles" we refer to prescriptions for a gendered division of labor within the context of social interaction, notably the idea that men and women have separate responsibilities for task and socio-emotional processes, respectively (Parsons & Bales, 1955). To the extent that the social situation calls forth women's responsibility to look out for people's emotional welfare, and to the extent that smiling serves this function (helping others feel included, at ease, accepted, etc.), then this role division would produce more female smiling. Feedback occurs here as well. Because it is likely to be rewarding both to be in charge of social processes and outcomes, to feel self-efficacious, and to make others feel good, we would expect that the fulfillment of this role function in turn promotes positive affect in women.[1]

By "gender affirmation" we refer to motives that are less complex, and probably more basic, than those identified so far. Underlying some gender-related nonverbal displays is the simple need to signal gender to oneself and others – what Birdwhistell called "tertiary sex characteristics" (Birdwhistell, 1970). As the first author's teenage daughter promptly replied when she was asked why boys smile less than girls, "They don't want to act like a girl." Thus, a woman could smile not because it conveys any particular message or emotional meaning, but simply because it affirms which social category she belongs to. As with the previous factors, this too would have a feedback effect insofar as reaffirming one's gender is rewarding.[2]

The next explanatory factor, *response to situation*, refers to a woman's perceptions of, and responses to, her social environment. To the extent that she believes other people expect her to smile more, *and* to the extent that she values others' approval, she is likely to smile more. By the same token, others' actual behaviors (which may be following from these expectations and their fulfillment) may induce more smiling; for example, others may treat her in a kindly manner, smile at her more, etc. There is indeed evidence that people smile at women more than at men (Rosenthal, 1976), and, moreover, that smiling is reciprocated in social interaction (Cappella, 1981). Here the concept of self-fulfilling prophecy is obviously relevant. And, to the extent that a woman finds it reward- ing to meet others' expectations, again there would be feedback creat- ing more positive affect in her.

Emotional contagion (Hatfield, Cacioppo, & Rapson, 1994) is yet another phenomenon relating to gender and positive affect: women have a stronger tendency to "catch" another's emotion compared to men (Doherty, 1997). Women's faces also show more emotion- appropriate electromyographic (EMG) response to various stimuli, for example, zygomatic muscle activity in response to positive stimuli and corrugator muscle activity in response to sad stimuli (Dimberg, 1990; Dimberg & Lundqvist, 1990; Lundqvist, 1995; Schwartz, Brown, & Ahern, 1980). When put together with the concept of facial feedback, it is only a small leap from the EMG studies to the hypothesis that women experience more emotion in response to affective stimuli. Therefore, if people display relatively high levels of positive affect toward women, then women's proclivity for contagion and facial responding could magnify their experience of positive affect.

As alluded to above, the question of how much a woman *wants* to conform to others' expectations is important. Obviously, such confor- mity can be reluctant and cynical. Smiling to avoid the negative conse- quences of violating gender expectations certainly occurs. In that case, fulfilling others' expectations may lead to more smiling, but may not have the positive effect on emotional experience shown in the model. Furthermore, a woman who finds others' expectations to be offensive might choose *not* to conform to them, which might have complex con- sequences for her affective state – she might feel pleased at not conform- ing but not pleased to receive negative responses from others.

The next situational element is "status relative to others" (Henley, 1977, 1995; LaFrance & Henley, 1994). It has been proposed that women's lower status compared to men underlies differences in women's and men's nonverbal behavior. This interpretation has the appeal of unifying a number of gender differences under one compre- hensive explanation: women's behavior differs from men's in the same way that weak, subordinate, or submissive people's behavior differs from that of strong, superior, or dominant people. It is unclear as of this writing, however, whether smiling has the hypothesized relation to status because experimental manipulations of status or power mostly have not produced more smiling in the subordinate than in the super- ior (e.g., Hecht, 1995; Johnson, 1994). A study that found the predicted difference is problematic because it confounded low power with the request to make a favorable impression (Deutsch, 1990). Another study, of employees in a company interacting with one another (Hall &

Friedman, 1998), found that higher and lower status employees differed on several behaviors, but not on smiling. If lower status does influence women to smile more, it is reasonable to hypothesize that any impact on positive affect would be weak at best.

The final situational element is the situation itself, which includes the kinds of people in it. If, for example, the situation had babies or children in it, women might experience heightened pleasure and therefore smile; they might also believe that children need or expect to be smiled at and therefore smile. Meta-analyses have found that situational characteristics do moderate the smiling gender difference (Hall & Halberstadt, 1986; LaFrance & Hecht, this volume). As an example, Hall and Halberstadt (1986) rated the tenseness of the situation and found that the tenser it was, the greater was the difference between men's and women's smiling. By itself this finding is ambiguous with respect to *women's* smiling, since one cannot tell which sex was influenced by the tension (Hall, 1987). But one possibility is that tension has more of an effect on women's smiling than on men's. It would still be important to uncover whether women smile more in tense situations because *they* are tense or because they are working to alleviate the tension of others.

The final category of explanation in the model is *social knowledge/learning,* under which the first element is "practice and modeling." Behaviors that are overlearned and mostly out of conscious awareness (as nonverbal behaviors often are) can take on a life of their own. Once a behavior is firmly entrenched in one's repertoire, it can occur with no attendant psychological meanings other than habit itself. One antecedent to the development of such habits is same-sex modeling that starts early in life, whereby girls imitate what they see their mothers and other women doing. Another antecedent of the smiling habit would be the accumulated experience of smiling reciprocally to others. As with the "gender affirmation" function of smiling, there need not be much message content to a behavior acquired in these ways.

The remaining elements in the model refer to social knowledge that women may possess. If females know the rules of social interaction better than males, then the successful application of this superior knowledge may entail more smiling (for example, as part of maintaining "face" for others). To the extent that a woman gains reward from the knowledge that she has successfully applied her store of social wisdom, there should be a positive effect on her emotional experience.

In summary, our model suggests a rich variety of possible influences on women's smiling. Perhaps the most important contribution of this model is the feedback arrows that suggest there are many routes through which women's positive affect may be related to their smiling.

In particular, it poses a challenge to the implication that much of what women show during social interaction bears little relation to what they actually feel.

The idea that there is a special discordance between women's expression and their emotion gained support from Bugental's well-known article on "perfidious feminine faces" (Bugental, Love, & Gianetto, 1971), in which the positivity of women's facial expressions showed a poorer match with the positivity of their words than was the case for men. However, Halberstadt, Hayes, and Pike (1988) found the opposite in a well-designed study (see also Merten, 1997). In the same vein, LaFrance and Hecht (this volume) cite unpublished work suggesting that women produce relatively more inauthentic smiles than men do (where "inauthentic" smiles involve the mouth muscles without involvement of the eyes; Frank et al., 1993). However, studies by Hecht (1995) and Merten (1997) indicate the opposite. Thus, great caution is in order in assuming a mismatch between women's inner experience and their outward displays.

What about men's smiling?

Space constraints do not permit a full discussion of how the model might be amended to account for men's smiling. Some effects for men would simply be the inverse of those for women. For example, gender affirmation would inhibit rather than facilitate smiling in men. But some relations may be more complex. Consider the gender-affirmation example. While gender affirmation by men would inhibit their smiling, men would at the same time experience positive affect as a consequence of successful gender affirmation, which should (other things being equal) facilitate their smiling. That men end up smiling less than women may indicate that the inhibitory effect is stronger than the facilitative one, and/or that men's overall level of positive affect is lower than women's, meaning that (again, other things being equal) their overall level of smiling would be lower.

For men, the feedback arrows going from smiling back to affect may also be more complex than for women. Though men's lower smiling would minimize the positive affect that would have resulted from facial feedback, at the same time not smiling might increase positive affect because of the reduction in anxiety, confusion, etc., that would have come with performing a behavior that violates the norms for men.

Conformity to gender roles/schemas would also have implications for men's smiling. Characteristics such as being task oriented, competitive, and expressing strength or expertise might all inhibit smiling in men either because of the stereotypic association of smiling with weakness or simply because smiling may not be functionally relevant to the fulfillment of these goals. This factor would also have a feedback arrow going to positive affect, because having and expressing these gender-linked motives might be intrinsically rewarding. For example, to the extent that less smiling makes it more difficult to "read" a person's emotional state, and to the degree to which remaining "unreadable" is associated with feelings of strength, mastery, competence, and "status" for men during interaction, we might expect men to feel good about smiling less. However, as above, there is a contradiction because this effect on positive feedback should promote, not inhibit, smiling.

Men's responses to the social situation could also serve to inhibit their smiling, and, again, the feedback processes could be complex. If people smile less at men, we would expect men's smiling to be reciprocally reduced, which could in turn reduce their positive affect through the reduction of facial feedback and also because they are experiencing a less positive social environment. However, it is also possible that a man's positive affect would be increased to the extent that fulfilling others' expectations is satisfying. Furthermore, when men are smiled at, an important consideration could be the gender of the other person. A man might feel increased positive affect when smiled at by a woman, but he may experience decreased positive affect when smiled at by a man, due to homophobia, suspicion, fear, etc., with further implications for his own smiling.

The final factor that might influence men's smiling is social knowledge/learning. The feedback arrows to positive affect from this factor could be both positive and negative. Positive affect would be experienced by successfully acting like those whose behavior has been modeled in the past. However, if the behaviors that males practice are less interpersonally oriented and less rewarding to others, the ultimate impact on emotional state could be negative. It is also reasonable to predict that if men do in fact possess less knowledge about norms, display rules, etc., then the feedback to their own affective state from this lack of knowledge would be negative. However, if men have different norms concerning smiling, then the feedback might be positive. For example, men might reserve smiling to those situations where there is a particular gain or they have a close relationship with the other person. Men may be aware of "others' needs" but choose not to smile because doing so would violate their internalized expectations. Thus the feedback to their affective state could be positive.

What is important to understand about how this model reflects on male smiling is that, as with women, there may be a pervasive relationship between expressed behaviors and internal emotional states.

However, for men the bidirectional relations between affective states, other proximal causes of smiling, and smiling itself may be more complex than is the case for women. In the case of women, a positive cycle exists such that virtually all of the hypothesized influences yield the same outcomes – positive affect and more smiling – which in turn reinforce one another. With men, there are contradictory processes such that some processes lead to more positive affect (and more smiling), while others lead to the reverse. The fact that some elements in the model are predicted to increase men's positive affect might explain why gender differences in smiling are not even greater than they are.

Expressiveness and expression accuracy

Overview of gender differences

We consider nonverbal expressiveness and expression accuracy together but it is important to point out how they differ. *Expressiveness* refers to facial and gestural animation. *Expression accuracy* refers to whether expressive movements accurately convey affective information to an audience. Within expression accuracy, there are two subtypes: *spontaneous* and *posed*. An expressor has high *spontaneous* expression accuracy if an observer can infer what the expressor's feelings are from his/her nonverbal behavior even though the expressor is not deliberately communicating. (The most common method for measuring spontaneous expression accuracy is the slide-viewing technique [Buck, 1984], in which expressors' faces are videotaped while they watch slides with emotional content, after which naive judges try to identify the slide from looking at the expressors' faces.) An expressor has high *posed* expression accuracy if he/she deliberately tries to convey affective messages through nonverbal cues and succeeds in doing so (in terms of an audience's judgments). These two kinds of expression accuracy are positively correlated.

Expressiveness

Hall's (1984) meta-analysis of facial expressiveness located only 5 studies but the average effect was $r = .45$, a rather strong tendency for females to be more facially expressive than males (EMG studies were not included). Gestural expressiveness, based on 7 results, also showed females to be more expressive ($r = .28$). Another 4 gestural results located since then had a very similar average effect size of $r = .27$ (citations available from first author).

Expression accuracy

Combining both spontaneous and posed expression accuracy, Hall (1984) found that females' nonverbal cues were more accurately judged than males' (average effect size $r = .25$, based on 35 studies). Ten more studies located for the present review yielded an average effect size r of .18 (citations available from first author). However, channel of communication is a moderator of this difference: the difference occurred for facial expression in the 1984 review but not for vocal cues, and, consistent with this, in the studies obtained for the present review the only one using vocal cues found a substantial male expressor advantage ($r = -.50$). If that result is omitted from the more recent summary, the average effect size is $r = .25$, identical to the 1984 review. Finally, in the Hall (1984) review, the gender difference was of equivalent magnitude for posed versus spontaneous accuracy.

In addition to this overall summary, one can ask whether the gender difference in expression accuracy varies depending on what emotion is being expressed. Based on the fact that some emotions are stereotyped as "female" (happiness, sadness, fear) and others as more "male" (anger, contempt, disgust) (Brody & Hall, 1993), one might predict a corresponding pattern of accuracy differences. We offer the following provisional summary of research on this question. Hall (1984) could discern no overall pattern in the studies available at that time, and the more recent study of Tucker and Friedman (1993) found the gender difference to be equally strong (in the female direction) for happiness and anger, and very small for sadness, a pattern that does not support the stereotypes. However, other studies done since the Hall (1984) review provide more support for the prediction based on stereotype. Tucker and Riggio (1988) found the gender difference to be greater (in the female direction) for happiness than for sadness, and smallest for disgust; and several studies found that the typical female expression advantage was diminished or reversed for anger (Coats & Feldman, 1996; Rotter & Rotter, 1988; Wagner, MacDonald, & Manstead, 1986).

But the cross-national study of Biehl, Matsumoto, Ekman, Hearn, Heider, Kudoh, & Ton (1997) challenges the conclusion that gender differences in expression accuracy parallel the gender stereotypy of different emotions. Biehl et al. administered standard photographs of facial expressions to samples in the United States and 5 other countries, 3 of which were Asian. Effect sizes were not available in their article, but an analysis of the percentage of judges in each country who successfully judged the Caucasian expressors shows some very surprising patterns. If one considers just the United States sample judging Caucasian faces, the data support the hypothesis that men and women are better at expressing gender-stereotypical emotions: accuracy was higher for men expressing anger, contempt, and disgust, and accuracy was higher for women expressing fear and happiness. However, data from the other national samples show some wide discrepancies from this pattern. For Japanese judges, the data suggest that women express anger and contempt better than men do; for Sumatrans and Vietnamese the data suggest that women express disgust better than men do; and for Sumatrans and Vietnamese, the data suggest that men express fear better than women do – all results that are inconsistent with the United States data and with the prevailing stereotype. What could account for these discrepant results, considering that the expressive stimuli were the *same* for all samples? The answer may be judgment biases: if judges believe "women don't show anger," then when presented with an angry female face they may choose other alternatives besides anger, which would lower her apparent accuracy at expressing anger. A bias to "see" female-stereotypic emotions in female faces would similarly inflate the apparent accuracy with which women express those emotions. Coats and Feldman (1996) were sensitive to this problem and applied Wagner's (1993) correction for rating bias, concluding that rating bias did not explain the stereotypic pattern they obtained. Encouraging though this is, other studies remain vulnerable to rating-bias artifacts, and the data of Biehl et al. (1997) suggest that these should be considered further.

Before concluding this summary, one more finding deserves mention. Coats and Feldman (1996) found that for women, those who were more accurate expressors of happiness were judged more popular (using sociometric methods), but for men, those who were more accurate expressors of anger were judged more popular. This finding suggests that there are negative consequences for a person who has a relatively weak ability to express gender-stereotypic emotions. When we discuss decoding accuracy, we shall see this pattern repeated.

Explanations

Because of space constraints, it is not possible to discuss the full spectrum of possible explanatory factors for women's expressiveness and expression accuracy. In brief, we believe that gender-linked social traits/values (see Zuckerman, DeFrank, Spiegel, & Larrance, 1982) and women's responses to situational cues remain important. However, the proximal affective cause of the nonverbal behavior would not be positive affect, as it was in the case of smiling, but would be the *intensity of emotional experience*. Consistent with such a view, women report experiencing higher levels of emotional intensity, both positive and negative, than men do (Diener, Sandvik & Larsen, 1985; Fujita, Diener, & Sandvik, 1991; Gross & John, 1985). Emotional contagion (Hatfield et al., 1994) may also play a significant part in this gender difference, as could women's greater ability to deliberately mimic expressions (Berenbaum & Rotter, 1992), both of which could, combined with internal feedback processes, serve to intensify women's emotional experience.

Another difference from the smiling model is that the feedback arrows that go from the proximal causes of the nonverbal behavior back to emotional state (those on the left side of the figure) would probably not be operative, the reason being that the proximal causes (identified in figure 5.1) should not serve to intensify one's feelings in a general sense. Finally, social knowledge/learning may play a stronger role than it did for smiling, especially for posed expression accuracy which obviously requires knowledge of nonverbal encoding rules. Success on posed expression tasks likely also draws on motivation (trying to do well), which is not likely to be the case for accuracy of spontaneous expression.

Nonverbal judgment accuracy

Overview of gender differences

The findings for accuracy in judging the meanings of nonverbal cues (decoding accuracy) are remarkably consistent across ages, gender of expressor, tasks, and cultures. In the first meta-analysis (Hall, 1978), women scored higher on average, with an effect size r of .20 (46 studies). In a second (nonoverlapping) review, Hall (1984) found an average effect size r of .25 (18 studies). In yet a third and non-overlapping review (done for this chapter, citations available from first author), the average effect size r was .26 (18 studies). The proportion of these studies showing females to score higher than males (regardless of p-value) is extremely high (84%, 91%, and 94% in the three summaries), and the proportion showing the difference to be statistically significant is also much higher than one would expect by chance.[3]

Underscoring the consistency and universality of this gender difference, Rosenthal, Hall, DiMatteo, Rogers, and Archer (1979) reported that females scored higher than males in 80% of 133 US and non-US samples that were administered the Profile of Nonverbal Sensitivity (PONS), a test of decoding face, body, and voice cues. The average effect size (r) was .20 – very close to that found in the summaries reported above. (Only a handful of the 133 PONS studies were included in those summaries, so the results are not redundant.) Other programs of research, using different tests, have also found cross-cultural consistency in this gender difference (e.g., Biehl et al., 1997; Izard, 1971). Biehl, for example, found an overall female decoding advantage across six groups (USA, Japanese, Sumatran, Vietnamese, Polish, and Hungarian), two cultures of encoders (USA and Japanese), and six emotions, with an overall effect size of $r = .25$, which is remarkably similar to the overall effects found in earlier reviews.

Such consistency over geography and hundreds of studies is truly remarkable. Although the specific judgment tasks varied (including both posed and spontaneous expressions), virtually all of the studies involved judgment of affect. Therefore it can be concluded that there is a gender difference in accuracy of identifying affective messages from nonverbal cues.

The question of whether the gender difference varies with different emotions has not been thoroughly studied. In an unpublished meta-analysis of gender and decoding accuracy (Bauer, Kulkarni, & McGowan, 1997), the largest gender difference was for fear, with anger and joy in the next ranks. Gender differences for surprise, love, and sadness were extremely small. This pattern does not well match predictions based on which emotions are stereotypically associated with the sexes.

A final topic for summary concerns correlates of judgment accuracy. Data from children suggest that there are gender differences in the consequences of being deficient in judgment of particular emotions. Social adjustment/acceptance appears to be lower for girls when they are deficient at judging happy, sad, and fearful nonverbal cues, but lower for boys when they are deficient at judging angry nonverbal cues (Nowicki & Mitchell, 1998). Thus, there may be social consequences for children whose pattern of decoding accuracy does not fit with gender-stereotypical expectations.

Explanations

In the case of judgment accuracy, the amendments we would make to the model are similar to those we mentioned for expression accuracy, with an even more reduced role for the level or nature of currently experienced affect. However, it is important to note that almost all research on judgment accuracy is so far based not on actual interpersonal interaction, but on accuracy in judging a standard set of affective stimuli. When considering actual interaction additional factors may become operative. Patterson's (1995) analysis of the cognitive demands of on-line encoding and decoding suggests that currently experienced emotion (anxiety, for example) may siphon cognitive resources away from one's capacity to process another interactant's cues and would therefore have an impact on judgment accuracy.

The path in the model pertaining to relative status follows from theoretical predictions that lower status people are more nonverbally sensitive (Henley, 1977; LaFrance & Henley, 1994). So far, the evidence does not support this hypothesis, and indeed some research finds the opposite (Hall & Halberstadt, 1997; Hall, Halberstadt, & O'Brien, 1997). As noted above, most research is based on standardized test scores. However, even when communication accuracy is measured between people engaged in actual interaction, the data do not suggest that the lower-status person is more motivated to decode cues accurately (Snodgrass, Hecht, & Ploutz-Snyder, 1998).[4]

Success on a nonverbal judgment task involves some mix of knowledge and effort. At present very little is known about the impact of motivation on nonverbal judgment accuracy (Nowicki & Richman, 1985), and in particular it is not known how differences in knowledge versus motivation may contribute to gender differences in nonverbal judgment accuracy (Graham & Ickes, 1997).

Conclusion

Our brief summary of findings showed that women smile more than men, are more expressive than men, and show higher levels of both expression accuracy and nonverbal judgment accuracy than men. In different ways, each of these differences is likely to be related to emotion. According to the theoretical model which we described most thoroughly for smiling in women, there are a number of distinct (though interrelated) causal factors, many of which have feedback arrows back to the expressor's emotional state. Thus, even when the direct cause of females' smiling is conformity to gender roles, positive affect may result from enacting those roles (stemming from both the act and its consequences), thus contributing to positive affect and more smiling.

We also mentioned some ways in which the factors influencing men's as opposed to women's smiling may be the same or different, the net result of which is the hypothesis that men actually experience less positive affect in interaction with predictable effects on behavior.

Expressiveness, expression accuracy, and judgment accuracy have, by definition, a relationship to emotion because typically the tasks and measures are based on affective cues. The question of which specific emotions are sent or judged with the greatest or least accuracy by each sex is not settled at the present time. There is, however, evidence that deficiencies in expressing and judging gender-stereotypic emotions may have negative social consequences.

Acknowledgment

Order of authorship of the second and third authors was determined alphabetically. This chapter was supported by a grant from the National Science Foundation to the first author.

Notes

1. For a persuasive literary demonstration of this aspect of women's role, the reader is referred to the dinner-table scene in Virginia Woolf's *To the Lighthouse* (1927, pp. 134–141).
2. With every element in this model, one can point to many exceptions as well as examples. In the present context one might predict that a woman who is insecure in her gender identity, who has a gender identity that conflicts with her biological sex, or who is homosexual, might experience ambivalent affect when engaging in behaviors that are stereotypically female, such as smiling obviously is, thus weakening or even reversing the positive feedback arrow.
3. Henley (1995) maintains that there is still room for doubt about the gender difference in decoding nonverbal cues. Henley misquotes the proportions of studies showing female advantage in the Hall (1984) review, and she fails to acknowledge that the proportion achieving statistical significance is far in excess of the chance level. Furthermore, she suggests that a female decoding advantage may not exist for spontaneous (versus posed) cues. This is not correct; for example, one of the strongest effects in the most recent review is for decoding of infants' facial expressions (Babchuck, Hames, & Thompson, 1985).
4. We believe that predictions based on status with respect to any nonverbal behavior will fare poorly until role-occupants' attitudes and motives toward their role and toward relevant other people are taken into account. For example, one would predict radically different behavior from a contented versus a resentful subordinate (Hall & Halberstadt, 1997).

References

Andersen, P. A. (1998). Researching sex differences within sex similarities: The evolutionary consequences of reproductive differences. In D. J. Canary & K. Dindia (Eds.), *Sex differences and similarities in communication: Critical essays and empirical investigations of sex and gender in interaction* (pp. 83–100). Mahwah, NJ: Erlbaum.

Babchuck, W. A., Hames, R. B., & Thompson, R. A. (1985). Sex differences in the recognition of infant facial expressions of emotion: The primary caretaker hypothesis. *Ethology and Sociobiology, 6,* 89–101.

Bauer, L. M., Kulkarni, M., & McGowan, S. (1997). Gender differences in nonverbal decoding of emotion: A meta-analysis. Unpublished manuscript, University at Albany, State University of New York.

Baumeister, R. F., & Leary, M. R. (1995). The need to belong: Desire for interpersonal attachment as a fundamental human motivation. *Psychological Bulletin, 117,* 497–529.

Berenbaum, H., & Rotter, A. (1992). The relationship between spontaneous facial expressions of emotion and voluntary control of facial muscles. *Journal of Nonverbal Behavior, 16,* 179–190.

Biehl, M., Matsumoto, D., Ekman, P., Hearn, V., Heider, K., Kudoh, T., & Ton, V. (1997). Matsumoto's and Ekman's Japanese and Caucasian Facial Expressions of Emotion (JACFEE): Reliability data and cross-national differences. *Journal of Nonverbal Behavior, 21,* 3–21.

Birdwhistell, R. L. (1970). *Kinesics and context.* Philadelphia: University of Pennsylvania Press.

Brody, L. R., & Hall, J. A. (1993). Gender and emotion. In M. Lewis & J. M. Haviland (Eds.), *Handbook of emotions* (pp. 447–460). New York: Guilford.

Brody, L. R., & Hall, J. A. (in press). Gender, emotion, and expression. In M. Lewis & J. M. Haviland (Eds.), *Handbook of emotions,* 2nd edition. New York: Guilford.

Brunner, L. J. (1979). Smiles can be back channels. *Journal of Personality and Social Psychology, 37,* 728–734.

Buck, R. (1984). *The communication of emotion.* New York: Guilford.

Buck, R. (1991). Social factors in facial display and communication: A reply to Chovil and others. *Journal of Nonverbal Behavior, 15,* 155–161.

Bugental, D. E., Love, L. R., & Gianetto, R. M. (1971). Perfidious feminine faces. *Journal of Personality and Social Psychology, 17,* 314–318.

Cappella, J. N. (1981). Mutual influence in expressive behavior: Adult-adult and infant-adult dyadic interaction. *Psychological Bulletin, 89,* 101–132.

Cappella, J. N. (1985). Controlling the floor in conversation. In A. W. Siegman and S. Feldstein (Eds.), *Multichannel integrations of nonverbal behavior* (pp. 69–103). Hillsdale, NJ: Erlbaum.

Chovil, N. (1991). Social determinants of facial displays. *Journal of Nonverbal Behavior, 15,* 141–154.

Coats, E. J., & Feldman, R. S. (1996). Gender differences in nonverbal correlates of social status. *Personality and Social Psychology Bulletin, 22,* 1014–1022.

Darwin, C. (1872/1965). *The expression of the emotions in man and animals.* University of Chicago Press.

Deutsch, F. M. (1990). Status, sex, and smiling: The effect of role on smiling in men and women. *Personality and Social Psychology Bulletin, 16,* 531–540.

Diener, E., Sandvik, E., & Larsen, R. J. (1985). Age and sex effects for emotional intensity. *Developmental Psychology, 21,* 542–546.

Dimberg, U. (1990). Facial reactions to auditory stimuli: Sex differences. *Scandinavian Journal of Psychology, 31,* 228–233.

Dimberg, U., & Lundqvist, L.-O. (1990). Gender differences in facial reactions to facial expression. *Biological Psychology, 30,* 151–159.

Doherty, R. W. (1997). The Emotional Contagion Scale: A measure of individual differences. *Journal of Nonverbal Behavior, 21,* 131–154.

Eagly, A. H. (1987). *Sex differences in social behavior: A social role interpretation.* Hillsdale, NJ: Erlbaum.

Eagly, A. H. (1995). The science and politics of comparing women and men. *American Psychologist, 50,* 145–158.

Fernández-Dols, J. M., & Ruiz-Belda, M. A. (1995). Are smiles a sign of happiness? Gold medal winners at the Olympic Games. *Journal of Personality and Social Psychology, 69,* 1113–1119.

Filsinger, E. E. (1981). A measure of interpersonal orientation: The Liking People Scale. *Journal of Personality Assessment, 45,* 295–300.

Frank, M. G., Ekman, P., & Friesen, W. V. (1993). Behavioral markers and recognizability of the smile of enjoyment. *Journal of Personality and Social Psychology, 64,* 83.

Fridlund, A. J. (1991). Sociality of solitary smiling: Potentiation by an implicit audience. *Journal of Personality and Social Psychology, 60,* 229–240.

Fridlund, A. J. (1994). *Human facial expression: An evolutionary view.* New York: Academic Press.

Friedman, H. S., & Miller-Herringer, T. (1991). Nonverbal display of emotion in public and private: Self-monitoring, personality, and expressive cues. *Journal of Personality and Social Psychology, 61,* 766–775.

Fujita, F., Diener, E., & Sandvik, E. (1991). Gender differences in negative affect and well-being: The case for emotional intensity. *Journal of Personality and Social Psychology, 61,* 427–434.

Graham, T., & Ickes, W. (1997). When women's intuition isn't greater than men's. In W. Ickes (Ed.)., *Empathic accuracy* (pp. 117–143). New York: Guilford.

Gross, J. J., & John, O. P. (1995). Facets of emotional expressivity: Three self-report factors and their correlates. *Personality and Individual Differences, 19,* 555–568.

Halberstadt, A. G., Hayes, C. W., & Pike, K. M. (1988). Gender and gender role differences in smiling and communication consistency. *Sex Roles, 19,* 589–604.

Hall, J. A. (1978). Gender effects in decoding nonverbal cues. *Psychological Bulletin, 85,* 845–857.

Hall, J. A. (1984). *Nonverbal sex differences: Communication accuracy and expressive style.* Baltimore, MD: The Johns Hopkins University Press.

Hall, J. A. (1987). On explaining gender differences: The case of nonverbal communication. *Review of Personality and Social Psychology, 7,* 177–200.

Hall, J. A. (1998). How big are nonverbal sex differences? The case of smiling and sensitivity to nonverbal cues. In D. J. Canary & K. Dindia (Eds.), *Sex differences and similarities in communication: Critical essays and empirical investigations of sex and gender in interaction* (pp. 155–177). Mahwah, NJ: Erlbaum.

Hall, J. A., & Friedman, G. (1998). Status, gender, and nonverbal behavior: A study of structural interactions between employees of a company. *Personality and Social Psychology Bulletin, 25,* 1082–1091.

Hall, J. A., & Halberstadt, A. G. (1986). Smiling and gazing. In J. S. Hyde & M. C. Linn (Eds.), *The psychology of gender: Advances through meta-analysis* (pp. 136–158). Baltimore, MD: The Johns Hopkins University Press.

Hall, J. A., & Halberstadt, A. G. (1997). "Subordination" and nonverbal sensitivity: A hypothesis in search of support. In M. R. Walsh (Ed.), *Women, men, and gender: Ongoing debates* (pp. 120–133). New Haven: Yale University Press.

Hall, J. A., Halberstadt, A. G., & O'Brien, C. E. (1997). "Subordination" and nonverbal sensitivity: A study and synthesis of findings based on trait measures. *Sex Roles, 37,* 295–317.

Hatfield, E., Cacioppo, J. T., & Rapson, R. L. (1994). *Emotional contagion.* Paris: Cambridge University Press.

Hecht, M. A. (1995). The effect of power and gender on smiling. Unpublished doctoral dissertation, Boston College.

Henley, N. M. (1977). *Body politics: Power, sex, and nonverbal communication.* Englewood Cliffs, NJ: Prentice-Hall.

Henley, N. M. (1995). Body politics revisited: What do we know today? In P. J. Kalbfleisch & M. J. Cody (Eds.), *Gender, power, and communication in human relationships* (pp. 27–61). Hillsdale, NJ: Erlbaum.

Izard, C. E. (1971). *The face of emotion.* New York: Appleton-Century-Crofts.

Johnson, C. (1994). Gender, legitimate authority, and leader-subordinate conversations. *American Sociological Review, 59,* 122–135.

Johnson-George, C., & Swap, W. C. (1982). Measurement of specific interpersonal trust: Construction and validation of a scale to assess trust in a specific other. *Journal of Personality and Social Psychology, 43,* 1306–1317.

Krauss, R. M., Chen, Y., & Chawla, P. (1996). Nonverbal behavior and nonverbal communication: What do conversational hand gestures tell us? In M. P. Zanna (Ed.), *Advances in experimental social psychology* (Vol. 28, pp. 389–450). San Diego: Academic Press.

Kraut, R. E., & Johnston, R. E. (1979). Social and emotional messages of smiling: An ethological approach. *Journal of Personality and Social Psychology, 37,* 1539–1553.

Kuebli, J., Butler, S., & Fivush, R. (1995). Mother-child talk about past emotions: Relations of maternal language and child gender over time. *Cognition and Emotion, 9,* 265–283.

LaFrance, M., & Henley, N. M. (1994). On oppressing hypotheses: Or differences in nonverbal sensitivity revisited. In H. L. Radtke and H. J. Stam (Eds.), *Power/gender: Social relations in theory and practice* (pp. 287–311). London: Sage.

Leakey, R. E., & Lewin, R. (1978). *People of the lake: Mankind and its beginnings.* New York: Avon.

Lundqvist, L.-O. (1995). Facial EMG reactions to facial expressions: A case of facial emotional contagion? *Scandinavian Journal of Psychology, 36,* 130–141.

Malatesta, C. A., Culver, C., Tesman, J. R., & Shepard, B. (1989). The development of emotion expression during the first two years of life. *Monographs of the Society for Research in Child Development,* No. 219.

Matlin, M. W., & Gawron, V. J. (1979). Individual differences in Pollyannaism. *Journal of Personality Assessment, 43,* 411–412.

Merten, J. (1997). Facial-affective behavior, mutual gaze, and emotional experience in dyadic interactions. *Journal of Nonverbal Behavior, 21,* 179–201.

Nowicki, S. Jr., & Mitchell, J. (1998). Accuracy in identifying affect in child and adult faces and voices and social competence in preschool children. *Genetic, Social, and General Psychology Monographs, 129,* 39–59.

Nowicki, S. Jr., & Richman, D. (1985). The effect of standard, motivation, and strategy instructions on the facial processing accuracy of internal and external subjects. *Journal of Research in Personality, 19,* 354–364.

Parsons, T., & Bales, R. F. (1955). *Family, socialization and interaction process.* Glencoe, IL: The Free Press.

Patterson, M. L. (1995). A parallel process model of nonverbal communication. *Journal of Nonverbal Behavior, 19,* 3–29.

Reis, H. T., Senchak, M., & Solomon, B. (1985). Sex differences in the intimacy of social interaction: Further examination of potential explanations. Journal of *Personality and Social Psychology, 48,* 1204–1217.

Rosenthal, R. (1976). *Experimental effects in behavioral research* (enlarged edition). New York: Irvington.

Rosenthal, R., Hall, J. A. DiMatteo, M. R., Rogers, P. L., & Archer, D. (1979). *Sensitivity to nonverbal communication: The PONS test.* Baltimore, MD: The Johns Hopkins University Press.

Rotter, N. G., & Rotter, G. S. (1988). Sex differences in the encoding and decoding of negative facial emotions. *Journal of Nonverbal Behavior, 12*, 139–148.

Snodgrass, S. E., Hecht, M. A., & Ploutz-Snyder, R. J. (1998). Interpersonal sensitivity: Expressivity or perceptivity? *Journal of Personality and Social Psychology.*

Schwartz, G. E., Brown, S.-L., & Ahern, G. L. (1980). Facial muscle patterning and subjective experience during affective imagery: Sex differences. *Psychophysiology, 17*, 75–82.

Stevens, L. E., & Fiske, S. T. (1995). Motivation and cognition in social life: A social survival perspective. *Social Cognition, 13*, 189–214.

Strack, F., Martin, L. L., & Stepper, S. (1988). Inhibiting and facilitating conditions of the human smile: A nonobtrusive test of the facial feedback hypothesis. *Journal of Personality and Social Psychology, 54*, 768–777.

Swap, W. C., & Rubin, J. Z. (1983). Measurement of interpersonal orientation. *Journal of Personality and Social Psychology, 44*, 208–219.

Tucker, J. S., & Friedman, H. S. (1993). Sex differences in nonverbal expressiveness: Emotional expression, personality, and impressions. *Journal of Nonverbal Behavior, 17*, 103–117.

Tucker, J. S., & Riggio, R. E. (1988). The role of social skills in encoding posed and spontaneous facial expressions. *Journal of Nonverbal Behavior, 12*, 87–97.

Vrugt, A., & Kerkstra, A. (1984). Sex differences in nonverbal communication. *Semiotica, 50*, 1–41.

Wagner, H. L. (1993). On measuring performance in category judgment studies of nonverbal behavior. *Journal of Nonverbal Behavior, 17*, 3–28.

Wagner, H. L., MacDonald, C. J., & Manstead, A. S. R. (1986). Communication of individual emotions by spontaneous facial expressions. *Journal of Personality and Social Psychology, 50*, 737–743.

Warr, P. B. (1971). Polyanna's personal judgments. *European Journal of Social Psychology, 1*, 327–338.

Wood, W., Christensen, P. N., Hebl, M. R., & Rothgerber, H. (1997). Conformity to sex-typed norms, affect, and the self-concept. *Journal of Personality and Social Psychology, 73*, 523–535.

Woolf, V. (1927). *To the lighthouse.* San Diego: Harcourt Brace Jovanovich.

Zuckerman, M., DeFrank, R. S., Spiegel, N. H., & Larrance, D. T. (1982). Masculinity-femininity and encoding of nonverbal cues. *Journal of Personality and Social Psychology, 42*, 548–556.

6. Gender and smiling: A meta-analysis

MARIANNE LAFRANCE AND MARVIN A. HECHT

A smile is the chosen vehicle for all ambiguity

Herman Melville

The human smile would seem to be among the most straightforward and least ambiguous of emotional expressions, yet it turns out to be one of the most variable and most complex facial displays. This ambiguity has in part contributed to confusion surrounding how best to explain why women appear to smile more than men. A decade ago the first meta-analysis of smiling documented that females smile more than males; moreover this difference was found to be significantly larger in situations involving social tension, and to a lesser extent, when there were variations in the amount of affiliation that was present (Hall & Halberstadt, 1986). As a result, Hall and Halberstadt (1986) concluded that little support was obtained for a dominance-status explanation of the sex difference since no significant correlations were found betweeen the size of the difference and the amount of power or status in the situation. The purpose of the present chapter is to take a second look at these and other potential moderators affecting the gender and smiling relationship by reviewing what is now nearly 20 years later a substantially larger body of research.

Like Hall and Halberstadt (1986), we conducted a meta-analysis of the relationship between sex and smiling. Meta-analyses statistically integrate the mathematical findings of independent research studies and are now considered by many to be superior to qualitative reviews (Cooper & Rosenthal, 1980) and vote counting methods (Hedges & Olkin, 1980) for summarizing research results. More importantly perhaps, meta-analysis permits systematic analysis of factors that potentially moderate the magnitude and nature of the relationship between sex and smiling.

There are a number of ways that the present meta-analysis differs from the oft-cited analysis by Hall and Halberstadt (1986). First, as mentioned, there is now a much larger data base of relevant studies. For example, we have drawn on unpublished studies as well as a new infu-

118

sion of studies deriving from current research in emotion. This expanded database allows a better test of some important moderators since there are now sufficient studies to cover different levels of a variable. Secondly, the present analysis tests the effects of a number of previously unexamined moderators that are likely to impact the size of the smiling difference. Specifically, the current review investigates the developmental and cultural generality of the tendency for women to smile more than men. Finally, we hope to advance current thinking of how gender affects smiling by proposing a theoretical model, the Demand Expressivity Theory, for understanding when sex differences in smiling are likely to increase and when they are likely to decrease.

Smiling as emotion indicator or social signal

For over 100 years, natural and social scientists have probed the meaning of the human smile (Darwin, 1872/1965). Although the most consistent finding is that smiles reflect positive affect (Ekman & Friesen, 1982; Ekman, Friesen, & Ancoli, 1980; Ekman, Davidson, & Friesen, 1990), it also appears that people smile when they are embarrassed (Edelmann, Asendorpf, Contarello, & Zammuner, 1989), uncomfortable (Ochanomizu, 1991), miserable (Ekman & Friesen, 1982), and socially apprehensive (Ickes, Patterson, Rajecki, & Tanford, 1982).

It also appears that smiling sometimes operates as a social signal not specifically indicative of experienced emotion. Kraut and Johnston (1979), for example, found that people smile more while interacting with others than when alone and that bowlers who had just succeeded in getting a strike or spare smiled more when they turned to face their friends than immediately following their accomplishment. More recently, Fridlund and his colleagues (Fridlund, 1991; Fridlund, Sabini, Hedlund, Schaut, Shenker, & Knauer, 1990) showed that even while affective states remained constant – that is when people were comparably happy – smiling increased with the real or imagined presence of a known other.

Particular contexts may also prompt one to smile because smiling is socially useful. Greetings are frequently associated with smiling (Eibl-Eibesfeldt, 1989), as are persuasion attempts aimed at patients (Burgener, Jirovec, Murrell, & Barton, 1992), students (Zanolli, Saudargas, & Twardosz, 1990) and potential dates (Walsh & Hewitt, 1985). Smiles have also been shown to elicit greater leniency for transgressors (LaFrance & Hecht, 1992) and to ward off others' displeasure (Elman, Schulte, & Bukoff, 1977; Goldenthal, Johnston, & Kraut, 1981). Finally, while it is true that smiles are often genuine and spontaneous (Ekman et al, 1980), it is also true that a smile can be among the most deliberate of facial actions. Anthropologists and sociologists have documented numerous instances where people smile because their role or situation requires them to do so. For example, Wierzbicka (1994) observed that cheerfulness is mandatory in many cultures, and within the United States Hochschild (1983) noted that many job holders are required to smile as part of the work they do. In short, smiling seems to serve different social functions in different social contexts. Consequently any assessment of sex differences in smiling needs to take these into account.

Expressivity Demand Theory

Expressivity Demand Theory begins with the recognition that smiling is highly variable and exquisitely related to social context. Moreover, several dimensions of context contribute to the observed variability. First, there are smile norms that are gender-based, specifically gender expressivity norms, which specify which sex is and/or should be more expressive in general and likely to smile more in particular. Secondly, different contexts impose different requirements to be or not to be expressive. Some situational demands for expressivity apply equally to both sexes (e.g., displaying pleasure at another's good news); other situational contexts may be such that one sex is expected to respond with greater expressivity than the other.

Gender expressivity norms

Like Eagly (1987), we hold that gender roles describe the norms that apply to people's behavior based on their socially identified sex. It is our contention that the norms governing facial display, and particularly smiling, are different for females and males with females are expected to show more smiling than males.

The belief that emotional expressivity characterizes women more than men is a strong and persistent stereotype (Shields, 1987). Investigations of the gender-emotion link, however, have revealed a pattern of beliefs about gender-based differences that is more complex than this gender stereotype would suggest. Interestingly, women are not believed to *experience* emotions more than men, but they are believed to *express* them more than men (Fabes & Martin, 1991). In a review of the literature, gender-related differences in emotionality were most likely found when emotional expression was assessed by observation of facial displays or direct self report measures (LaFrance & Banaji, 1992), but are more equivocal when indirect measures are taken. Recent findings by Levenson and his colleagues provide support for the important distinction between emotion and expression. In their study of married couples, husbands and wives did not differ significantly in the degree to which they displayed the Duchenne smile – that is the smile indicative of genuine positive feeling – but they did differ with respect to non-Duchenne smiles with wives showing significantly more non-Duchenne smiles (Levenson, personal communication).

Some sex differences in expressivity may derive from actual differences in anxiety or sociability; they may also be the result of self-fulfilling prophecies (Fischer, 1993) or prescriptive guides (Fiske & Stevens, 1993). Thus women may be obligated to be more emotionally expressive than men. For example, a recent study investigated how male and female college students felt about having expressed or failed to express a positive emotion toward a friend who had achieved a personal success. Both sexes expected more favorable reactions when they imagined themselves being expressive but women expected more negative responses when they imagined themselves not expressing positive emotion (Stoppard & Gunn Gruchy, 1993).

We tested whether women expect more negative reactions if they do not smile (LaFrance, 1998). Instead of expressing positive emotion, the target person was described as displaying a smile or a neutral expression as they said, "Congratulations." This was done to control for the possibility that participants in prior work had imagined different kinds of "positive emotion" being expressed by males and females. Results strongly supported the idea that women anticipate greater costs in not smiling than men. Specifically, non-smiling females felt less comfortable and less appropriate and believed that they would be regarded less positively than men who do not smile. They also believed that the other's impression of them would change more if they do not smile while men reported that whether they smiled or not does not affect others' impression of them. In sum, there is credible evidence that gender norms exist with respect to smiling.

Situational demands for expressivity

But there are also rules for expressivity that can apply to everyone depending on the situation. Greetings and farewells, funerals and weddings, interviews and first dates, classrooms and conventions all have expressivity norms. Although some situations prescribe different levels of expressivity for each sex, nonetheless we argue that in many situations both women and men are expected to show the same relative level of smiling. In fact, some social roles rather than gender norms may be responsible for what looks like sex differences in expressivity. The caregiving role is a case in point. Some paid jobs are characterized by attending to others in emotionally responsive ways. For example, nurses and primary school teachers are expected to provide tender loving care to patients and young children respectively, and the caring required in these jobs is usually stressed more than the skills (Nieva & Gutek, 1981). Other occupations also call for high levels of expressivity. Hochschild (1983), for example, observed that flight attendants and receptionists show high degrees of emotional expressivity and do so because it is a prerequisite for the work.

One role thought to be linked with greater smiling is having less power relative to someone else. The argument has been that powerlessness should be associated with more smiling because smiling is a sign of deference or appeasement (Keating, 1985). While some studies have found that lower-power people smile more than those with higher power (Deutsch, 1990; Dovidio, Brown, Heltman, Ellyson, & Keating, 1988) not every study has found this effect (Burgoon, Buller, Hale, & deTurck, 1984; Hall & Friedman, 1998; Halberstadt & Saitta, 1987).

We recently collected data showing that the inconsistency in findings can be resolved by recognizing that high-power people have the option to smile if they feel like it, whereas low-power people are obligated to smile some amount irrespective of how positive they feel (Hecht & LaFrance, in press; see also LaFrance & Hecht, 1999). For high-power people, there was a significant positive correlation between smiling and felt positive affect, but there was no such correlation for low-power people, whose smiling was tied more to feelings of ingratiation. The study showed that when the smiling of high-power men and high-power women was compared, there were no significant differences. Nor were there differences in the amount of smiling shown by low-power men and low-power women. The only sex difference that emerged in the equal power condition was that women were found to smile significantly more than men. These results support the contention that when men and women are in the same role or engaged in the same task then they will show similar expressive behavior. It is only when the situation is ambiguous or where gender norms are salient that they will differ, with men smiling less than women.

Expressivity Demand Theory specifies how gender expressivity norms and situational expressivity demands combine to affect facial expressivity and smiling. Like Deaux and Major (1987), we believe that men and women are likely to behave differently according to the degree that gender is salient in a particular context. However, we also contend that sex differences may be even more evident when situational demands are absent or ambiguous. In unstructured contexts, gender norms, for expressivity are thought to be the default option. In other words, gender norms for greater expressivity of women relative to men come to the fore and affect facial displays when situational demands for greater or lesser expressivity are minimal. Finally, while situational demands take priority over gender norms, and hence act to reduce sex differences, they can, on occasion, dovetail with gender norms creating even a larger sex difference in expressivity.

A meta-analysis of sex and smiling

Method

Sample of studies. An extensive search of the research literature was undertaken to retrieve studies that documented the relationship between sex and smiling, even if that relationship was not the central one of the investigation. We included not only published materials, but also unpublished materials such as conference papers, student theses, dissertations, and unpublished papers in order to counter the publication bias toward positive results (Rosenthal, 1979). For example, if a reference was unpublished or a dissertation, the author was contacted for the report. If a dissertation was not available by that route, a copy was obtained from University Microfilms International. The datebase also includes several articles written in German, French, and Japanese. Thus our data set differs from that described by Hall and Halberstadt (1986) in that it includes unpublished reports as well as research that was available throughout 1994.

Several methods were used for obtaining relevant reports. First, computer searches were conducted using the keywords "smile," "smiles," and "smiling" on various databases.[1] Second, several reference lists were searched for relevant studies.[2] Third, we included all the smile studies used by Hall and Halberstadt (1986) in their meta-analysis of sex differences in smiling and gazing, and we included the studies of non-social smiling mentioned in Hall (1984). Fourth, the ancestry method in which the reference list of retrieved studies is scanned for additional reports was used (Rosenthal, 1991). These included our own personal files. Finally, we used the invisible college method (Rosenthal, 1991) whereby investigators known to have conducted research on facial expression (Buck, Ekman, Levenson) and nonverbal behavior (Feldman, Riggio) were also contacted with requests to furnish any relevant data.

The obtained sample was then evaluated for inclusion based on the following criteria: (a) the study measured smiling (e.g., frequency, duration, rated amount) or facial positivity as a dependent variable and (b) both males and females were assessed. Studies were omitted from the sample if they tested only unique populations such as clinically abnormal or institutionalized populations. Studies were also excluded from the sample if they only included children under the age of 13. Unfortunately, it was not possible to examine type of smile (Ekman & Friesen, 1982), since only a few studies reported sex differences in smiling broken down by smile type. If a study did not report a separate test of sex differences in smiling or if there was insufficient data to calculate an effect size, its authors were contacted and asked to provide either the appropriate statistics or raw data, including breakdown by experimental condition.

Variables coded from each study.   In addition to coding variables necessary to compute an overall effect size (e.g., number of female and male participants), an extensive set of variables was recorded for each report including aspects of the study itself (e.g., year of publication, sex of authors and experimenters) as well as those variables thought to be potential moderators. In this chapter, we report on three sets of moderator variables based on the theoretical reasons outlined previously. These sets of variables were: (a) participant characteristics, (b) gender expressivity norms, and (c) situational expressivity demands. For each of these, coding was performed by four coders, two of each sex. We checked reliability by calculating the average correlation between each pair of judges (reliability of the single average judge) and the aggregate reliability of raters using the Spearman–Brown formula (Rosenthal, 1991). Across all variables, the reliability of a single judge averaged .63 and the aggregate reliability of raters averaged .85.

Participant characteristics.   Age was coded as one of three age subgroups: 13–17 years, 18–23 years, and 24–64 years. These age groupings correspond to the age groupings most commonly used in the existing literature from which the data were obtained. If the article did not report age but described the population in terms of level in school (e.g., high school students, college students) the average age corresponding to the school level was assigned (e.g., age 18–23 for college students). If the article noted that the sample consisted of adults, these were coded in the 24–64 year old group.

While the substantial proportion of the studies were conducted in the United States or Canada, several reports included data collected in Europe and Asia. Consequently culture was coded as Caucasian, African-American, and Asian. Of the 303 effect sizes involving Caucasians, 18 were British, 1 was Canadian, 26 Belgium, 4 Australian, 3 Italian, and approximately 25 were German. Of the 12 Asian effect sizes, 7 were Japanese from Japan and 2 were either Chinese or Chinese/American.

Gender expressivity norms. The second set of moderator variables are subsumed under the rubric of gender expressivity norms. These included (a) camera visibility, (b) presence of others, (c) getting acquainted format, and (d) self-disclosure. The first two, namely camera visibility and presence of others, are conjectured to make subjects aware that their behavior is being scrutinized. That awareness should lead women and men to adopt behaviors that they believe are normative for their sex. The second two variables, namely instruction to get acquainted and self-disclosure, are specifically designed to tap situations in which gender is salient.

Camera visibility. The scale used for this ranged from (a) the camera being visible to (b) knowledge that the session was being taped with a non-visible camera to (c) awareness of the possibility of being recorded in some manner to (d) concealed observation, as used in studies where participants are unobtrusively recorded while presumably waiting to participate in a study.

Presence of others. Presence of others was coded in 2 ways. First, the absolute number of others with whom the subject would be interacting – the total number of people in the subject's immediate vicinity – was coded as one of 4 levels: the subject was alone or one other person was present; 2–3 others were present, or 4 or more others were present. The second way "presence of others" was coded had to do with the level of social engagement required by the subjects. This was coded as one of 4 levels: situations in which the subject was alone, or coacting with another (e.g., parallel activity with another as in watching a movie together), or one-way communication with another (e.g., delivering a speech to a camera), or two-way interaction (e.g., sharing, debating).

Getting acquainted format. The getting acquainted format consisted of 3 levels: (1) no experimental instructions to get acquainted which made up the majority of the effect sizes (2) a situation in which people might aim to establish some contact, such as being put together in a waiting room but with no explicit instructions to get to know the other; and (3) a condition where subjects were expressly told to get acquainted with the other. *Self-disclosure* consisted of 2 levels, either no explicit self-disclosure, which made up the majority of the effect sizes, or explicit experimental instructions to subjects to be forthcoming with the other about important aspects of themselves.

The third set of variables were those where there was a clear *situational demand.* Situational demands required that the subject performed a specific task to adopt a particular role. Two tasks were coded – one where subjects were required to deceive and one where they were required to compete. *Deception* was coded at 2 levels, either one where subjects were told to lie to their partner or those where lying was not the issue. Similarly *competition* was coded at 2 levels, where subjects competed with their partner or where competition was not relevant.

Finally, social power was coded as one way of being required to perform a particular role. *Power* was defined as one of 3 levels, where the subject had lower, equal, or higher power than their partner. Having power meant that the participant had the capacity to reward another – such as being able to hire, promote, choose, or praise – or was in the position to punish another by imposing penalties or withholding some benefit, or had expertise wanted or required by another.

Computation and analysis of effect sizes. The effect size index used in the present study is Cohen's d, defined as the difference between the means for females and males divided by the pooled within-sex standard deviation. Positive values for d signify greater smiling by females than by males.[3] Studies which reported a non-significant sex difference were assigned an effect size of zero. This is considered a conservative estimate (Rosenthal, 1991). Unlike previous meta-analyses on smiling, ds were also calculated separately for each reported experimental condition. Because the resulting effect sizes often had quite small ns, we applied the correction for small sample size (Hedges, 1981). If a study used different metrics were used for coding smiling (such as frequency and intensity), the different measures were averaged to get a single measure using the procedure outlined by Rosenthal and Rubin (1986).

After the mean weighted effect size was tested for significance (as indicated by a 95% confidence interval not including zero), the homogeneity of the effect sizes was tested by Q_w, which has an approximate chi-square distribution with k-1 degrees of freedom, where k is the number of effect sizes. A significant Q_w means that the set of effect sizes tested is heterogeneous. Heterogeneity indicates that the variability of the effect sizes is not due to sampling error alone (Hedges, 1994).

If the summary analysis of the effect sizes indicated heterogeneity, we conducted tests for the moderator variables. These contrasts were achieved by dividing the effect sizes into categories and then comparing their mean effect sizes.[4]

Results

Characteristics of sample. A total of 59,076 participants in 147 reports is approximately 7 times the 20 reports cited in the Hall and Halberstadt (1986) meta-analysis. Since many reports included several experimental conditions, the total was 347 effect sizes. For the whole sample, analysis yielded a mean weighted effect size of $d = .40$, with a 95% confidence interval of .38 to .41. This positive effect size indicates that females smiled significantly more than men. We also calculated the mean weighted effect size eliminating the 33 effect sizes that were assigned a zero value, and this yielded a very similar value of $d = .41$, with a 95% confidence interval of .40 to .43.

Although the summary analyses showed that females displayed greater smiling, homogeneity analyses indicated that the set of effect sizes was heterogeneous, $Q_w (346) = 1391.52$, $p < .0001$; hence, examination of potential moderator variables was warranted.

Impact of moderator variables: Participant characteristics. Table 6.1 displays the results for participant characteristics. Because some of these categories contained more than 2 classes, contrasts between the mean weighted effect sizes were computed to allow interpretation of any significant between classes effects (e.g., Hedges & Olkin, 1980).

Age group. As expected, the analysis of age group produced a significant between classes effect, indicating that age moderated the observed relationship between sex and smiling ($Q_b = 65.22$, $p < .00001$). As can be seen in table 6.1, the effect sizes were positive favoring females for all age groups. However, the effect size of the oldest age group (24–64 year olds) was significantly smaller than both the younger groups ($z^2 = 29.70$, $p < .0001$). Individual contrasts specifically indicated that this older group differed significantly from the youngest group (13–17 year olds) ($z^2 = 19.25$, $p < .0001$) and the older group also differed significantly from the middle group of 18–23 year olds ($z^2 = 53.23$, $p < .0001$). The youngest group had a marginally significantly larger effect size than the young adult group ($z^2 = 2.65$, $p < .10$). In short, the difference between female and male smiling is greatest when subjects are teens or young adults and drops off significantly with subjects who are older. Hall (1984) reported similar findings with regard to age (see below).

Related to age is the variable which classified participants as either college students or non-college students (the latter more often older than the former). As expected, this distinction produced a significant between classes effect ($Q_b = 41.01$, $p < .0001$). College students were significantly more likely to show sex differences in smiling (females smiling more) than were non-college students.

Culture. Culture was also a significant moderator of the overall effect size ($Q_b = 27.11$, $p < .0001$). Among Caucasian subjects, a significant effect size of $d = .41$ indicated that females showed greater smiling

Table 6.1. Tests of categorical moderators of effect sizes for participant characteristics

Variable and class	Between classes effect (Q_b)	Mean weighted effect size		95% CI for d		Homogeneity within each class (Q_w)
		k	(d)	Lower	Upper	
Age	65.22					
13–17		34	.43	.38	.48	79.94
18–23		156	.48	.45	.51	575.81
24–64		68	.28	.24	.33	141.22
Unspecified		69	.37	.34	.39	529.34
College	41.01					
No		173	.36	.34	.38	737.24
Yes		174	.47	.44	.50	613.27
Culture	27.31					
Caucasian		303	.41	.39	.43	1310.38
African–American		8	.23	.12	.35	6.11
Asian		12	.34	.22	.45	9.34
Other		22	.19	.08	.29	38.88

than males. Smaller but still significant effect sizes were observed for Asian ($d = .34$) and African-American ($d = .23$) populations. Contrasts revealed that the effect size for Caucasians was significantly greater than both the Asian and African American populations combined, ($z^2 = 8.78$, $p < .003$). However, this difference was mostly due to the African-American samples, since comparing only Caucasian and African-Americans revealed a significant difference ($z^2 = 8.71$, $p < .003$), but comparing Caucasians and Asians revealed no significant difference. There was also no significant difference between the effect sizes for Asians and African-Americans.

Impact of moderator variables: Gender expressivity norms. We next examined whether gender norms account for some of the observed variability. Specifically, we predicted that there are norms that prescribe greater smiling for females and/or lesser smiling for males. Although we did not feel it was possible to reliably and validly code whether gender norms were differentially operating across the various samples (that determination requiring too much conjecture on the part of coders), we believe that several variables serve as proxies for the presence of gender norms. Specifically, we contend that if the differences in smiling between women and men are greater (a) when a surveillance device like a camera is visible than when it is hidden, (b) when they are in the company of others or engaged with others than when they are alone, (c) when they are given explicit instructions to get acquainted as opposed to when there are no directions, and (d) when they are asked to self-disclose than when they are not, then there is reason to suspect that participants are responding to perceived gender-related expectations for how much smiling they should display. Table 6.2 provides the results of these analyses.

Camera visibility. As expected, camera visibility produced a significant between-classes effect, indicating that as the camera became more apparent, the effect size favoring greater smiling by females became larger ($Q_b = 100.41$, $p < .0001$). As can be seen from table 6.2, effect sizes for all levels of camera surveillance were positive (favoring females), but the largest effect size was for the camera-visible situation ($d = .44$), and the smallest when there was no awareness of a camera ($d = .23$). The contrast comparing a camera being visible with all situations in which it was variously hidden yielded a significant effect ($z^2 = 25.71$, $p < .0001$), as was the contrast comparing camera visible and non-awareness conditions ($z^2 = 98.76$, $p < .0001$). The contrast for linear trend across all 5 groups was also significant ($z^2 = 20.52$, $p < .0001$).

Table 6.2. *Tests of categorical moderators of effect sizes for gender expressivity norms*

Variable and class	Between classes effect (Q_b)	Mean weighted effect size		95% CI for d		Homogeneity within each class (Q_w)
		k	(d)	Lower	Upper	
Camera Visibility	100.31					
Visible		226	.44	.42	.46	958.84
Known taping		42	.38	.29	.48	108.25
Possible taping		34	.34	.24	.44	100.64
Concealed taping		13	.38	.24	.52	14.46
Non-awareness		32	.23	.19	.27	109.01
Others Present	23.93					
0		15	.19	.05	.33	56.58
1		283	.43	.41	.45	982.29
2-3		6	.34	.28	.41	15.98
4		1	.54	.03	1.06	0
Unspecified		42	.36	.33	.39	312.74
Engagement with others	90.47					
None		10	.01	-.16	.17	25.99
Coaction		8	.34	.21	.48	15.92
One-way		21	.72	.64	.80	70.52
Two-way		308	.39	.37	.40	1188.92
Getting Acquainted	5.62					
No instructions		309	.40	.38	.41	1298.13
Unstructured		17	.33	.20	.45	35.04
Explicit instructions		21	.54	.41	.67	52.72
Self Disclosure	5.62					
No		306	.39	.37	.40	1209.00
Yes		41	.66	.58	.75	145.05

Presence of others. The prediction was that the difference in smiling would be greater when the subject interacted with others than when the subject was alone and results are clearly supportive. There were significant differences in effect size as a function of how many other participants were present (Qb $= 23.93$, $p = .0003$). The smallest effect size ($d = .19$) occurred when subjects were alone and the largest occurred when the subject was interacting with 4 or more others ($d = .54$). The prediction was that the difference in smiling would be greater when the participant interacted with any other people than when the participant was alone and results indicate support for that notion ($z^2 = 4.73$ $p = .03$). There was also a highly significant difference between being alone and being with one other person ($z^2 = 10.83$, $p = .001$). In summary, the difference in smiling favoring females significantly increased when subjects were face-to-face with one or more other people.

Presence of engaged others. We also predicted that the effect size for smiling would be greater when subjects were more rather than less engaged with others. Data supported this speculation ($Q_b = 90.47$, $p < .00001$). When subjects were alone and unengaged, the effect size was almost zero ($d = .01$). Thus there is no reliable relationship between sex and smiling when subjects are not engaged with anyone else. In contrast, when subjects are required to interact, the effect sizes differ significantly from zero (coaction $d = .34$, one-way interaction $d = .72$, two-way interaction $d = .39$). With all of these "involved" situations are compared with the no-involvement condition, the contrast is significant ($Q_b = 27.78$, $p < .0003$).

Getting acquainted. Our assumption was that when subjects were explicitly told to get to know another person whom they did not initially know, this would activate the gender-related expectation that females should be more social than males. This would translate into a number of communicative behaviors including smiling, which is strongly linked with sociability. And that is what happened. The effect size in smiling favoring females was significantly greater ($d = .54$) when subjects were given explicit instructions to get acquainted than when subjects were in an unstructured getting acquainted situation ($d = .33$). Although the overall variance between groups was marginal ($Q_b = 5.62$, $p = .06$), the contrasts were significant. The effect size in smiling favoring females was significantly greater when subjects were given explicit instructions to get acquainted ($d = .54$) than when subjects were in an unstructured getting acquainted situation ($d = .33$), $z^2 = 5.27$, $p = .02$. Explicit getting acquainted instructions ($d = .54$) also led to a significantly greater effect size than no getting acquainted instructions at all ($d = .40$), $z^2 = 4.33$, $p = .04$).

Self-disclosure. Our logic with respect to self-disclosure was similar to that for getting acquainted. Women tend to be more self-disclosing than men, especially to other women (Dindia & Allen, 1992). Hence if participants are in a situation in which they are asked to share intimate details of themselves, this should trigger gender-related norms that call for men to do less self-disclosing (and expressing) than women. While the effect size itself cannot tell us whether greater self-disclosure leads to greater smiling, it should show itself in a larger effect size than where there is no explicit requirement to self-disclose. And that is what we found. The effect size favoring greater smiling for women occurred more when self-disclosure was expected than when it was not ($Q_b = 37.37, p < .001$)

Impact of moderator variables: Situational demands. We next explored the second tenet of Expressivity Demand Theory, that situational demands account for some of the variability observed in smiling rates between females and that of males. With respect to situations not specifically associated with gender, but which have expressivity demands of their own, our theorizing led us to predict that the differences in smiling between women and men would be less. In other words, many social situations impose their own specific expectations about what is appropriate expressive behavior. Thus, the differences between women and men in these situations should be less because both are responding to the same demands. That would include smiling. As noted earlier, a number of studies have in fact shown reduced sex differences when people are given identical goals or expectations (Chase, 1988; Moskowitz, Suh, & Desaulniers, 1994). Analysis of three of these situations are described below and are shown in table 6.3.

Deception. Regarding the requirement to lie to someone else, our thinking was that all subjects would be more focused on how to accomplish this goal than on how to be gender-appropriate, that is, that the deception requirement would override gender norms. Consequently, we predicted that the effect size would be less in a deception context than in one not so marked. The evidence bore us out. The effect size favoring greater smiling by females was significantly smaller when subjects were required to lie than where deception was not explicitly required ($d = .19$ and $d = .40$, respectively, $Q_b = 7.43, p < .006$)

Competition. The logic regarding competition was the same as that outlined above for deception situations. Again we predicted that the effect size would be less in a competitive context than in one where competition was not the operative dynamic and again, the evidence is

Table 6.3. *Tests of categorical moderators of effect sizes for situation demand*

Variable and class	Between classes effect (Q_b)	Mean weighted effect size		95% CI for d		Homogeneity within each class (Q_w)
		k	(d)	Lower	Upper	
Deception	7.43					
No		334	.40	.38	.42	1350.68
Yes		13	.19	.04	.34	33.40
Competition	9.39					
No		344	.40	.38	.42	1379.74
Yes		3	.06	-.16	.28	2.38
Power	14.47					
More Power		43	.29	.22	.37	98.75
Equal Power		241	.41	.39	.43	956.03
Less Power		63	.38	.34	.41	325.28
Status	14.47					
High Status		55	.25	.17	.33	108.70
Equal Status		148	.39	.36	.42	392.79
Low Status		38	.45	.37	.54	142.20
Not Applicable		106	.41	.39	.43	733.34
Vulnerability	12.57					
Less Vulnerability		7	.32	.08	.56	6.32
Equal Vulnerability		277	.40	.38	.42	1054.18
More Vulnerability		56	.47	.39	.55	222.33

supportive. The effect size favoring greater smiling by females was significantly smaller when subjects were required to compete than where competition was not the issue ($Q_b = 9.39$, $p = .002$). In fact, the effect size was minimal and non significant when the situation involved competition ($d = .06$). In contrast, the effect size for non-competitive contexts was $d = .40$, which is the overall effect size.

Social power. As noted previously, the question as to whether power differences between women and men could be used to explain the greater smiling of women relative to men has been much debated. Previously, the approach has been to determine whether variations in the size of the sex difference is correlated with the presence/absence of a power differential between the subject and the person they are interacting with. Following this strategy, Hall and Halberstadt (1986) concluded that power did not significantly moderate the size of the effect for sex differences in smiling.

Our analysis lead to a different conclusion and interpretation. First, social power significantly moderated the sex difference effect size for smiling. More importantly, we tested the idea that power is similar to other situational demands, in that smiling differences between women and men would decrease when they both have more or both have less power than their partner than when they are on equal footing with each other. The reason is that in powerful positions expressive behaviors like smiling are a response to the demands of that role; in a power-equal condition, where power is not manifestly evident, gender norms are likely more salient.

The results endorse this thinking ($Q_b = 14.47$, $p = .0007$). Although the effect sizes for all levels of power are positive, favoring greater smiling by women, the lowest effect size of $d = .29$ occurred for those who had more power than their partner and the highest effect size was for those with equal power ($d = .41$). The two effect sizes differed significantly from each other ($z^2 = 9.61$, $p = .002$). Low-power participants had an intermediate effect size of $d = .38$, which was marginally lower than equal-power participants ($z^2 = 3.09$, $p = .08$), but significantly higher than the high-power participants ($z^2 = 4.40$, $p = .04$).

The predicted pattern was replicated when the "power" moderator variable was coded as status ($Q_b = 14.47$, $p = .002$) and vulnerability ($Q_b = 12.57$, $p = .002$). Consistent with our theory, those with higher status than their partner had the lowest effect size ($d = .25$), and the contrast between higher status and equal status was significant ($z^2 = 9.74$, $p = .002$). Similarly, those with less vulnerability than their partner also had the lowest effect size ($d = .25$), and the contrast between those with less vulnerability and equal vulnerablity was again significant ($z^2 = 9.15$, $p =$

.003). Where status and vulnerability differed from power was that the highest effect sizes were found for the lowest status ($d = .45$) and most vulnerable persons ($d = .47$). But similar to the results for power, these slight variations turned out not to be significantly different from the equal status condition ($z^2 = 1.77$, $p = .17$, and $z^2 = 3.04$, $p = .08$, respectively).

Conclusions

Do women and men differ in how much they smile? This meta-analysis indicates that they do and also that it depends. If one focuses on the magnitude of the overall effect size, the evidence clearly indicates that women and men smile in different amounts with women smiling more than men. According to Cohen (1977), effect sizes of .20, .50, and .80 indicate small, medium, and large effects respectively. By these criteria, the overall effect sizes of $d = .40$ (including zeros) and $d = .41$ (excluding zeros) verge on a medium size effect and hence are noteworthy. These overall effect sizes are quite similar to those reported by Hall and Halberstadt (1986). They reported average effect sizes of $d = .39$ (including zeros) and $d = .63$ (excluding zeros).

Participant characteristics

It is also true that this analysis of nearly 150 reports indicates that the magnitude of this sex effect for smiling differs depending on participant characteristics, gender expressivity norms, and situational demands. In other words, focusing on overall differences between males and females without considering these moderating variables ignores important effects associated with one's position in the larger social structure and in one's immediate circumstances. Specifically, variations in effect size depending on participant characteristics indicate that smiling must be considered within a larger cultural context and suggests that men and women may measure themselves against culture-specific as well as age-specific standards of what is appropriate (e.g., Josephs, Markus, & Tafarodi, 1992).

Our meta-analysis indicates that age is a significant moderator of the relationship between sex and smiling. This pattern is consistent with early theorizing that gender cues should become increasingly visible as a child moves toward early adulthood and thereafter decline (Birdwhistell, 1970; Saarni & Weber, 1999). We found that the effect size favoring greater smiling by women was at its greatest in the 18–23 year old group and least for the 24–64 year old group. This differentiation shows that sex differences in smiling do not increase with age in a linear fashion. The relationship is better described as a curvilinear one, moderate for the teen group, increasing for the young adult group and dropping off again for the middle-age adult group. Although research evidence for the linkages between sex and age groupings and expressivity is somewhat sketchy, there are indications that sex differences in many nonverbal displays are maximal at precisely that time in early adulthood when there is pressure for greater sex differentiation (Brody, 1985).

The findings showing that the effect size was significantly greater among college students than for those not in college are compatible with the notion that greater smiling by women may be particularly critical at a time when women and men are negotiating heterosexual relationships. Whether smiling is by itself a gender marker or whether its presence or absence documents expected differences between the sexes in terms of such gender-related attributes as communality and agency is not known. Nonetheless, these data point to the importance of considering developmental stages and their associated social contexts in attempting to understand why women and men smile at different rates.

The findings for culture particularly illustrate the importance of considering cultural differences. Across studies, the differences in smiling favoring women were consistent yet differed in size depending on cultural or racial group. Caucasian subjects showed the largest effect size which was significantly greater than African-American subjects who showed the smallest sex differences in smiling (see also Fischer & Manstead, this volume).

Gender expressivity norms

A basic premise of Expressivity Demand Theory is that gender norms exist for nonverbal expressivity in general and smiling in particular. Research shows that women and men not only smile in different amounts but they are expected to do so too (LaFrance, 1998).

Specifically, we predicted that the effect size favoring greater smiling by women should be greater when subjects are aware that their behavior is being videotaped; when there are others present than when one is alone; when there are explicit instructions to get acquainted; and when participants are specifically charged with the task of self-disclosing. What ties these moderators together is the idea that subjects adjust their behavior to be in compliance with expressivity norms when they know they are being observed. Hence, if women smile more than men when they are engaged than when they are alone, there is the strong suggestion that women are expected to smile more than men. Part of women's role that they are expected to perform is to be cheerful and affiliative (Eagly, 1987; Hall, 1984).

The second major tenet of Expressivity Demand Theory is that men and women smile at more comparable levels when they are in the same role or required to engage in the same activity. This is because either the situation has its own norms for appropriate expressivity or because the situation takes priority over gender norms. Several situations were evaluated in order to see whether there was support for such thinking. When subjects are given the task of deceiving or competing with another person, our theory predicted that the sex difference effect size would be smaller than when no such demand is imposed. Results were strongly supportive. When subjects were required to lie, the smiling effect size was significantly smaller than when no lying is required. In other words, when women and men are both in the business of deception, the differences between them with respect to smiling become much smaller. The same pattern was observed when subjects were in a competitive situation.

With respect to power, we predicted that when both men and women have more power or less power than their partner, there should be a smaller effect size than when they have equal power. Again there was clear support for this idea. The sex difference effect size was significantly smaller when subjects had higher power than when they were on equal footing. When the low power condition was contrasted with the equal power condition, the difference was marginally significant. In sum, many situations impose their own demands with the result that the sex difference in smiling gets dampened because both sexes are responding to where they are and what they are required to do.

The aim in the present meta-analysis has been to move the discussion of sex differences in smiling beyond a debate over single explanations like power or affiliation for why women smile more than men. Instead, we have proposed that different characteristics of the participants and different gender-role norms can account for variations in the size of the gender difference. There are also times when the situation has priority, such that both men and women are required to deal with it by turning up or turning down their smile volume. The data are clearly in support of the idea that both men and women change their smiling behavior in response to situational variations like having power or being required to perform a task such as lying.

Throughout, sex differences in smiling have tended to be framed in terms of women smiling more than men. However, sex differences in smiling could be described with equal accuracy by saying that men smile less than women. Some of the emphasis on women smiling more rather than men smiling less may stem from linguistic, cultural, and/or cognitive proclivities which favor "more than" constructions over "less than" forms of comparison. Hall (1987) herself notes that describing group differences in terms of the group with the higher mean is an established convention.

No matter what the basis is for phrasing the result as "women smile more," the formulation should not be taken to mean that sex differences are caused by women's behavior and that changes in the size of the difference are a result of changes in the smiling of women alone. Among other consequences of such phrasing has been that there has been a neglect of factors that affect men's smiling. Even here when we have described gender norms for expressivity it has tended to be cast in terms of the pressure on women to smile. There is empirical evidence for that (LaFrance, 1998), but there are ample anecdotal requirements that men should actively limit their facial expressiveness ("keep a stiff upper lip" and "poker face"). Consequently, gender norms for expressivity could be the result of the prescripton for women to smile more or for men to smile less or as some combination of these two.

Similarly, when the size of the smiling sex differences decreases, meta-analysis by itself cannot tell us whether it comes about by women smiling less or men smiling more or by a combination. Meta-analysis cannot capture information about how much men and women are actually smiling at different levels of a factor which has been shown to moderate the relationship (Hall & Rosenthal, 1991; Noyes, Hecht, & LaFrance, 1996).

Herman Melville suggested that the smile is the chosen vehicle for all ambiguity. What our meta-analysis has suggested instead, is that the smile is not so much ambiguous as it is a very social and multi-purpose expression. The sexes sometimes smile at different rates and sometimes there appears to be a convergence which is moderated by important developmental, cultural, and social factors.

Acknowledgments

Preparation of this chapter was supported by grants from the National Science Foundation and the Social Science and Humanities Council of Canada. Portions of this research were presented at the October 1994 meeting of the Society for Experimental Social Psychology, Lake Tahoe, Nevada. We thank Alison Noyes, Larry DeSalvatore, and Leathe Allard for their assistance with coding. Address all correspondence concerning this chapter to Marianne LaFrance, Department of Psychology, Yale University, PO Box 208205, New Haven, CT 06520–8205, USA; email: marianne.lafrance@yale.edu or to Marvin A. Hecht, Department of Psychology, Louisiana College, Pineville, LA 71359, USA; email: hecht@andria.lacollege.edu.

Notes

1. The following databases were used: *ABI/Inform* (1971–1992), Harvard's Tozzer Library *Anthropological Index* (1975–1992), *Boston Library Consortium UnCover* (1988–1992), *Dissertations Abstracts International* (1861–1992), ERIC (1966–1992), *EPIC* books in psychology (1980–1992), *Medline* (1975–1992),

OCLC (1972–1992), *Social Science Citation Index* (1973–1992), *Wilson Periodicals Index* (1983–1992), *Psychological Abstracts* (1974–1992), and *Sociofile* (1974–1992). Several other abstract resources, not available on computer, were manually searched using the same smile keywords as above and also "nonverbal communication" and "facial expression." These included *Communication Abstracts* (1978–1992), *Language and Behavior Abstracts* (1967–1992), *London Bibliography of the Social Sciences* (1983–1987), and *Pascal International Bibliography: Psychology, Psychopathology, Psychiatry* (1981–1992).

2. These included several bibliographies of research on nonverbal behavior (e.g., Davis, 1972; Davis & Skupien, 1982; Obhudho, 1979; Thorne & Henley, 1975); several texts on nonverbal communication (e.g., Argyle, 1988; Knapp & Hall, 1997; LaFrance & Mayo, 1978), several texts on gender (e.g., Eagly, 1987; Eakins & Eakins, 1978; Hall, 1984; Matlin, 1993; Perry, Turner, & Sterk, 1992); previous reviews (meta-analytic or otherwise) of nonverbal signs of deception (Zuckerman & Driver, 1985), impressions created by nonverbal behavior (DePaulo, 1992; Tickle-Degnen, Hecht, Harrigan, Ambady & Rosenthal, 1998), and expectancy effects (Hall & Briton, 1993; Harris & Rosenthal, 1985).

3. A complete listing of the effect sizes for all studies is available from the second author. Most of the effect sizes were estimated directly from a *t* or *F* or chi square, and less frequently they were converted from a *r* using the *r* to *d* formula (Rosenthal, 1991).

4. This comparison is done by computing Q_b, which has an approximate chi-square distribution with p-1 degrees of freedom where p is the number of categories within each moderator variables (Hedges, 1994; Hedges & Olkin, 1980). We then computed contrasts to determine which categories differed significantly from one another.

References

Argyle, M. (1988). *Bodily Communication* (2nd Edn.). London: Methuen.

Birdwhistell, R. L. (1970). *Kinesics and context*. Philadelphia, PA: University of Pennsylvania Press.

Brody, L. R. (1985). Gender differences in emotional development: A review of theories and research. *Journal of Personality, 53*, 102–149.

Burgener, S. C., Jirovec, M., Murrell, L., & Barton, D. (1992). Caregiver and environmental variables related to difficult behaviors in institutionalized, demented elderly persons. *Journal of Gerontology, 47*, 242–249.

Burgoon, J. K., Buller, D. B., Hale, J. L., & deTurck, M. A. (1984). Relational messages associated with nonverbal behaviors. *Human Communication Research, 10*, 351–378.

Chase, S. E. (1988). Making sense of "The women who becomes man". In A. D. Todd & S. Fisher (Eds.)., *Gender and discourse: The power of talk* (pp. 275–295). Norwood, NJ: Ablex.

Cohen, J. (1977). *Statistical power analysis for the behavioral sciences* (Rev. Edn.). New York: Academic Press.

Cooper, H.M., & Rosenthal, R. (1980). Statistical versus traditional procedures for summarizing research findings. *Psychological Bulletin, 87*, 442–449.

Darwin, C. (1872/1965). *The expression of the emotions in man and animals*. New York: Appleton.

Davis, M. (1972). *Understanding body movement, an annotated biography*. New York: Arno Press.

Davis, M., & Skupien, J. (Eds.) (1982). *Body movement and nonverbal communication: An annotated bibliography, 1971–1980*. Bloomington, IN: Indiana University Press.

Deaux, K., & Major, B. (1987). Putting gender into context: An interactive model of gender-related behavior. *Psychological Review, 94,* 369–389.

DePaulo, B. M. (1992). Nonverbal behavior and self presentation. *Psychological Bulletin, 111,* 203–243.

Deutsch, F. M. (1990). Status, sex, and smiling: The effect of role on smiling in men and women. *Personality and Social Psychology Bulletin, 16,* 531–540.

Dindia, K., & Allen, M. (1992). Sex differences in self-disclosure: A meta-analysis. *Psychological Bulletin, 112,* 106–124

Dovidio, J. F., Brown, C. E., Heltman, K., Ellyson, S. L., & Keating, C. F. (1988). Power displays between women and men in discussions of gender-linked tasks: A multichannel study. *Journal of Personality and Social Psychology, 55,* 580–587.

Eagly, A. H. (1987). *Sex differences in social behavior: A social role interpretation.* Hillsdale, NJ: Lawrence Erlbaum Associates.

Eakins, B. W., & Eakins, R. G. (1978). *Sex differences in human communication.* Boston, MA: Houghton Mifflin.

Edelmann, R. J., Asendorpf, J., Contarello, A., & Zammuner, V. (1989). Self-reported expression of embarrassment in five European cultures. *Journal of Cross Cultural Psychology, 20,* 357–371.

Eibl-Eibesfeldt, I. (1989). *Human ethology.* New York: Aldine de Gruyter.

Ekman, P., Davidson, R. J., & Friesen, W. (1990). The Duchenne smile: Emotional expression and brain physiology II. *Journal of Personality and Social Psychology, 58,* 342–353.

Ekman, P., & Friesen, W. V. (1982). Felt, false, and miserable smiles. *Journal of Nonverbal Behavior, 6,* 238–252.

Ekman, P., Friesen, W. V., & Ancoli, S. (1980). Facial signs of emotional experience. *Journal of Personality and Social Psychology, 39,* 1125–1134.

Elman, D., Schulte, D. C., & Bukoff, A. (1977). Effects of facial expression and stare duration on walking speed: Two field experiments. *Environmental Psychology and Nonverbal Behavior, 2,* 93–99.

Fabes, R. A., & Martin, C. L. (1991). Gender and age stereotypes of emotionality. *Personality and Social Psychology Bulletin, 17,* 532–540.

Fischer, A. H. (1993). Sex differences in emotionality: Fact or stereotype? *Feminism and Psychology, 3,* 303–318.

Fiske, S. T. & Stevens, L. E. (1993). What's so special about sex? Gender stereotyping and discrimination. In S. Oskamp & M. Costanzo (Eds.), *Gender issues in contemporary society* (pp. 173–196). Newbury Park, CA: Sage.

Fridlund, A. J. (1991). Sociality of solitary smiling: Potentiation by an implicit audience. *Journal of Personality and Social Psychology, 60,* 229–240.

Fridlund, A. J., Sabini, J. P., Hedlund, L. E., Schaut, J. A., Shenker, J. I., & Knauer, M. J. (1990). Audience effects on solitary faces during imagery: Displaying to the people in your head. *Journal of Nonverbal Behavior, 142,* 113–137.

Goldenthal, P., Johnston, R. E., & Kraut, R. E. (1981). Smiling, appeasement, and the silent bared-teeth display. *Ethology and Sociobiology, 2,* 127–133.

Halberstadt, A. G., & Saitta, M. B. (1987). Gender, nonverbal behavior, and perceived dominance: A test of theory. *Journal of Personality and Social Psychology, 53,* 257–272.

Hall, J. A. (1984). *Nonverbal sex differences: Communication accuracy and expressive style*. Baltimore, MD: Johns Hopkins University Press.

Hall, J. A. (1987). On explaining gender differences: The case of nonverbal communication. In P. Shaver & C. Hendrick (Eds.), *Sex and Gender* (pp. 177–200). Newbury Park, CA: Sage.

Hall, J. A., & Briton, N. J. (1993). Gender, nonverbal behavior, and expectations. In P. D. Blanck (Ed.)., *Interpersonal expectations: Theory, research, and applications* (pp. 276–295). Cambridge University Press.

Hall, J. A., & Friedman, G. (1998). Status, gender, and nonverbal behavior: A study of structural interactions between employees of a company. *Personality and Social Psychology Bulletin, 25*, 1082–1091.

Hall, J. A. & Halberstadt, A.G. (1986). Smiling and gazing. In J. S. Hyde and M. C. Linn (Eds.), *The psychology of gender: Advances through meta-analysis* (pp. 136–185). Baltimore: Johns Hopkins University Press.

Hall, J. A. & Rosenthal, R. (1991). Testing for moderator variables in meta-analysis: Issues and methods. *Communication Monographs, 58*, 437–448.

Harris, M. J., & Rosenthal, R. (1985). Mediation of interpersonal expectancy effects: 31 meta-analyses. *Psychological Bulletin, 97*, 363–386.

Hecht, M. A. & LaFrance, M. (in press). License or obligation to smile: Power, sex and smiling. *Personality and Social Psychology Bulletin.*

Hedges, L. V. (1981). Distibution theory for Glass's estimator of effect size and related estimators. *Journal of Educational Statistics, 6*, 107–128.

Hedges, L. V. (1994). Fixed effects models. In H. Cooper & L. V. Hedges (Eds.), *The handbook of research synthesis* (pp. 285–299). New York: Russell Sage Foundation.

Hedges, L.V., & Olkin, I. (1980). Vote-counting methods in research synthesis. *Psychological Bulletin, 88*, 359–369.

Hochschild, A. R. (1983). *The managed heart: Commercialization of human feeling*. Berkeley, CA: University of California Press.

Ickes, W., Patterson, M. L., Rajecki, D. W., & Tanford, S. (1982). Behavioral and cognitive consequences of reciprocal versus compensatory responses to preinteraction expectancies. *Social Cognition, 1*, 160–190.

Josephs, R. A., Markus, H. R., & Tafarodi, R. W. (1992). Gender and self-esteem. *Journal of Personality and Social Psychology, 63*, 391–402.

Keating, C. F. (1985). Human dominance signals: The primate in us. In S. L. Ellyson & J. F. Dovidio (Eds.), *Power, dominance and nonverbal behavior* (pp. 89–108). New York: Springer.

Knapp, M. L., & Hall, J. A. (1997). *Nonverbal Communication in Human Interaction* (4th Edn.). New York: Harcourt Brace Jovanovich.

Kraut, R. E., & Johnston, R. E. (1979). Social and emotional messages of smiling: An ethological approach. *Journal of Personality and Social Psychology, 37*, 1539–1553.

LaFrance, M. (1998). Pressure to be pleasant: Effects of sex and power on reactions to not smiling. *International Review of Social Psychology, 2*, 95–108.

LaFrance, M., & Banaji, M. (1992). Towards a reconsideration of the gender emotion relationship. In M. S. Clark (Ed.), *Emotions and Social Behavior* (Review of Personality and Social Psychology, Vol. 14, pp 178–201). Beverly Hills, CA: Sage.

LaFrance, M., & Hecht, M. A. (1999). Obliged to smile: The effect of power and gender on facial expression. In P. Philippot, R. S. Feldman, & E. J. Coats (Eds.), *The social context of nonverbal behavior*. Cambridge University Press.

LaFrance, M., & Mayo, C. (1978). *Moving bodies: Nonverbal communication in social relationships*. Monterey, CA: Brooks/Cole.

Matlin, M. M. (1993). (2nd Edn.). *The psychology of women*. New York: Harcourt Brace.

Moskowitz, D. S., Suh, E. J., & Desaulniers, J. (1994). Situational influences on gender differences in agency and communion. *Journal of Personality and Social Psychology, 8*, 249–270.

Nieva, V. F., & Gutek, B. A. (1981). *Women and work: A psychological perspective*. New York: Praeger.

Noyes, A., Hecht, M. A., & LaFrance, M. (August 1995) *Do women really smile more or do men smile less?* Paper presented at the annual convention of the American Psychological Association, New York.

Obudho, C. E. (1979). *Human nonverbal behavior: An annotated bibliography*. Westport, CT: Greenwood Press.

Ochanomizu, U. (1991). Representation forming in Kusyo behavior. *Japanese Journal of Developmental Psychology, 2*, 25–31.

Perry, L. A. M., Turner, L. H., & Sterk, H. M. (1992). (Eds), *Constructing and reconstructing gender: The links among communication, gender, and language*. Albany, NY: State University of New York Press.

Rosenthal, R. (1979). The "file-drawer problem" and tolerance for null results. *Psychological Bulletin, 85*, 638–641.

Rosenthal, R. (1991). *Meta-analytic procedures for social research* (Rev. Edn.). Newbury Park, CA: Sage.

Rosenthal, R., & Rubin, D. B. (1986). Meta-analytic procedures for combining studies with multiple effect sizes. *Psychological Bulletin, 99*, 400–406.

Saarni, C., & Weber, H. (1999). Emotional displays and dissemblance in childhood: Implications for self-presentation. In R. Feldman, P. Philippot, & E. Coats (Eds.), *The social context of nonverbal behavior* (pp. 71–106). New York: Cambridge University Press.

Shields, S.A. (1987). Women, men and the dilemma of emotion. In P. Shaver & C. Hendrick (Eds.), *Sex and Gender* (Review of Personality and Social Psychology, Vol. 7, pp. 229–251). Beverly Hills: Sage.

Stoppard, J. M., & Gunn Gruchy, C. D. (1993). Gender, context and expression of positive emotion. *Personality and Social Psychology Bulletin, 19*, 143–150.

Thorne, B., & Henley, N. M. (1975). *She said/he said: an annotated bibliography of sex difference in language, speech, and nonverbal communication*. Pittsburgh, PA: Know, Inc.

Tickle-Degnen, L., Hecht, M. A., Harrigan, J. A., Ambady, N., & Rosenthal, R. (1998). *The effect of nonverbal behavior on favorability of impressions formed: Eight meta-analsyses*. Manuscript in preparation.

Walsh, D. G., & Hewitt, J. (1985). Giving men the come-on: Effect of eye contact and smiling in a bar environment. *Perceptual and Motor Skills, 61*, 873–874.

Wierzbicka, A. (1994). Emotion, language and cultural scripts. In S. Kitayama, & H. R. Markus (Eds.), *Emotion and culture: Empirical studies of mutual influence* (pp. 133–197). Washington, DC: American Psychological Association.

Zanolli, K., Saudargas, R., & Twardosz, S. (1990). Two-year olds' responses to affectionate and caregiving teacher behavior. *Child Study Journal, 20*, 35–54.

Zuckerman, M., & Driver, R. E. (1985). Telling lies: Verbal and nonverbal correlates of deception. In A. W. Siegman & S. Feldstien (Eds.), *Multichannel integration of nonverbal behavior* (pp. 129–147). Hillsdale, NJ: Lawrence Erlbaum.

7. Sex differences in crying: Empirical findings and possible explanations

AD VINGERHOETS AND JAN SCHEIRS

Crying or weeping[1] can best be described as a typically human form of emotional expression. However, despite the vast literature on emotions and emotional disorders, this phenomenon surprisingly appears to have been neglected in behavioral science literature, as was already recognized by Borgquist (1906). Since that time no significant increase in the interest of researchers for this topic has been noted. In recent handbooks on emotions (e.g., Lewis & Haviland, 1993; Magai & McFadden, 1996; Oatley & Jenkins, 1996) hardly any attention is paid to adult crying.

The functions of crying

There is no doubt that crying is by nature a response to an emotional event, or to memories of or reflections on emotional events. The scarce literature on crying reveals the following two functions of this emotional expression: tension relief or catharsis (see, however, Cornelius, 1997) and communication, that is, making clear to others that one feels helpless and in need of comfort and support (e.g., Cornelius, 1997; Kottler, 1996). In addition, there is some evidence that crying can be used to manipulate others (Buss, 1992; Frijda, 1997; Kottler, 1996).

In current stress theory, the term "coping" refers to the behaviors and cognitions of an individual who is exposed to stressful situations, with the aim of eliminating stressors, reducing their intensity, or dampening emotional distress brought about by the confrontation with stressful events (Lazarus, 1991). It thus seems reasonable to assume that crying fulfills some of these coping functions. A global distinction can be made between problem-focused coping and emotion-focused coping (Lazarus & Folkman, 1984; Steptoe, 1991). Problem-focused coping refers to efforts to remove the stressors or to reduce their intensity. Emotion-focused coping, in contrast, implies efforts to diminish the intensity of emotions and to regulate one's emotions adequately. Seeking social support deserves some specific attention, because it refers to attempts to mobilize informational, emotional, and/or instrumental support from one's social network. Social support thus may imply both problem-focused coping and emotion-focused coping. Crying may also fulfil both functions. Crying is supposed to relieve tension and to elicit emotional support (comfort), but as pointed out above, crying sometimes can also be used purposefully to manipulate people, turning it into a true problem-focused strategy. We contend that crying should be considered as an ultimate response, which occurs in particular when one does not have any behavioral responses available to deal with the situation. The accompanying emotional state thus can best be described as helplessness (cf. Bindra, 1972; Frijda, 1986; Vingerhoets, Van Geleuken, Van Tilburg, & Van Heck, 1997). Further, we want to emphasize that this state may also apply to positive situations, for example, when people are overwhelmed by positive feelings. Such feelings may prevent them to display appropriate behavior, resulting in the flowing of tears.

Methodological issues in the study of adult crying

Before we continue, it seems useful to discuss some measurement issues in crying research. There are different approaches to examine the question of why and how often people cry, and what the effects may be for the individuals themselves and for their environment. Dependent on the specific nature of the measures and the design of the study, different aspects of crying can be examined. First, one can focus on actual *crying frequency*. How often do men and women cry in a certain time period? This can be examined by asking people to estimate how often they have cried within a given time period (e.g., last week, last 4 weeks, last year) (e.g., Williams & Morris, 1996), or, alternatively, by requesting participants to keep a diary for a certain period, which probably yields more reliable information than retrospective estimates (e.g., Frey, Hoffman-Ahern, Johnson, Lykken, & Tuason, 1983). Still another approach is to consider the time since the last actual crying episode as an index for the person's crying frequency (cf., Wallbott & Scherer, 1986).

In a third type of studies, participants are requested to rate how likely it is that one will cry when being exposed to a specific situation or when experiencing a certain emotion (e.g., De Fruyt, 1997). When applying such an approach, we prefer to speak of measuring *crying proneness* rather than crying frequency. Unfortunately, some authors failed to make this distinction and examined crying proneness while using the term frequency (e.g., De Fruyt, 1997; Williams, 1982; see also table 7.1 for an overview of different studies). The difference between both concepts may become most evident if one realizes that people may prefer to avoid situations that are likely to make them cry. In other words, people might report rather paradoxically that it is unlikely that they would cry in a situation that generally has a high potential of eliciting tears (Gross, 1998; Gross & Munoz, 1995). Thus, crying frequency may tell us more about one's preference to avoid crying, rather than one's tendency to cry.

Finally, there are also examples of observational studies in crying research (e.g., Eibl-Eibesfeldt, 1997), and of experiments in which crying behavior of both sexes in response to a laboratory stimulus like a sad movie has been examined (see Cornelius, 1997). In all types of studies except in observational studies, data have been most frequently collected by means of self-reports. The method of self-report, however, is not without problems. People's limited capability of remembering mood, as well as specific response biases, might distort their reports in a manner and to a degree that we have little knowledge of to date (Stone, 1995).

Gender differences in crying: Empirical evidence

We traced 14 studies in the literature in which the relationship between sex and any aspect of adult crying was investigated. We further decided to add the preliminary data obtained by Vingerhoets and Becht (1996) (see table 7.1 for a summary of these studies). Table 7.1 shows that crying has mostly been investigated by asking questions about the estimated proneness, frequency, intensity and duration of a past crying episode. In addition, questions have been asked about the reasons for crying and the effects of crying on mood. As was argued above, sex differences in actual crying behavior might well be determined by two factors: differences in crying proneness and differences in the actual situations that men and women are confronted with in their daily lives (or that they successfully seek or avoid).

A quick look at the listed studies reveals that the methodology, i.e. the questions that were asked and their exact wording, as well as the length of the time period that the subjects had to describe, substantially differs among the reported studies. In addition, the composition of the study samples shows considerable variation in age, background, and the relationship between male and female participants. These different methods and subject samples may partly account for some of the seemingly contradictory results in the table, for instance on crying duration.

Despite this variety, however, we can safely conclude that women report a greater propensity to cry, a greater actual crying frequency and

Table 7.1. *Summary of gender differences in crying*

Article	N (men and women)	Method/period covered	Frequency	Intensity	Duration	Proneness[1]	Reasons for actual crying[2]	Effects on mood
Young, 1937	48 M 8 W	Questionnaire/past 24 hours	W>M	*	*	*	No data on gender differences	*
Bindra, 1972	25 M 25 W	Questionnaire/description of recent episode	*	W>M	W>M	*	W> due to anguish; M> due to elation and dejection	*
Williams, 1982	70 M 70 W	Questionnaire/last year	*	W>M	*	W>M No sex differences in antecedents[3]	*	*
Frey et al., 1983	45 M 286 W	Record keeping for 30 days	W>M	W>M	No sex difference	*	Data only presented for women	More improvement for M than W
Lombardo et al., 1983	285 M 307 W	Questionnaire/no specific period	W>M	W>M	*	W>M No sex difference in antecedents	*	W stronger feelings than M. No sex difference in importance
Ross & Mirowsky, 1984	680 husbands 680 wives	Questionnaire/last week	W>M	*	*	*	*	*

Study	Subjects	Method						
Hastrup et al., 1986	77 husbands (young) 145 wives (young) 20 M (old) 44 W (old)	Questionnaire/ last year	W>M, not significant in oldest subjects	*	*	*	No exact data reported.	*
Kraemer & Hastrup, 1986	23 M 33 W	Questionnaire and record keeping for 9 weeks	W>M	*	*	*	No sex differences found	*
Choti et al., 1987	58 M 56 W	Questionnaire after watching films	W>M	*	*	*	*	*
Delp & Sackeim, 1987	37 M 43 W	Observation: measuring wetting of filter paper	*	M and W different reactions to mood manipulation	*	*	*	*
Labott & Martin, 1987	161 M 219 W	Questionnaire/ last year	W>M[4]					
Williams & Morris, 1996	224 M 224 W 2 countries	Questionnaire/ one year in general	W>M	W>M	W>M	W>M Differences smallest for "death of a close person"; and for positive emotions		*
De Fruyt, 1997	25 M 79 W	Questionnaire/ no specific period	*	*	*	W>M in general[3] No data on antecedents	No data reported	No sex differences for neg. and pos. emotions after crying

Table 7.1. (cont.)

Article	N (men and women)	Method/period covered	Frequency	Intensity	Duration	Proneness[1]	Reasons for actual crying[2]	Effects on mood
Wagner et al., 1997	83 M 169 W (health professionals)	Questionnaire/ no specific period	W>M	*	*	*	*	*
Vingerhoets & Becht, 1996[5]	1687 M 2280 W (30 countries)	Questionnaire/ last four weeks	W>M	W>M	W>M	W>M. Sex differences smallest for positive emotions	W more due to conflict; M more due to loss and positive events	Improvement of mood for both sexes; effect larger in women

Note:

*. Aspect of crying not investigated

[1]. The label "proneness" refers to the extent to which different situations or emotions may elicit crying. Subjects were asked to indicate how likely it was that they would cry in certain situations.

[2]. Subjects were asked to describe the precipitating factors of the crying episode that had occurred on a recent occasion and that was still vivid in their memories.

[3]. Proneness to cry was erroneously called "weeping frequency" in this study.

[4]. The number of different situations in which subjects had sometimes cried was considered as a measure of crying frequency in this study.

[5]. Preliminary data of this large cross-cultural study were first presented at "The international conference on the (non)expression of emotions in health and disease," which was held at Tilburg University (The Netherlands, August 1996). The data have not yet been published.

more intense crying than do men. Whether women also cry for longer periods needs further exploration. To give an indication of how large the sex difference in crying frequency really is, we would like to refer to Frey et al. (1983). To date only they have collected data of men (45) and women (286), who kept records of both irritant and emotional crying during a 30 day period. Leaving out those who gave evidence of any psychiatric illness, their results showed a mean crying frequency of 5.3 ± 0.3 episodes per month for normal women and of 1.4 ± 0.4 episodes per month for normal men (the modes were 3 and 0 respectively).

Some investigators (e.g., Bindra, 1972; Vingerhoets & Becht, 1996, see table 7.1) provided evidence on the reasons why men and women cry. It appeared that men cry relatively more often in positively appraised situations and in loss situations, whereas women cry more frequently in conflict situations. In addition, Buss (1992) showed that women tend to use crying more frequently as a way to manipulate others than do men.

Explaining gender differences in crying

The assumption of a close association between crying and coping potential is crucial for the present purpose, because there is a large body of evidence on sex differences in coping that may be helpful to gain a better understanding of sex differences in crying. Although there are notable exceptions, the general picture that emerges is that women are more inclined to emotion-focused coping and seeking emotional support in comparison with men, who instead favor problem-focused coping strategies (Ptacek, Smith, & Dodge, 1994; Vingerhoets & Van Heck, 1990). Women also feel helpless and powerless more often, not in the least when angry (Crawford, Kippax, Onyx, Gault, & Benton, 1992). Crying thus seems to fulfil the coping functions that women generally apply and attach much value to. Of further interest is the methodology used to establish whether men and women indeed differ in the type of coping strategies they use. According to Lazarus' (1991) stress model, the nature of coping at least partly depends on the nature of the stressor and the way the stressor is appraised. Therefore, it is important to know more about differences in the kind of stressors men and women are confronted with, as well as about the way they perceive stressors.

Ptacek, Smith, and Zanas (1992) mention two hypotheses that have guided research on sex differences in coping: the *socialization* hypothesis and the *structural* hypothesis. The socialization hypothesis states that boys and girls are socialized to deal with stressful events in different ways. Because of gender role expectations, boys learn to deal with stressors in an instrumental way, whereas girls are encouraged to express their emotions and to seek social support. The structural hypothesis, in contrast, holds that sex differences in coping can be attributed to differences in the type of stressful situations that men and women typically encounter. Although at first glance it might be reasonable to apply both the socialization and the structural hypotheses to crying (e.g., Blier & Blier-Wilson, 1989; Brody, 1985), we have serious doubts concerning the implied distinction between the two hypotheses, because it fails to recognize that men and women also may "learn" to seek and to avoid certain situations, as may be evidenced, among other things, by differences in career choice. Since we further believe that there are good reasons to evaluate the possible *biological basis* of sex differences in crying, we will limit the discussion of possible explanations of these differences to the socialization hypothesis and biological aspects. It is interesting to note that biological factors are also considered to be potentially relevant to explain sex differences in depression (Halbreich & Lumley, 1993; Harris, Surtees, & Bancroft, 1991; Nolen-Hoeksema & Girgus, 1994). In our view, the intrinsic links between depressive mood and psychological states related to crying such as sadness, helplessness, and despair, justify the attention for factors relevant for the development of depression.

Sex differences in crying might also be explained from an evolutionary point of view. It could be speculated that the main tasks of our male ancestors were hunting and the defense of their tribe. Showing weakness under such circumstances may have been dangerous, not only for themselves, but also for the women, who may have felt unprotected and insecure.

Preliminary model of adult crying

In an attempt to obtain more insight into the precise nature of the sex differences in crying, we base ourselves on a preliminary model of adult crying (see figure 7.1) that was derived from emotion and stress models.

The model distinguishes between (1) objective situations; (2) (re-)appraisal, resulting in a subjective internal representation of the situations, such as loss, personal inadequacy, conflict, etc.; (3) an emotional response. Together with (4) moderating variables (both personal and situational factors), these exposure and appraisal variables determine whether or not a crying response will occur. By analogy with the previously described structural hypothesis, we assume that differences in crying behavior between men and women may – at least partly – result from differences in each of these components of the model. To make this clear, we will briefly review the literature with respect to sex differences for each of these components.

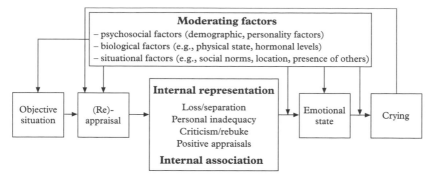

Figure 7.1 Preliminary model of adult crying
Based on Vingerhoets et al. (1997). *The (non)expression of emotions in health and disease* (p. 334). Tilburg University Press.

Gender differences in exposure to objective situations

Several studies have focused on the issue of whether men and women differ in the quality or quantity of stressful conditions they encounter. These studies, however, have yielded inconsistent results, which may partly be explained by the specific nature of the stressors under investigation. For example, there is evidence that women (and girls) face more negative events like sexual abuse which may have dramatic long-term effects. They may also meet other parental and peer expectations than men and boys (Cutler & Nolen-Hoeksema, 1991; Nolen-Hoeksema, 1994). In addition, it has been shown that women – due to their higher empathic capabilities and their greater emotional involvement in the lives of their intimates (Eisenberg & Lennon, 1983; Kessler & McLeod, 1984; Turner & Avison, 1989) – are more sensitive to events occurring to others. Women further report more stressors related to health and the family, whereas men experience more job-related stressors and miscellaneous problems (Porter & Stone, 1995). Recent not-yet-published data from our own group revealed that women more than men reported to have been exposed to situations and feelings that were identified as very likely to induce crying.

There is thus at least some evidence that women experience different stressors than do men. Crucial, however, is whether this also holds for events that elicit crying. It seems reasonable to assume that events like the death of intimates are experienced by men and women with a similar frequency. However, one might argue that women's stronger empathic skills and their more intimate relationships with other women, make women also more liable to cry for events occurring to their intimates or even to people more distant from them. In addition, there is some evidence suggesting that women may be more prone – and even enjoy – to watch sad television programs and films and read books with high emotional contents (cf. Tellegen, unpublished data; Van der Bolt & Tellegen, 1995–1996). Frey (1985) indicated that the media are an important trigger of shedding tears. Table 7.1 (see "Reasons for actual crying") reveals that only few studies to date reported data on this topic. Men and women may thus differ both in the type of situations that they are passively exposed to, as well as in the type of situations that they deliberately seek or avoid. Additional research is needed to establish this difference more definitely.

Gender differences in appraisal

Gillespie and Eisler (1992) have identified stressors related to gender role, which are perceived as more stressful by women than by men. These include fear of unemotional relationships, fear of being unattractive, fear of victimization, fear of behaving assertively, and fear of not being nurturant. In addition, Eisler and Skidmore (1987) devised an inventory of masculine gender role stressors. They found that men perceived physical inadequacy, emotional expressiveness, subordination to women, intellectual inferiority, and performance failure as more threatening than women.

   Fischer, Manstead, and Scheepers (in preparation) used vignettes in order to study sex differences in appraisal and crying. They found that powerlessness and a negative self-image were more important for female participants than for men. Applying multiple regression analysis with crying as the dependent variable and appraised powerlessness and social norms as predictors revealed that for women powerlessness was the single main predictor, whereas for men powerlessness and social norms were significant predictors.

   There is further evidence that women generally appraise stressful life events as having greater impact on their lives and that women need more time to recover compared to men (Jorgensen & Johnson, 1990). Similar results were obtained in a study on the appraisal of the conflict environment in Northern Ireland by 8 to 11 years old boys and girls (Muldoon & Trew, 1995). On the other hand, there are also indications that in the case of severe events such as the loss of one's spouse, no sex differences in appraisal emerge (e.g., Gass, 1988).

Gender differences in emotional response

Differences in appraisal may not only affect the emotional response to the event, but also the psychophysiological reaction. For example, Lash, Eisler, and Southard (1995) presented some evidence that cardiovascular responses to the cold pressor test depend on the appraised gender relevance of the stressor. The manipulation of gender relevance was achieved by varying the instructions, suggesting a relationship between the ability to keep one's hands in the ice-water and maternal and social bonding in the "female" version, whereas in the "male" version an association with testosterone was suggested, which is important in physical coping and good performance. The results partly supported the predictions that men showed higher reactivity when having received the "male" version of the instruction, whereas female participants responded more strongly in the "female" condition. Needless to say that, also in this case, the possible different appraisal of specific crying-inducing events is most crucial. Unfortunately, we do not know of any studies addressing this issue directly.

A final and important question refers to the quality and/or intensity of emotional responses, in particular when identical stressors have been appraised similarly by both sexes. Women have been found to be more prone than men to react to stressful events with helplessness and depression (Nolen-Hoeksema & Girgus, 1994), just as there is empirical support for women preferring emotion-focused coping strategies (e.g., Ptacek, Smith, & Dodge, 1994; Vingerhoets & Van Heck, 1990). However, there is little empirical evidence that men and women differ in coping when stressor and appraisal do not differ. An exception is the study by Ptacek et al. (1994), who examined the appraisal and (preparatory) coping reactions in relation to a laboratory lecturing task. These investigators demonstrated that women reported seeking social support and using emotion-focused coping to a greater extent than men in a similar situation, which had also been appraised identically by both sexes. The authors interpreted these results as consistent with the notion that men and women are socialized to cope with stressors in different ways. It is not clear, however, to what extent the results of this single study with a specific laboratory stressor, which has doubtful ecological validity, can be generalized and extrapolated to real life stressors.

Moderating factors

In the model presented in figure 7.1, both person and environmental influences are included as moderating factors. Examples of person factors are psychological and biological trait and state variables, including sex, personality, physical states (fatigue, sleeplessness, phase of the menstrual cycle, pregnancy) and psychological (depressed mood) states. Environmental factors that may act as moderators are parenting style, the sociocultural context, the specific setting, and the presence of others. It is important to note that the different (personal and environmental) factors that may act as moderators may affect different components of the model and, in addition, may exert additive as well as interactive effects.

Personality may be important because it may at least partially determine what kind of situations one seeks or avoids, it may affect appraisal and coping processes, as well as be closely associated with the tendency to express emotions. One thus may wonder whether sex differences in crying are maintained after having controlled for differences in relevant personality attributes like empathy, depression, neuroticism, emotional expressiveness, and disclosure proneness. Vingerhoets, Van den Berg, Kortekaas, Van Heck, and Croon (1993) observed that men with high self-esteem cry more frequently or at least are more willing to admit in questionnaires that they shed tears, as compared to male individuals low in self-esteem. Unfortunately, to date we do not have any insight into how much of the variance in sex differences in crying may be attributed to differences in personality between the sexes.

As far as environmental factors are concerned, Ross and Mirowsky (1984) found evidence suggesting that the behavioral expression of emotions, in particular crying, is socially conditioned. They emphasized the importance of the relation between adherence to traditional role patterns and crying behavior in men. Men in more traditional roles cried less frequently than those who defined their gender role more flexibly. The willingness to cry when feeling sad was high in women, intermediate in non-traditional men, and low in traditional men. There is further evidence suggesting that women feel more confident in expressing emotions including crying (cf. Fischer, 1993). Since educational level, socioeconomic status and role patterns are closely related, one may expect that higher educated males generally cry more often. Interesting in this respect are the comments by Kottler (1996) stating that a reverse development can be seen in women in higher functions, who reportedly are less prone to cry than women in general.

Another important environmental factor may be that more women than men spend their time at home, where there are less stringent forces, such as the presence of strangers, that inhibit crying. There is evidence that people cry most often at home (e.g., Vingerhoets et al., 1997) and it has been speculated that crying in the work situation is generally not tolerated, particularly not for women (Cornelius, 1986; Kottler, 1996; Plas & Hoover-Dempsey, 1988). Kottler (1996) suggested that it is the professional context and not one's sex that determines whether or not an individual cries. He argued that therapists and nurses frequently cry, whereas doctors rarely cry. There is some empirical support for this suggestion (e.g., Wagner et al., 1997). It should be kept in mind, however, that sex itself may be a confounding factor in this case, since most nurses are female and the majority of the responding doctors were males.

Finally, it appears that the sex of an occasional accompanying subject may also be a relevant environmental factor. Choti et al. (1987) observed that both men and women cry more easily when in male company. This finding suggests that in a heterosexual relationship, crying is more likely and acceptable for the wife than for her male partner.

In conclusion, we do not pretend that we have exhaustively discussed all possible moderating factors that may help to explain sex differences in crying. The major problem is the simple lack of data that prevents any more definitive statements.

Biological factors in crying

Genetic basis of crying behavior

To date, little is known about the role of genetics in crying proneness and actual crying behavior. Frey (1985) concluded in an exploratory study with monozygotic and dizygotic twins that there was no genetic basis underlying crying. However, Lensvelt and Vingerhoets (unpublished data) distinguished in a similar study with 35 monozygotic and 30 dizygotic female twins, between crying frequency and crying proneness which yielded discrepant findings. Actual crying frequency appeared to be environmentally determined to a large extent, whereas crying tendency appeared to be more genetically based.

Interestingly, Flint, Corley, DeFried, Fulker, Gray, Miller, and Collins (1995) have provided evidence in support of a genetic basis for emotionality in mice, which is often used as a model for anxiety and neuroticism in humans. Boomsma and Slagboom (1997) argue that Flint et al.'s results suggest that an important part of the variance in human emotionality may be explained by genetic factors.

Thus, it seems reasonable to assume that some aspects of crying tendency have a genetic basis. The question of whether this can also explain sex differences in crying remains to be examined, however. In this respect it would be of interest to know whether male and female newborns already differ in their crying behavior, because this may increase our understanding of the development and backgrounds of adult crying.

Sex differences in newborns

It can be assumed that cultural influences are not yet at work and that sex differences in personality do not yet exist in newborns and very young children. Therefore, it seems justified to attribute inter-individual and sex differences in crying behavior at this age to genetic or biological factors. However, when significant sex differences are found in very young children, this should not be taken as evidence that environmental factors can be excluded. There is always the possibility of a third, contaminating variable affecting the "true" relationship between sex and crying. For example, there is some evidence that circumcision affects several behaviors including crying of new-born males (Feldman, Brody, & Miller, 1980; Philips, King, & Dubois, 1978) and that mothers might interact differently with babies, depending on their sex (Philips et al., 1978).

Most important is the finding that sex differences do not exist in newborns or in children up to two years old. There is even some support for the reversed pattern, namely that boys of this age cry more frequently than girls. Examples of studies failing to show sex differences in crying among babies are those by Feldman, Brody, and Miller (1980) and St. James-Roberts and Halil (1991). In contrast, studies by Moss (1967), Philips et al. (1978), and Kohnstamm (1989) suggest that boys cry more often than girls. However, due to the fact that small sample studies generally have low statistical power, the failure to find a difference in a particular study does not necessarily imply that this difference does not exist on the population level.

Taken together, the evidence leads us to conclude that there are no or only very small sex differences in the amount of crying that is displayed by young infants (St. James-Roberts, 1993). Moreover, the expression of emotions in general does not differ for boys and girls who are a few months old (Cossette et al., 1996).

Unfortunately, the study of emotional expressions including crying has largely been confined to very young children and adults. We are not aware of any published studies that have addressed crying behavior in school children or adolescents. According to Löfgren (1966), the sex difference observed in babies, namely boys crying more than girls, reverses at a certain age between nursery school and college time. Frey (1985) refers to an unpublished study by Hastrup showing that sex differences in the frequency of crying emerge at about age thirteen. To get a clearer picture of the development of sex differences in crying, additional data on child and adolescent crying are strongly needed. A further issue is whether young children's crying is qualitatively and functionally equivalent to the crying of older subjects: newborns and young infants cry a lot and for varying reasons. These reasons might only partly coincide with the reasons for crying in older children and adults (Lester, 1985). Often, it is impossible to observe or reasonably infer the cause of a young child's crying. Moreover, crying frequency data obtained from only two age categories will not suffice. In order to draw any valid conclusions, there is a need of life span data.

Based on the above arguments, it may be concluded that the sex difference in crying frequency that can be observed in adults is not present at birth. The difference seems to unfold from the child's schoolyears onwards. It is appealing to take this as evidence of the role of social factors in the development of crying. Such an argument would fit the common belief that when boys grow up they learn to withhold their tears, even when they are sad, because of the negative evaluation that has traditionally been associated with men who cry, at least in Western society (Lombardo et al., 1983). However, as we will demonstrate next, the possibility that biological factors also play an important role may not be excluded.

Hormonal factors as possible determinants of crying behavior

Frey (1985) has put forth the hypothesis that the hormone prolactin, released by the pituitary, lowers the threshold for crying. This is an interesting speculation because men and women differ in plasma prolactin levels during fertile years. Frey points to three observations which have led him to formulate his hypothesis. First, sex differences in crying frequency become manifest during puberty (see above), when prolactin levels in girls are rising. Second, an illustrative case of a woman suffering from excessive crying spells showed a significant decrease in her crying after prolactin levels had been reduced pharmacologically. Third, marine ducks show an increase in the secretory activity of the salt glands, which are similar in location and innervation to the human lacrimal gland, after prolactin had been administered. We can further add the arguments that prolactin increases during pregnancy and especially just after labour, when the mother breast feeds her baby. It is tempting to speculate about a relationship with well-known post-partum phenomena like the maternity blues (cf. Beck, 1991). This is a transitory phenomenon of mood changes starting in the first days after delivery through approximately the first 10 post-partum days. Not only depression, anxiety, irritability, and lability of mood, but especially tearfulness are most characteristic symptoms. Finally, Theorell (1992) has argued that prolactin is the hormone that mirrors passivity and inability to cope, the psychological state particularly characteristic of crying.

On the basis of Frey's theory, we might expect that women are more prone to cry during pregnancy. In order to test this hypothesis, we[2] examined the responses of a sample of 396 primiparous pregnant women and 275 age-matched "normal" controls on two crying-related items ("Lump in throat" and "Prone to cry") from the Dutch version of the Hopkins Symptom Checklist (HSCL; Derogatis, Lipman, Rickets,

Uhlenhuth, & Covi, 1974; Dutch version by Luteijn, Hamel, Bouman, & Kok, 1984). It appeared that the pregnant women indeed reported a higher crying propensity. The pregnant women had completed the questionnaires three times during their pregnancy (weeks 12–13, 24–25, and 35–36), but there were no significant changes during the course of pregnancy. Lutgens (1998) provided preliminary evidence suggesting that crying proneness in pregnant women shows a U-shape over trimesters, with the second trimester as the most emotionally stable phase of pregnancy. Since prolactin levels show an almost linear increase from the first weeks of pregnancy until delivery, this pattern clearly does not parallel crying proneness data. A further observation by Lutgens disfavoring the prolactin hypothesis was that there was a strong effect of parity on post-partum tears. First-time mothers reported much more crying during the first month post-partum than multiparous women. Although we are aware of the fact that these data are far from conclusive due to the retrospective character of the studies, the unclear relation between crying proneness and actual crying and to the neglect of the role of other important psychosocial factors (cf. Paarlberg, Vingerhoets, Passchier, Heinen, Dekker, & Van Geijn, 1996), the data nevertheless fail to support the prolactin hypothesis. On the other hand, one should realize that the relationship between biological processes and behavior or mood seldom can be represented by simple linear functions. More evidence for the role of prolactin may be obtained by comparing crying behavior in breastfeeding and bottlefeeding mothers and, most directly, by comparing prolactin levels of frequent criers and individuals who have a high crying threshold.

Another speculation is that crying proneness varies as a function of phase of the menstrual cycle. A link with the premenstrual syndrome seems obvious, although one should be aware that it may make a big difference whether women actually cry or whether they feel like crying or feel they are more inclined to do so. To date, there are only few data available. Moos (1968) asked 839 women to rate 47 symptoms associated with their most recent and their worst menstrual cycles. Crying was one of the negative symptoms, like depression, tension, irritability, and mood swings. Crying was 5 times increased during the premenstrual period and 4 times during menstruation, as compared to the intermenstrual period. From additional comments made by the subjects, it appeared that some women indeed showed very low thresholds for shedding tears, as evidenced by the reports of crying without any obvious reasons, and without feeling depressed or sad.

Horsten, Becht and Vingerhoets (1997) collected retrospective data on the relation between crying and the menstrual cycle. Their data first of all revealed impressive cross-cultural differences in percentages of women (mainly arts or social sciences students) reporting an association between crying proneness and menses. Of the total sample of 2,018 participants, 44.9% answered positively to the question "Is your crying tendency dependent on the phase of your menstrual cycle?" However, the percentages ranged from as low as 15.4% and 18.9% in countries like China and Ghana, to as high as 69.2% and 68.9% in Australia and Turkey. In other words, in some countries stronger associations were reported than in other countries. To what extent these cross-cultural differences are indicative of a minimal role of biological factors is not clear. The finding of a remarkable correspondence in the data from contraceptive pill-users in comparison with no-pill-users further challenges the role of biological factors. The data revealed a significant increase in self-reported crying proneness from the seventh day before menstruation until the second day of the periods. In addition, some slight elevations were found on the first day after menstruation and around ovulation. This study, however, has two major weaknesses. First, a retrospective design has been used. Second, as mentioned earlier, the question is whether it is justified to equate self-reported crying proneness with actual crying behavior.

As far as we know, two studies have collected data on actual crying behavior, applying a crying diary in a concurrent design. The first one was conducted by Frey and co-workers (cited in Frey [1985] and in Frey, Ahern, Gunderson, & Tuason [1986]). These investigators examined the number and length of the crying episodes of 85 normal female subjects, who were not using anticonceptives nor any other hormone medication. Unfortunately, further information concerning the sample (such as age, marital, and socio-economic status) was not provided. Per cyclus, three consistent peaks of 3 to 4 days of increased crying were observed. The first one occurred 6–4 days *before* the menstrual period, the second 3–5 days *after* the onset of the period, and a third on 13–16 days *after* the onset of menses (around ovulation). Remarkably, the three days immediately preceding the menstrual cycle were quite low with regard to self-reported crying frequency. Frey further noted that the three "crying" peaks did not correspond with the changes in levels of female sex hormones, such as progesterone or estrogen.

In an attempt to replicate these findings, we[3] conducted a pilot-study in which we asked women to complete a crying diary, very similar to the one applied by Frey and co-workers. Data were collected from 21 contraceptive pill-users and 21 no-pill-users. Although the samples differed too much in terms of age, education and marital status to draw definite conclusions concerning the role of oral anticonceptives in mood change, two interesting observations could be made. First, the pill-users failed to report differences in crying frequency during the different phases of the menstruation, thereby challenging the retrospective data of Horsten et al. (1997). Second, in the no-pill users group, most frequent crying was not reported preceding the onset of the menstruation, but rather during its first days. These data thus do neither correspond strongly with Frey's observations nor with Horsten et al.'s findings. In conclusion, there is a remarkable lack of correspondence in findings of these three studies. An indepth analysis of the causes that induce crying during menstruation versus before and after may be helpful to establish to what extent psychological or social factors, for example not being available for sex, rather than biological factors may be part of the story to explain possible differences in crying behavior during the periods.

To summarize, Frey (1985) advanced an interesting hypothesis arguing that prolactin may lower the threshold to shed tears. Some data have indirectly supported this hypothesis, but other observations seem to contradict it. Thus, conclusions are still speculative, until there is more evidence based on actual measurements of plasma prolactin combined with an adequate and valid assessment of crying. There is further evidence that women do not cry more frequently during the days preceding their menses, thus refuting a relationship between crying and pre-menstrual tension.

In conclusion, we strongly believe that research on the possible biological determinants of crying, in particular the "prolactin hypothesis," deserves further attention in order to gain a better understanding of the possible biological causes of sex differences in crying.

Conclusion

We have shown that there is substantial evidence that adult women are more prone to cry and also actually cry more frequently than men. Without doubt, socialization plays an important role. This socialization process may not be limited to teaching boys to withhold their tears and encouraging girls to let them flow, but may also be related to differential exposure to crying-inducing situations and dissimilar appraisal processes. No clear differences have been reported in crying frequency between newborn girls and boys. At what age or in what developmental phase these gender differences become manifest has not yet been established. More insight into developmental trends can be expected to contribute significantly to a better understanding of the underlying mechanisms explaining sex differences in crying. We strongly feel that in addition to socialization and differential exposure to crying-inducing situations, biological factors should be considered. Although the prolactin hypothesis has received little support in the above-mentioned studies, it should be realized that to date there have been no studies in which prolactin was measured directly. In future studies, other biological factors (e.g., sex hormones, differences in brain functioning and biochemistry) should also be seriously considered when investigating sex differences in crying and tearfulness.

Author note

All correspondence concerning this chapter should be sent to the first author at the Department of Psychology, Tilburg University, PO Box 90153, 5000 LE Tilburg, the Netherlands (tel.: 31–13–4662078; e-mail: vingerhoets@kub.nl).

Notes

1. Although we are aware that some authors make a distinction between these two terms we will use them as synonyms in the present chapter.
2. The authors would like to thank Marieke Paarlberg for her willingness to provide us with the data of the pregnant women and Nienke Bosma, Marieke Brouwer, Evan van Essen, Nadine Lommers, Aafke Seebregts, and Shiela Vermaas for their help in further data collection and analysis.
3. We are indebted to Mariëlle van de Rijt, Angelina Klokgieters, Stannie Simonis, Inge Stuifbergen, and Colinda Boers for their help in data collection.

References

Beck, C. T. (1991). Maternity blues research: A critical review. *Issues in Mental Health Nursing, 12*, 291–300.

Bindra, D. (1972). Weeping, a problem of many facets. *Bulletin of the British Psychological Society, 25*, 281–284.

Blier, M. J., & Blier-Wilson, L. A. (1989). Gender differences in self-rated emotional expressiveness. *Sex Roles, 21*, 287–295.

Boomsma, D. I., & Slagboom, E. (1997). Op zoek naar de genen voor angst en depressie [In search for the genes for fear and depression]. *Mediator, 8 (September)*, 9–10.

Borgquist, A. (1906). Crying. *American Journal of Psychology, 17*, 149–205.

Brody, L. R. (1985). Gender differences in emotional development: A review of theories and research. *Journal of Personality, 53*, 102–149.

Buss, D. M. (1992). Manipulation in close relationships: Five personality factors in interactional context. *Journal of Personality, 60*, 477–499.

Choti, S. E., Marston, A. R., Holston, S. G., & Hart, J. T. (1987). Gender and personality variables in film-induced sadness and crying. *Journal of Social and Clinical Psychology, 5*, 535–544.

Cornelius, R. R. (1986, April). *Prescience in the pre-scientific study of weeping? A history of weeping in the popular press from the mid-1800s to the present.* Paper presented at the 57th Annual Meeting of the Eastern Psychological Association, New York, NY.

Cornelius, R. R. (1997). Toward a new understanding of weeping and catharsis? In A. J. J. M. Vingerhoets, F. J. Van Bussel, & A. J. W. Boelhouwer (Eds.), *The (non)expression of emotions in health and disease* (pp. 303–321). Tilburg University Press.

Cossette, L., Pomerleau, A., Malcuit, G., & Kaczorowski, J. (1996). Emotional expressions of female and male infants in a social and a nonsocial context. *Sex Roles, 35*, 693–709.

Crawford, J., Kippax, S., Onyx, J., Gault, U., & Benton, P. (1992). *Emotion and gender: Constructing meaning from memory*. London: Sage.

Cutler, S. E., & Nolen-Hoeksema, S. (1991). Accounting for sex differences in depression through female victimization: Childhood sexual abuse. *Sex Roles, 24*, 425–438.

Delp, M. J., & Sackeim, H. A. (1987). Effects of mood on lacrimal flow: Sex differences and asymmetry. *Psychophysiology, 24*, 550–556.

De Fruyt, F. (1997). Gender and individual differences in adult crying. *Personality and Individual Differences, 22*, 937–940.

Derogatis, L. R., Lipman, R. S., Rickets, K., Uhlenhuth, E. H., & Covi, L. (1974). The Hopkins Symptom Checklist (HSCL): A self-report symptom inventory. *Behavioral Science, 19*, 1–15.

Eibl-Eibesfeldt, I. (1997). *Die Biologie des menschlichen Verhaltens. Grundriss der Humanethologie* [The biology of human behavior. Principles of human ethology]. (3rd Edn.). Weyarn: Seehamer Verlag.

Eisenberg, N., & Lennon, R. (1983). Sex differences in empathy and related capacities. *Psychological Bulletin, 94*, 100–131

Eisler, R. M., & Skidmore, J. R. (1987). Masculine gender role stress. *Behavior Modification, 11*, 123–136.

Feldman, J. F., Brody, N., & Miller, S. A. (1980). Sex differences in non-elicited neonatal behaviors. *Merrill-Palmer Quarterly, 26*, 63–73.

Fischer, A. H. (1993). Sex differences in emotionality: Fact or stereotype? *Feminism and Psychology, 3*, 303–318.

Fischer, A. H., Manstead, A. S. R., & Scheepers, D. (in preparation). Gender differences in crying.

Flint, J., Corley, R., DeFried, J. C., Fulker, D. W., Gray, J. A., Miller, S., & Collins, A. C. (1995). A simple genetic basis for a complex psychological trait in mice. *Science, 269*, 1432–1435.

Frey, W. H. (1985). *Crying: The mystery of tears*. Minneapolis, MN: Winston Press.

Frey, W. H., Ahern, C., Gunderson, B. D., & Tuason, V. B. (1986). Biochemical, behavioral, and genetic aspects of psychogenic lacrimation: The unknown function of emotional tears. In F. J. Holly (Ed.), *The preocular tear film in health, disease, and contact lens wear*. Lubock, TX: Dry Eye Institute.

Frey, W. H., Hoffman-Ahern, C., Johnson, R. A., Lykken, D. T., & Tuason, V. B. (1983). Crying behavior in the human adult. *Integrative Psychiatry, 1*, 94–100.

Frijda, N. H. (1986). *The emotions*. New York, NY: Cambridge University Press.

Frijda, N.H. (1997). On the functions of emotional expression. In A. J. J. M. Vingerhoets, F. J. Van Bussel, & A. J. W. Boelhouwer (Eds.), *The (non)expression of emotions in health and disease* (pp. 1–14). Tilburg University Press.

Gass, K.A. (1988). Aged widows and widowers: Similarities and differences in appraisal, coping, resources, type of death, and health dysfunction. *Archives of Psychiatric Nursing, 2*, 200–210.

Gillespie, B. L., & Eisler, R. M. (1992). Development of the Feminine Gender Role Stress Scale. *Behavior Modification, 16*, 426–438.

Gross, J. J. (1998). Antecedent and response-focused emotion regulation: Divergent consequences for experience, expression, and physiology. *Journal of Personality and Social Psychology, 74*, 224–237.

Gross, J. J., & Munoz, R. F. (1995). Emotion regulation and mental health. *Clinical Psychology: Science and Practice, 2*, 151–164.

Halbreich, U., & Lumley, L. A. (1993). The multiple interactional biological processes that might lead to depression and gender differences in its appearance. *Journal of Affective Disorders, 29,* 159–173.

Harris, T., Surtees, P., & Bancroft, J. (1991). Is sex necessarily a risk factor to depression? *British Journal of Psychiatry, 158,* 708–712.

Horsten, M., Becht, M., & Vingerhoets, A. J. J. M. (1997). *Crying and the menstrual cycle.* Poster presented at the Annual Meeting of the American Psychosomatic Society, Santa Fe, NM (Abstract in *Psychosomatic Medicine, 59,* 102–103).

Jorgensen, R. S., & Johnson, J. H. (1990). Contributors to the appraisal of major life changes: Gender, perceived controllability, sensation seeking, strain, and social support. *Journal of Applied Social Psychology, 20,* 1123–1138.

Kessler, R. C., & McLeod, J. D. (1984). Sex differences in vulnerability to undesirable life events. *Amercian Sociological Review, 49,* 620–631.

Kohnstamm, G.A. (1989). Temperament in childhood: cross-cultural and sex differences. In G. A. Kohnstamm, J. E. Bates, & M. K. Rothbart (Eds.), *Temperament in childhood* (pp. 483–508). Chicester: John Wiley & Sons.

Kottler, J. A. (1996). *The language of tears.* San Francisco, CA: Jossey-Bass.

Kraemer, D. L. & Hastrup, J. L. (1986). Crying in natural settings. *Behavioural Research and Therapy, 24,* 371–373.

Labott, S. M., & Martin, R. B. (1987). The stress-moderating effects of weeping and humor. *Journal of Human Stress, 13,* 159–164.

Lash, S. J., Eisler, R. M., & Southard, D. R. (1995). Sex differences in cardiovascular reactivity as a function of the appraised gender relevance of the stressor. *Behavioral Medicine, 21,* 86–94.

Lazarus, R. S. (1991). *Emotion and adaptation.* New York: Oxford University Press.

Lazarus, R. S., & Folkman, S. (1984). *Stress, appraisal, and coping.* New York: Springer.

Lester, B. M. (1985). Introduction: There's more to crying than meets the ear. In B. M. Lester & C. F. Z. Boukydis (Eds.), *Infant crying: theoretical and research perspectives* (pp. 1–27). New York: Plenum Press.

Lewis, M., & Haviland, J. M. (Eds.) (1993). *Handbook of emotions.* New York: The Guilford Press.

Lombardo, W. K., Cretser, G. A., Lombardo, B., & Mathis, S. L. (1983). Fer cryin' out loud – There's a sex difference. *Sex Roles, 9,* 987–995.

Löfgren, L. B. (1966). On weeping. *International Journal of Psychoanalysis, 47,* 375–381.

Luteijn, F., Hamel, L. F., Bouman, T. K., & Kok, A. R. (1984). *HSCL Hopkins Symptom Checklist: Manual.* Lisse: Swets & Zeitlinger.

Lutgens, C. (1998). *Mood and crying during pregnancy and postpartum: A pilot study.* Unpublished masters thesis. Tilburg University, Tilburg, The Netherlands.

Magai, C., & McFadden, S. H. (Eds.) (1996). *Handbook of emotion, adult development and aging.* San Diego: Academic Press.

Moos, R. H. (1968). The development of a Menstrual Distress Questionnaire. *Psychosomatic Medicine, 30,* 853–867.

Moss, H. A. (1967). Sex, age, and state as determinants of mother-infant interaction. *Merrill-Palmer Quarterly, 13,* 19–36.

Muldoon, O., & Trew, K. (1995). Patterns of stress appraisal in a conflict environment: A Northern Irish study. *Children's Environments, 12,* 49–56.

Nolen-Hoeksema, S. (1994). An interactive model for the emergence of gender differences in depression in adolescence. *Journal of Research on Adolescence*, 4, 519–534.

Nolen-Hoeksema, S., & Girgus, J. S. (1994). The emergence of gender differences in depression during adolescence. *Psychological Bulletin, 115*, 424–443.

Oatley, K., & Jenkins, J. M. (1996). *Understanding emotions*. Cambridge, MA: Blackwell Publishers.

Paarlberg, M., Vingerhoets, A., Passchier, J., Heinen, A., Dekker, G., & Van Geijn, H. (1996). Maternal well-being in pregnancy, pregnancy complaints, and psychosocial factors in nulliparous women. *Journal of Psychosomatic Gynecology & Obstetrics, 17*, 93–102.

Philips, S., King, S., & DuBois, L. (1978). Spontaneous activities of female versus male newborns. *Child Development, 49*, 590–597.

Plas, J. M., & Hoover-Dempsey, K. V. (1988). *Working up a storm: Anger, anxiety, joy and tears on the job*. New York: W. W. Norton.

Porter, L. S., & Stone, A. A. (1995). Are there really gender differences in coping? A reconsideration of previous data and results from a daily study. *Journal of Social and Clinical Psychology, 14*, 184–202.

Ptacek, J. T., Smith, R. E., & Zanas, J. (1992). Gender, appraisal, and coping: A longitudinal analysis. *Journal of Personality, 60*, 747–770.

Ptacek, J. T., Smith, R. E., & Dodge, K. L. (1994). Gender differences in coping with stress: When stressors and appraisals do not differ. *Personality and Social Psychology Bulletin, 20*, 421–430.

Ross, C. E., & Mirowsky, J. (1984). Men who cry. *Social Psychology Quarterly, 47*, 138–146.

Steptoe, A. (1991). Psychological coping, individual differences and physiological stress responses. In C. L. Cooper & R. Payne (Eds.), *Personality and stress: Individual differences in the stress process* (pp. 205–234). Chichester: Wiley.

St. James-Roberts, I. (1993). Infant crying: normal development and persistent crying. In I. St. James-Roberts, G. Harris, & D. Messer (Eds.), *Infant crying, feeding and sleeping* (pp. 7–25). New York: Harvester Wheatsheaf.

St. James-Roberts, I., & Halil, T. (1991). Infant crying patterns in the first year: normal community and clinical findings. *Journal of Child Psychology and Psychiatry, 32*, 951–968.

Stone, A. A. (1995). Measurement of affective response. In S. Cohen, R. C. Kessler, & L. Underwood Gordon (Eds.), *Measuring stress. A guide for health and social scientists* (pp. 148–171). New York: Oxford University Press.

Theorell, T. (1992). Prolactin – a hormone that mirrors passiveness in crisis situations. *Integrative Physiological and Behavioral Sciences, 27*, 32–38.

Turner, R. J., & Avison, W. R. (1989). Gender and depression: Assessing exposure and vulnerability to life events in a chronically strained population. *Journal of Nervous and Mental Disease, 177*, 443–455.

Van der Bolt, L., & Tellegen, S. (1995–96). Sex differences in intrinsic reading motivation and emotional reading experience. *Imagination, Cognition and Personality, 15*, 337–349.

Vingerhoets, A. J. J. M., & Becht, M. C. (1996, August). The ISAC study. Some preliminary results. Paper presented at the International Study on Adult Crying (ISAC) symposium. Tilburg, The Netherlands.

Vingerhoets, A. J. J. M., Van den Berg, M., Kortekaas, R. Th., Van Heck, G. L., & Croon, M. (1993). Weeping: Associations with personality, coping, and subjective health status. *Personality and Individual Differences, 14*, 185–190.

Vingerhoets, A. J. J. M., Van Geleuken, A. J. M. L., Van Tilburg, M. A. L., & Van Heck, G. L. (1997). The psychological context of crying episodes: Toward a model of adult crying. In A. J. J. M. Vingerhoets, F. J. Van Bussel, & A. J. W. Boelhouwer (Eds.), *The (non)expression of emotions in health and disease* (pp. 323 – 336). Tilburg University Press.

Vingerhoets, A. J. J. M., & Van Heck, G. L. (1990). Gender, coping and psychosomatic symptoms. *Psychological Medicine, 20*, 125–135.

Wagner, R. E., Hexel, M., Bauer, W. W., & Kropiunigg, U. (1997). Crying in hospitals: A survey of doctors', nurses', and medical students' experience and attitudes. *Medical Journal of Australia, 166*, 13–16.

Wallbott, H. G., & Scherer, K. R. (1986). How universal and specific is emotional experience? Evidence from 27 countries on five continents. *Social Science Information, 25*, 763–795.

Williams, D. G. (1982). Weeping by adults: Personality correlates and sex differences. *Journal of Psychology, 110*, 217–226.

Williams, D. G., & Morris, G. H. (1996). Crying, weeping or tearfulness in British and Israeli adults. *British Journal of Psychology, 87*, 479–505.

Young, P. T. (1937). Laughing and weeping, cheerfulness and depression: A study of moods among college students. *Journal of Social Psychology, 8*, 311–334.

8. Masculine identity and restrictive emotionality

JEROEN JANSZ

Men and psychology have a somewhat awkward relationship. From its earliest days in the last quarter of the nineteenth century until its mature age in the 1960s, psychology was largely concerned with studying one half of humankind: men. The people who provided the data by participating in psychological experiments were mostly of the male sex, and so was the majority of psychologists reporting about these experiments. As a matter of consequence, a male bias could be discerned in the theories that were advocated, and the topics that were investigated. But, despite the overrepresentation of men in psychology, men were hardly ever studied *as men*. They were generally seen as representatives of the human species and treated as if they had no gender (Kimmel & Messner, 1989).

Ironically, it took the feminist criticism of the male bias in psychology before a substantial psychology of men was developed. In the 1970s a number of psychologists pioneered in this new field using bits of psychological knowledge to understand masculinity. Most of them were concerned with consciousness raising in accordance with the political aims of their feminist sisters: emancipation required as many personal and structural changes in the lives of men as in women's lives. In academic research, psychologists undertook empirical analyses of the vicissitudes of the male role. In clinical settings, new therapies were developed that confronted men with their personal behavior under patriarchy. In retrospect we can see that the psychological researchers and therapists of those days initiated a tradition in men's studies which continues to be productive till the present day (Levant & Pollack, 1995; Parker, 1995; Pleck, 1995).

This chapter aims at a specific contribution to the psychology of men by discussing the ways in which men cope with their feelings. It argues that men tend to lace up most of their feelings, a phenomenon called "restrictive emotionality" (Levant, 1995). The argument will be developed in the following way. I will first introduce 4 focal attributes of contemporary masculinity: autonomy, achievement, aggression, and stoicism. The stoic attribute amounts to a strict control of pain, grief, and

166

vulnerable feelings. Then, I will argue that male stoicism generally leads to restrictive emotionality: most men are reluctant to disclose intimate feelings, and they also inhibit the expression of their emotions, with anger as the proverbial exception to the rule. The third step in my argument is concerned with the dysfunctional nature of restrictive emotionality: the inhibition of (tender) feelings has a negative impact on men's health. The last section of this chapter aims at an explanation of restrictive emotionality. It tries to argue that the general inhibition of emotions among men is not "given" in men's nature, but rather the result of a lack of practice.

A cautionary note is in order before I start unfolding my argument. Most research in the psychology of men is based on the statements of men in Western Europe, the United States, and Canada who are relatively young, well-educated and white. Most studies do not report the sexual orientation of the participants, but it is highly probable that the large majority is heterosexual. Empirical research among men in ethnic minorities is not as well developed to date as research among the ethnic majority. Therefore, attention paid to the ways in which men from ethnic minorities cope with their emotions is modest. In conclusion, the following account of restrictive emotionality is necessarily of a limited scope.

Contemporary masculinity

Like every other culture, Western culture has its public conception of masculinity: members of this culture know what "being a man" amounts to. These shared, conventional ideas about masculinity that individuals learn by talking and acting with their fellows are subsumed here under the notion of a cultural model (Holland, 1992; Quinn & Holland, 1987). The knowledge structures of the model are linked to practices of masculinity as diverse as, for example, being a son, being a partner, or being a father. In these everyday practices the cultural model may gain motivational force (Jansz, 1996; Strauss, 1992), for example, when a 10-year-old takes great pains to develop an identity like his father's.

The cultural model is easiest to disentangle by looking at the identities of men who appear in public. The examples of what a man is (and must be) are set by showbusiness stars, and political leaders, but also by "ordinary" men who appear in talkshows. These public resources of masculinity are rich in diversity. Take, for example, the differences in identity between the smart, daring, and adventurous womanizer James Bond, the successful and determined Tony Blair, who also is very kind, and the "coolness" of Michael Jordan with his stylish dunking of the basketball and high-five handshakes. Their different styles provide the audience with enacted examples of masculine identities that may inspire some and frighten others.

Over the past decades, a number of researchers has studied the extent to which culturally available models of masculinity have been endorsed by individual men. The participants in these surveys could express on Likert-type scales to what extent they attributed particular characteristics to "men in general," and on self-report instruments they could state which characteristics they attributed to themselves (Levant & Pollack, 1995; Pleck, Sonenstein, & Ku, 1993; Thompson, Pleck, & Ferrara, 1992). The results of these studies show that despite the variety in male styles and roles, there is a dominant set of characteristics attributed to contemporary men, that is to say to men in the subculture of the Western, white middle class. The dominant attributes can be labeled in different ways: some authors have used metaphors, like "sturdy oak" and "big wheel" (Brannon, 1976), others have used common roles like "boss," "worker," and "standard bearer" (Harris, 1995). Here, I will characterize contemporary masculinity by 4 attributes that echo the categorizations proposed by others (Brannon, 1976; Harris, 1995; Pleck, 1981):

Autonomy: A man stands alone, bears the tribulations of life with a stiff upper lip, and does not admit his dependences on others.

Achievement: A man is achieving in work and play in order to be able to provide bread for his loved one and family.

Aggression: A man is tough, and acts aggressively if the circumstances require so.

Stoicism: A man does not share his pain, does not grieve openly, and avoids strong, dependent and warm feelings.

Taken together, the attributes characterise the dominant cultural model of masculinity in the Western world. It is no coincidence that these attributes overlap with the features that have been attributed to personhood (Harré, 1983; Jansz, 1991): Western personhood is largely, though not exclusively, woven out of male fabric, which is a reflection of the power structures under patriarchy (Fischer & Jansz, 1995).

Surveys underline the shared conventions about "traditional" Western masculinity (Pleck, 1995), and self-reports show that the normative properties of the cultural model are translated to the level of personal identities. Masculine identity conceptualizes "who one is as a man"; it embraces the knowledge and feelings of a man about who he is, both with regard to an audience and with regard to himself (Bosma,

1995; Jansz, in press). A masculine identity does not "bubble up" to consciousness from the biological make-up of a male, but is created in social interaction (Kimmel, 1994). In this constructive process, individual men borrow from the public resources of masculinity, but they also lend to them: "doing" masculine identity at an individual level always sustains the public, or cultural, conception of masculinity (Shotter, 1989).

Surveys and self-reports show that men generally construct their identities within the confines of the cultural model of masculinity. But men's conformism is not without problems. Recent research has confirmed what Pleck (1981) argued earlier: living according to the standards of traditional masculinity is a source of stress for many men. Several investigators studied role strain, and related constructs like role conflict and role stress among relatively young, well-educated, and predominantly white men. Particularly this group of participants had persistent worries about their achievements. They were afraid not to meet the standards for success, and they also worried about their physical inadequacy in sports and sex, as well as about their intellectual inferiority (Eisler, 1995; O'Neil, Good, & Holmes, 1995; Thompson, Pleck, & Ferrera, 1992).

Pleck (1981) suggested that when men fail at one aspect of masculinity they may blow up other aspects. Men who find it difficult to meet the cultural standards of achievement and success tend to compensate these feelings of career failure by behaving aggressively. Ethnic minorities are particularly vulnerable to this kind of compensatory behavior, because they generally face a disadvantaged societal position (Pleck, 1981). Immigrant Mexican men, for example, were found to display toughness, "bravado," and exaggerated aggression as a way to compensate for their lack of societal power (Hondagneu-Sotelo & Messner, 1994). A defensive kind of toughness was also found among a group of black British youth called "The Rasta Heads" (Mac An Ghaill, 1994). They were able to survive in a hostile environment because they amplified a specific form of masculinity that overemphasized toughness. In the words of one of them: "you can't let the white man use you all the time . . . you see it's the image. You've got to act tough to survive here, to survive in this country" (Mac An Ghaill, 1994, p. 188).

In sum, I have argued that the cultural model of masculinity provides the resources for the construction of personal identities: men require other men and themselves to be autonomous, achieving, aggressive and stoic. The stoic attribute is of particular interest in this chapter because it embraces the emotional life of men.

The emotional inexpressiveness of men

If men are – and must be – stoic, which means that they do not show their vulnerability and restrict their emotions, it will be problematic for them to engage in intimate relationships in which feelings are shared. In this section we will see whether man's emotional life is as inhibited as the dominant conception of masculinity suggests. First, I will present research about the extent in which men express intimate feelings in general, and second I will discuss research about the experience and expression of specific emotions.

Disclosing intimate feelings

In his clinical practice, and in his counseling project for fathers (Levant & Kelly, 1989), Levant observed that many men were genuinely unaware of their feelings. When they, for example, were asked to identify their feelings, they tended to rely on their knowledge-base and tried to deduce logically how they should feel in particular circumstances. Levant borrows the term *alexithymia* from the clinical literature to label the condition these men are in (Levant, 1995). Alexithymia is a condition in which patients are unable to identify and describe their feelings in words (Sifneos, 1996). In its radical form it is only observed among patients who are severely disturbed, but in a mild form alexithymia is widespread among adult men, according to Levant.

Repressing emotions has been measured with a variety of (sub)scales about the inhibition of emotion. A few examples of the scales concerned with men's emotional life are: "concealing emotions" (Brannon, 1985), with items like "When a man is feeling a little pain he should try not to let it show very much"; "restrictive emotionality" (Levant, Hirsch, Celentano, Cozza, Hill, MacEachern, Marty, & Schnedeker, 1992) containing items like "A man should never reveal worries to others": and "restrictive affectionate behavior between men" (O'Neil, Helms, Gable, David, & Wrightsman, 1986), of which an illustrative item is "Hugging other men is difficult for me." Results of the studies that used these scales showed that participants had difficulty with finding words for their feelings. They also found it difficult to express emotions and often feared the consequences of becoming emotional. The men further reported difficulties in dealing with other people's vulnerable feelings. The problems summarized here mostly concerned feelings that imply a non-masculine image of oneself: fear, insecurity, sadness, disappointment, envy, and jealousy (Eisler, 1995; O'Neill et al., 1995; Thompson, et al., 1992).

The interviews reported by Harris (1995) provide another kind of insight into the actual workings of the stoic normative attribute, as may be illustrated by the following statement of a 38-year-old manager:

> The strongest message was emotional control with others. This primary message was obtained at the cost of emotional awareness. The internal controls were so strong by adulthood that my own knowledge of emotions consisted of only knowing the fear of being out of control, i.e., showing any emotion at all. (Harris, 1995, p. 111)

Other researchers have focused on the communicative aspects of (intimate) feelings by studying *self-disclosure*, that is the extent to which a person communicates personal feelings (and other intimate matters) to another person (Derlega, Metts, Petronio, & Margulis, 1993). Dindia and Allen (1992) have done a meta-analysis about verbal self-disclosure in order to determine whether there are sex differences in self-disclosure. They found a significant effect indicating that men disclose their feelings less than women. But the gender differences are not as large as the stereotype of "rational men" and "emotional women" would suggest. The differences between men and women are largest in same sex interactions: men share less intimate information in conversation with other men in comparison with women conversing with women. Gender differences are also dependent on the sex of the target. When a man talks to a woman, he discloses less about himself than a woman does when she talks to another woman. But this gender difference disappeared when the target is a man: women disclose as little to men as men do. Another important moderator of gender differences in disclosure is the kind of relationship the interactants have. When the actors have an intimate relationship, women disclose more than men, however when the target is a stranger, women disclose about the same amount of intimate information as men (Dindia & Allen, 1992). In addition, men generally do not disclose much, because they prefer to converse about relatively impersonal topics such as their work, shared activities, sports, and politics as compared to women who generally prefer to discuss more intimate matters (Bischoping, 1993).

In sum, men are generally reluctant to share personal feelings, which can be understood as a way to protect their identity, because expressing tender feelings exposes vulnerability, which is generally taken as a sign of weakness. The protection of identity is underlined by the results of the few studies in which men disclosed more than women. Derlega, Winstead, Wong, and Hunter (1985), for example, found that men exceed women in self-disclosure during the very first opposite-sex encounters to initiate the relationship and exert control over its development. Another goal of disclosing at an initial encounter is to elicit intimate information from an attractive woman (Cross & Madson, 1997). The instrumental nature of male self-disclosure was also found in a study about self-disclosure among opposite-sex friends (Leaper, Carson, Baker, Holliday, & Myers, 1995). The authors suggest that the high frequency of male disclosure in this study was probably due to the fact that the men felt they had to perform well in conversation with a female friend.

The experience and expression of specific emotions

Self-reports about the *experience* of specific emotions generally show that men report less intro-punitive emotions, like, for example, shame, guilt, sadness, and fear, than do women (Brody & Hall, 1993; Fischer, 1993). In her detailed analysis of self-reports about fear, Fischer (1991) found that the majority of men argued that they never were really afraid; they did not label their feelings as fear, but rather employed labels like "worry" or "concern." With respect to love and disgust a different picture emerges from several studies. Men have a romantic and erotic orientation toward love, they tend to "fall in love" faster than women and they attach greater importance to falling in love, which results in a higher incidence of the experience of love among male participants (Dion & Dion, 1985; Rubin, Peplau, & Hill, 1981). Disgust is an outward-directed negative emotion which is reported more by men than by women. Other negative emotions that are directed toward others hardly show any gender differences: men experience as much anger and contempt as women (Averill, 1983; Brody, 1993; Brody & Hall, 1993). Self-reports about experiencing the positive emotion joy did not show any gender difference either (Fischer, 1993).

The *expression* of emotions by men seem to differ from the experience of them. The general result of the research is that men conceal their emotions (Brody & Hall, 1993; Fischer, 1993). Consequently, male non-verbal behavior is less expressive than female's (Brody & Hall, 1993). The most conspicuous result in this respect is that men hardly ever cry (LaFrance & Banaji, 1992; Shields, 1991). Cultural norms regarding gender seem to have an impact on the frequency of crying, because traditional men cry less than non-traditional men (Ross & Mirowski, 1984). The results of a recent study suggest we may face a change in the norms regarding crying men: Labott, Martin, Eason and Berkey (1991) found that both women and men consider men who cry during an emotional film fragment to be more sympathetic than women who cry watching the same fragment. The crying man was also rated as more sympathetic than a non-emotional or laughing man. However, sympathy for male sadness was not found in another study among college students. The results showed that men who express their depressed state are evaluated negatively, whereas their female counterparts are not (Siegel & Alloy, 1990).

Men generally inhibit the expression of emotions, but anger is the proverbial exception to the rule: many studies have confirmed that men express their anger far more frequently than women (Averill, 1983; Fischer, 1993; McConatha, Leone, & Armstrong, 1997). In addition, men show more facial expressiveness when role-playing anger than when they enact fear (Eisler, 1995). Long (1987) argued on the basis of case material that the high incidence of anger among men is the result of the fact men tend to funnel non-masculine emotions such as disappointment, shame, and fear into the expressive channel of anger, because anger is in accordance with their masculine identity. The prototypical nature of male anger is underlined by Fischer's observation (1991) that the male participants in her study never felt uneasy about the anger they had expressed in earlier social situations.

A particular way of emotional expression can be observed among men in African-American subcultures. Many African-Americans, in particular the younger ones, have adopted a "cool pose" (Majors & Mancini Billson, 1992). It is enacted in a range of behaviors that stress independence and invulnerability, but also in ritual displays of powerful masculinity, such as "playing the dozens" (that is, the rapid exchange of insults), and high-five handshakes (Rybarczyk, 1994). Emotional toughness is a core characteristic of the cool pose: vulnerable emotions are suppressed, because they are at odds with the desired image of masculinity. Pride, anger, and distrust are displayed powerfully for their sustenance of the same image, and often directed toward the dominant society for many years of hostile mistreatment and discrimination (Majors & Mancini Billson, 1992). Lazur and Majors (1995) link being cool with self-diclosure. They argue that "cool men" may be successful in proving themselves, but they do it at the cost of intimacy. Labeling the expression of many emotions as "uncool" unavoidably hinders the social sharing of intimate feelings with partners, family, and friends. The cool pose has been well-documented among African-American (young) men, but its appeal is far wider (Lazur & Majors, 1995; Majors & Mancini Billson, 1992). Many men in minority groups, as well as in the majority, seem to be attracted to the cool pose, which is probably due to its wide popularization in rap music videos, movies, and sports.

In sum, psychological research has found that men hardly disclose their personal feelings, and tend to conceal the expression of emotions like fear, sadness, shame, and guilt. This can be understood as a strategy to boost conventional masculine identity: the expression of tender feelings and intro-punitive emotions is generally seen as an indication of vulnerability and weakness. Further, refraining from self-disclosure extends the psychological distance between audience and self, which impedes predicting and controlling the individual's behavior. This may contribute to the sustenance of the individual's autonomy (cf. Cross & Madson, 1997). In addition, the enactment of a cool pose and the expression of (controled) anger can be understood as a way to exert power and gain control in a situation, which also contributes to conventional masculine identity.

Masculinity, emotionality, and health

One of the pioneers in the field of men studies, Jourard (1974), asserted about a quarter of a century ago that the male gender role, which "requires man to appear tough, objective, striving, achieving, instrumental and emotionally unexpressive" (Jourard, 1974, p. 22) is an important factor in explaining why men die younger than women. Recent research about the health of men supports Jourard's assertion, although the balance is redressed a bit by the fact that stereotypical masculine behaviors such as being assertive, decisive, and independent may contribute to individual well-being (Copenhaver & Eisler, 1996). Men live approximately seven fewer years, on average, than do women. Men's death-rate is higher than women's at all ages and in all leading causes of death (Copenhaver & Eisler, 1996). The higher morbidity of men is generally attributed to gender-related lifestyles: men smoke more than women, they drink more alcohol, and they are more often engaged in dangerous and violent activities (Cleary, 1987). Among African-American men the situation is worse. They are overrepresented in deaths caused by AIDS, accidents, suicides, and homicides. Majors and Mancini Billson (1992) have proposed that this may be the result of the urge some African-American men feel to undertake risky behaviors in order to prove their masculinity as a way to compensate for their disadvantaged societal position.

Research about cardiovascular processes has been done against the background of the stress generating aspects of contemporary masculine identity. The results of these experiments show that men who are highly committed to traditional masculinity are more likely than others to become strongly emotionally aroused when faced with a situation that threatens or challenges their identity: their blood pressure rose when they had to complete a task which emphasized, for example, a good performance, or physical fitness (Lash, Eisler, & Schulman, 1990; Lash, Gillespie, Eisler, & Southard, 1991). The observation that men tend to express dysphoric emotions through physiological responses, rather than translate them in actions was also confirmed in an experiment with couples in long-term marriages. Physiological measures were taken when they discussed an issue of continuing disagreement in their marriage. Most husbands showed increased physiological arousal in these difficult interactions, whereas wives did not. The gender differences disappeared when they discussed the events of the day or a pleasant topic (Levenson, Carstensen, & Gottman, 1994). The authors conjecture that the oft-observed tendency of men to withdraw during conflict-ive marital interaction results from men experiencing states of high physiological arousal as unpleasant. They try to reduce arousal by seeking isolation.

Research about the consequences of men's restrictive emotionality is of special interest in this chapter. Pennebaker and his colleagues have developed the theory that inhibition of unpleasant emotions is a major cause of chronic nervous system arousal, and psychosomatic health problems (Pennebaker, Hughes, & O'Heeron, 1987). In their experiments, they invited participants to self-disclose traumatic experiences. It was found that participants who self-disclosed actively had lower physiological arousal, and better immune responses than participants in the control condition (Pennebaker, Hughes, & O'Heeron, 1987; Pennebaker, Kiecolt-Glaser, & Glaser, 1988). Although the results of the experiments were not analyzed for sex differences, they warrant the conclusion that "the masculine characteristic of inhibiting emotional expressiveness surrounding painful or stressful events may have adverse effects on health" (Copenhaver & Eisler, 1996, p. 228).

In addition to its negative effects on health, restrictive emotionality impairs social interaction. Concealing emotions is related to a communicative problem many men are confronted with: they are not as good as women in identifying feelings from nonverbal cues of face, body, and voice (Brody & Hall, 1993). The identification of anger seems to be different from other emotions: men outperform women at decoding anger-cues (Wagner, McDonald & Manstead, 1986). Difficulties with reading the emotions of others seriously handicaps men with respect to intimate relationships, which is underlined by the empirical finding that men who score high on scales of restrictive emotionality report low intimacy in their relationships (O'Neill, et al. 1995).

In some cases, restrictive emotionality results in pathological social interaction. These serious consequences of the structural inhibition of feelings have largely been documented by psychoanalysts. Their theorizing is built upon case histories, which provide indepth reports about the conflict-laden construction of masculine identities. The report about a patient HL is an example of the psychoanalytic approach (Munder Ross, 1996). This 34-year-old man is quoted saying:

> Sometimes I think my treating S. mean is a big coverup. I don't want to show her my fears. I'm real soft inside and care for her, and I get so scared for her [weeps]. I don't think you should be involved with someone and not care for them (Munder Ross, 1996, p. 58).

He hints at an explanation for the difficult relationship with his girl-friend S.: he compensates his own vulnerability with aggressive behavior towards her.

At this point in my argument it must be noted that restrictive emotionality has a paradoxical status with respect to male functioning. On the one hand, researchers and clinicians have found that it is dysfunctional with respect to individual health and building social relationships. On the other hand, inhibiting emotions is functional in terms of appropriate male behavior: "real men" do not cry, inhibit their tender feelings, and express their anger strategically. The resulting emotional toughness, or coolness, has become an important display of masculine identity in a variety of (sub)cultures.

Toward an explanation of restrictive emotionality

If we want to understand how restrictive emotionality becomes a focal part of masculine identity, we must focus on the construction of this particular gender-identity. For most boys, the family is the production site in which the cultural model of masculinity is translated into a personal masculine identity. I will first discuss the constructive process in general, and then concentrate on emotional communication within families. The empirical base of this section is – again – limited: most studies were done in white, middle-class Western nuclear families.

The interactive production of a masculine identity

As soon as parents know that their child is of the male sex the social construction of masculine identity starts (cf. Harré, 1991). Parents, and others, attribute all kinds of characteristics to the infant, and will interpret actions of the neonate within the frame of conventional masculinity. The attributes of "what a man (or a boy) is and must be" are communicated in all kinds of ordinary, day-to-day activities. As a result of the communicative interaction between parents and child, public resources of masculinity are internalized (Vygotsky, 1978; Wertsch & Stone, 1985). Public resources are transformed rather than copied in this process, and they may undergo further transformation as a result of the individual's agency (Harré, 1983). In due course, the individual gains control over meaning structures that were external to him (Wertsch & Stone, 1985), and they become part of his internal world. The new identity-related information is generally linked to autobiographical meaning-structures that exist already in memory (Barclay, 1993).

When the male individual grows older, agency becomes more important. He gains the capacities to select purposively among the elements of the cultural model, but he may also have to negotiate between social pressures to adopt particular aspects of a masculine identity, and his own preferences. The intentional construction of a particular kind of masculine identity is very well illustrated by Duindam's research among "caring fathers," who share the burden of child-care and domestic duties with their partners (Duindam, 1997; Duindam & Spruijt, 1997). He found that most of them said they constructed their identities in opposition to their own fathers, as if they wanted to compensate for the lack of involvement of their own fathers. In addition, this study underlines that (re)constructing an identity is an interactionist project: many caring fathers stressed the role of their partners in the practical reconstruction of their own identities. Their partners, who in most cases were "working mothers," created a context of interaction in which a reconstruction of traditional masculinity was both necessary and possible (Duindam & Spruijt, 1997).

Thus far, family interaction was sketched as if both parents interact on an equal base with their sons. In actual practice, however, this is not the case. The sexual division of labor in Western families has resulted in a situation in which mothers spend a large amount of time with their children, and fathers have far less interaction with them. This situation is still widespread according to recent surveys in Australia, Israel, the Netherlands, Sweden, and the United States (Duindam & Spruijt, 1997). The social organization of family life has consequences for the affective relations that contribute to the construction of a masculine identity, which will be shown in the next paragraphs.

The sexual division of labor together with the biological given that children are born from the bodies of their mothers guarantee a symbiotic bond between mother and child during the first months after birth. It is in this relational context that the first steps of the social construction of masculine identity are taken. The psychoanalyst Greenson (1968) was among the first to argue that a successful dis-identification from mother is necessary for the little boy in order to adequately complete the separation-individuation process (Mahler, 1972). But, dis-identifying is difficult for the boy, because men have spent an important part of their young lives "totally in the care of women who wiped their bottoms, fed their mouths and their egos, and held their hands whenever there was danger or difficulty" (Cooper, 1996, p. 113; Greenson, 1968). The little boy will only succeed in breaking the early psychological bond with his mother, if he is able to solve his Oedipus complex positively, that is, by identifying with his father. The feminist theorist Chodorow (1978) has added a critical note to this psychodynamic account by arguing that the interaction between mother and son will always proceed under the banner of differences: "mothers tend to experience their daughters as more like, and continuous with themselves . . . By contrast, mothers experience their sons as a male opposite" (Chodorow, 1978, p. 166).

On his side, the son must fend off the earlier sense of symbiotic "oneness" with his mother rather strictly, because he is of a different sex. He cannot borrow from his mother in the construction of his masculine identity, but he cannot use his father either, because fathers are absent from the family home most of the time. For the little boy "learning what it is to be masculine comes to mean learning to be . . . not womanly" (Chodorow, 1989, p. 109). Boys are theorized to identify with a *position* rather than with a example of masculinity in flesh and blood, which generally means that they lean heavily on culturally stereotypic attributes of masculinity in construing their own identity.

As boys grow up, they may continue to long for the kind of relational closeness they once had with their mother, but these yearnings tend to become associated with a "fear of engulfment," that dates back to the pre-Oedipal period (Levant, 1995, p. 242). This fear is fundamental, because it threatens the integrity of the individual (Cooper, 1996). For some men, it leads to a defensive kind of autonomy that can result in serious maladaption because they shy away from any kind of social contact (Pollack, 1990). Most men cope with the fear of losing their integrity by building psychological fences around themselves. They continue to favor independent functioning over interdependent ways of relating to others (Cross & Madson, 1997).

Thus, the organization of family life is important in explaining why many men have problems with close relationships, emotional bonding, and the expression of tender feelings. Both intimacy and emotions like grief, shame, fear, and guilt expose vulnerable sides of oneself, which is at odds with conventional masculinity in Western culture.

Emotional communication within families

If we want to explain the restrictive emotionality of men, we must also look at they ways in which emotions are dealt with in socialization. In research on neonates it was found that males and females differ in expressiveness as a result of biologically based temperamental predispostions. In their review, Haviland and Malatesta (1981) concluded that infant boys are more emotionally reactive and expressive than infant girls: they become more easily excited and startled, do not tolerate frustration very well, cry sooner and more often, and show a rapid fluctuation between emotional states. In addition, male neonates show higher levels of (motor) activity than females (Eaton & Enns, 1986). Given these biological differences between the sexes, it is conceivable that parents interpret the behavior of their male infant as expressive. But it is not only a question of perceiving differences that are "given" in biology: when judges were misinformed about the actual sex of the child, they still perceived the infant "boys" as more intensely emotionally expressive than the infant "girls" (Brody & Hall, 1993). Presumably, the perception of biological differences is co-determined by expectations that stem from the cultural model of masculinity.

Culturally embedded expectations also occur in later socialization practices. Dunn, Bretherton, and Munn (1987) observed, for example, that mothers used less emotion words when interacting with their 18-to 24-month-old sons than with their same aged daughters. A study in which parents were asked to "read" wordless storybooks to their sons and daughters provides us with another example (Brody & Hall, 1993). In the stories the parents told, it occurred that fathers used less emotion words in reading for their sons than for their daughters.

The expressive temperament of infant boys may make it easier for caretakers (i.e., mothers in most cases) to read the emotional expressions of infant boys. Brody (1993, this volume) has argued that this emotional expressivity may stimulate parents, especially mothers, to contain the expressivity of their infant sons. This is both an adaptive response to their son's initial temperament, and a conscious or unconscious application of the cultural norms regarding masculinity to their son's behavior. Because of the interactive nature of socialization, the parent's containing efforts are translated into the boy's actions: he learns to control, or possibly inhibit, the emotional arousal of his earliest years in due course. Girls, by contrast, must amplify their expressions, and parents must take greater pain to read the (emotional) expressions of their daughters. This results in more fine-tuning in the emotional communication between daughters and parents, in most cases mothers (Brody, 1993).

Detailed observations of mother-child interaction underline the differences in emotional communication. Fivush (1989) observed mothers and their sons and daughters between 2½ and 3 years of age who had a conversation about past (emotional) experiences. Mothers used more negative emotion words with their sons than with their daughters. For example, they spoke about anger with their sons, but never did with their daughters. It was also found that mother–son conversations focussed on the causes and consequences of the emotion, while mother–daughter dyads elaborated on the emotional state itself. This difference can be interpreted as mothers teaching their sons to analyze the context of their feeling, probably in order to gain control over it, while daughters are taught to be sensitive to the feeling itself. In general, it can be concluded from this study and other studies about emotional communication in Western nuclear families that parents discuss less emotions with their sons than with their daughters, and display a smaller range of emotions to their sons than to their daughters (Brody & Hall, 1993).

Some recent studies indicate that emotional communication will change when family life is organized in a different way. In families where partners share the burden of care, fathers are far more intimately involved with their children than is generally the case (Brody, 1997; Duindam & Spruijt, 1997). Brody (1997) studied boys' emotional expressiveness when fathers spend more time with their children. She found that "boys with more involved fathers express more interpersonal affiliation themes, fewer competition themes, more fear, more warmth, less anger, and less aggression than boys with less involved fathers" (Brody, 1997, p. 383). In other words, a non-traditional division of labor in which fathers spend more time on care work than they do conventionally, has consequences for the kind of feelings boys and young men express: boys show less anger, but more fear (see also Brody, this volume).

Two more factors contribute to the development of inhibited emotional expressiveness among men. The first one is concerned with the verbalization of feeling states. In general, boys are less good at verbal language than girls (Gleason, 1989). In a context where parents are focused on containing their son's earliest expressiveness, the little boy's feeling states are de-emphasized. Consequently, the little boy will not receive much training in the verbalization of emotions, which partly explains later difficulties in finding words for feelings (Brody, 1993; Levant, 1995). The second factor has to do with life outside the family. Observations of nursery school interactions, and children's play groups corroborate what was found within families (Tannen, 1990). Boys at play tend to emphasize competition and explicit kinds of self-promotion. They like, for example, to identify with heroes like Batman and Zorro. This competitive and "autonomous" play fosters aggression and dominance, often at the expense of affiliation and cooperation (Maccoby, 1990). In this kind of play, boys tend to maximize feelings of hostility and anger, and minimize emotions that have to do with vulnerability, guilt, fear, and hurt (Brody & Hall, 1993). This pattern also occurred in a study of boys and girls of 7 and 12 years of age in which the expression of anger and sadness was studied. Boys reported more anger and an aggressive strategy of expression. Girls, by contrast, were more likely to express sadness. All children reported controlling their sadness and anger more in the presence of peers than when they were with their parents, because they expected negative interpersonal interaction following disclosure (Zeman & Garber, 1996).

Theories and research about the construction of masculine identity and emotional communication indicate that the male sex experiences a "cross-over" (Haviland & Malatesta, 1981) with respect to the expression of emotions. In their first months of life, little boys are more active and expressive with regard to their feeling states than little girls, but when they grow up, they tend to restrict the expression of emotions. The cross-over has its origin in socialization practices. Parents who themselves were socialized in the traditional attributes of gender will consciously and unconsciously communicate in such a way that the emotional expressions of their sons are constrained.

Conclusion

Earlier in this chapter, a paradoxical status has been attributed to restrictive emotionality: the inhibition of feelings is a focal characteristic of masculinity, but it is also detrimental in its effects on health and social interaction. The paradox cannot be solved easily, because restrictive emotionality is linked inextricably to the construction of masculine identity in traditional families. The gendered nature of emotional communication creates a context of interaction in which boys and (young) men do not learn to talk about or act upon emotions that imply vulnerability. As a result, men tend to deny their experience of this class of emotions, and conceal their expression. In situations where feelings like disappointment, shame, sadness, fear, and guilt cannot be denied, they will generally be experienced as a threat to masculine identity.

The restrictions on (the expression of) emotions that were found among adult (young) men are therefore the result of many years of interactive learning. The attributes of the cultural model are ascribed to the (neonate) boy by his parents and others, and the boy also constructs his own ideal of masculinity in virtual and practical interaction. In other words, restrictive emotionality is not a biological given, but the result of a lack of practice: boys and men do not have the opportunity to practice sensibility instead of toughness. They lack the examples during socialization, and must face the danger of social rejection when they transgress the stoic norm of the cultural model. Brannon (1976) underlined this normative aspect and its consequences by introducing "No Sissy Stuff" as one of the attributes of traditional masculinity.

Contrasting masculine restrictive emotionality with the greater emotional expressivity and the higher level of intimacy among women is not without dangers. The first of these is that the contrast may imply a sexual dichotomy between men and women, thus denying the fact that gender and not sex is at issue here: non-traditional androgynous men may be as sensitive to their tender feelings as women are. The second danger is that female emotionality and intimacy come to function as the exclusive standards for evaluating masculine feelings. The particular nature of affective interaction between men may be overlooked easily when these standards are employed. Baumeister and Sommer (1997) have paved the way for future research in this respect with their discussion of masculine forms of relating closely. They acknowledge that men are not intimate, as it is commonly understood, but they take issue with the observation that men desire independence (Cross & Madson, 1997). Men favor other kinds of sociality, they argue, in which social connections are established in different ways, for example through shared activities. It is worthwile to investigate minutely the emotional communication in these relationships. It may reveal masculine forms of emotionality that do not fit in with current frameworks, because they are of a non-intimate nature.

Current psychological research about masculine identity and emotionality warrants the conclusion that the ways in which men cope with their feelings will change when parents succeed in socializing their sons in less traditional ways. Next to this, adult men will experience a less restricted kind of emotionality when they take the trouble to reconstruct their identities. Whether the actual changes in male experience and expression of emotions will be as they are predicted by current psychological knowledge is a question that must be answered in future research about the emotional life of men.

References

Averill, J. R. (1983). Studies on anger and aggression: Implications for theories of emotion. *American Psychologist, 38*, 1145–1160.

Barclay, C. R. (1993). Remembering ourselves. In G. M. Davies & R. H. Logie (Eds.), *Memory in everyday life* (pp. 285–310). Amsterdam: Elsevier.

Baumeister, R. F., & Sommer, K. L. (1997). What do men want? Gender differences and two spheres of belongingness: Comment on Cross and Madson (1997). *Psychological Bulletin, 122*, 38–44.

Bischoping, K. (1993). Gender differences in conversation topics, 1922–1990. *Sex Roles, 28*, 1–13.

Bosma, H. A. (1995). Identity and identity processes: What are we talking about? In A. Oosterwegel & R. A. Wicklund (Eds.), *The self in European and North-American culture: Development and processes* (pp. 5–17). Dordrecht: Kluwer Academic Publishers.

Brannon, R. (1976). The male sex-role: Our culture's blueprint for manhood, what it's done for us lately. In D. David & R. Brannon (Eds.), *The forty-nine percent majority: The male sex role* (pp. 1–49). Reading, MA: Addison-Wesley.

Brannon, R. (1985). A scale for measuring attitudes toward masculinity. In A. Sargent (Ed.), *Beyond sex-roles* (2nd Edn., pp. 110–116). St-Paul, MN: West.

Brody, L. R. (1993). On understanding gender differences in the expression of emotions. In S. Ablon, D. Brown, J. Mack, & E. Khantazian (Eds.), *Human feelings: Explorations in affect development and meaning* (pp. 87–121). Hillsdale, NJ: Analytic Press.

Brody, L. R. (1997). Gender and emotion: beyond stereotypes. *Journal of Social Issues*, *53*, 369–394.

Brody, L. R., & Hall, J. A. (1993). Gender and emotion. In M. Lewis & J. Haviland (Eds.), *Handbook of emotions* (pp. 447–460). New York: Guilford Press.

Chodorow, N. (1978). *The reproduction of mothering: Psychoanalysis and the sociology of gender*. Berkeley: University of California Press.

Chodorow, N. (1989). *Feminism and psychoanalytic theory*. New Haven, CT: Yale University Press.

Cleary, P. D. (1987). Gender differences in stress related disorders. In R. C. Barnett, L. Biener, & G. K. Baruch (Eds.), *Gender and stress* (pp. 39–72). New York: Free Press.

Cooper, A. M. (1996). What men fear: The facade of castration anxiety. In G. I. Fogel, F. M. Lane, & R. S. Liebert (Eds.), *The psychology of men* (pp. 113–130). New Haven: Yale University Press.

Copenhaver, M. M., & Eisler, R. M. (1996). Masculine gender role stress. A perspective on men's health. In P. M. Kato & T. Mann (Eds.), *Handbook of diversity issues in health psychology* (pp. 219–236). New York: Plenum Press.

Cross, S. E., & Madson, L. (1997). Models of the self: self-construals and gender. *Psychological Bulletin*, *122*, 5–37.

Derlega, V. J., Metts, S., Petronio, S., & Margulis, S. T. (1993). *Self-disclosure*. Newbury Park, CA: Sage.

Derlega, V. J., Winstead, B., Wong, P., & Hunter, S. (1985). Gender effects in an initial encounter: A case where men exceed women in disclosure. *Journal of Social and Personal Relationships*, *2*, 25–44.

Dindia, K., & Allen, M. (1992). Sex differences in self-disclosure: A meta-analysis. *Psychological Bulletin*, *112*, 106–124.

Dion, K. K., & Dion, K. L. (1985). Personality, gender, and the phenomenology of romantic love. In Ph. Shaver (Ed.) *Review of personality and social psychology* (Vol. 6, pp. 209–239). London: Sage.

Duindam, V. (1997). *Zorgende vaders* [Caring fathers]. Amsterdam: Van Gennep.

Duindam, V., & Spruijt, E. (1997). Caring fathers in the Netherlands. *Sex Roles*, *36*, 149–171.

Dunn, J., Bretherton, I., & Munn, P. (1987). Conversations about feeling states between mothers and their children. *Developmental Psychology*, *23*, 132–139.

Eaton, W. O., & Enns, L. R. (1986). Sex differences in human motor activity level. *Psychological Bulletin*, *100*, 19–28.

Eisler, R. M. (1995). The relationship between masculine gender role stress and men's health risk: The validation of a construct. In R. F. Levant & W. S. Pollack (Eds.), *A new psychology of men* (pp. 229–252). New York: Harper Collins.

Fischer, A. H. (1991). *Emotion scripts – a study of the social and cognitive facets of emotions*. Leiden: DSWO Press.

Fischer, A. H. (1993). Sex differences in emotionality. *Feminism and Psychology*, *3*, 303–318.

Fischer, A. H., & Jansz, J. (1995). Reconciling emotions with Western personhood. *Journal for the Theory of Social Behaviour*, *25*, 59–81.

Fivush, R. (1989). Exploring sex differences in the emotional content of mother-child conversations about the past. *Sex Roles*, *20*, 675–691.

Gleason, J. (1989). Sex differences in parent-child interaction. In S. Philips, S. Steel, & C. Tanz (Eds.), *Language, gender, and sex in comparative perspective* (pp. 189–199). Cambridge University Press.

Greenson, R. (1968). Disidentification from mother: Its special importance for the boy. *International Journal of Psychoanalysis, 49,* 370–374.

Harré, R. (1983). *Personal being.* Oxford: Blackwell.

Harré, R. (1991). *Physical being: A theory for corporeal psychology.* Oxford: Blackwell.

Harris, I. A. (1995). *Messages men hear. Constructing masculinities.* London: Taylor & Francis.

Haviland, J. J., & Malatesta, C. Z. (1981). The development of sex-differences in non-verbal signals: Fallacies, facts, and fantasies. In C. Mayo & N. M. Henly (Eds.), *Gender and nonverbal behavior* (pp. 183–208). New York: Springer.

Holland, D. C. (1992). How cultural systems become desire: a case study of American romance. In R. D'Andrade & C. Strauss (Eds.), *Human motives and cultural models* (pp. 61–90). Cambridge: Cambridge University Press.

Hondagneu-Sotelo, P., & Messner, M. A. (1994). Gender displays and men's power: the 'New Man' and the Mexican immigrant man. In H. Brod & M. Kaufman (Eds.), *Theorizing masculinities* (pp. 200–219). Thousand Oaks, CA: Sage.

Jansz, J. (1991). *Person, self, and moral demands. Individualism contested by collectivism.* Leiden: DSWO Press.

Jansz, J. (1996). Constructed motives. *Theory and Psychology, 6,* 471–484.

Jansz, J. (in press). Doing identity. A conceptual framework for the study of contemporary masculinity. In: W. Maiers (Ed.). *Conceptual issues in psychology.* North York: Captus Press.

Jourard, S. (1974). Some lethal aspects of the male role. In J. H. Pleck & J. Sawyer (Eds.), *Men and masculinity* (pp. 21–29). Englewood Cliffs, NJ: Prentice Hall.

Kimmel, M. S. (1994). Masculinity as homophobia: Fear, shame, and silence in the construction of gender identity. In H. Brod & M. Kaufman (Eds.), *Theorizing masculinities* (pp. 119–142). Thousand Oaks, CA: Sage.

Kimmel, M. S., & M. A. Messner (Eds.) (1989). *Men's lives.* New York: MacMillan.

Labott, S. M., Martin, R. B., Eason, P. S., & Berkey, E. Y. (1991). Social reactions to the expression of emotion. *Cognition and Emotion, 5,* 397–417.

LaFrance, M., & Banaji, M. (1992). Toward a reconsideration of the gender-emotion relationship. In M. S. Clark (Ed.), *Emotion and social behavior. Review of Personality and Social Psychology* (Vol. 14, pp. 178–201). London: Sage.

Lash, S. J., Eisler, R. M., & Schulman, R. S. (1990). Cardiovascular reactivity to stress in men. *Behavior Modification, 14,* 3–20.

Lash, S. J., Gillespie, B. L., Eisler, R. M., & Southard, D. R. (1991). Sex differences in cardiovascular reactivity: Effects of the gender relevance of the stressor. *Health Psychology, 6,* 392–398.

Lazur, R. F., & Majors, R. (1995). Men of color: Ethnocultural variations of male gender role strain. In R. F. Levant & W. S. Pollack (Eds.), *A new psychology of men* (pp. 337–359). New York: HarperCollins.

Leaper, C., Carson, M., Baker, C., Holliday, H., & Myers, S. (1995). Self-disclosure and listener verbal support in same-gender and cross-gender friends' conversations. *Sex Roles, 33,* 387–405.

Levant, R. F. (1995). Toward the reconstruction of masculinity. In R. F. Levant & W. S. Pollack (Eds.), *A new psychology of men* (pp. 229–252). New York: HarperCollins.

Levant, R. F., Hirsch, L., Celentano, E., Cozza, T., Hill, S., MacEachern, M., Marty, N., & Schnedeker, J. (1992). The male role: An investigation of norms and stereotypes. *Journal of Mental Health Counseling, 14,* 325–377.

Levant, R. F., & Kelly, J. (1989). *Between father and child.* New York: Viking.

Levant, R. F., & Pollack, W. S. (Eds.) (1995). *A new psychology of men.* New York: Harper Collins.

Levenson, R., Carstensen, L., & Gottman, J. (1994). The influence of age and gender on affect, physiology, and their interrelations: A study of long-term marriages. *Journal of Personality and Social Psychology, 67,* 56–68.

Long, D. (1987). Working with men who batter. In M. Scher, M. Stevens, C. Good, & G. A. Eichenfield (Eds.), *Handbook of counseling and psychotherapy with men* (pp. 305–320). Newbury Park, CA: Sage.

Mac An Ghaill, M. (1994). The making of black English masculinities. In H. Brod & M. Kaufman (Eds.), *Theorizing masculinities* (pp. 183–200). Thousand Oaks, CA: Sage.

Maccoby, E. (1990). Gender and relationships: A developmental account. *American Psychologist, 45,* 513–520.

Mahler, M. S. (1972). On the first three sub-phases of separation-individuation process. *International Journal of Psychoanalysis, 53,* 333–338.

Majors, R., & Mancini Billson, J. (1992). *Cool pose: The dilemmas of black manhood in America.* New York: Lexington Books.

McConatha, J. T., Leone, F. M. & Armstrong, J. M. (1997). Emotional control in adulthood. *Psychological Reports, 80,* 499–507.

Munder Ross, J. (1996). Beyond the phallic illusion: Notes on man's heterosexuality. In G. I. Fogel, F. M. Lane & R. S. Liebert (Eds.), *The psychology of men* (pp. 49–70). New Haven: Yale University Press.

O'Neil, J. M., Helms, B. J., Gable, R. K., David, L., & Wrightsman, L. S. (1986). Gender role conflict scale: College men's fear of femininity. *Sex Roles, 14,* 335–350.

O'Neil, J. M., Good, G. E., & Holmes, S. (1995). Fifteen years of theory and research on men's gender role conflict: New paradigms for empirical research. In R. F. Levant, & W. S. Pollack (Eds.), *A new psychology of men* (pp. 164–207). New York: Harper Collins.

Parker, I. (1995). Masculinity and cultural change: Wild men. *Culture and Psychology, 1,* 455–475.

Pennebaker, J. W., Hughes, C. F., & O'Heeron, R. C. (1987). The psychophysiology of confession: Linking inhibitory and psychosomatic processes. *Journal of Personality and Social Psychology, 52,* 781–793.

Pennebaker, J. W., Kiecolt-Glaser, J., & Glaser, R. (1988). Disclosure of trauma's and immune function: Health implications for psychotherapy. *Journal of Consulting and Clinical Psychology, 56,* 239–245.

Pleck, J. H. (1981). *The myth of masculinity.* Cambridge, MA: MIT Press.

Pleck, J. H. (1995). The gender-role strain paradigm. An update. In R. F. Levant & W. S. Pollack (Eds.), *A new psychology of men* (pp. 11–33). New York: Harper Collins.

Pleck, J. H., Sonenstein, F. L., & Ku, L. C., (1993). Masculinity ideology: Its impact on adolescent males' heterosexual relationships. *Journal of Social Issues, 49,* 11–29.

Pollack, W. S. (1990). Men's development and psychotherapy: A psychoanalytic perspective. *Psychotherapy, 27,* 316–321.

Quinn, N., & Holland, D. (1987). Culture and cognition. In: D. Holland, & N. Quinn, *Cultural models in language and thought* (pp. 3–40). New York: Cambridge University Press.

Ross, C. E., & Mirowski, J. (1984). Men who cry. *Social Psychological Quarterly, 47,* 146–159.

Rubin, Z., Peplau, L. A., & Hill, C. T. (1981). Loving and leaving: Sex differences in romantic attachments. *Sex Roles, 8*, 625–638.

Rybarczyk, B. (1994). Diversity among American men: The impact of aging, ethnicity, and race. In C. T. Kilmartin (Ed.), *The masculine self* (pp. 113–132). New York: MacMillan.

Shields, S. A. (1991). Gender in the psychology of emotion: A selective research review. In K. T. Strongman (Ed.), *International Review of Studies on Emotion* (Vol. 1, pp. 227–245). Chichester: Wiley.

Shotter, J. (1989). Social accountability and the social construction of 'you'. In J. Shotter & K. J. Gergen (Eds.), *Texts of identity* (pp. 133–152). London: Sage.

Siegel, S., & Alloy, L. (1990). Interpersonal perceptions and consequences of depressive-significant other relationships: A naturalistic study of college roommates. *Journal of Abnormal Psychology, 99*, 361–373.

Sifneos, P. E. (1996). Alexithymia: Past and present. *American Journal of Psychiatry, 153*, 137–142.

Strauss, C. (1992). Models and motives. In R. D'Andrade & C. Strauss (Eds.) *Human motives and cultural models* (pp. 1–21). Cambridge University Press.

Tannen, D. (1990). *You just don't understand.* New York: Ballantine Books.

Thompson, E. H., Pleck, J. H., & Ferrera, D. (1992). Men and masculinities: Scales for masculinity ideology and masculinity-related constructs. *Sex Roles, 27*, 573–607.

Vygotsky, L. S. (1978). *Mind in society. The development of higher psychological processes.* Cambridge, MA: Harvard University Press.

Wagner, H. L., MacDonald, C. J., & Manstead, A. S. R. (1986). Communication of individual emotions by spontaneous facial expressions. *Journal of Personality and Social Psychology, 50*, 737–743.

Wertsch, J. V., & Stone, C. A. (1985). The concept of internalization in Vygotsky's account of the genesis of higher mental functions. In J. V. Wertsch (Ed.), *Culture, communication, and cognition: Vygotskian perspectives* (pp. 162–179). New York: Cambridge University Press.

Zeman, J., & Garber, J. (1996). Display rules for anger, sadness, and pain: It depends on who is watching. *Child Development, 67*, 957–973.

PART III

Distinct emotions

9. Women, men, and positive emotions: A social role interpretation

MICHELE G. ALEXANDER AND WENDY WOOD

Considerable publicity has surrounded research on sex differences in negative emotional experiences, especially the tendency for women to experience greater depression, personal discomfort, and mental disorganization than men (e.g., Gove, 1978; Nolen-Hoeksema, 1987). However, an exclusive focus on sex differences in negative affect could suggest that women's emotional states in general are more negative than men's. Adopting a broader perspective on emotion that includes positive emotions reveals quite a different picture of sex differences. As we will demonstrate in our present review of the research literature, women not only report experiencing more negative feelings, but also more positive emotions.

The seemingly paradoxical finding that women report more positive as well as negative emotions than men can be understood if positive and negative affect are conceptualized as separate, unipolar dimensions. When research participants rate their global experience of good versus bad emotions, these two dimensions typically emerge as statistically independent (Diener, 1984; Diener & Emmons, 1985; Warr, Barter, & Brownbridge, 1983; although see Green, Goldman, & Salovey, 1993). The independence of positive and negative affect in reports of global emotions is apparently due to the combined effects of two qualities of emotion, intensity and frequency. Ratings of emotional intensity typically are positively correlated, so that people possess a characteristic level of emotional intensity across both positive and negative dimensions. That is, some people typically experience intense, passionate emotions (both positive and negative ones) and others experience relatively placid, subdued emotions (Diener, Larsen, Levine, & Emmons, 1985; Diener, Suh, Smith, & Shao, 1995; Moore & Isen, 1990). In contrast, frequency of emotional experience in the two hedonic domains is inversely related, so that at any given time, the experience of either positive or negative emotions apparently suppresses the experience of the other. With global ratings, which essentially collapse across intensity and frequency, positive and negative emotions emerge as independent of each other.

In this chapter, emotions will be defined as a broad syndrome of socially regulated experiences that includes subjective labeling, physiological reactions, expressive reactions, and behavior (Cornelius, 1996; Smith & Pope, 1992). According to social constructivist theories, these aspects of emotional response are regulated by social norms and arise from beliefs about the appropriate and valued responses associated with emotion in a given culture (Averill, 1982). In Western societies, for example, joy and happiness are pleasant experiences that most often arise in relationships with friends, and are associated with warmth, relaxed muscles, increased heartbeat, smiling facial expression, laughter, and enthusiastic speech (Mesquita & Frijda, 1992; Shaver, Schwartz, Kirson, & O'Connor, 1987). In contrast, love is a relatively enduring state or relationship with a highly valued other person, associated with proximity- and contact-seeking, with an intense desire for the other's interest and reciprocation, and, for romantic love, with sexual arousal (Cornelius, 1996; Shaver et al., 1987). Although other positive emotions, such as hope and surprise, might also represent discrete emotions that yield meaningful sex differences (see the extensive discussions of basic emotions by Plutchik [1984] and Shaver, Wu, and Schwartz [1992]), the present review targets those emotions that have been the primary focus of research to date, specifically love and the constellation of happiness, joy, and well-being.

Social roles and sex differences in emotion

Why might men and women differ in their experience and expression of positive emotions? In our view, sex differences in emotion, much like other sex differences in social behavior, arise from the social roles held by men and women in a society (Eagly, 1987; Eagly & Wood, 1991, 1999).[1] According to Social Role Theory, sex differences in social behavior stem from a society's gender hierarchy and from its sex-typed division of labor.

In contemporary American society, as in many world societies, women have less power and status than men and control fewer resources. In addition, as the division of labor is realized in the United States and in many other nations, women spend fewer hours in paid employment than men and perform more domestic work. Although most women in the United States are employed in the paid workforce, they have lower wages than men, are disproportionately represented in caretaking positions (e.g., nurse, teacher, social worker), and are thinly represented at the highest levels of organizational hierarchies (Anderson & Tomaskovic-Devey, 1995; Reskin & Padavik, 1994). Within the home, women are more likely to be involved in child care than men and, regardless of women's employment status, women perform a large share of household duties (Biernat & Wortman, 1991; Calasanti & Bailey, 1991; Hochschild, 1989). Similarly, caretaking of the elderly is still predominantly performed by women in Western societies, with the majority of caretakers being daughters, wives, and female in-laws (Horowitz, 1985; Stone, Cafferata, & Sangl, 1987).

Caretaking activities are linked to the experience and expression of positive emotions because emotions are important in establishing and maintaining relations with others. Sensitivity to others' emotions and emotional expressiveness are skills that enhance caretakers' effectiveness and should be especially useful with infants, infirm, and elderly who are unable to communicate verbally. Positive emotions such as happiness and love generally facilitate relationship formation and maintenance by enhancing one's attractiveness to others, improving interaction partners' well-being, and maintaining intimacy, trust, and interdependent relations with others (Berry & Hansen, 1996; Leary, 1995).

Sex differences in emotion may also arise from differences in the status of men's and women's roles in society. Although social status is multifaceted (including, for example, political power and ownership of property), and men and women do not differ in all societies on all dimensions, when differences in status are found, men tend to hold higher status positions than women (Whyte, 1978). Occupants of low-status roles are likely to be discouraged from expressing negative emotions that challenge authority. Expression of positive emotions allows low status people to establish affective ties with those in power and to demonstrate their own positive motivation in support of the goals of higher status others (Meeker & Weitzel-O'Neill, 1977; Ridgeway & Berger, 1986; Wood & Karten, 1986).

The social role analysis, then, anticipates sex differences in specific kinds of positive emotional experiences, those associated with maintaining relationships, caring for others, and expressing solidarity and support. Women are not likely to demonstrate especially high levels of positive emotions that are not associated with these relationship-type goals, such as pride in one's own performance and favorable self-evaluation. Some support for this idea comes from Stoppard and Gunn Gruchy's (1993) research on sex differences in emotional responses to success. Their participants judged positive self-directed emotions (i.e., pride over own success) as more likely to be experienced by men than by women and other-directed positive emotions (i.e., joy for a friend's success) as more likely to be experienced by women. In addition, the social consequences of expressing these positive emotions may differ for women and men (Stoppard & Gunn Gruchy, 1993); women may expect greater social rewards for expressing happiness over others' success than pride over own success, whereas men anticipate social rewards for both emotions.

According to social role theory, the greater power and status associated with men's roles in most societies and the different activities associated with men's and women's roles generate sex differences in individuals' behavior through psychological and social processes. One set of processes involves gender role beliefs, in which persons of each sex are believed to have characteristics that equip them for sex-typical work roles and for the relative social status and power of those roles. The normative expectations associated with gender roles foster behaviors consistent with the demands of sex-typical activities.

The content of gender roles within a society can be inferred from the generally held social stereotypes about the sexes. When Western college students are asked to describe men and women, the typical woman in our society is believed to be more emotionally expressive, concerned with her own and others' feeling states, and emotionally labile than the typical man (Broverman, Vogel, Broverman, Clarkson, & Rosenkrantz 1972; Swim, 1994; Williams & Best, 1990). The expression of positive feeling in particular is believed to be more characteristic of women than of men (Birnbaum, Nosanchuk, & Croll, 1980; Stoppard & Gunn Gruchy, 1993). These stereotypic beliefs about sex differences represent socially learned rules about how men and women, for example, appraise emotionally relevant situations, how they behave in response to the appraisal, and how they interpret bodily reactions.

To the extent that normative expectations about emotional behavior appropriate to women and men become internalized as part of individuals' self-concepts and personalities, people can be described as forming dispositions or traits that are consistent with gender roles (Feingold, 1994; Wood, Christensen, Hebl, & Rothgerber, 1997). Women and others who have many opportunities in daily life to express positive emotions and engage in nurturant behavior are likely to develop a self-concept of themselves as happy and nurturant. Indeed, women score higher than men on personality scales assessing communal attributes such as gentle and compassionate (e.g., the BSRI, Bem, 1981; the PAQ, Spence & Helmreich, 1978). People may also behave consistently with their gender roles without necessarily acquiring dispositions that foster such behavior (see Olson, Roese, & Zanna, 1996; Skrypnek & Snyder, 1982; Wood & Karten, 1986).

A second set of processes that fosters sex differences in emotion is the acquisition by men and women of different skills and beliefs through performance of sex-typed social roles (e.g., for girls, performing child-care) and through other socialization experiences. Brody and Hall's (1993) review of socialization processes in Western societies suggests that parents encourage happiness in girls more than boys through mod-eling, smiling, and conversing (Dunn, Bretherton, & Munn, 1987; Fivush, 1989; Halberstadt, Fox, & Jones, 1993; Malatesta & Haviland, 1982; see also Brody, this volume; Fivush & Buckner, this volume). These kinds of sex-typed socialization experiences equip males and females to perform sex-appropriate tasks within society.

Empirical evidence for sex differences in positive emotional experiences

From a social role perspective, men and women are likely to possess sex-differentiated skills, beliefs, and subjective experiences that con-tribute to successful enactment of sex-typed social roles (Eagly & Wood, 1999). Thus, women's socialization and past role-related experi-ence are likely to instil the subjective emotions and external emotional responding that facilitate the performance of caretaking and nurturing roles. In addition, consistency between public and private expressions of emotion is anticipated by classic theories in social psychology out-lining the processes by which people's self-reports shift to correspond to their behavior (Bem, 1972; Festinger, 1957). Thus, it is possible that sex differences will emerge in all of the components of emotional expe-rience, reflecting an overall tendency for women to respond more pos-itively than men.

Reports of happiness and well-being

Most of the research on sex differences in happiness, well-being, and life satisfaction has relied on self-reports of emotion. Consistent with social role predictions, when exposed to specific emotional stimuli, women report experiencing pleasant stimuli (e.g., pictures of babies) more intensely than do men (Grossman & Wood, 1993; Lang, Greenwald, Bradley, & Hamm, 1993), and when asked to report intensity of reaction to stories with positive outcomes, women report more intense happi-ness than do men (Brody, 1993). Sex differences have also been found in global reports of happiness and joy, with women reporting more intense experiences and expressions than do men (Allen & Haccoun, 1976; Brody, 1996). In addition, on self-report inventories of subjective expe-rience, women report more intense positive affect than do men (e.g., Larsen, Diener, & Emmons's [1986] Affect Intensity Measure; Diener,

Sandvik, & Larsen, 1985; Fujita, Diener, & Sandvik, 1991; Larsen & Diener, 1987), and on self-report measures of outward expression of emotions, women score higher than men (e.g., King & Emmons' [1990] Emotional Expressiveness Questionnaire). In summary, then, sex differences in *intensity* of happiness appear to hold for both experience and expression.

Less consensus has emerged among researchers concerning sex differences in the *frequency* of positive emotions. Although a number of studies have found that women report more frequent experience of joy than do men (Balswick & Avertt, 1977; Fujita et al., 1991; Sprecher & Sedikides, 1993), no sex difference was obtained by Allen and Haccoun (1976). In an attempt to directly compare intensity measures with frequency measures (called "hedonic level"), Fujita and his colleagues (1991) estimated sex differences on a variety of indices and concluded that consistent differences emerge only on intensity. We question this conclusion, however, because the research did not clearly distinguish between frequency and intensity. For example, the number of emotions participants could recall experiencing within the last year was classified as a measure of intensity, whereas the extent to which participants experienced emotions daily (with each emotion rated on a scale ranging from *not at all* to *extremely much*) was classified as a measure of frequency. Despite the inconsistent labeling of the measures, for our purposes Fujita et al.'s (1991) important finding is that all indices yielded at least trends for more extreme positive responses of women than men, and none yielded effects in the reverse direction. It thus appears that, when sex differences emerge on measures of frequency, women report experiencing positive emotions more frequently than do men.

In addition to self-reports of joy and happiness, sex differences appear in subjective well-being, as reflected in ratings of overall life happiness and satisfaction with life. Subjective well-being has been defined as frequent positive affect, infrequent negative affect, and global life satisfaction (Myers & Diener, 1995). Women appear to report slightly higher levels of happiness and life satisfaction on a variety of indicators and across a variety of cultures than do men (Inglehart, 1990; Lee, Seccombe, & Shehan, 1991; Wood, Rhodes, & Whelan, 1989). Given that women also report greater negative affect and distress than men (e.g., Gove, 1978), few sex differences are likely to be found on scales that tap both aspects of emotion (e.g., including items assessing both positive and negative affect, or assessing well-being on bipolar scales that range from positive to negative affect). With these kinds of measures women's greater reports of negative affect are likely to cancel their greater reports of positive affect (Wood et al., 1989).

Experience and expression of love and affection

On self-report measures that directly assess love, liking, and affection, women have been found to report more intense warmth, love, and concern for others than do men (Balswick, 1982, 1988; Spence & Helmreich, 1978). The sex difference in self-reports of love intensity may, however, be limited to certain targets, or recipients of love (Rubin, 1970). Although women report more intense love for same-sex friends than do men, men and women report experiencing equally intense love feelings for romantic partners. It is also interesting that men and women have been found to differ in the way they experience romantic love, with women emphasizing intimacy and passion more than men and men emphasizing sexuality more than women (e.g., Hendrick & Hendrick, 1991; Singelis, Choo, & Hatfield, 1995).

Although little empirical research has examined directly sex differences in expressions of love in relationships, men and women differ on a number of factors associated with emotional expression. Women report that they express greater intimacy than do men in interactions with others (King & Emmons, 1990), women self-disclose more than do men (Dindia & Allen, 1992), women appear to be more skilled in communicating love to others (Golding, 1990), and women report more confidence, or self-efficacy, in their ability to express love, liking, and affection than do men (Blier & Blier-Wilson, 1989). These findings are consistent with women expressing love more frequently and intensely than men.

Physiological indicators of emotion

Most of what we know about sex differences in psychophysiological responding comes from comparisons between husbands' and wives' responses during marital conflict. Consequently, we know more about the sexes' physiological behavior during negative experiences than during positive ones and we cannot be certain that differences between husbands and wives in marital relationships represent general differences between men and women. Despite these limitations, psychophysiological research has yielded intriguing sex differences.

Early research on the relation between psychophysiological responses and overt expression of emotion suggested that men and women differ in the ways they experience emotions (Buck, 1984; Buck, Savin, Miller, & Caul, 1972; Buck, Miller, & Caul, 1974). Men supposedly are internalizers of emotional experience who have inhibited overt emotional expression and as a result use "hidden internal avenues of affect discharge" (Buck et al., 1974, p. 595). Women, in contrast, are thought to be externalizers who express their emotions outwardly rather than at an internal, physiological level. Contrary to a social role analysis, then, this perspective anticipates that sex differences in psychophysiological responding are likely to reflect more extreme reactions by men than by women.

Among the many physiological indicators of emotion that tap arousal, larger changes in skin conductance response appear to be associated with extremely pleasant or extremely unpleasant stimuli or experiences (Bradley, Cuthbert, & Lang, 1990; Levenson, 1992). The sex differences that have been found in electrodermal responding do not yield clear interpretation. Although men have been found to display higher levels of skin conductance responses than women at resting levels (Hare, Wood, Britain, & Frazelle, 1971) and during the negative experience of discussing conflict topics in distressed marriages (Gottman & Levenson, 1992), a sex difference in skin conductance has not been found during positive affective experiences (Kring & Gordon, 1998).

For cardiovascular activity, as represented in measures of heart rate and blood pressure, men and women have also been found to differ during negative emotional experiences, but no clear pattern of sex differences has emerged for positive experiences. Specifically, wives in distressed marriages experience greater heart rate and blood pressure elevation during conflict discussions than do wives in nondistressed marriages and than do husbands in general (Ewart, Taylor, Kraemer, & Agras, 1991; Gottman & Levenson, 1992). During positive or supportive experiences, however, no differences have emerged between the change in men's and in women's blood pressure (Kiecolt-Glaser et al., 1993), nor in men's and in women's heart rate (Lang et al., 1993; Levenson, Ekman, & Friesen, 1990).

Endocrine functioning is also related to emotional experience, with greater levels of the hormones epinephrine, norepinephrine, and cortisol reflecting stronger arousal and stress reactions. In general, women generate stronger endocrine responses to both positive and negative emotional events than do men. Specifically, when husbands and wives engage in negative conflict behavior (e.g., criticizing), wives but not husbands reveal increased cortisol, greater norepinephrine release, and increased epinephrine (Kiecolt-Glaser, Newton, Cacioppo, MacCallum, Glaser, & Malarkey, 1996; Kiecolt-Glaser, Glaser, Cacioppo, MacCallum, Snydersmith, Kim, & Malarkey, 1997; Malarkey, Kiecolt-Glaser, Pearl, & Glaser, 1994). Similarly, during positive interactions, wives but not husbands show decreased epinephrine levels (Kiecolt-Glaser et al., 1996).

Measures of facial muscle movements, or electromyography (EMG), tap valence of emotional experience. In general, the evidence for sex differences in EMG responses are consistent with findings from nonverbal research that women are more facially expressive than men (see Hall, Carter, & Horgan, this volume; LaFrance & Hecht, this volume). The motor responses tapped by EMG measures, however, are more subtle than the overt displays in encoding research; they typically are not detectable by an observer and thus are unlikely to reflect social responses to others (Cacioppo, Petty, Lorsch, & Kim, 1986). It is noteworthy that women's facial EMG responses correspond more highly with their self-reports of negative and positive affect than do men's (Grossman & Wood, 1993; Schwartz, Brown, & Ahern, 1980), and men's autonomic arousal levels correspond more highly with their self-reports than do women's (Harver, Katkin, & Bloch, 1993; Levenson, Carstensen, & Gottman, 1992; Pennebaker & Roberts, 1992). The different patterns in correspondence imply that men and women may draw on different physiological events in their subjective experience of emotion, rather than rely on internal versus external cues (Roberts & Pennebaker, 1995).

In short, when sex differences have been found on neuroendocrine and EMG responses, these generally reflect more intense positive emotional responses of women than men. Even though the majority of research has focused on negative affective stimuli and much of it has been limited to married couples, sufficient evidence is available to counter the notion that men are internalizers of emotional experience who respond at a physiological level whereas women are externalizers with minimal physiological reactivity (cf. Buck et al., 1974). Instead, physiological indicators of positive emotion either reveal no sex difference or find that women are more internally reactive and more facially expressive than men.

Summary

Our review of the research literature on the various components of emotional experience revealed a relatively consistent sex difference. Women report more intense positive emotions than men, they more frequently express such emotions to others, and they respond more extremely on certain psychophysiological measures, especially endocrine levels and facial muscle movement.

Some inconsistency also emerged across study findings, which is to be expected given that past research has sometimes evaluated discrete positive and negative emotions and sometimes aggregated positive and negative dimensions together into a single index of general emotionality. Women are likely to report more intense and more frequent emotions than men on scales that assess positive emotions separate from negative ones, whereas on scales that collapse across positive and negative dimensions, the tendency for women to experience greater positive as well as negative emotion is likely to yield no overall sex difference (Wood et al., 1989).

Evidence for the social role account of sex differences in positive emotions

Indirect evidence for a normative, role-based account of sex differences in positive emotions comes from the finding that sex differences in positive emotions vary with the social roles held by men and women. In particular, sex differences in happiness and life satisfaction vary with respondents' marital status.

Marital roles and sex differences in emotion

Reports of well-being are higher among married people than among unmarried ones (Lee et al., 1991; Wood et al., 1989). Furthermore, the sex difference of women's greater well-being is found primarily among married respondents (Wood et al., 1989); unmarried men and women do not differ in overall well-being. One explanation for this sex differences in positive emotion among married people is that women invest more in close relationships than do men and they play the role of emotional specialists in their marriages (Wood et al., 1989). Indeed, social expectations are that women are more responsible than men for the emotional tenor of the marriage (Cancian & Gordon, 1988).

The greater effects of marital status on women's than men's happiness is part of the general phenomenon that women's happiness is linked to relationships with others more than is men's. For example, women's well-being is facilitated by social support from others more than is men's (Cohen & Wills, 1985). Women college students more than men report that their important life goals depend on social resources such as emotional control, social skills, family and friend support, and romantic relationships (Diener & Diener, 1995; Diener & Fujita, 1995). Similarly, conveying friendliness has been found to be female college students' primary concern in the impressions they make on others (Leary, 1995). Male college students also include friendliness among their top four impression goals, but their primary concern is to be perceived as intelligent and accomplished.

Sex differences in the expression of positive emotions among the married arise in part because of the different activities performed by wives than husbands: wives engage in nurturing activities and assume responsibility for relationship maintenance, activities that involve expressing positive emotions to others. In addition, given the importance of close relationships to women's successful role performance, women are especially likely to experience well-being and other positive emotions when they establish and maintain such relations with others, both inside and outside of marriage. In this account, women more than men are sensitive to and place value on the benefits of close relations and are more likely to experience well-being upon successfully enacting such relations with others (Wood et al., 1997). According to our social role perspective, then, the closer link for women than men between positive emotions and relations with others arises from the behaviors required to perform their respective social roles and the emotions they experience as part of role performance and as a consequence of those roles.

Sex differences in emotions and experimental manipulations of norms

Direct evidence that stereotyped expectations and roles influence positive emotions comes from research that has examined the relation between normative expectations and men's and women's emotions. In an initial study, Grossman and Wood (1993) investigated whether participants' beliefs in sex-role norms concerning emotion covaried with their personal experience of emotions. Overall, women reported more extreme feelings and expressions of love, joy, fear, and sadness than men and participants endorsed sex stereotypes for emotionality, judging typical women more extreme on these emotions. Most importantly, participants' own emotional experiences were correlated with their stereotypic expectations about the sexes; women who endorsed the stereotype that women are more emotional than men reported more extreme emotions themselves and men who endorsed the same stereotypes reported relatively subdued emotions.

To test directly whether sex differences in emotion are a function of social norms, Grossman and Wood (1993) experimentally manipulated normative expectations for men's and women's emotional behavior in a second study. Experimental instructions established norms for participants to enhance or to attenuate responses while viewing a series of positive or negative emotion-inducing slides. A control condition was also included in which no explicit information was given concerning appropriate response. As expected, participants' self-reports varied with normative expectations: greater extremity emerged when participants were to enhance than to attenuate their responses. Furthermore, when norms were specified by the experimenter, no sex differences were found, presumably because expectations were comparable for both sexes. In the no-instructions control condition, however, participants appeared to rely on broader social norms and women reported more intense responding than men and, when viewing negative slides, demonstrated greater EMG corrugator activity. In sum, this research provides strong support for the idea that sex role expectations underlie sex differences in self-reports of emotion as well as sex differences in psychophysiological responding.

Emotional sex differences in a cross-cultural context

If, as we have argued, sex differences in positive emotions arise from the different social roles of men and women in society, then the nature and direction of emotion sex differences should vary between societies with different cultural norms (see also Fischer & Manstead, this volume). One of the authors of this chapter recently conducted a cross-cultural survey to assess whether the variation in gender role norms across two societies, Pakistan and the United States, indeed corresponds to individual men's and women's reports of their own positive emotional experiences (Alexander, Chaudry & Najam, 1999).

These two countries were chosen for comparison because they potentially vary with respect to collective versus individualistic norms for emotional behavior (Hofstede, 1980). Indian and Asian cultures, in comparison to US culture, place greater emphasis on the familial self and have a stronger family orientation (Roland, 1988; Sethi & Allen, 1984). Qualities of the familial self include emotional interdependence, reciprocal demands for intimacy and support, mutual caring, empathy, and sensitivity to others' needs. Sex differences in emotionality are likely to vary between collective and individualistic societies. Because Asians consider expressive characteristics and displays of family-centred orientation (e.g., family loyalty, obligation to the elderly) to be socially desirable for both men and women (Ward & Sethi, 1986), expression of positive, other-supportive emotions may be aspects of both men's and women's role relations. If so, emotional expression in both sexes may be encouraged in collectivist cultures such as Pakistan.

Thirty-four male and 57 female undergraduate students at Ohio State University in the US, and 34 male and 36 female undergraduates at the University of Lahore in Pakistan individually rated the intensity and frequency of their typical experiences of joy and love. Participants also reported their stereotypical, or normative, beliefs concerning these emotions by judging the intensity and frequency of experience for a typical man and typical woman in their respective countries.[2]

The results revealed an impressive correspondence between the normative expectations for men and women in a given culture and personal emotional behavior. Specifically, within each culture, stereotypic beliefs about feelings were related to self-reports of feelings, suggesting that men and women who believe sex-role stereotypes tend to behave consistently with them. That is, American women reported more intense and frequent feelings and expressions of joy and of love than did men, and participants reported that the typical woman feels and expresses these emotions more intensely and frequently than does the typical man. Most importantly, analyses on the correspondence between own self-reports of emotional experience and endorsement of sex stereotypes revealed positive correlations for female raters, indicating that women who believe strongly in the stereotype that women are more emotional also report greater emotionality themselves. The correlations were uniformly negative for male raters, indicating that men who believe strongly in the stereotype that women are more emotional report less emotionality themselves (see also Grossman & Wood, 1993).

For the Pakistani sample, only personal experience of emotions and not emotional expression yielded sex differences. That is, men's and women's self-reports yielded sex differences in the frequency and intensity of both love and joy, with women reporting more frequent and intense feelings. However, no differences emerged between men and women in self-reported expressions of love and joy. As we would expect, social stereotypes paralleled these sex effects in own ratings. The typical Pakistani woman was believed to feel joy and love more intensely than the typical man, but not to express these emotions any more intensely than the typical man. The correlations between Pakistani subject's own experience and their stereotypic beliefs were in the anticipated direction for personal feelings, with women reporting intense experiences of love and joy to the extent that they endorsed the stereotype that women experience more intense emotions than men, and men reporting less intense experiences of emotion to the extent that they endorsed the sex-stereotypic belief. However, consistent with the lack of sex differences in expression of emotions, weak or no correspondence emerged between either sexes' reports of own expression and their endorsement of expression stereotypes.

Several aspects of Alexander et al.'s (1999) findings are consistent with a social role interpretation. In collectivistic cultures, in which both men and women are expected to establish communal relations with others and presumably both express positive emotions to maintain close relationships, sex differences are not found in ratings of own emotional expression or in stereotypic beliefs about expression. Sex differences in personal experience and stereotypes about experience were, however, found in both countries. In addition, within each culture, subjective experience and stereotypic beliefs proved to be related. To the extent that participants believed that typical women are more emotional than typical men, women reported more emotional responsiveness themselves, and men reported less responsiveness.

Functions of women's emotional positivity

The social constructivist perspective (Averill, 1982) and our social role analysis of emotions converge in the assumption that emotions are functional and oriented to the achievement of individual and social goals. Positive emotions yield clear benefits to self and others: good feelings are an aspect of general well-being (Myers & Diener, 1995), and expression of positive emotions is associated with popularity and liking from others (Sommers, 1984) and contributes to effective group functioning (Ridgeway & Johnson, 1990; Wood, 1987). In addition, we argued in the introduction to this chapter that positive emotions have a special significance for women in Western societies, given that the experience and expression of such emotions contribute to women's effective performance of nurturing roles. Positive emotions may also be sanctioned by women's lower status positions in many societies; supportive behaviors do not challenge status hierarchies and can demonstrate low status persons' commitment to powerful others.

The assumption that positive emotions are uniquely functional for women has received support in a recent study on determinants of popularity within college student groups (Coats & Feldman, 1996). If the expression of happiness is important in woman's social networks, then a woman's ability to convey happy experiences should be linked to her social success. Indeed, popularity of members of a sorority group (i.e., sociometric status) was found to correlate more strongly with these individuals' ability to convey happiness through nonverbal facial expressions than with their ability to convey sadness or anger. The better a woman's ability to encode happiness, the greater her popularity in the group. The authors conclude that maintenance of women's friendships involves establishing rapport with others and communicating support and understanding. Among fraternity members, in contrast, ability to encode happiness was unrelated to status. Instead, the expression of anger was related to popularity in fraternities (but not in sororities), suggesting that men's friendships do not depend on social support as much as do women's.

A very different functional perspective on emotions than we have taken in this chapter is suggested by evolutionary psychology. Psychological tendencies such as sex differences in the experience and expression of positive emotions are thought to represent evolved psychological mechanisms that developed early in our species' history as adaptive responses to sex-linked reproductive problems (Buss & Schmitt, 1993; Tooby & Cosmides, 1992). In this view, sex differences reflect the differing adaptive problems faced early in human history (Buss & Schmitt, 1993), especially women's greater parental investment in each child than men's (i.e., for women, a minimum of nine months' gestation). Building on the ideas of sexual selection theory (Trivers, 1972), evolutionary psychologists have sometimes argued that women's reproductive success is maximized by ensuring the survival of each child and men's success is maximized by numbers of sexual encounters with fertile partners (e.g., Buss & Schmitt, 1993). Women's greater experience and expression of love than men's thus reflects the importance of maintaining stable, supportive long-term relationships in order to obtain the social and material resources from others that maximizes women's reproductive success (i.e., ensuring survival of each child). Women might also experience greater attachment and love for their offspring than do men, given women's greater parental investment in each child. Within this model of evolutionary processes, men and women would be expected to differ generally in the experience and expression of love. Cultural effects on evolved dispositions are potentially compatible with evolutionary analyses. Findings such as the lack of sex differences in expression of positive emotions among Alexander and Chaudry's (1999) Pakistani sample potentially can be explained through the expression of evolved dispositions being dependent on developmental processes and current social context (Tooby & Cosmides, 1992). However, evolutionary psychology approaches have rarely considered cross-cultural variability in their predictions and have typically emphasized uniformity in sex differences across cultures (e.g., Buss & Schmitt, 1993).

The general question of the validity of such evolutionary theorizing is beyond the scope of this chapter, and we refer readers to recent debates on this point (e.g., Eagly & Wood, 1999). For our purposes, it is important to note that a variety of possible evolutionary explanations are relevant to sex differences in positive emotions. In addition to perspectives that build on sexual selection theories of evolution (e.g., Buss & Schmitt, 1993), alternate theories have emphasized the common evolutionary pressures on men and women (e.g., Caporeal & Brewer, 1991; Miller & Fishkin, 1997).

Conclusion: sex differences in positive affect in everyday life

The sex differences in positive emotion that we have identified in this chapter are one component of a broader pattern of sex-typed goals, values, and attitudes concerning social relationships. Indeed, men's and women's differing goals and values in everyday relations with others is a recurring theme in the popular psychology literature. Tannen's (1990) best-seller, *You just don't understand*, suggests that women's "conversations are negotiations for closeness in which people try to seek and give confirmation and support, and to reach consensus" (p. 25), whereas men's are "negotiations in which people try to achieve and maintain the upper hand if they can, and protect themselves from others' attempts to put them down and push them around" (p. 25). Similarly, Gray's (1992) popular book, *Men are from Mars, women are from Venus*, outlines sex-typed value systems, with men oriented toward "power, competency, efficiency, and achievement" (p. 16) and women toward "love, communication, beauty, and relationships" (p. 18).

We believe that the divergent orientations of men and women have been featured so extensively in the popular literature because these differences reflect a basic organizing principle of our society. That is, sex differences in social behavior emerge from the differing social roles held by men and women. Women's roles more than men's are likely to involve caretaking and nurturing activities and to be relatively low in social status and power. Although it is probably an overstatement to treat the differing emotional responses of men and women as comparable to cross-cultural differences between societies (cf. Tannen, 1990) or to the likely differences between creatures from different worlds (cf. Gray, 1992), the differing roles that men and women fill within post-industrial Western societies have a sufficiently consistent, powerful effect to yield greater emotional responsiveness of women than men in the majority of research we reviewed. From this perspective, then, the sex differences we have noted in positive emotion are part of a broader syndrome of sex-typed skills, motivations, and behaviors that arise with sex-differentiated roles in the broader society.

Notes

1. The determinants of the distribution of men and women into social roles are many (see Wood & Eagly, 1999) and include the biological endowment of women and men. The sex-differentiated physical attributes that influence role occupancy include men's greater size and strength, and women's reproductive activities (childbearing, lactating). These physical sex differences, in interaction with a society's economic system and cultural beliefs, influence the roles held by men and women (Wood & Eagly, 1999).

2. All questionnaires were administered in English, as all subjects were fluent speakers and readers. The term "love" on the Pakistani questionnaires was replaced with "affection," given that Pakistani's direct interpretation of "love" contains a strong sexual implication.

References

Alexander, M. G., Chaudry, Z. & Najam, N. (1999). Social roles and sex differences: Evidence for the cultural construction of emotion. Manuscript in preparation. University of Maine, Orono.

Allen, J. G., & Haccoun, D. M. (1976). Sex differences in emotionality: A multidimensional approach. *Human Relations, 29,* 711–722.

Anderson, C. D., & Tomaskovic-Devey, D. (1995). Patriarchal pressures: An exploration of organizational processes that exacerbate and erode gender earnings inequality. *Work & Occupation, 22,* 328–356.

Averill, J. R. (1982). *Anger and aggression: An essay on emotion.* New York: Springer.

Balswick, J. O. (1982). Male inexpressiveness: Psychological and social aspects. In K. Soloman & M. Levy (Eds.), *Men in transition: Theory and therapy* (pp. 131–150). New York: Plenum.

Balswick, J. O. (1988). *The inexpressive male.* Lexington, MA: Lexington Books.

Balswick, J., & Avertt, C. P. (1977). Differences in expressiveness: Gender, interpersonal orientation, and perceived parental expressiveness as contributing factors. *Journal of Marriage and the Family, 2,* 112–127.

Bem, D. J. (1972). Self-perception theory. In L. Berkowitz (Ed.), *Advances in experimental social psychology* (Vol. 6, pp. 1–62). San Diego, CA: Academic Press.

Bem, S. L. (1981). Gender schema theory: A cognitive account of sex typing. *Psychological Review, 88,* 354–364.

Berry, D. S., & Hansen, J. S. (1996). Positive affect, negative affect, and social interaction. *Journal of Personality and Social Psychology, 71,* 796–809.

Biernat, M., & Wortman, C. B. (1991). Sharing home responsibilities between professionally employed women and their husbands. *Journal of Personality and Social Psychology, 60,* 844–860.

Birnbaum, D. W., Nosanchuk, T. A., & Croll, W. L. (1980). Children's stereotypes about sex differences in emotionality. *Sex Roles, 6,* 435–443.

Blier, M. J. & Blier-Wilson, L. A. (1989). Gender differences in self-rated emotional expressiveness. *Sex Roles, 21,* 287–295.

Bradley, M. M., Cuthbert, B. N., & Lang, P. J. (1990). Startle reflex modification: Emotion or attention? *Psychophysiology, 27,* 513–522.

Brody, L. R. (1993). On understanding gender differences in the expression of emotion: Gender roles, socialization, and language. In S. Ablon, D. Brown, E. Khantzian, & J. Mack (Eds.), *Human feelings: Exploration in affect development and meaning.* New York: Analytic Press.

Brody, L. R. (1996). Gender, emotional expression, and parent-child boundaries. In R. D. Kavanaugh, B. Zimmerberg, & S. Fein (Eds.), *Emotion: Interdisciplinary perspectives* (pp. 139–170). Mahwah, NJ: Lawrence Erlbaum.

Brody, L. R., & Hall, J. A. (1993). Gender and emotion. In M. Lewis & J. Haviland (Eds.), *Handbook of emotions* (pp. 447–461). New York: Guilford Press.

Broverman, I., Vogel, S., Broverman, D., Clarkson, F. E., & Rosenkrantz, P. S. (1972). Sex role stereotypes: A current appraisal. *Journal of Social Issues, 28,* 59–78.

Buck, R. (1984). *The communication of emotion.* New York: Guilford.

Buck, R., Miller, R. E., & Caul, W. F. (1974). Sex, personality, and physiological variables in the communication of affect via facial expression. *Journal of Personality and Social Psychology, 30,* 587–596.

Buck, R., Savin, V., Miller, R., & Caul, W. F. (1972). Communication of affect through facial expressions in humans. *Journal of Personality and Social Psychology, 23,* 362–371.

Buss, D. M., & Schmitt, D. P. (1993). Sexual strategies theory: An evolutionary perspective on human mating. *Psychological Review, 100,* 204–232.

Cacioppo, J. T., Petty, R. E., Losch, M. E., & Kim, H. S. (1986). Electromyographic activity over facial muscle regions can differentiate the valence and intensity of affective reactions. *Journal of Personality and Social Psychology, 50,* 260–268.

Calasanti, T. M., & Bailey, C. A. (1991). Gender inequality and the division of household labor in the United States and Sweden: A socialist-feminist approach. *Social Problems, 38,* 34–53.

Cancian, F. M., & Gordon, S. L. (1988). Changing emotion norms in marriage: Love and anger in US women's magazines since 1900. *Gender & Society, 2,* 308–342.

Caporeal L. R., & Brewer, M. B. (1991). The quest for human nature: Social and scientific issues in evolutionary psychology. *Journal of Social Issues, 47,* 1–9.

Coats, E. J., & Feldman, R. S. (1996). Gender differences in nonverbal correlates of social status. *Personality and Social Psychology Bulletin, 22,* 1014–1022.

Cohen, S., & Wills, T. A. (1985). Stress, social support, and the buffering hypothesis. *Psychological Bulletin, 98,* 310–357.

Cornelius, R. R. (1996). *The science of emotion: Research and tradition in the psychology of emotions.* Upper Saddle River, NJ: Prentice-Hall.

Diener, E. (1984). Subjective well-being. *Psychological Bulletin, 95,* 542–575.

Diener, E., & Diener, M. (1995). Cross-cultural correlates of life satisfaction and self-esteem. *Journal of Personality and Social Psychology, 68,* 653–663.

Diener, E., & Emmons, R. A. (1985). The independence of positive and negative affect. *Journal of Personality and Social Psychology, 47,* 1105–1117.

Diener, E., & Fujita, F. (1995). Resources, personal strivings, and subjective well-being: A nomothetic and ideographic approach. *Journal of Personality and Social Psychology, 68,* 926–935.

Diener, E., Larsen, R., Levine, S., & Emmons, R. (1985). Intensity and frequency: Dimensions underlying positive and negative affect. *Journal of Personality and Social Psychology, 48,* 1253–1265.

Diener, E., Sandvik, E. & Larsen, R. J. (1985), Age and sex effects for emotional intensity. *Developmental Psychology 21,* 542–546.

Diener, E., Suh, E., Smith, H., & Shao, L. (1995). National and cultural differences in reported well-being: Why do they occur? *Social Indicators Research, 34,* 7–32.

Dindia, K., & Allen, M. (1992). Sex differences in self-disclosure: A meta-analysis. *Psychological Bulletin, 112,* 106–124.

Dunn, J., Bretherton, I., & Munn, P. (1987). Conversations about feeling states between mothers and their young children. *Developmental Psychology, 23,* 132–139.

Eagly, A. H. (1987). *Sex differences in social behavior: A social role interpretation.* Hillside, NJ: Erlbaum.

Eagly, A. H., & Wood, W. (1991). Explaining sex differences in social behavior: A meta-analytic perspective. *Personality and Social Psychological Bulletin, 17,* 306–315.

Eagly, A. H., & Wood, W. (1999). The origins of sex differences in human behavior: Evolved dispositions versus social roles. *American Psychologist, 54,* 408–423.

Ewart, C. K., Taylor, C. B., Kraemer, H. C., & Agras, W. S. (1991). High blood pressure and marital discord: Not being nasty matters more than being nice. *Health Psychology, 10,* 155–163.

Feingold, A. (1994). Gender differences in personality: A meta-analysis. *Psychological Bulletin, 116,* 429–456.

Festinger, L. (1957). *A theory of cognitive dissonance.* Evanston, IL: Row, Peterson.

Fivush, R. (1989). Exploring sex differences in the emotional content of mother–child interactions about the past. *Sex Roles, 20,* 675–691.

Fujita, F., Diener, E., & Sandvik, E. (1991). Gender differences in negative affect and well-being: The case for emotional intensity. *Journal of Personality and Social Psychology, 61,* 427–434.

Golding, J. M. (1990). Division of household labor, strain, and depressive symptoms among Mexican American and non-Hispanic Whites. *Psychology of Women Quarterly, 14,* 103–117.

Gottman, J., & Levenson, R. W. (1992). Marital processes predictive of later dissolution: Behavior, physiology, and health. *Journal of Personality and Social Psychology, 63,* 221–233.

Gove, W. R. (1978). Sex differences in mental illness among adult men and women: An evaluation of four questions raised regarding the evidence on the higher rates of women. *Social Science and Medicine, 12,* 187–198.

Gray, J. (1992). *Men are from Mars, women are from Venus.* New York: Harper Collins.

Green, D. P., Goldman, S. L., & Salovey, P. (1993). Measurement error masks bipolarity in affect ratings. *Journal of Personality and Social Psychology, 64,* 1029–1041.

Grossman, M., & Wood, W. (1993). Sex differences in intensity of emotional experience: A social role interpretation. *Journal of Personality and Social Psychology, 65,* 1010–1022.

Halberstadt, A. G., Fox, N., & Jones, N. A. (1993). Do expressive mothers have expressive children? The role of socialization in children's affect expression. *Social Development, 2,* 48–65.

Hare, R., Wood, K., Britain, S., & Frazelle, J. (1971). Autonomic responses to affective visual stimulation: Sex differences. *Journal of Experimental Research in Personality, 5,* 14–22.

Harver, A., Katkin, E. S., & Bloch, E. (1993). Signal-detection outcomes on heartbeat and respiratory resistance detection tasks in male and female subjects. *Psychophysiology, 30,* 223–230.

Hendrick, C., & Hendrick, S. S. (1991). Dimensions of love: A sociobiological interpretation. *Journal of Social and Clinical Psychology, 10,* 206–230.

Hochschild, A. (1989). *The second shift: Working parents and the revolution at home.* New York: Viking Press.

Hofstede, G. (1980). *Culture's consequences: International differences in work-related values.* Beverly Hills, CA: Sage.

Horowitz, A. (1985). Sons and daughters as caregivers to older parent: Differences in role performance and consequences. *The Gerontologist, 25,* 612–617.

Inglehart, R. (1990). *Culture shift in advanced industrial society.* Princeton University Press.

Kiecolt-Glaser, J. K., Glaser, R., Cacioppo, J. T., MacCallum, R. C., Snydersmith, M., Kim, C., & Malarkey, W. B. (1997). Marital conflict in older adults: Endocrinological and immunological correlates. *Psychosomatic Medicine, 59,* 339–349.

Kiecolt-Glaser, J. K., Malarkey, W. B., Chee, M., Newton, T., Cacioppo, J. T., Mao, H., & Glaser, R. (1993). Negative behavior during marital conflict is associated with immunological down-regulation. *Psychosomatic Medicine, 55,* 395–409.

Kiecolt-Glaser, J. K., Newton, T., Cacioppo, J. T., MacCallum, R. C., Glaser, R., & Malarkey, W. B. (1996). Marital conflict and endocrine functioning: Are men really more physiologically affected than women? *Journal of Consulting and Clinical Psychology, 64,* 324–332.

King, L. A, & Emmons, R. A. (1990). Conflict over emotional expression: Psychological and physical correlates. *Journal of Personality and Social Psychology, 58,* 864–877.

Kring, A. M., & Gordon, A. H. (1998). Sex differences in emotion: Expression, experience, and physiology. *Journal of Personality and Social Psychology, 74,* 686–703.

Lang, P. J., Greenwald, M. K., Bradley, M. M., & Hamm, A. O. (1993). Looking at pictures: Affective, facial, visceral and behavioral reactions. *Psychophysiology, 30,* 261–273.

Larsen, R. J., & Diener, E. (1987). Affect intensity as an individual difference characteristic: A review. *Journal of Research in Personality, 21,* 1–39.

Larsen, R. J., Diener, E., & Emmons, R. A. (1986). Affect intensity and reactions to daily life events. *Journal of Personality and Social Psychology, 51,* 803–814.

Leary, M. (1995). *Self-presentation: Impression management and interpersonal behavior.* Madison, WI: Brown & Benchmark.

Lee, G. R., Seccombe, K., & Shehan, C. L. (1991). Marital status and personal happiness: An analysis of trend data. *Journal of Marriage and the Family, 53,* 839–844.

Levenson, R. W. (1992). Autonomic nervous system differences among emotions. *Psychological Science, 3,* 23–27.

Levenson, R. W., Ekman, P. & Friesen, W. V. (1990). Voluntary facial action generates emotion-specific autonomic nervous system activity. *Psychophysiology, 27,* 363–384.

Malarkey, W., Kiecolt-Glaser, J. K., Pearl, D., & Glaser, R. (1994). Hostile behavior during marital conflict alters pituitary and adrenal hormones. *Psychosomatic Medicine, 56,* 41–51.

Malatesta, C. Z., & Haviland, J. M. (1982). Learning display rules. *Child Development, 53,* 991–1003.

Meeker, B. F., & Weitzel-O'Neill, P. A. (1977). Sex roles and interpersonal behavior in task-oriented groups. *American Sociological Review, 42,* 91–105.

Mesquita, B., & Frijda, N. H. (1992). Cultural variations in emotion: A review. *Psychological Bulletin, 112,* 179–204.

Miller, L. C., & Fishkin, S. A. (1997). On the dynamics of human bonding and reproductive success: Seeking windows on the adapted-for-human-environmental interface. In J. A. Simpson & D. T. Kenrick (Eds.), *Evolutionary social psychology* (pp. 197–235). Mahwah, NJ: Lawrence Erlbaum.

Moore, B. S., & Isen, A. M. (1990). Affect and social behavior. In B. S. Moore, & A. M. Isen (Eds.), *Affect and social behavior* (pp. 1–21). Cambridge University Press.

Myers, D. G., & Diener, E. (1995). Who is happy? *Psychological Science, 6,* 10–19.

Nolen-Hoeksema, S. (1987). Sex differences in unipolar depression: Evidence and theory. *Psychological Bulletin, 101,* 259–282.

Olson, J. M., Roese, N. J., & Zanna, M. P. (1996). Expectancies. In E. T. Higgins & A. W. Kruglanski (Eds.), *Social psychology: Handbook of basic principles* (pp. 211–238). New York, NY: Guilford Press.

Pennebaker, J. W., & Roberts, T. (1992). Toward a his and hers theory of emotion: Gender differences in visceral perception. *Journal of Social and Clinical Psychology, 11*, 199–212.

Plutchik, R. (1984). Emotions and imagery. *Journal of Mental Imagery, 8*, 105–111.

Reskin, B. F., & Padavik, I. (1994). *Women and men at work*. Thousand Oaks: Pine Forge Press.

Ridgeway, C. L., & Berger, J. (1986). Expectations, legitimation, and dominance behavior in task groups. *American Sociological Review, 51*, 603–617.

Ridgeway, C. L., & Johnson, C. (1990). What is the relationship between socio-emotional behavior and status in task groups? *American Journal of Sociology, 95*, 1189–1212.

Roberts, T., & Pennebaker, J. W. (1995). Gender differences in perceiving internal state: Toward a his-and-hers model of perceptual cue use. In M. P. Zanna (Ed.), *Advances in experimental social psychology* (Vol. 27, pp. 143–175). San Diego, CA: Academic Press.

Roland, A. (1988). *In search of self in India and Japan*. Princeton University Press.

Rubin, Z. (1970). Measurement of romantic love. *Journal of Personality and Social Psychology, 16*, 265–273.

Schwartz, G.E., Brown, S., & Ahern, G.L. (1980). Facial muscle patterning and subjective experience during affective imagery: Sex differences. *Psychophysiology, 17*, 75–82.

Sethi, R. R., & Allen, M. J. (1984). Sex-role stereotypes in Northern India and the United States. *Sex Roles, 11*, 615–626.

Shaver, P., Schwartz, J., Kirson, D., & O'Connor, C. (1987). Emotion knowledge: Further exploration of a prototype approach. *Journal of Personality and Social Psychology, 52*, 1061–1086.

Shaver, P. R., Wu, S., & Schwartz, J. C. (1992). Cross-cultural similarities and differences in emotion and its representation: A prototype approach. In M. S. Clark (Ed.), *Emotion: Review of Personality and Social Psychology* (Vol. 13, pp. 175–212). Newbury Park, CA: Sage.

Singelis, T., Choo, P., & Hatfield, E. (1995). Love schemas and romantic love. *Journal of Social Behavior and Personality, 10*, 15–36.

Skrypnek, B. J., & Snyder, M. (1982). On the self-perpetuating nature of stereotypes about women and men. *Journal of Experimental Social Psychology, 18*, 277–291.

Smith, C. A., & Pope, L. K. (1992). Appraisal and emotion: The interactional contributions of dispositional and situational factors. In M. S. Clark (Ed.), *Emotion and social behavior: Review of personality and social psychology* (Vol. 14, pp. 32–62). Newbury Park, CA: Sage.

Sommers, S. (1984). Reported emotions and conventions of emotionality among college students. *Journal of Personality and Social Psychology, 46*, 207–215.

Spence, J. T., & Helmreich, R. L. (1978). *Masculinity and femininity: Their psychological dimensions, correlates, and antecedents*. University of Texas Press.

Sprecher, S., & Sedikides, C. (1993). Gender differences in perceptions of emotionality: The case of close heterosexual relationships. *Sex Roles, 28*, 511–530.

Stone, R., Cafferata, G. L. & Sangl, J. (1987). Caregivers of the frail elderly: A national profile. *The Gerontologist*, 616–626.

Stoppard, J. M., & Gunn Gruchy, C. D. (1993). Gender, context, and expression of positive emotion. *Personality and Social Psychology Bulletin, 19*, 143–150.

Swim, J. (1994). Perceived versus meta-analytic effect sizes: An assessment of the accuracy of gender stereotypes. *Journal of Personality and Social Psychology, 66*, 21–36.

Tannen, D. (1990). *You just don't understand: Men and women in conversation.* New York: Ballantine Books.

Tooby, J., & Cosmides, L. (1992). Psychological foundations of culture. In J. Barkow, L. Cosmides, & J. Tooby (Eds.), *The adapted mind: Evolutionary psychology and the generation of culture* (pp. 19–136). New York: Oxford University Press.

Trivers, R. L. (1972). Parental investment and sexual selection. In B. Campbell (Ed.), *Sexual selection and the descent of man* (pp. 136–179). Chicago: Aldine Press.

Ward, C. & Sethi, R. R. (1986). Cross-cultural validation of the Bem Sex Role Inventory: Malaysian and South African research. *Journal of Cross-Cultural Psychology, 17*, 300–314.

Warr, P., Barter, J., & Brownbridge, G. (1983). On the independence of positive and negative affect. *Journal of Personality and Social Psychology, 44*, 644–651.

Whyte, M. K. (1978). *The status of women in preindustrial societies.* Princeton, NJ: Princeton Univ. Press.

Williams, J. E., & Best, D. L. (1990). *Sex and psyche: Gender and self viewed cross-culturally.* Newbury Park, CA: Sage

Wood, W. (1987). A meta-analytic review of sex differences in group performance. *Psychological Bulletin, 102*, 53–71.

Wood, W., Christensen, N., Hebl, M., & Rothgerber, H. (1997). Sex-typed norms, affect, and the self. *Journal of Personality and Social Psychology, 73*, 523–535.

Wood, W., & Eagly, A. (1998). *A social role account of the origin of sex differences in social behavior.* Manuscript in preparation. Texas A&M University, College Station.

Wood, W., & Karten, S. J. (1986). Sex differences in interaction style as a product of perceived sex differences in competence. *Journal of Personality and Social Psychology, 50*, 341–347.

Wood, W., Rhodes, N. & Whelan, M. (1989). Sex differences in positive well-being: A consideration of emotional style and marital status. *Psychological Bulletin, 106*, 249–264.

10. Gender and anger

ANN M. KRING

Anger is momentary madness

Horace

Like women's anger, impotent and loud

Dryden

What happens when we approach a lane closure while driving on the freeway, and a car cuts rapidly in front of us just before the lane closes, forcing us to brake abruptly? What happens when a romantic partner accuses us of flirting when we have done no such thing? What happens when we hear a news report telling us that 4 million children in the United States go hungry every day? Perhaps the most common response to these scenarios is anger. Anger is a commonly experienced and expressed emotion, and contrary to persistent myths and stereotypes, women and men both get angry in response to these types of situations. Indeed, conventional wisdom suggests that anger is a "male" emotion: women don't get angry, and if they do, they certainly don't show it. Yet, as this chapter will show, the bulk of the empirical evidence does not support these contentions. The literature on anger clearly demonstrates the need to modify questions about gender differences in emotion from the more global (e.g., do men and women differ?) to the more specific (e.g., under what conditions and in the presence of whom might men and women differ?). Differences in the experience and expression of anger have as much to do with other variables such as social context, status, and gender role as they do with gender.

Although a number of excellent reviews of gender differences in emotion more generally have recently been published (e.g., Brody & Hall, 1993; Fischer, 1993; Shields, 1991), few reviews have specifically considered gender differences in anger. In this chapter, I will first consider definitions of anger , and then I will review the empirical literature on gender differences in anger in adults, including an explication of the rules, norms, and stereotypes for the expression and experience of anger. I will then consider how theories of anger address gender. Finally, I will conclude with directions for research and suggestions for dispelling the persistent myths about women's anger.

Emotions are multichannel (e.g., facial, vocal, verbal) response systems that have developed through the course of human evolutionary history to help us deal with challenges and problems in our environment (e.g., Frijda, 1986; Keltner & Kring, 1998; Kring & Bachorowski, 1999; Levenson, 1992; Scherer, 1986). An emotion response consists of multiple components, including a cognitive or appraisal component, an expressive or behavioral component, an experiential component, and a physiological component. The coordinated engagement of these emotion components subserves a number of intra- and interpersonal functions (e.g., Averill, 1982; Campos, Campos, & Barrett, 1989; Ekman, 1992; Levenson, 1992; Keltner & Kring, 1998). To be complete, assessments of anger should consider multiple components of emotional responding.

By most accounts, anger is an unpleasant or negative emotion. It typically occurs in response to an actual or perceived threat, a disruption in ongoing behavior, or in response to the perception of deliberate or unjustifiable harm or negligence (Averill, 1982; de Rivera, 1977; Thomas, 1993). Anger is also a social emotion: it is often elicited in response to the actions or words of others; it is often directed toward others; and the consequences of the experience and expression of anger are often interpersonal (Averill, 1982; Scherer, Matsumoto, Wallbott, & Kudoh, 1988; Wallbott & Scherer, 1989). Moreover, the motivation for anger often involves revenge or punishment, typically directed towards another individual. Averill (1982) argues that anger is a socially constructed syndrome, consisting of expressive displays, physiological responses, and subjective experience, but that is largely determined by social rules and functions that are embedded within a given culture. Anger is believed to have a universally recognized facial display (e.g., Ekman, 1992, 1994; Izard, 1971; but see Russell, 1994, 1995), and a distinct psychophysiological signature (Ekman, Levenson, & Friesen, 1983; Levenson, Ekman, & Friesen, 1990). In cross-cultural studies of facial expression recognition, the anger facial expression is among the most difficult to label or recognize, although it is recognized above chance levels (Ekman, 1994; Russell, 1994).

Anger is similar in many respects to a number of other emotions, such as frustration, distress, upset, hostility, and rage (Russell & Fehr, 1994). Ortony and colleagues (Clore, Ortony, Dienes, & Fujita, 1993; Ortony, Clore, & Collins, 1988) have argued that there are four "anger-like" emotions, including anger, reproach, frustration, and resentment. These 4 emotions differ with respect to the conditions under which they are likely to be experienced and the types of situations that elicit them. Although these other emotions and traits are similar to anger, my focus in this chapter will be on anger.

Literature review on gender and anger

A number of studies have either directly or indirectly examined whether men and women differ in their expression, experience, and perception of anger as well as in the antecedents, concomittants, and rules or norms for the experience and expression of anger. Several different methods have been used to measure anger, including self-reports, the coding of facial expressions, and psychophysiological indices, such as heart rate and skin conductance. Moreover, the contexts in which anger has been studied vary, from more naturalistic settings to the experimental manipulation of other persons present. Given the variety of methods used to study gender and anger, it is perhaps not surprising that there are a variety of divergent findings. Yet, it is precisely the variations in method and context that help us understand under what conditions and in what situations men and women might differ in their expression and experience of anger.

Causes and antecedents of anger

Theorists have long noted a number of reasons why people get angry. For example, Frijda (1992) notes that anger is caused almost universally by harm inflicted on kin, possessions, or social status (see also Mesquita & Frijda, 1992). Ekman and Friesen (1975) suggested 5 antecedents to anger: (1) frustration, most often due to some type of interference; (2) physical threat; (3) insult; (4) witnessing someone else being violated; and (5) being the recipient of another's anger. Wallbott and Scherer (1989) cite the most common elicitor of anger to be personal relationships, followed by being treated unfairly, interaction with strangers, and unnecessary inconvenience. Unfortunately, few theorists have addressed the extent to which these reasons for anger apply equally to men and women. A comprehensive study of anger among women that included interviews and several self-report measures, found the most common elicitors of anger among women to be interpersonal, intrapersonal, and societal (Denham & Bultemeier, 1993).

Some studies that have directly examined gender differences in anger antecedents failed to find differences between men and women (e.g., Frodi, 1977; Campbell & Muncer, 1987). For example, both men and women reported feeling angry after being provoked by the opposite sex (Frodi, 1977). However, other studies did find differences (e.g., Buss, 1989; Fehr & Baldwin, 1996; Harris, 1993), such as men reporting more anger following female aggression than male aggression, and women reporting greater anger following aggression from a male (Harris, 1993). One important factor that distinguishes studies that do and do not find gender differences is the context in which the reasons for anger are asked about. Specifically, in the context of close relationships or interactions between men and women, the reasons for anger appear to differ for men and women. For instance, Fehr and Baldwin (1996) found that although both men and women reported betrayal of trust to be the most anger-provoking elicitor, women reported more anger following betrayal of trust, rebuff, negligence, and unwarranted criticism than men. Similarly, Buss (1989) found that women reported greater anger and upset than men following condescending remarks, inconsiderate, neglecting, or rejecting behavior, alcohol abuse, and their partner's emotional constriction. By contrast, men reported more anger and upset in response to women's moodiness and self-absorption. Other studies have also found that women reported more anger than men following condescension from men (Frodi, 1977; Harris, 1993). Thus, in the context of close relationships, the reasons why men and women get angry appear to differ. Specifically, women tend to be angered by the negative behaviors of men, whereas men tend to be angered by womens' negative emotional reactions and self-focused behavior.

Frequency and quality of experienced anger

The context within which individuals are asked to report about their experience of anger differs quite a bit from study to study. For example, some studies asked participants to complete questionnaires designed to assess the extent to which they generally feel anger; other studies asked participants to report on their anger following the presentation of an emotional stimulus, and still others asked individuals to report on how much anger they would feel if they were the active participants in different presented stories or vignettes.

General self-report measures. Self-report studies have used general measures of emotion that include items about anger (e.g., Emotionality Survey, Allen & Haccoun, 1976) or specific measures of anger experience (e.g., Trait and State Anger scales, Spielberger, 1988). State anger is defined as the momentary experience of anger that occurs in response to some event or person in the environment. By contrast, trait anger is construed as a stable, personality disposition that reflects an individual's propensity to experience anger across a variety of situations (Spielberger, 1988; Spielberger, Johnson, Russell, Crane, Jacobs, & Worden, 1985; Spielberger, Krasner, & Solomon, 1988). Individuals high in trait anger are hypothesized to experience more intense and frequent state anger. Studies comparing men and women on these state and trait anger scales have generally failed to find gender differences (e.g., Deffenbacher, Oetting, Thwaites, Lynch, Baker, Stark, Thacker, & Eiswerth-Cox, 1996b; Kopper, 1991; Kopper & Epperson, 1991,1996; but see Fischer, Smith, Leonard, Fuqua, Campbell, & Masters, 1993).

Similarly, studies employing more general scales of emotional experience did not find support for sex differences in the frequency or intensity of anger either (e.g., Allen & Haccoun, 1976; Averill, 1983). In one of the most comprehensive studies of anger, Averill (1982) collected daily reports of anger among college students and community residents. Although a few sex differences were noted, no sex differences in reported experience across both samples were found.

Experimental manipulations. A number of emotion induction techniques have been used in studies designed to assess gender differences in emotion and anger, including slides, films, pictures of facial expressions, audiotaped conversations, and vignettes. In vignette studies, participants are asked to report what they would do *if* they were in the depicted scenario. By contrast, in studies that directly manipulate emotional experience participants report on their actual responses to that particular stimulus.

Manstead and Fischer (1995) presented men and women a series of vignettes that were designed to elicit what they referred to as "powerless" emotions (sadness, despair, anxiety, disappointment) and "powerful" emotions (anger, rage, irritation, and disgust). Vignettes included stories about romantic rejection, academic failure, work rejection, romantic criticism, robbery, work criticism, being ignored, and being passed over. Across these scenarios, women did not significantly differ from men in their reports of how much anger they would feel in these situations. However, as predicted, women reported feeling more powerless in these situations and reported that they would experience more despair than men. Brody, Lovas, and Hay (1995) obtained slightly different results. They examined gender differences in experienced anger by presenting vignettes to adult men and women (also to children and adolescents) that varied in terms of the emotional nature of the story (anger, envy, warmth, fear) and the gender and sex-typed behavior of the participants (targets and instigators) in the story. Women tended to report that they would experience *more* anger than men, and in particular that they would experience more anger towards men than women. Harris (1994) also presented 4 vignettes designed to elicit anger to college men and women. These vignettes varied in terms of the familiarity and sex of the other people involved (e.g., being yelled at by another driver following a minor traffic accident, a professor gave you a failing grade and accused you of cheating). No sex differences in reported anger were found, except for the dating scenario, in reaction to which women reported that they would feel more anger than men.

Studies that directly manipulate participants' anger by presenting emotional stimuli, showed few gender differences in the experience of anger. For example, Kring and Gordon (1998) found no gender differences in the experience of unpleasant emotions following an anger-eliciting film clip. Additional analyses indicated that men and women also did not differ in their reports of anger. Wagner, Buck, and Winterbotham (1993) presented emotional slides to men and women and found no gender differences in reports of experienced anger in response to any of the slides. However, Strachan and Dutton (1992) had participants listen to an audiotaped recording of a couple having a conflict related to sexual jealousy and they found that women reported feeling more anger-related emotions (angry, hostile, irritable, annoyed) than men. Thus, in studies where anger involves an interpersonal situation, women may report feeling more anger than men. By contrast, in studies where the anger stimulus reflects an injustice toward others, as in the case of the film study by Kring and Gordon (1998) or in various of the scenarios used in the vignette studies, men and women report feeling angry to a similar extent. These findings are consistent with the literature on anger elicitors: women report experiencing more anger than men in the context of close relationships.

Clinical literature. In both the lay and professional clinical and counseling literatures, some treatment professionals perpetuate stereotypes about women and anger that often are not supported by the research literature. For instance, various clinicians have suggested that women do not experience anger, do not know how to express anger, actively suppress their anger, and have difficulty expressing their anger (Tavris, 1989; for a review, see Sharkin, 1993). Consider the following quotes by treatment professionals:

> "[Anger] is an emotion that women express far less frequently than do men." (Halas 1981)

> "Many women find the idea of anger unthinkable, no matter how much justification there might seem to be." (Collier 1982)

The reasons for these assertions could be due, as Sharkin (1993) suggested, to clinicians' experiences with women in therapy who really have trouble with anger. Unfortunately, these literatures are often misinterpreted to suggest that all women have trouble with anger, not just those who are seeking treatment. Lest one think that men's anger is not also pathologized, Sharkin (1993) noted that since anger is argued to be one of the "acceptable" emotions for men, they are also considered likely candidates for trouble with anger control and expression. Although many of the assertions of clinicians and counselors are quite consistent with the empirical findings on stereotypes (reviewed below), these writings also unintentionally serve to strengthen the stereotypes which are not, for the most part, supported by the majority of empirical studies.

Expression of anger

Similar to the studies that have examined the experience of anger, a number of different methods for measuring anger expression have been used, such as self-report, coding of facial and vocal expression, judges accuracy ratings of posed and spontaneous facial displays, and psychophysiological measures of facial muscle activity.

General self-report measures. Although women tend to score higher than men on self-report measures of general emotional expressivity (e.g., Gross & John, 1995; Kring, Smith, & Neale, 1994), differences between men and women in their reports of anger expression are not as widely found (e.g., Burrowes & Halberstadt, 1987; King & Emmons, 1990). For example, Allen and Haccoun (1976) asked men and women to report how frequently and intensely they expressed different emotions, including anger. While women reported expressing fear and sadness more often than men, they did not differ in their reports of anger or joy expression. Similarly, Balswick and Avertt (1977) found that women reported being more expressive of happiness, love, and sadness, but did not differ in their reports of hate/anger (see also Dosser, Balswick, & Halverson, 1983; Ganong & Coleman, 1985).

Using Spielberger's Anger Expression Inventory (AEI, Spielberger et al., 1985), a number of studies have examined whether men and women differ in their reports of anger suppression (termed "anger-in" on the AEI), anger expression towards others, often in an unhealthy manner (termed "anger-out"), or their anger control (controlling both the experience and expression of anger). Contrary to the clinical literature noted above, women do not report suppressing their anger more often than men nor do men report expressing their anger outwardly more often than women (e.g., Deffenbacher, Oetting, Lynch, & Morris, 1996a; Deffenbacher, et al., 1996b; Faber & Burns, 1996; Kopper, 1991; Kopper & Epperson, 1996; Stoner & Spencer, 1987; Thomas, 1989; Thomas & Williams, 1991; but see Fischer et al., 1993).

It is important to point out that some gender differences in the reports of anger expression have been found, but these differences typically have to do with the manner of expression and not with the frequency of expression. Specifically, men report that they physically assault objects and people (e.g., hitting, throwing) and verbally assault people (e.g., name calling, sarcasm) more often than women (Deffenbacher, et al., 1996a), whereas women cry more often when angry (e.g., Crawford, Kippax, Onyx, Gault, & Benton, 1992; Eagly & Steffen, 1986; Frost & Averill, 1982; Hoover-Dempsey, Plas, & Wallston, 1986; Lombardo, Cretser, Lombardo, & Mathis, 1983; Timmers, Fischer, & Manstead, 1997; Thomas, 1993; Zemen & Garber, 1996). Blier and Blier-Wilson (1989) also found that men reported more confidence in expressing their anger to other men than to women. Moreover, women were more confident expressing their anger to other women than men were.

Although there appear to be few gender differences in reports of anger expression, Kopper and colleagues have found gender role differences (Kopper, 1991; Kopper & Epperson, 1996). Specifically, men and women who endorse a number of masculine personality characteristics tend to score higher on Spielberger's Anger-Out scale than men and women who endorse a number of feminine personality characteristics. By contrast, men and women with more feminine characteristics score higher on the Anger-In Scale, suggesting that feminine sex role characteristics are associated with suppressing anger and masculine sex role characteristics are associated with outwardly expressing anger.

Experimental manipulations. Although self-report studies failed to find many significant gender differences in anger expression, vignette studies that asked men and women to report on what they would express and to whom they would express it across various scenarios yield some interesting gender differences. Contrary to conventional wisdom, however, these studies typically showed that women reported that they would express *more* anger than men, depending upon the situation. For example, Dosser et al. (1983) found that women reported that they would express more anger in situations requiring expression to both male and female friends. Brody (1993) in contrast found that women reported that they would express more anger if the target of their anger was male. Timmers et al. (1998) found that women reported being more likely to express anger when the object and target of the anger were different (e.g., expressing anger about vandalism to a friend), whereas men reported being more likely to express anger when the object and target of anger were the same (e.g., expressing anger at a friend who ruins your jacket). Timmers et al. also found that the manner in which anger was expressed differed: men reported that they would yell or name-call; women reported that they would cry. Interestingly, women also reported more often than men that they would not show any anger.

Findings on gender differences in posing anger expressions are equivocal. Some studies find no gender differences (e.g., Levenson et al., 1990); other studies find that women are better posers than men (e.g., Friedman, Riggio, & Segall, 1980; Zuckerman, Lipets, Hall Koivumaki, & Rosenthal, 1975), and still others find that men are better posers than women (e.g., Rotter & Rotter, 1988). Methodological differences might account for these variable findings. Findings from studies of spontaneous facial expression are more consistent: either women tend to be more expressive than men or no differences between men and women are found. For example, Schwartz, Brown, and Ahern (1980) found that women exhibited greater facial muscle activity (as assessed via electromyography) than men while imagining an angry situation. Kring and Gordon (1998) found that women displayed more negative expressions than men in response to an anger-eliciting film clip (unfortunately, specific anger expressions were not coded). Wagner et al. (1993) found that women's expressions of anger in response to emotional slides were more accurately rated than men's expressions; however, using a different set of slides and a different communication accuracy measure, Wagner, MacDonald, and Manstead (1986) in contrast, failed to find gender differences in anger expression accuracy. Similarly, Bonanno and Keltner (1997) found no gender differences in the frequency of anger expressions during a bereavement interview 6 months after the loss of a spouse or partner. Moreover, a higher frequency of anger expressions was associated with more grief symptoms at 14 and 25 months post-loss for both men and women.

Finally, it is important to consider gender differences in the target of anger expressions, however, only a few studies have directly examined this question. In general, men seem to be the targets of anger expression more often than women (Brody et al., 1995; Dosser et al., 1983; Eagly & Steffen, 1986; Frost & Averill, 1982; Harris, 1994), particularly when they are strangers (Averill, 1982; Harris, 1994). Other evidence indicates that women are more likely to direct their anger toward a male relationship partner, whereas men are more likely to direct their anger toward male strangers (Allen & Haccoun, 1976; Blier & Blier-Wilson, 1989). In the context of close friendships, however, one study found that both men and women reported being more likely to express anger to female best friends (Dosser et al., 1983).

In sum, similar to the findings on experienced anger, men and women do not differ in their reports of the general extent to which they express anger. However, men and women do differ in their expression of anger in response to emotional films or slides. Moreover, the manner in which anger is expressed may differ between men and women (e.g., men hit and throw things more often, and women cry more often), and the targets of men and women's anger expressions differ. Men are more likely to express anger towards other males or strangers, particularly if the object and target of their anger are the same. By contrast, women are more likely to express anger towards familiar or close others, whether they be male or female, particularly if the object and target of their anger are different.

Consequences of anger expression and experience

Psychophysiological components of anger: Linkage to health

The psychophysiological responses associated with either suppressing or expressing anger appear to be different for men and women. In response to an anger-eliciting film, Kring and Gordon (1998) found that men exhibited greater skin conductance reactivity than women, yet women displayed more facial expressions than men. Studies from the health psychology literature indicate that anger expression among women in response to stress or provocation is associated with lower heart rate reactivity and more rapid systolic blood pressure recovery (Faber & Burns, 1996; Shapiro, Goldstein, & Jamner, 1995; but see Lai & Linden, 1992). By contrast, anger expression among men and higher scores on trait measures of hostility are associated with heart rate increases and sustained blood pressure (Burns, 1995; Burns & Katkin, 1993; Faber & Burns, 1996; Lai & Linden, 1992; Shapiro, et al., 1995). In addition, women who express their anger, but do not score high on trait measures of hostility are better able to adjust to chronic pain (Burns, Johnson, Mahoney, Devine, & Pawl, 1996). Thus, the healthy expression of anger may have a protective benefit for women, at least with respect to psychophysiological indicators that have been linked with coronary heart disease and adjustment to chronic pain.

Perceived concomittants of anger episodes

Gender differences in perceived psychological consequences of anger have also been observed. For example Deffenbacher and colleagues have found that women report experiencing other negative emotions following anger episodes more often than men, whereas men reported more negative consequences of their anger, including physical assaults on others and property and hurting oneself more often than women (Deffenbacher et al., 1996a; Deffenbacher et al., 1996b). However, both men and women reported experiencing negative consequences following a particularly severe anger episode (Deffenbacher, 1996b). In the context of close relationships, men reported expecting that their partner will display hurt feelings or reject them in response to their anger, whereas women expected that they would be mocked by their partner (Fehr & Baldwin, 1996).

Regulation, norms, and stereotypes about anger

Although recent studies of emotion regulation suggest that the expressive, experiential, and physiological effects of emotional suppression do not differ between men and women (e.g., Gross, 1998; Gross & Levenson, 1993, 1997), these and other studies have not directly considered the regulation of anger. However, research on stereotypes indicates that women are perceived to express less anger than men (Birnbaum & Croll, 1984; Fabes & Martin, 1991), yet they are perceived no differently than men with respect to the experience of anger (Fabes & Martin, 1991; Johnson & Shulman, 1988; Smith, Ulch, Cameron, Cumberland, Musgrave, & Tremblay, 1989). Men's and women's anger is also judged differently by men and women. For example, a vignette study by Smith et al. (1989) indicated that men rated anger from men and women as more appropriate than women did.

These differences in sex stereotypes and anger judgments may be directly linked to the different display rules for men and women. Display rules are conceptualized as the rules or standards for showing emotions and are specified by situation, target, and instigator. Most research on anger display rules has been conducted with children since it is through the course of development that most theorists believe display rules are acquired. In this developmental literature, results on adult stereotyping are replicated: children report thinking that anger displays are more acceptable from boys than girls (Birnbaum, 1983; Fuchs & Thelen, 1988). Very few studies, however, have examined the extent to which adults' expressive behavior is or is not governed by display rules. This is particularly unfortunate since researchers often interpret failures to confirm predictions about expressive behavior as an indication that display rules are operating. However, without an explicit theory about how and when display rules modify expressive behavior, these contentions are post hoc at best and circular at worst.

Conclusions: Explaining gender in relation to anger

Throughout the studies of gender and anger reviewed here, it seems apparent that both similarities and differences have been found. In cases where differences between men and women are found, these are restricted to specific contexts. Thus, the accumulated evidence does not allow us to conclude that men are more angry than women or that women are more angry than men or that men and women do not differ. This same conclusion has been drawn by a number of other theorists and researchers (e.g., Averill, 1982; Brody, 1985; Fischer, 1993; Shields, 1991; Tavris, 1989). Yet, other predominantly feminist writers continue to suggest that women differ markedly and cross-situationally from men when it comes to anger (e.g., Halas, 1981; Lerner, 1977). For example, Lerner (1977) postulates that because women live in a patriarchal society, they have to suppress their anger. In a similar way, other feminists have suggested that a woman's expression of anger is inconsistent with her nurturant role as wife and mother (e.g., Friday, 1977). Yet, generally speaking, empirical studies do not support this claim that women are less expressive of anger or that they suppress their anger. So why the disparity? If stereotypes matched behavior, we would expect to see converging evidence that women rarely display their anger and men constantly display their anger, but this is not the case.

The data suggest that men and women's anger may differ *depending upon the situation*, and this may explain the divergence in findings. It is within the context of interpersonal relationships where gender differences in anger are most often found. Specifically, the reasons for anger differ between men and women in close relationships: women report more anger than men following betrayal, condescension, rebuff, unwarranted criticism, or negligence; whereas, men report more anger than women if their partner is moody or self-absorbed. Similarly, women report experiencing more anger than men in response to male aggression and conflict between couples, and women are more likely to express their anger to a familiar person rather than to a stranger or when the target and object of their anger are different. By contrast, men are more likely to express their anger when the target and object of their anger are similar or to male strangers. In general, men are more often the target of anger, but this too, depends on the nature of the relationship between instigator and target. Contrary to stereotypes that suggest men should experience and express more anger than women, these data suggest otherwise. These may not be startling revelations, yet they have failed to make much of an impact on changing stereotypes about gender and anger, nor have they led to systematic theorizing about the relation between anger and gender.

However, despite evidence that stereotypes are not confirmed by behavior, stereotypical beliefs nonetheless impact perceptions about anger among men and women. For example, it was shown that women believe that anger displays are less appropriate than men (Smith et al., 1989), and female anger expressions are rated as more hostile and angry than male expressions (Dimberg & Lundquist, 1990). Compared to men, women also report feeling more embarrassed, ashamed, and bad about themselves after an anger episode (Deffenbacher et al., 1996a; Deffenbacher et al., 1996b); and they report feeling as if they will be mocked or denounced by their male romantic partners for their anger displays (Campbell & Muncer, 1987; Fehr & Baldwin, 1996). Moreover, these beliefs are reflected in the terms used to describe men and women's anger. For example, angry women are more likely to be called hostile or bitchy, whereas men who display anger may be referred to as strong (Shields, 1987; Tavris, 1989). Taken together, these findings suggest that although women readily experience and express anger, they may feel uncomfortable doing so.

Finally, an important caveat to consideration of theories about gender and anger is warranted. Specifically, findings that are not entirely consistent with theoretical predictions are often "explained" by invoking terms such as socialization differences. But as Deaux and Major (1990) candidly note, using socialization as an explanation for why men and women differ is not much more complete or any less circular than saying "people are different because they are different." To be sure, socialization must be considered, but simply referring to socialization as an explanation for gender differences without first articulating what is meant by socialization and the conditions under which one would predict that differential socialization would lead to different behaviors, we are left without an explanation. In order for research to progress, it seems that theoretically derived hypotheses about how and when women might differ in their anger response will ultimately answer tell us more about gender and anger than a post hoc application of socialization factors. A number of theories that make explicit statements about how socialization impacts emotion and thus hold promise for the study of gender and anger can be found in the developmental literature (e.g., Garber & Dodge, 1991; Fivush, 1989, 1991; Lewis & Saarni, 1985; Ratner & Stettner, 1991; Saarni, 1990; Walden & Ogan, 1988).

I would be remiss if I did not consider methodological differences and shortcomings of the empirical approaches discussed in this chapter. First, individual's self-reports of emotion may be influenced by stereotypes and are certainly dependent upon memory (Fischer, 1993). Feldman Barrett (1997) has shown that retrospective reports of emotions are influenced by an individual's perceptions of their personality. So, for example, individuals who describe themselves as neurotic are more likely to recall more negative emotions. Second, in most studies in which observable displays of anger were coded, the coders were not blind to the sex of subject. Thus, stereotypes about men and women's expressive behavior may have influenced these ratings (Brody, 1985; Brody & Hall, 1993). Third, studies that present emotionally evocative vignettes are "what-if" experiments. Participants are asked what they would do in a given situation, but this may differ dramatically from what they would actually do in the same situation. That anger is a social emotion suggests that we ought to be studying anger in the context of social interactions and interpersonal relationships (Keltner & Kring, 1998). Finally, very few studies have assessed multiple components of emotional response in the same study (but see Kring & Gordon, 1998), thus it is difficult to make complete statements about how men and women may differ in anger.

Future directions

These critiques are not intended to paint a bleak picture of the research on gender and anger. Rather, they should serve as an impetus for future research. First, researchers need to study anger using multiple methods. Self-report measures are worthwhile, but we cannot rely solely on them to tell us about how men and women deal with anger. Rather, a combination of observational, self-report, and physiological measures should be used to assess anger. Second, anger should be studied in social situations. Although gender differences are far outnumbered by gender similarities in anger, differences that do exist are typically within the context of close relationships. Thus studying emotional behavior in ongoing interactions, as has been done in the marital literature (e.g., Gottman & Levenson, 1986, 1988) will likely tell us a great deal about the social nature of anger. New theoretical and empirical developments on the social functions of emotion have recently been articulated (e.g., Keltner & Kring, 1998) which can provide a framework for studying gender and anger within interpersonal relationships and interactions.

Shields (1991) has also argued that any consideration of gender differences must necessarily consider the context in which the observations were made. For example to conclude that women's reasons for getting angry differ from men's in the context of close relationships, it would be important to examine whether or not women's reasons for getting angry are similar in the context of lesbian relationships. Shields (1991) makes the important point that it is also important to consider how men and women use their knowledge of emotion (in our case, anger) in gender-salient interactions to better understand the discrepancy between beliefs and behaviors.

Third, research needs to consider how power, status, and gender role might moderate the relationship between gender and anger (Cupach & Canary, 1995; Kogut, Langley, & O'Neil, 1992; Manstead & Fischer, 1995; Strachan & Dutton, 1992; Tavris, 1989). Tavris (1989) argues that stereotypes about anger may say more about status differences than gender differences, since women have historically occupied positions of lower status in society. Both men and women have trouble expressing anger to high status individuals (e.g., Keltner, Young, Oemig, Heerey, & Monarch, 1998; Kring, 1998; Strachan & Dutton, 1992), yet there is some evidence indicating that men and women report experiencing more anger when in a lower status position (Strachan & Dutton, 1992). Other research finds gender role differences in anger, with some studies showing that individuals who ascribe a number of masculine characteristics to themselves experience and express more anger (e.g., Kopper & Epperson, 1991; Kogut et al., 1992), and other studies demonstrating that individuals who ascribe both masculine and feminine characteristics to themselves (androgynous) are more expressive of many emotions, including anger (Ganong & Coleman, 1984; Kring & Gordon, 1998). These results say less about whether gender role identity is linked to anger and more about how certain personality characteristics are linked to anger. Nonetheless, there are theoretical frameworks about gender role identity and gender-typed characteristics that allow for testable predictions about how personality and identity might modify the relationship between gender and anger (e.g., Bem, 1993; Spence, 1993).

In conclusion, there are as many similarities as differences resulting from an analysis of gender and anger, yet it is noteworthy that the differences that are found are within the context of close relationships. A social functional account of emotion that stresses the interpersonal characteristics of anger, provides a theoretical framework from which predictions can be made and tested about the relationship between gender and anger. Moreover, developmental theories that articulate how emotions are socialized also hold promise for understanding the conditions under which anger may be more salient for men and women.

References

Allen, J. G., & Haccoun, D. M. (1976). Sex differences in emotionality: A multi-dimensional approach. *Human Relations, 29*, 711–722.

Averill, J. R. (1980). A constructivist view of emotion. In R. Plutchik & H. Kellerman (Eds.), *Emotion: Theory, research, and experience* (pp. 305–339). New York: Academic Press.

Averill, J. R. (1982). *Anger and aggression*. New York: Springer-Verlag.

Averill, J. R. (1983). Studies on anger and aggression: Implications for theories of emotion. *American Psychologist, 38*, 1145–1160.

Balswick, J., & Avertt, C. (1977). Differences in expressiveness: Gender, interpersonal orientation, and perceived parental expressiveness as contributing factors. *Journal of Marriage and Family, 39*, 121–127.

Bem, S. L. (1993). *The lenses of gender: Transforming the debate on sexual inequality*. New Haven, CT: Yale University Press.

Birnbaum, D. W. (1983). Preschoolers' stereotypes about sex differences in emotionality: A reaffirmation. *Journal of Genetic Psychology, 143*, 139–140.

Birnbaum, D. W. & Croll, W. L. (1984). The etiology of children's stereotypes about sex differences in emotionality. *Sex Roles, 10*, 677–691.

Blier, M. J., & Blier-Wilson, L. A. (1989). Gender differences in self-rated emotional expressiveness. *Sex Roles, 21*, 287–295.

Bonanno, G. A., & Keltner, D. (1997). Facial expressions of emotion and the course of conjugal bereavement. *Journal of Abnormal Psychology, 106*, 126–137.

Brody, L. R. (1985). Gender differences in emotional development: A review of theories and research. *Journal of Personality, 53*, 102–149.

Brody, L. R. (1993). On understanding gender differences in the expression of emotion: Gender roles, socialization, and language. In S. Ablon, D. Brown, E. Khantzian, & J. Mack (Eds.), *Human feelings: Explorations in affect development and meaning* (pp. 87–121). New York: Analytic Press.

Brody, L. R., & Hall, J. A. (1993). Gender and emotion. In M. Lewis & J. M. Haviland (Eds.), *Handbook of emotions* (pp. 447–460). New York, NY: The Guilford Press.

Brody, L. R., Lovas, G. S. , & Hay, D. H. (1995). Gender differences in anger and fear as a function of situational context. *Sex Roles, 32*, 47–78.

Burns, J. W. (1995). Interactive effects of traits, states, and gender on cardiovascular reactivity during different situations. *Journal of Behavioral Medicine, 18*, 279–303.

Burns, J. W., Johnson, B. J., Mahoney, N., Devine, J., & Pawl, R. (1996). Anger management style, hostility, and spouse responses: Gender differences in predictors of adjustment among chronic pain patients. *Pain, 64*, 445–453.

Burns, J. W., & Katkin, E. S. (1993). Psychological, situational, and gender predictors of cardiovascular reactivity to stress: A multivariate approach. *Journal of Behavioral Medicine, 16*, 445–465.

Burrowes, B. D., & Halberstadt, A. G. (1987). Self- and family-expressiveness styles in the experience and expression of anger. *Journal of Nonverbal Behavior, 11*, 254–268.

Buss, D. M. (1989). Conflict between the sexes: Strategic interference and the evocation of anger and upset. *Journal of Personality and Social Psychology, 5*, 735–747.

Campos, J. J., Campos, R. G., & Barrett, K. C. (1989). Emergent themes in the study of emotional development and emotion regulation. *Developmental Psychology, 25*, 394–402.

Campbell, A. & Muncer, S. (1987). Models of anger and aggression in the social talk of women and men. *Journal for the Theory of Social Behaviour, 17*, 498–511.

Clore, G. L., Ortony, A., Dienes, B. & Fujita, F. (1993). Where does anger dwell? In R. S. Wyer & T. K. Srull (Eds.), *Perspectives on anger and emotion. Advances in social cognition* (vol. VI, pp. 57–88). Hillsdale, NJ: Lawrence Erlbaum.

Collier, H. V. (1982). *Counseling women: A guide for therapists.* New York, NY: Free Press.

Crawford, J., Kippax, S., Onyx, J., Gault, U., & Benton, P. (1992). *Emotion and gender: Constructing meaning from memory.* London: Sage.

Cupach, W. R., & Canary, D. J. (1995). Managing conflict and anger: Investigating the sex stereotype hypothesis. In P. J. Kalbfleish & M. J. Cody (Eds.), *Gender, power, and communication in human relationships* (pp. 233–252). Hillsdale, NJ: Lawrence Erlbaum.

Deaux, K., & Major, B. (1990). A social psychological model of gender. In D. L. Rhode (Ed.), *Theoretical perspectives on sexual difference* (pp. 89–99). New Haven, CT: Yale University Press.

Deffenbacher, J. L., Oetting, E. R., Lynch, R. S., & Morris, C. A. (1996a). The expression of anger and its consequences. *Behavior Research and Therapy, 34,* 575–590.

Deffenbacher, J. L., Oetting, E. R., Thwaites, G. A., Lynch, R. S., Baker, D. A., Stark, R. S., Thacker, S., & Eiswerth-Cox, L. (1996b). State-Trait anger theory and the utility of the trait anger scale. *Journal of Counseling Psychology, 43,* 131–148.

Denham, G. & Bultemeier, K. (1993). Anger: Targets and triggers. In S. Thomas (Ed.), *Women and anger.* (pp. 68–90). New York: Springer Publishing Company.

de Rivera, J. (1977). *A structural theory of the emotions.* New York: International Universities Press.

Dimberg, U., & Lundquist, L. O. (1990). Gender differences in facial reactions to facial expressions. *Biological Psychology, 30,* 151–159.

Dosser, D., Balswick, J., & Halverson, C. (1983). Situational context of emotional expressiveness. *Journal of Counseling Psychology, 30,* 375–387.

Dryden, J. *To Sir Godfrey Kneller* 1.84.

Eagly, A. H., & Steffen, V. (1986). Gender and aggressive behavior: A meta-analytic review of the social psychological literature. *Psychological Bulletin, 100,* 3–22.

Ekman, P. (1992). An argument for basic emotions. *Cognition and Emotion, 6,* 169–200.

Ekman, P. (1994). Strong evidence for universals in facial expressions: A reply to Russell's mistaken critique. *Psychological Bulletin, 115,* 268–287.

Ekman, P., & Friesen, W. V. (1975). *Unmasking the Face.* Englewood Cliffs, NJ: Prentice-Hall.

Ekman, P., Levenson, R. W., & Friesen, W. V. (1983). Autonomic nervous system activity distinguishes among emotions. *Science, 221,* 1208–1210.

Faber, S. D., & Burns, J. W (1996). Anger management style, degree of expressed anger, and gender influence cardiovascular recovery from interpersonal harassment. *Journal of Behavioral Medicine, 19,* 31–53.

Fabes, R. A., & Martin, C. J. (1991). Gender and age stereotypes of emotionality. *Personality and Social Psychology Bulletin, 17,* 532–540.

Fehr, B. & Baldwin, M. (1996). Prototype and script analyses of laypeople's knowledge of anger. In G. J. O. Fletcher & J. Fitness (Eds.), *Knowledge structures in close relationships: A social psychological approach.* (pp. 219–245). Mahwah, NJ: Lawrence Erlbaum.

Feldman Barrett, L. (1997). The relationship among momentary emotion experiences, personality descriptions, and retrospective ratings of emotion. *Personality and Social Psychology Bulletin, 23,* 1100–1110.

Fischer, A. H. (1993). Sex differences in emotionality: Fact or stereotype? *Feminism and Psychology, 3,* 303–318.

Fischer, P. C., Smith, R. J., Leonard, E., Fuqua, D. R., Campbell, J. L., & Masters, M. A. (1993). Sex differences on affective dimensions : Continuing examination. *Journal of Counseling and Development, 71,* 440–443.

Fivush, R. (1989). Exploring sex differences in mother–child conversations about the past. *Sex Roles, 20,* 675–691.

Fivush, R. (1991). Gender and emotion in mother–child conversations about the past. *Journal of Narrative and Life History, 1,* 325–341.

Friday, N. (1977). *My mother/my self.* New York: Delacorte.

Friedman, H. S., Riggio, R. E., & Segall, D. O. (1980). Personality and the enactment of emotion. *Journal of Nonverbal Behavior, 5,* 35–48.

Frijda, N. (1986). *The emotions*. Cambridge University Press.

Frijda, N. (1992). Universal antecedents exist and are interesting. In P. Ekman & R. J. Davidson (Eds.), *The nature of emotion: Fundamental questions* (pp. 155–162). New York: Oxford University Press.

Frodi, A. (1977). Sex differences in the perception of a provocation: A survey. *Perceptual and Motor Skills, 44,* 113–114.

Frost, W. D. & Averill, J. R. (1982). Differences between men and women in the everyday experience of anger. In J. R. Averill, *Anger and aggression: An essay on emotion* (pp. 281–317). New York: Springer-Verlag.

Fuchs, D., & Thelen, M. H. (1988). Children's expected interpersonal consequences of communicating their affective state and reported likelihood of expression. *Child Development, 59,* 1314–1322.

Ganong, L. H., & Coleman, M. (1985). Sex, sex roles, and emotional expressiveness. *Journal of Genetic Psychology, 146,* 405–411.

Garber, J., & Dodge, K. A. (Eds.) (1991). *The development of emotion regulation and dysregulation*. New York: Cambridge University Press.

Gottman, J. M., & Levenson, R. W. (1986). Assessing the role of emotion in marriage. *Behavioral Assessment, 8,* 31–48.

Gottman, J. M., & Levenson, R. W. (1988). The social psychophysiology of marriage. In P. Noller & M. A. Fitzpatrick (Eds.), *Perspectives on marital interactions* (pp. 182–200). San Diego: College Hill Press.

Gross, J. J. (1998). Antecedent- and response-focused emotion regulation: Divergent consequences for experience, expression, and physiology. *Journal of Personality and Social Psychology, 74,* 224–237.

Gross, J. J., & John, O. P. (1995). Facets of emotional expressivity: Three self-report factors and their correlates. *Personality and Individual Differences, 19,* 555–568.

Gross, J. J., & Levenson, R. W. (1993). Emotional suppression: Physiology, self-report, and expressive behavior. *Journal of Personality and Social Psychology, 64,* 970–986.

Gross, J. J., & Levenson, R. W. (1997). Hiding feelings: The acute effects of inhibiting negative and positive emotion. *Journal of Abnormal Psychology, 106,* 95–103.

Halas, C. (1981). *Why can't a woman be more like a man?* New York: Macmillan.

Harris, M. B. (1993). How provoking! What makes men and women angry? *Aggressive Behavior, 19,* 199–211.

Harris, M. B. (1994). Gender of subject and target as mediators of aggression. *Journal of Applied Social Psychology, 24,* 453–471.

Hoover-Dempsey, K. V., Plas, J. M, & Wallston, B. S. (1986). Tears and weeping among professional women: In search of new understanding. *Psychology of Women Quarterly, 10,* 19–34.

Horace. *Epistles,* bk. 1, no. 2, 1.62.

Izard, C. (1971). *The face of emotion*. New York: Appleton-Century-Croft.

Johnson, J. T., & Shulman, G. A. (1988). More alike than meets the eye: Perceived gender differences in subjective experience and its display. *Sex Roles, 19,* 67–79.

Keltner, D., & Kring, A. M. (1998). Emotion, social function, and psychopathology. *Review of General Psychology, 2,* 320–342.

Keltner, D., Young, R. C., Oemig, C., Heerey, E., & Monarch, N. D. (1998). Predictors and social consequences of teasing: face threat and redressive action in hierarchical and intimate relations. *Journal of Personality and Social Psychology, 75,* 1231–1247.

King, L., & Emmons, R. A. (1990). Conflict over emotional expression: Psychological and physical correlates. *Journal of Personality and Social Psychology, 58,* 864–877.

Kogut, D., Langley, S. & O'Neil, E. C. (1992). Gender role masculinity and angry expression in women. *Sex Roles, 26,* 355–368.

Kopper, B. A. (1991). Role of gender, sex role identity, and Type A behavior in anger expression and mental health functioning. *Journal of Counseling Psychology, 40,* 232–237.

Kopper, B. A., & Epperson, D. L. (1991). Women and anger. Sex and sex role comparisons in the expression of anger. *Psychology of Women Quarterly, 15,* 7–14.

Kopper, B. A., & Epperson, D. L. (1996). The experience and expression of anger: Relationships with gender, gender role socialization, depression, and mental health functioning. *Journal of Counseling Psychology, 43,* 158–165.

Kring, A. M. (1998, April). *Emotion in social interaction: Teasing among women.* Paper presented at the meeting of the Emotion Research Group. Martha's Vineyard, MA.

Kring, A. M., & Bachorowski, J.-A. (1999). Emotion and psychopathology. *Cognition and Emotion, 13,* 575–600.

Kring, A. M. & Gordon, A. H. (1998). Sex differences in emotion: Expression, experience, and physiology. *Journal of Personality and Social Psychology, 74,* 686–703.

Kring, A. M., Smith, D.A., & Neale, J. M. (1994). Individual differences in dispositional expressiveness: Development and validation of the Emotional Expressivity Scale. *Journal of Personality and Social Psychology, 66,* 934–949.

Lai, J. Y, & Linden, W. (1992). Gender, anger expression style, and opportunity for anger release determine cardiovascular reaction to and recovery from anger provocation. *Psychosomatic Medicine, 54,* 297–310.

Lerner, H. (1977). The taboos against female anger. *Menninger Perspective,* 5–11.

Levenson, R. W. (1992). Autonomic nervous system differences among emotions. *Psychological Science, 3,* 23–27.

Levenson, R. W., Ekman, P. , & Friesen, W. V. (1990). Voluntary facial action generates emotion-specific autonomic nervous system activity. *Psychophysiology, 27,* 363–384.

Lewis, M., & Saarni, C. (Eds.) (1985). *The socialization of emotions.* New York: Plenum Press.

Lombardo, W. K., Cretser, G. A., Lombardo, B., & Mathis, S. L. (1983). Fer cryin' out loud – There is a sex difference. *Sex Roles, 9,* 987–996.

Manstead, A. S. R., & Fischer, A. H. (1995, August). *Gender and emotions: The role of powerlessness.* Paper presented at the meeting of the International Society for Research on Emotion, Toronto, Canada.

Mesquita, B., & Frijda, N. H. (1992). Cultural variations in emotions: A review. *Psychological Bulletin, 112,* 179–204.

Ortony, A., Clore, G. L., & Collins, G. L. (1988). *The cognitive structure of emotions.* New York: Cambridge University Press.

Ratner, H., & Stettner, L. (1991). Thinking and feeling: Putting Humpty Dumpty back together again. *Merrill-Palmer Quarterly, 37,* 1–26.

Rotter, N. G., & Rotter, G. S. (1988). Sex differences in the encoding and decoding of negative facial emotions. *Journal of Nonverbal Behavior, 12,* 139–148.

Russell, J. A. (1994). Is there universal recognition of emotion from facial expression? A review of the cross-cultural studies. *Psychological Bulletin, 115,* 102–141.

Russell, J. A. (1995). Facial expressions of emotion: What lies beyond minimal universality? *Psychological Bulletin, 118,* 379–391.

Russell, J. A., & Fehr, B. (1994). Fuzzy concepts in a fuzzy hierarchy: The varieties of anger. *Journal of Personality and Social Psychology, 67,* 186–205.

Saarni, C. (1990). Emotional competence: How emotions and relationships become integrated. In R. Thompson (Ed.), *Nebraska symposium on motivation* (Vol. 36, pp. 115–182). Lincoln: University of Nebraska Press.

Scherer, K. R. (1986). Vocal affect expression: A review and model for future research. *Psychological Bulletin, 99,* 143–165.

Scherer, K. R., Matsumoto, D., Wallbott, H. G., & Kudoh, T. (1988). Emotional experience in cultural context: A comparison between Europe, Japan, and the United States. In K. Scherer (Ed.), *Facets of emotion research: Recent research* (pp. 5–30). Hillsdale, NJ: LEA.

Schwartz, G. E., Brown, S.-L., & Ahern, G. L. (1980). Facial muscle patterning and subjective experience during affective imagery: Sex differences. *Psychophysiology, 17,* 75–82.

Shapiro, D., Goldstein, I. B., & Jamner, L. D. (1995). Effects of anger/hostility, defensiveness, gender, and family history of hypertension on cardiovascular reactivity. *Psychophysiology, 32,* 425–435.

Sharkin, B. S. (1993). Anger and gender: Theory, research, and implications. *Journal of Counseling and Development, 71,* 386–389.

Shields, S. A. (1987). Women, men, and the dilemma of emotion. In P. Shaver & C. Hendrick (Eds.), *Sex and Gender. Review of Personality and Social Psychology* (Vol. 7, pp. 229–250). Newbury Park, CA: Sage.

Shields, S. A. (1991). Gender in the psychology of emotion: A selective research review. In K. T. Strongman (Ed.), *International Review of Studies on Emotion* (pp. 227–245). New York: Wiley.

Smith, K. C., Ulch, S. E., Cameron, J. E., Cumberland, J. A., Musgrave, M. A., & Tremblay, N. (1989). Gender-related effects in the perception of anger expression. *Sex Roles, 20,* 487–499.

Spence, J. T. (1993). Gender-related traits and gender ideology: Evidence for a multifactorial theory. *Journal of Personality and Social Psychology, 64,* 624–635.

Spielberger, C. D. (1988). *State-trait anger expression inventory.* Orlando, FL: Psychological Assessment Resources.

Spielberger, C. D., Johnson, E., Russell, S., Crane, R., Jacobs, G., & Worden, T. (1985). The experience and expression of anger: Construction and validation of an anger expression scale. In M. A. Chesney & R. H. Rosenman (Eds.), *Anger and hostility in cardiovascular and behavioral disorders* (pp. 5–30). New York: McGraw Hill.

Spielberger, C. D., Krasner, S., & Solomon, E. (1988). The experience, expression, and control of anger. In H. Kassinove (Ed.), *Anger disorders: Definition, diagnosis, and treatment* (pp. 49–67). Washington, DC: Taylor & Francis.

Stoner, S. B., & Spencer, W. B. (1987). Age and gender differences with the Anger Expression Scale. *Educational and Psychological Measurement, 47,* 487–492.

Strachan, C. E., & Dutton, D. G. (1992). The role of power and gender in anger responses to sexual jealousy. *Journal of Applied Social Psychology, 22,* 1721–1740.

Tavris, C. (1989). *Anger: The misunderstood emotion.* New York: Simon & Schuster.

Thomas, S. P. (1989). Gender differences in anger expression: Health implications. *Research in Nursing and Health, 12,* 389–398.

Thomas, S. P. (Ed.) (1993). *Women and anger.* New York: Springer Publishing Company.

Thomas, S. P., & Williams, R. L. (1991). Perceived stress, trait anger, modes of anger expression, and health status of college men and women. *Nursing Research, 40,* 303–307.

Timmers, M., Fischer, A. H., & Manstead, A. S. R. (1998). Gender differences in motives for regulating emotions. *Personality and Social Psychology Bulletin, 24,* 974–986.

Wagner, H. L., Buck, R., & Winterbotham, M. (1993). Communication of specific emotions: Gender differences in sending accuracy and communication measures. *Journal of Nonverbal Behavior, 17,* 29–53.

Wagner, H. L., MacDonald, C. J., & Manstead, A. S. R. (1986). Communication of individual emotions by spontaneous facial expressions. *Journal of Personality and Social Psychology, 50,* 737–743.

Walden, T. A., & Ogan, T. A. (1988). The development of social referencing. *Child Development, 59,* 1230–1240.

Wallbott, H. G. & Scherer, K. S. (1989). Assessing emotion by questionnaire. In R. Plutchik & H. Kellerman (Eds.) *Emotion: Theory, research, and practice: The measurement of emotion* (Vol. 4, pp. 55–82). San Diego, CA: Academic Press.

Zemen, J., & Garber, J. (1996). Display rules for anger, sadness, and pain: It depends on who is watching. *Child Development, 67,* 957–973.

Zuckerman, M., Lipets, M. S., Hall Koivumaki, J., & Rosenthal, R. (1975). Encoding and decoding nonverbal cues of emotion. *Journal of Personality and Social Psychology, 32,* 1068–1076.

11. Gender, sadness, and depression: The development of emotional focus through gendered discourse

ROBYN FIVUSH AND JANINE P. BUCKNER

Sadness is, undeniably, a universal human emotion. We all experience loss – the death of loved ones, the ending of significant relationships, the loss of prized possessions, as well as the more mundane losses and disappointments of everyday life. The "natural" response to such loss is sadness (Stein, Liwag, & Wade, 1996). But as with all other emotions, while there is a universal, biological component (Ekman, 1972; Izard, 1971), culture and context exert a ubiquitous influence on the definition, understanding, interpretation and expression of what it means to be sad (e.g., Lutz & White, 1986; Rosaldo, 1984). In this chapter, we explore the ways in which sadness comes to be understood and expressed differently by females and males. Just as different cultures develop different "emotion scripts" that modulate the understanding of emotional experience, we argue that females and males come to understand and integrate emotional experience into their lives in different ways as a result of participating in gender-differentiated activities and interactions.

Gender differences in sadness are particularly compelling because of the large gender differences in depression. Although many theories have been advanced to account for this disparity, little research has explicitly examined the ways in which females and males understand their sad experiences. As we will argue in this chapter, females may both self-report and be diagnosed with more depressive symptoms because they express sadness in more intense ways than do males. However, it must be emphasized at the outset that, although our focus in this chapter is on gender differences, there is a great deal of variability within each gender group as well as differences between them. Moreover, as we will try to demonstrate, gender might be better conceived of as a process, or a way of interacting in the world, rather than as a category (Deaux & Major, 1987).

Gender, culture and emotional learning

Gender, like culture, provides a coherent, interrelated set of understandings about experience. Being a member of a particular gender, like being a member of a particular culture, leads one to engage in activities considered "appropriate" for the group, and through these participatory interactions, one learns the skills deemed necessary to be a member of that group. More specific to emotion, it is quite clear that emotional experience and expression is culturally mediated (see Lutz & Abu-Lughod, 1990, for an overview). On the simplest level, different cultural groups have different emotion vocabularies (see Russell, 1989, for a review). Some cultures do not differentiate between particular emotion states that other cultures do. For example, in some African languages, there is no distinction between anger and sorrow.

Emotion vocabulary matters, because it is emotion words that fundamentally inform members of the culture about the meaningful division of emotional experience. A language that does not differentiate easily between anger and sorrow informs the language user that this is not an important distinction to make in the experience and expression of emotion. In addition to the specific emotion words available, cultures also define the contexts in which emotions are experienced and expressed (Abu-Lughod, 1990). These "emotion scripts" (e.g., Gordon, 1989; White, 1990) define the extended interactional scenarios surrounding an emotion. Although underlying physiological arousal may be a necessary part of experiencing an emotion, the way in which this arousal is interpreted and evaluated depends on the social/cultural context. The culturally appropriate causes of particular emotions, as well as the behavioral expression and consequences of emotional experience are embodied in the culturally transmitted stories, scripts, and sanctions governing the experience.

From this perspective, emotions are clearly social constructs (Sarbin, 1989). Emotions function within social interactions and serve to regulate social interactions (Campos & Barrett, 1984). Moreover, cultural definition and transmission of emotion knowledge is carried through discourse (Lutz & Abu-Lughod, 1990). The ways in which emotions are talked about both inform and constitute emotional experience. The emotion vocabulary available through the culture fundamentally influences how individuals within that culture categorize emotional experience. And the ways in which the causes and consequences of emotional experience are discussed form the emotion scripts which, in turn, modulate an understanding of how emotions are integrated into the ongoing interactions of everyday life. Members of a culture learn what their emotional experience means through participating in everyday activities and discourse imbued with emotion. Most important, this is a developmental process. Through participating in adult-guided interactions, children learn the skills necessary for becoming competent in their culture (Rogoff, 1990), and much of this learning takes place through discourse (Schieffelin & Ochs, 1986). Given this theoretical framework, gender differences in emotion and sadness can be elucidated by examining the ways in which emotion and sadness are integrated into everyday activities and practices, as well as the ways in which emotion and sadness are talked about with others.

Gender, emotionality, and depression

Both historically and in contemporary society, women are perceived to be more emotionally fragile than men (Chesler, 1972). Related to stereotypes of women being more emotional than men overall, women are also perceived to have less control over their emotional life than do men (Labouvie-Vief, 1994). Although the traditional stereotype of the weeping female and the stoic male have softened somewhat over the past twenty years (Basow, 1992), one of the strongest stereotypes related to gender continues to centre on emotionality. Both men and women believe that women experience and express emotions more frequently and more intensely than do men (Fabes & Martin, 1991; Strauss, Munday, McNall, & Wong, 1997). Moreover, this stereotype is particularly strong for sadness.

Gender stereotypes about emotions do seem to have some basis in real behavior (see Brody & Hall, 1993, for a review). In conformity with the stereotypes, women report experiencing emotion more frequently than do men, women show more frequent and intense facial displays of emotion, and women report talking about and valuing emotional experience more than do men (Aries & Johnson, 1983; Balswick & Avertt, 1977). These gender differences appear to emerge during childhood.

At the extreme of emotionality, women are diagnosed with affective disorders more frequently than are men, especially with depression. Although the statistics vary depending on how depression is defined and evaluated, most researchers agree that women are diagnosed with depression 2 to 4 times as frequently as are men (Sprock & Yoder, 1997). Similar to the developmental patterns for expression of emotion overall, there are no differences in the incidence of depression in early childhood, but, beginning in adolescence, gender differences become substantial and remain so until old age.

Of course, the experience of sad emotions is not the same as a prolonged clinical state of depression. Sadness or disappointment in response to a specific event or circumstance is not as intense, nor as pathological, as severe depression, although sadness may lead to the expression of depressive symptoms. While the relations between having the "blues" and clinical depression are somewhat controversial, these kinds of emotional experiences certainly seem to be related.

Of course, depression is an extremely complicated disorder, and in all likelihood there is no simple etiologic explanation either for depression per se, or for gender differences in depression. Although we can discuss specific factors independently for purposes of explication, ultimate explanations will undoubtedly rely on complex interactions of multiple factors. A recent review by Sprock and Yoder (1997) provides a clear and concise discussion of the various explanations of gender differences in depression, which we summarize only briefly here. Basically, there are three classes of explanations advanced: biological influences, psychological theories, and gender bias in description and diagnosis of depression (see also Golombok & Fivush, 1994, and Nolen-Hoeksema, 1987, for discussions).

Biological theories fall into three types. One line of evidence suggests that there is a genetic basis to mood disorders, such as depression. However, although there is some evidence for genetic linkage, the relation between genes and gender differences in depression is unclear. A second class of biological explanations links depression to levels of sex hormones. Women who suffer from pre-menstrual syndrome and postpartum depression are also more likely to show other episodes of depression, suggesting a link between estrogen levels and depressed mood. Moreover, the emergence of gender differences in depression during adolescence suggests that the onset of puberty may play a role. But there are no relations between menopause and depression, undermining at least part of this argument. A final class of biological explanations point to the role of neurotransmitters. There do seem to be gender differences in monoamine synthesis and uptake, one of the key neurotransmitters implicated in depressed state, and there also seem to be gender differences in rates of glucose utilization, which may also be related to depression. Taken together, however, the data on biological differences are not overwhelming; biology alone cannot account for the large observed gender differences in depression.

Psychological theories implicate either the individual's coping styles, or the social conditions conducive to depressed state. Intra-individual explanations rest on the argument that the traditional female role, which is passive and submissive and involves giving up control, may lead to feelings of helplessness and depression. Related to this, females are more likely than males to seek support when feeling depressed than are males. Nolen-Hoeksema (1987) developed this particular gender difference into a theory of depression based on rumination. Because females tend to seek out others with whom to discuss their sad feelings, they fall into a style of ruminating over sad events, leading to a focus on sadness, which in turn, can lead to depression. Males, in contrast, tend to use a distracting style; when sad, men try to evade the situation by thinking about or doing something else. In this way, men do not ruminate on feeling sad and do not spiral down into depression. Still, it must be emphasized that distraction is not a perfect coping strategy either, as not dealing with one's feelings can lead to externalizing disorders such as alcoholism and violent behavior. The point is that either strategy, rumination or distraction, when taken to the extreme is detrimental, but because women are more likely than men to use rumination as a coping strategy, they are more likely to develop internalizing disorders such as depression.

A somewhat different class of explanations focuses on gender biases in the diagnosis of depression. In particular, several theorists have argued that because therapists share the cultural stereotypes, they are more likely to see women as depressive than men, and are more likely to interpret the same symptoms as indicating depression in women than in men. In addition, because women express more emotion, and are more likely to ruminate on sad feelings than are men, they are more likely to talk about sadness and depression with therapists than are men, again leading to differential diagnosis. That is, men may feel just as depressed as women, but because women talk about their feelings more than men, they are perceived by others, including therapists, as more depressed.

Overall, then, whereas biology is a factor which must be considered, gender differences in depression appear to be largely socially based. Women focus more on emotional experience, women acknowledge and discuss emotions more openly, and women seem to ruminate more on sadness than do men, leading to a greater propensity for emotionally based disorders such as depression. But this explanation of depression leads to an intriguing paradox. Women are more likely to suffer depression than are men because they are more likely to express and discuss the sad events of their lives with others. Yet we also know that having a strong social support network, and being able to discuss personal experiences and feelings with others buffers one against depression, and that women have larger and more intimate social networks than males (see Turner, 1994, for a review). Given that a critical social factor implicated in depression is lack of social support, why would women, who have larger social support networks than do men, simultaneously be at greater risk of depression? An answer must lie in the quality of women's social support networks.

Gender, friendship, and social disclosure

An integral part of being human is relating to other people, and both males and females develop deep and meaningful relationships. Yet there are pervasive gender differences in the ways in which females and males relate to others. Females report valuing friendship more than do males, and females spend more time with their friends in one-on-one intimate conversations, whereas males tend to participate in various kinds of activities with their friends (Aries & Johnson, 1983; Balswick & Avertt, 1977). Across adulthood, women are more expressive in their relationships than are men; they talk more frequently and more intimately with their friends than do men (Fox, Gibbs, & Auerbach, 1985). Conversational topics also vary by gender (Bischoping, 1993). Women tend to discuss personal experiences, feelings, hopes, and dreams, whereas men are more likely to discuss politics, sports, and current events. When discussing the personal past, females tend to focus on events with social motives, such as wanting to be loved, to help another, and to increase emotional closeness to another, whereas males tend to highlight themes of separation, or uniqueness from others (Adams, 1997; Adcock & Ross, 1983; Thorne, 1995). As a consequence of such differences, women's friendships have generally been characterized as "expressive," whereas men's friendships are usually labeled "instrumental."

Along these lines, Mazur (1989) examined college students' written responses to a thematic apperception test, and related these stories to students' evaluations of their friendships. Female students wrote stories strikingly higher in affiliation themes than did their male peers; their stories focused on interactants' desires to relate to each other and to share their lives. Females also reported their own friendships to involve more disclosure than did males, and females reported being more involved with their friends than did males.

In examining disclosure in more detail, Snell and his colleagues (Snell, Miller, & Belk, 1988; Snell, Belk, Flowers, & Warren, 1988; Snell Miller, Belk, Garcia-Falconi, & Hernandez-Sanchez, 1989) found that women and men disclose equally about nonemotional topics, but women consistently disclose more about emotions than do men. Even more interesting, women are significantly more likely to talk with friends about negative emotions, such as depression, anxiety, and fear, than are men. Further, women talk about these negative emotions with a greater variety of people than do men. These patterns indicate that women discuss sad and depressing events more frequently than do men. Moreover, when men do discuss these emotions, they are more likely to discuss them with women than with men. Thus women not only disclose more of their own negative emotions to others, but they also listen to other's discussions of negative emotions more than do men.

In general, when discussing their friendships, females are substantially more likely than males to talk about feelings of empathy and responsibility for others. Empathy is most often defined as the vicarious experience of another's emotional state (Feshbach, 1975, as cited in Robinson, Zahn-Waxler, & Emde, 1994). This emotion is focused on relieving others' distress and is contingent upon sensitivity to others' emotional experiences. Females at all ages report and are rated as having higher empathy than males (Eisenberg, Shell, Pasternack, Lennon, Beller, & Mathy, 1987; Robinson et al., 1994).

Gender differences in empathy are surely related to differences in self-concept. Women define themselves in relation to other people; they are embedded in a web of relationships and see their self definition stemming from these relationships (Gilligan, 1982; Markus & Oyserman, 1989; Thorne, 1995). Men, in contrast, tend to define themselves more autonomously. They see themselves as independent and separate from others. In a sense, women define themselves *in concert with* other people whereas men define themselves *in contrast to* other people. And because women define themselves more in terms of relationships with others than do men, it stands to reason that they are also more centrally concerned with others' well-being than are men.

Related to this, females generally place their emotional experience in the context of interpersonal relationships. Females are significantly more likely than males to talk about emotional experience as occurring around, about and with others, both in adulthood and adolescence, and these effects are particularly strong when experiencing and expressing sadness (Adams, 1997; Stapley & Haviland, 1989). Thus females place themselves in a web of interconnectedness and experience themselves and their emotions as interpersonally situated. This is a consistent thread in the literature on gender differences in friendship patterns and self-disclosure.

These findings point to two ways in which gender differences in friendship patterns and self-concept may relate to gender differences in sadness and depression. First, given that females tend to invest more emotionally in friendships, rely on this social support in coping with emotional experiences, and largely see others as integral parts of their own self-concepts, disturbances in social networks may be more disruptive and distressing for females than for males, leading to greater vulnerability to depression. Second, because females' friendships are more intimate than are males', females engage in more self-disclosure, and more discussion of sad and distressing events with their friends than do males. This pattern of talking about and listening to sadness may in turn lead females to a more ruminative coping style.

Moreover, females and males may depend differentially on the support provided by social networks. For example, Robbins and Tanck (1991) found that female and male college students reported comparable occurrences of interpersonal problems, but females were significantly more likely than males to experience depressive symptoms following these disturbances. Similarly, Slavin and Rainer (1990) found that social support had more impact on adolescent girls' depressive symptoms than boys'. Whereas boys' symptoms were independent of the quality of social relationships, girls had higher reports of perceived non-family adult and friend support, as well as higher depressive symptoms. The patterns in family relations in relation to the occurrence of depressive symptoms suggest that females are significantly more sensitive and vulnerable to ruptures in their support networks than are males, and that stressful life events, particularly those which test relationships, may negatively affect mental health.

Paradoxically, then, females' strong emotional ties to others provide both a buffer and a vulnerability to depression. As females disclose more about their emotional life with others, particularly negative feelings of depression, sadness, and anxiety, they may extend this style inappropriately and ruminate about sad and depressing feelings. Similarly, by responding too empathetically to others' sad and distressing experiences, women may take on too much responsibility for others' well-being. Thus, what is normally a healthy emotional attachment to others, which provides critical social support, may become unhealthy when taken to its extremes.

Socialization of sadness

Provocatively, gender differences in friendship patterns and emotional expressivity appear to emerge extremely early in development. As early as the preschool years, girls engage in more nurturing and cooperative play, whereas boys engage in more aggressive and competitive play (Leaper, 1991; Sheldon, 1990). These patterns become even more exaggerated during middle childhood. Girls form more close and intimate "best friends" with whom they engage in one-on-one play, and oftentimes, this "play" involves a great deal of conversation. Boys, in contrast, engage friends in group activities which emphasize team membership, conformity to rules, and little conversational interaction (Lever, 1976). Even when with their "best friend," 8-year-old boys talk about sports and television, whereas 8-year-old girls are already sharing problems and discussing emotions (Camerena, Sarigiani, & Petersen, 1990; Tannen, 1990).

Such themes of connectedness for females and separation for males are also seen more generally in children's talk about their personal past. For example, Buckner and Fivush (in press) report that 8-year-old girls included more affiliative themes, made more mention of other people, and used more emotion talk than boys in their autobiographical narratives. Empathetic concern, particularly for others' reactions of sadness, is also evident quite early in development, with females expressing empathy more strongly than males (Zahn-Waxler, Robinson, & Emde, 1992; Strayer, 1989).

A critical question is how to account for these gender differences in disclosure and discussion of sad events. From our position, gender, like culture, is a way of interacting in the world, and we argue that gender-appropriate activities and skills are learned through gender-differentiated interactions with others. Early on, children are aware of the ramifications of emotional expression, and the cultural appropriateness of emotions in specific contexts. For example, Zeman and Shipman (1996) found that as early as middle childhood, both boys and girls expect supportive reactions from others in response to their own expressions of sadness, but girls reported feeling better after expressing sadness and pain, as compared with boys. Moreover, girls and boys reported different methods for communicating their emotions. Girls expressed sadness through verbalization and crying. Boys, on the other hand, reported expressing negative emotions through aggression, mainly for anger, but also for sadness. Interestingly, girls, more so than boys, believed one should always express feelings, particularly pain and sadness.

Furthermore, children also hold expectations about the interpersonal consequences of emotion (for a review see Zeman & Shipman, 1996). Fuchs and Thelen (1988, as cited in Zeman & Shipman, 1996) found elementary school children to be sensitive to the fact that parents approve of and encourage the expression of emotions differently depending upon the gender of the child and the particular emotion in question. More specifically, children perceived mothers to support sadness more than fathers, but there were no differential predictions for anger. Boys also expected less parental support for expressing negative emotions as they got older, but girls showed no differences over time. Throughout middle childhood, girls continued to expect parents to support the expression of negative and sad emotions.

Individual differences in empathy and other emotional expressions are linked to the amount and quality of emotional support provided by significant others, particularly parents. There is considerable evidence that lack of parental warmth and support and rejecting parenting styles lead to little empathetic development, limited emotional closeness to others (Camarena, et al., 1990), low self-worth and depressed affect in adolescents (Whitbeck, Hoyt, Miller, & Kao, 1992). In general, such a relationship between parental support and depressed affect are stronger for girls than for boys.

These patterns indicate that the kinds of support children receive for their emotional displays are a critical part of how children learn to understand and express their emotional experience. Moreover, there is some suggestion that displays of emotion, and particularly sadness, may follow different developmental pathways for girls and for boys. Indeed, a series of studies from our research laboratory has demonstrated that gender differentiated socialization of emotion, and especially sadness, begins very early in development. We have examined the ways in which parents and their preschool children discuss specific past experiences, with a focus on how emotions are integrated into these reminiscences. We are interested in examining systematically the ways in which parents and children talk about emotional experiences in order to understand one process by which children learn "gender-appropriate" emotional expressions.

Talking about past emotions may play a particularly important role in emotional socialization for several reasons (see Fivush, 1993, and Fivush & Kuebli, 1997, for full theoretical discussions). First, in talking about past emotions, the child is not in the heat of the emotional moment, and may be in a better position to reflect on and interpret emotional experience. Second, in reminiscing, parents can select to focus on specific emotions over others. For example, parents may talk a great deal about the child's feelings of sadness and hardly at all about feelings of anger. In this way, the parent is implicitly informing the child that sadness is a more appropriate and self-defining emotion than is anger. Finally, in reminiscing, parents and children have more opportunity to reflect on the causes and consequences of emotional experience, and in this way, parents and children co-construct appropriate "emotional scripts."[1]

In all of our studies, families are visited in their homes, and parents are asked to sit with their children and discuss specific past events. In a preliminary study (Fivush, 1989), mothers were asked to select several distinctive events and discuss them with their 30- to 35-month old children in as natural a way as possible. Instructions to mothers made no mention of emotion, and conversations were audiotaped for transcription. On average, mothers and children spontaneously used emotion language in 54% of the events they discussed. Mothers used about the same number of emotion words per event with daughters (M = 2.22) and sons (M = 2.70), but mothers and sons were more likely to discuss negative emotions than were mothers and daughters. Interestingly, boys themselves initiated 50% of the mother–son conversations about negative emotions, but girls initiated only 18% of the mother–daughter conversations about negative emotions, although there were no gender differences for conversations about positive emotions.

A closer examination showed that both mother–son and mother–daughter dyads used specific positive emotion words such as "happy," "love," and "like" with similar frequency. However, interesting gender differences emerged in the specific negative words used; in particular, 54% of all negative emotion terms mentioned by mothers of girls referred to "sad/cry," but such terms accounted for just 14% of the negative emotion words used with sons (the remaining words referred to anger, fear or general dislike). Because the children themselves at this young age used so few emotion words, separate analyses on their emotion talk could not be performed.

From this study it appears that maternal conversations about emotion with children not yet 3 years old are moderated by gender. To investigate these patterns further, Adams, Kuebli, Boyle and Fivush (1995) conducted a longitudinal study of parent–child emotion talk across the preschool years. Parents and children were visited in their homes when children were 40 months old and again when they were 70 months old, and asked at each time point to discuss, in as natural a way as possible, several distinctive past events. In addition to mother–child conversations, fathers were also asked to discuss specific past experiences with their children in a separate session. Given the previous findings in the literature that females and males discuss emotions in different ways, Adams et al. were interested in both parental and child gender differences in emotion talk. Again, no mention was made as to the inclusion of emotion in these conversations. The resulting narratives from each time point were coded for the number of spontaneously occurring emotion terms, as well as the variety of emotions discussed.

Somewhat surprisingly, mothers and fathers did not differ from each other in amount or variety of emotion terms used. However, whereas Fivush (1989) had previously reported no differences in mothers' overall amount of emotion talk with their 30- to 35-month old daughters and sons, in this study, both mothers and fathers used more emotion words with daughters than with sons at 40- and 70 months of age. Again, there were no differences between mothers and fathers in their use of positive terms; in general, both parents focused on positive evaluations with both sons and daughters at both time points. Two differences emerged, however, in negative emotion talk. By 70 months, parents made more general negative evaluations (e.g., "You hated that party, didn't you?" or "You were fussy") with daughters than with sons. And across time, parents mentioned sadness more often with girls (29 times) than with boys (12 times).

Because the children in this study were older than in the previous study, they were better able to contribute to the emotional content of the conversations. Thus, it was possible to conduct analyses on children's use of emotion terms as well. Predictably, children's talk about emotion increased as they grew older. However, whereas at 40 months, girls and boys used about the same number and variety of emotion terms, by 70 months of age girls used twice as many unique emotion words (M = 4.2) as did boys (M = 1.7). Due to the limited number of emotion terms used by children, however, it is unclear how much children talked about sadness per se.

These findings suggest that by the end of the preschool years, parent–child conversations about past events spontaneously take on different emotional tones depending upon the gender of the child. When talking about the past, emotions are part of the story, helping to guide evaluations and personal significance of experience. In conversations with young preschoolers, mothers tend to discuss more negative emotional aspects of experience with boys than girls, although even early on, mothers discuss sadness more with daughters than with sons. But as children grow older, it appears that parents are discussing emotions – particularly sadness and negative evaluations – more often with daughters than with sons. And by the end of the preschool years, daughters are contributing more emotion talk on their own than are sons.

Whereas these studies explore how emotions are spontaneously incorporated into parent–child reminiscing, they do not examine how specific kinds of emotional experiences are constructed in retrospect. To address such concerns, Fivush (1991) investigated the influence of gender on conversations explicitly focused on children's past *emotional* experiences. Mothers were asked to converse at home with their 32- to 35-month-old children about 4 specific past events in which their child experienced happiness, sadness, anger, or fear. Narratives were transcribed and emotion words within them were identified. All emotional utterances were coded as being an attribution (e.g., "I was really sad," or "You were angry, huh?") or an explanation (e.g., "I felt sad when I fell," or "That bee really scared me.").

In examining the specific emotions discussed, mothers, overall, talked more about sadness in conversation with daughters than with sons, and mothers made more explanations about sadness than simple attributions, and did so almost twice as much with girls than with boys. Coupled with differences in explanation were more qualitative observations about mothers' provision of resolutions. Mothers provided comforting responses when discussing sadness with daughters, but offered little comfort to sons, suggesting "mothers are more concerned with reassuring and comforting daughters feeling sad than sons" (Fivush, 1991, p. 334).

The most recent study from our laboratory of parent–child emotion narratives adds to the emerging pattern in emotion socialization. Extending the findings above to fathers as well, Fivush, Brotman, Buckner, and Goodman (1997) asked mothers and fathers independently to discuss 4 specific past events with their 40- to 45-month children during which the child experienced happiness, anger, sadness, and fear. In contrast to Adams et al.'s (1995) findings of no differences in the quantity of mothers' and fathers' emotion talk, Fivush et al. (1997) found mothers talked more overall, talked more about emotional aspects of events, and used more specific emotion words than did fathers, although mothers and fathers used about the same percentage of negative and positive words. When discussing sadness, however, both mothers and fathers made more emotional utterances with daughters (M = 7.05) than with sons (M = 6.20). Further, of these emotional utterances, parents made proportionately more statements about causes of sadness with girls (M = .55) than with boys (M = .25). These findings support those previously reported by Adams et al.

Several differences between parents were paralleled in children's narrative contributions. While girls did not talk more than boys overall, like their mothers, a larger portion (M = 37%) of their narratives focused on the emotional aspects of experience than boys (M = 21%). More specific analyses revealed that girls gave proportionately more emotional propositions about the causes of sadness (M = .59) than did boys (M = .23), but there were no differences for the other emotions. Considering the overall theme of the narratives, parents and daughters placed the majority of emotional experiences within an interpersonal scenario (52%) (e.g., sister teasing child, friend hurting another friend). With sons, narratives were most often set in autonomous activities (64%) (i.e., getting an A on a math test, hurting his finger in the woods).

A final finding in the Fivush et al. (1997) data is worth noting. When discussing events during which children experienced happy, angry, sad, or scared feelings, both parents and children often discussed a wide range of emotions. For instance, in talking about "scared" events parents often talked about other emotional feelings and behaviors, such as anger or sadness. As is evident from table 11.1, the majority of "sad" words were spoken during narratives about sadness. However, sadness was also discussed within the other emotion narratives as well, particularly when discussing fear. Chi-square analyses indicated that, regardless of the target emotion being discussed, mothers used more "sad"

Table 11.1. *Number of "sad" words mentioned by parents and children, by dyad type and target emotion*

Dyad Participants	Emotion				
	Sad	Angry	Scared	Happy	Total
PARENTS					
Mothers					
with daughters	43	2	12	1	58
with sons	23	2	6	1	32
Fathers					
with daughters	40	1	5	0	46
with sons	22	6	0	0	28
CHILDREN					
Daughters					
with mothers	15	1	7	0	23
with fathers	7	2	1	0	10
Sons					
with mothers	4	0	0	0	4
with fathers	7	4	0	0	11

Note:
[a] Total category is the total number of "sad" words mentioned within all emotion narratives.
Source:
Data from Fivush, Brotman, Buckner, & Goodman, 1997.

words with both daughters and sons than did fathers. Moreover, both mothers and fathers used almost twice as many "sad" words with daughters than with sons, $X^2 = 35.22$, $p < .001$. Children mentioned sadness more with mothers than with fathers, and daughters referred to sadness twice as often as sons, $X^2 = 7.78$, $p < .05$.

The results from our research reveal a complex pattern in the ways in which parents and children discuss emotional aspects of experience, and different studies have yielded somewhat different findings. In spite of these discrepancies, however, one consistent finding emerges in every study: mothers and fathers talk more about sadness with daughters than with sons. This pattern is apparent in the length of parents' conversations about sadness, and in the frequency and variety of specific "sad" words used. And, by the end of the preschool years, girls independently talk more than do boys about their sad experiences.

These quantitative patterns in parent–child talk about sadness may be observed qualitatively as well, as seen in the following excerpts from

Fivush et al. (1997). In the first excerpt, a mother and her 40-month old daughter, Ellen, are discussing a specific time when the child felt sad. They focus on an incident with a friend:

> M: You were very sad, and what happened? Why did you feel sad?
> C: Because Malaika, Malaika, she was having [unintelligible word].
> M: Yes.
> C: And then she stood up on my bed and it was my bedroom. She's not allowed to sleep in there.
> M: Is that why you were sad?
> C: Yeah. Now it makes me happy. I also [unintelligible word]. It makes me sad but Malaika just left . . . and then I cried.
> M: And you cried because . . .
> C: Malaika left.
> M: Because Malaika left? And did that make you sad?
> C: And then I cried [makes crying sounds] like that. I cried and cried and cried and cried.
> M: I know, I know. I thought you were sad because Malaika left, but I didn't know you were sad because Malaika slept in your bed.

In this interchange, the issues surrounding the experience of sadness are complex. Ellen explains she was sad because her friend both slept in her bed and then left. Ellen is therefore dealing with two very different reasons for feeling sad, a violation of her own private space, and the loss of her friend when she leaves the house. Interestingly, Ellen's mother expects Malaika's leaving to be the cause of sadness. But as they talk about the event, she recognizes, and then validates, her daughter's own perspective of the event. These are very complicated feelings linked to a special relationship in a little girl's life. In another conversation, Jackson, about 40 months, and his mother also discuss a theme of "leaving," but in this case, a different kind of interchange ensues.

> M: Do you remember when we were at Debbie's house yesterday and it was time to go home?
> C: Yeah.
> M: When I came in the door and you cried? Do you remember? Why did you cry?
> C: Because I wanted to.
> M: Why did you cry when you saw me?
> C: Because um the movie was over and you and I had to go and I wanted more grape juice.
> M: You knew that it was time to go and the movie was over and you wanted your grape juice?
> C: Uhhuh.
> M: Why didn't you want to come home?
> C: Because I didn't want to.
> M: Did that feel good or bad?
> C: Bad!

Although Jackson and his mother also talk about feeling sad about leaving, the theme of this conversation is very different from that between Ellen and her mother. Ellen's sadness is clearly interpersonal in nature. Both she and her mother explicitly link her feelings to her friend, Malaika. Jackson's mother, however, is unsuccessful in getting Jackson to acknowledge Debbie's role in his own experience of feeling sad. While she attempts to relate his sadness to the interpersonal scenario, Jackson responds by focusing on his own wishes. When asked about the reason for his feelings, Jackson simply explains he just didn't want to leave. Furthermore, he states, he was sad because he couldn't get more of what he wanted – more grape juice.

Several other differences may be found in these two conversations. In the first example, we see a rich conversation between a mother and daughter who are both very much engaged in negotiating the circumstances leading to Ellen's sadness. It is a fairly long interchange, and much mention is made of sadness itself and crying by both mother and child. In contrast to this dialogue, however, the mother and son in the second excerpt have considerably less to say on the subject. In fact, sadness is mentioned only 4 times, by the mother, and Jackson's participation, which hardly makes mention of any emotion, is limited to two bits of information. His one emotional utterance ("Bad") was only in reply to a generic, forced-choice question from his mother ("Did that feel good or bad?"). Mom carries all the weight in this emotional conversation. Most interestingly, in the first conversation, Ellen's mother realizes and confirms a new side to her daughter's experience; Jackson's mother, on the other hand, never comments on his explanation, beyond repeating what he said.

Such differences in the ways parents, daughters, and sons elaborate upon emotions certainly impact the ways children themselves come to interpret, understand, and later talk about their experiences. In fact, by middle childhood, girls and boys are telling very different stories about personally significant life experiences. Buckner and Fivush (in press) asked 8-year old children to narrate about several emotionally laden personal experiences and found that girls mentioned sadness, crying, and other depression-related emotion words twice as often (17 times) as boys did (6 times). Furthermore, girls not only used more "sad" words, but used more emotion language in general, talked more than boys overall, and tended to mention interpersonal themes more often than did their male peers. For example, in response to an experimenter´s prompt to tell about feeling alienated, girls more often defined their feelings in terms of broken relationships, whereas boys typically referred to activities that were not acknowledged or rewarded by others.

Conclusions

Although there is little research on adult gender differences in sadness per se, research on friendship and emotional disclosure patterns indicate that females and males discuss sad experiences very differently. Females talk more about sad events to others, hear more about sad events from others, and place sadness in interpersonal contexts to a greater extent than do males. Obviously both women and men experience sadness in their lives, but when feeling sad, women are more likely than men to seek out others with whom they can share these feelings. And the others sought are most often females, who not only listen to others' sadness, but respond more empathetically than do males. Thus women are more likely to focus on both their own and other's experiences of sadness than are men, and are also more likely to feel sad themselves about other's experiences. In essence, females learn to focus on emotions in general, and sadness in particular, by participating in gendered discourse about emotions which begins in early parent–child interactions and continues throughout childhood and adulthood.

Because females talk more about sad events, they may also come to understand sadness in qualitatively different ways than do males. Females may come to understand sadness as a more integral part of everyday life. Moreover, women may conceptualize sadness as an emotion that links people together, through sharing and communicating, more so than do men. Sadness is both a cause and a consequence of interconnectedness for females. These patterns conform to a style of rumination about sadness that has been described in the literature as a contributing factor to depression. As Nolen-Hoeksema (1987) has argued, one reason why women may experience depression more often than men is because women are more likely to ruminate on the sad events of life.

Gender differences between adults in the discussion and disclosure about sadness raise the obvious question of the origins of these differences. Biology undoubtedly plays some role, but biological gender differences must be articulated in particular social-cultural contexts. The qualities that are valued and/or sanctioned by particular cultures modulate which biological propensities will be reinforced or downplayed. Indeed, examining the social interactions in which females and males engage beginning very early in development, suggests that gender differences in sadness are at least partly produced in gender differentiated forms of discourse, especially when reminiscing about emotionally laden past events. In general, parents seem to talk more about emotion overall with daughters than with sons, although the patterns are complex. But for sadness, clear and consistent gender differences emerge beginning as early as age 2 to 3 years. Specifically, parents talk more about sad events, explicitly mention sadness more frequently, and talk more about the causes of sadness when reminiscing with daughters than with sons. Although there are no gender differences between girls and boys in discussing sadness early in the preschool years, by the end of the preschool years, girls are discussing sadness with their parents overwhelmingly more than are boys. And it is not just when conversing with their parents, even when discussing their experiences with friends or strangers, girls talk more about sadness than do boys.

In addition to a focus on sadness, women also place sad experiences in a more interpersonal context than do men. Again, we see this difference already emerging in early parent–child conversations. When reminiscing with their preschoolers, parents discuss emotions in a more interpersonal context with daughters than with sons. Parent–daughter conversations include more references to social interactions, and to other people's emotions during these interactions than do parent–son conversations. And again, by middle childhood we see this same pattern in girls' discussion of their past experiences in conversation with friends and strangers. Thus the patterns that begin in parent-guided conversations soon become an aspect of the individual's style, such that little girls focus more on sadness than boys, and place sad experiences in a more interpersonal context than do boys.

It is through discourse about emotion that individuals learn what it means to be sad. For females, at least within white middle-class Western culture, sadness is a frequent and reportable emotion. Talking about sadness with others is an acceptable and important form of social interaction, and through talk about sadness, sadness becomes a self-defining aspect of females' experience more so than males'. Moreover, sadness is often caused by other people's distress, emphasizing the connections between people. In many ways this is a positive aspect of female identity, as sadness links people together in a web of interconnectedness. Sharing the emotional experiences of our lives creates interpersonal bonds. But when taken to an extreme, talking about sadness can have disastrous outcomes. By focusing too heavily on sad events, and by empathetically feeling others' sadness to too great a degree, females become vulnerable to depressive symptoms. The very bonds that link females together in healthy support networks can negatively impact the individual's self-concept when strained or ruptured.

In contrast, males learn that sadness is not an appropriate topic of conversation. Conversations about sad events are short and the emotion of sadness is rarely mentioned explicitly. Causes of sadness are more likely to center on themes of autonomy than on themes of interconnectedness. Thus, for males, sadness does not link people together, either through discussions about sadness or through an understanding of the causes of sadness. This may buffer males against depressive symptoms, but simultaneously make them more vulnerable to externalizing disorders. Because sad experiences cannot be discussed to a great extent, and because males' self-concept becomes defined as separate from others, males are vulnerable to isolation, leading to aggressive reactions, such as addictive and violent behavior.

What does it mean to be sad? Certainly sadness involves loss. But for females, sadness is a loss of self-in-relation, whereas for males, sadness is a loss of self-in-control. Obviously this is an overly simplistic and extreme characterization; the experience and expression of all emotions, including sadness, is multiply determined and complex, and there are as many similarities between the genders as there are differences. However, females and males discuss sadness with others in different ways, and through these gender-differentiated discourses, females and males construct different understandings of sadness. To be sad is an inevitable part of life; how one is sad is part of being female or male.

Author note

Please address correspondence to: Robyn Fivush, Department of Psychology, Emory University, Atlanta, GA 30322, USA (e-mail: fivush@social-sci.ss.emory.edu).

Notes

1. It is important to note that our research has focused on white middle-class families, and our results may not generalize to other populations. Because we believe that gender can be conceptualized in similar ways to culture, and that cultures help define and modulate emotional experience, we also believe that different sub-cultures may construct gender-differentiated emotion scripts in different ways. Thus this research should be viewed as a first step in understanding the myriad ways in which gender and culture interact in producing emotional behavior.

References

Abu-Lughod, L. (1990). Shifting politics in Bedouin love poetry. In C. A. Lutz & L. Abu-Lughod (Eds.), *Language and the politics of emotion* (pp. 24–45). New York: Cambridge University Press.

Adams, S. (1997). *Gender differences in emotion and self-concept*. Unpublished doctoral dissertation, Emory University, Atlanta, GA.

Adams, S., Kuebli, J., Boyle, P. A., & Fivush, R. (1995). Gender differences in parent–child conversations about past emotions: A longitudinal investigation. *Sex Roles, 33*, 309–323.

Adcock, N. V., & Ross, M. W. (1983). Early memories, early experiences and personality. *Social Behavior and Personality, 11*, 95–100.

Aries, E., & Johnson, F. (1983). Close friendship in adulthood: Conversational content between same-sex friends. *Sex Roles, 9,* 1183–1196.

Balswick, J., & Avertt, C. P. (1977). Differences in expressiveness: Gender, interpersonal orientation and perceived parental expressiveness as contributing factors. *Journal of Marriage and the Family, 38,* 121–127.

Basow, S. A. (1992). *Gender stereotypes and roles.* Belmont, CA: Brooks-Cole.

Bischoping, K. (1993). Gender differences in conversation topics: 1922–1990. *Sex Roles, 28,* 1–18.

Brody, L. R., & Hall, J. A. (1993). Gender and emotion. In M. Lewis & J. M. Haviland (Eds.), *Handbook of emotions* (pp. 447–460). New York: Guilford Press.

Buckner, J. P., & Fivush, R. (in press). Gender and self in children's autobiographical narratives. *Applied Cognitive Psychology.*

Camarena, P. M., Sarigiani, P. A., & Petersen, A. C. (1990). Gender-specific pathways to intimacy in early adolescence. *Journal of Youth and Adolescence, 19,* 19–32.

Campos, J. J., & Barrett, K. C. (1984). Toward a new understanding of emotions and their development. In C. E. Izard, J. Kagen, & R. B. Zajonc (Eds.), *Emotions, cognition and behavior* (pp. 229–263). New York, NY: Cambridge University Press.

Chesler, P. (1972). *Women and madness.* New York, NY: Doubleday.

Deaux, K., & Major, B. (1987). Putting gender into context: An interactive model of gender-related behavior. *Psychological Review, 94,* 369–389.

Ekman, P. (1972). Universals and cultural differences in facial expressions of emotion. In J. Cole (Ed.), *Nebraska Symposium on Motivation* (pp. 207–284). Lincoln, NB: University of Nebraska Press.

Eisenberg, N., Shell, R., Pasternack, J., Lennon, R., Beller, R., & Mathy, R. M. (1987). Prosocial development in middle childhood: A longitudinal study. *Developmental Psychology, 23,* 712–718.

Fabes, R. A., & Martin, C. L. (1991). Gender and age stereotypes of emotionality. *Personality and Social Psychology Bulletin, 17,* 532–540.

Fivush, R. (1989). Exploring sex differences in the emotional content of mother–child conversations about the past. *Sex Roles, 20,* 675–691.

Fivush, R. (1991). Gender and emotion in mother-child conversations about the past. *Journal of Narrative and Life History, 1,* 325–341.

Fivush, R. (1993). Emotional content of parent-child conversations about the past. In C. A. Nelson (Ed.), *The Minnesota Symposium on Child Psychology: Memory and affect in development* (pp. 39–77). Hillsdale, NJ: Lawrence Erlbaum.

Fivush, R. (in press). Interest, gender and personal narrative: How children construct self-understanding. In A. Karp, A. Renninger, J. Baumeister, & L. Hoffman (Eds.), *Interest and gender in education.*

Fivush, R., & Kuebli, J. (1997). Making everyday events emotional: The construal of emotion in parent–child conversations about the past. In N. Stein, P. A. Ornstein, C. A. Brainerd, & B. Tversky (Eds.), *Memory for everyday and emotional events* (pp. 239–266). Hillsdale: NJ: Lawrence Erlbaum.

Fivush, R., Brotman, M., Buckner, J.P., & Goodman, S. (1997). *Gender differences in parent–child emotion narratives.* Submitted manuscript.

Fox, M., Gibbs, M., & Auerbach, D. (1985). Age and gender dimensions of friendship. *Psychology of Women Quarterly, 9,* 489–502.

Gilligan, C. (1982). *In a different voice: Psychological theory and women's development.* Cambridge, MA: Harvard University Press.

Golombok, S., & Fivush, R. (1994). *Gender development.* New York, NY: Cambridge University Press.

Gordon, S. L. (1989). The socialization of children's emotions: emotional culture, competence, and exposure. In C.A. Saarni & P. L. Harris (Eds.), *Children's understanding of emotion* (pp. 293–318). New York, NY: Cambridge University Press.

Izard, C.E. (1971). *The face of emotion.* New York, NY: Appletome-Century-Crofts.

Labouvie-Vief, G. (1994). *Psyche and Eros.* New York, NY: Cambridge University Press.

Leaper, C. (1991). Influence and involvement in children's discourse: Age, gender and partner effects. *Child Development, 62,* 797–811.

Lever, J. (1976). Sex differences in the games children play. *Social Problems, 23,* 478–487.

Lutz, C. A., & Abu-Lughod, L. (1990) (Eds.). *Language and the politics of emotion.* New York, NY: Cambridge University Press.

Lutz, C., & White, G. M. (1986). The anthropology of emotions. *Annual Review of Anthropology, 15,* 405–436.

Markus, H., & Oyserman, D. (1989). Gender and thought: The role of the self-concept. In M. Crawford, & M. Gentry (Eds.), *Gender and thought: Psychological perspectives.* New York, NY: Springer-Verlag.

Mazur, E. (1989). Predicting gender differences in same-sex friendships from affiliation motivation and value. *Psychology of Women Quarterly, 13,* 277–291.

Nolen-Hoeksema, S. (1987). Sex differences in unipolar depression: Evidence and theory. *Psychological Bulletin, 101,* 259–282.

Robbins, P. R., & Tanck, R. H. (1991). Gender differences in the attribution of causes for depressive feelings. *Psychological Reports, 68,* 1209–1210.

Robinson, J. L., Zahn-Waxler, C., & Emde, R. N. (1994). Patterns of development in early empathic behavior: Environmental and child constitutional influences. *Social Development, 3,* 125–145.

Rogoff, B. (1990). *Apprenticeship in thinking.* New York, NY: Oxford University Press.

Rosaldo, M. Z. (1984). Toward an anthropology of self and feeling. In R. A. Schweder & S. R. LeVine (Eds.), *Culture theory: essays on mind, self and emotion* (pp. 137–157). New York: Cambridge University Press.

Russell, J. (1989). Culture, scripts and children's understanding of emotion. In C. Saarni & P. L. Harris (Eds.), *Children's understanding of emotion* (pp. 293–318). New York, NY: Cambridge University Press.

Sarbin, T. (1989). Emotion as situated actions. In L. Cirillo, B. Kaplan, & S. Wapner (Eds.), *Emotions in ideal human development* (pp. 77–99). Hillsdale, NJ: Lawrence Erlbaum.

Schieffelin, B. B., & Ochs, E. (1986). *Language socialization across cultures.* New York, NY: Cambridge University Press.

Sheldon, A. (1990). Pickle fights: Gendered talk in preschool disputes. *Discourse Processes, 13,* 5–31.

Slavin, L. A., & Rainer, K. L. (1990). Gender differences in emotional support and depressive symptoms among adolescents: A prospective analysis. *American Journal of Community Psychology, 18,* 407–421.

Snell, W. E., Jr., Miller, R. S., & Belk, S. S. (1988). Development of the Emotional Self-Disclosure Scale. *Sex Roles, 18*, 59–73.

Snell, W. E., Jr., Belk, S. S., Flowers, A., & Warren, J. (1988). Women's and men's willingness to self-disclose to therapists and friends: The moderating influence of instrumental, expressive, masculine and feminine topics. *Sex Roles, 18*, 769–776.

Snell, W. E., Jr., Miller, R. S., Belk, S. S., Garcia-Falconi, R., & Hernandez-Sanchez, J. E. (1989). Men's and women's emotional self-disclosure: The impact of disclosure recipient, culture and the masculine role. *Sex Roles, 21*, 467–486.

Sprock, J., & Yoder, C. Y. (1997). Women and depression: An update on the report of the APA Task Force. *Sex Roles, 36*, 269–303.

Stapley, J. C., & Haviland, J. M. (1989). Beyond depression: Gender differences in normal adolescents' emotional experience. *Sex Roles, 20*, 295–308.

Stein, N. L., Liwag, M. D., & Wade, E. (1996). A goal-based approach to memory for emotional events: Implications for theories of understanding and socialization. In R. D. Kavanaugh, & B. Zimmerberg (Eds), *Emotion: Interdisciplinary perspectives* (pp. 91–118). Mahwah, NJ: Lawrence Erlbaum.

Strauss, J., Munday, T., McNall, K., & Wong, M. (1997). Response Style Theory revisited: Gender differences and stereotypes in rumination and distraction. *Sex Roles, 36*, 771–792.

Strayer, J. (1989). What children know and feel in response to witnessing affective events. In C. Saarni, & P. L. Harris (Eds.), *Children's understanding of emotion* (pp. 259–289). New York, NY: Cambridge University Press.

Tannen, D. (1990). Gender differences in topical coherence: Creating involvement in best friend's talk. *Discourse Processes, 13*, 73–90.

Thorne, A. (1995). Developmental truths in memories of childhood and adolescence. *Journal of Personality, 63*, 140–163.

Turner, H. A. (1994). Gender and social support: Taking the bad with the good? *Sex Roles, 30*, 521–541.

Whitbeck, L. B., Hoyt, D. R., Miller, M., & Kao, M. (1992). Parental support, depressed affect, and sexual experience among adolescents. *Youth & Society, 24*, 166–177.

White, G. (1990). Moral discourse and the rhetoric of emotion. In C. A. Lutz, & L. Abu-Lughod (Eds.), *Language and the politics of emotion* (pp. 46–48). New York, NY: Cambridge University Press.

Zahn-Waxler, C., Robinson, J., & Emde, R. N. (1992). The development of empathy in twins. *Developmental Psychology, 28*, 1038–1047.

Zeman, J. & Shipman, K. (1996). Children's expression of negative affect: Reasons and methods. *Developmental Psychology, 32*, 842–849.

12. Engendering gender differences in shame and guilt: Stereotypes, socialization, and situational pressures

TAMARA J. FERGUSON AND HEIDI L. EYRE

Characteristics of shame and guilt

During the past decade, shame and guilt have increasingly captured the attention of many social scientists. One sign of this growing interest is the proliferation of instruments available to measure the two constructs (see table 12.1 for a brief overview of the instruments most widely used to measure adults' self-reports of guilt and shame). Although the instruments differ greatly, they reflect a growing consensus regarding fundamental differences between the two emotions in terms of their situational antecedents, appraisals, experiential aspects, and action tendencies. Shame involves a focus on one's global self – who I am and who I do not want to be – with its source being an *unwanted identity*. Because of the focus on one's own or others' (imagined) evaluation of the self as inferior or deficient, the ashamed person feels exposed, small, passive, and unable. We frequently hide or privately manage shame, because of its painful nature. At the same time, "being" ashamed communicates an awareness that we are somehow inadequate and need to defer or change lest someone launch further attacks on our identity and bases for our mutual relationships.

While shame involves the *global* self, some construe guilt as a reaction to a *specific* act of omission or commission that violates moral standards. We prefer to view guilt as arising from people's belief that their behavior somehow disadvantages a valued other. Immoral deeds (e.g., infidelity) can provoke guilt in some people, some of the time. But many guilt-inducing events do not necessarily involve unethical behaviors (e.g., outperforming your best friend on an exam; getting invited to a party when your friend did not). People's perceptions that they could have done something to avoid disadvantaging the other are salient aspects of the guilty experience. Compared to shame, then, the guilty person's sense of self as a competent individual remains relatively intact. The self in guilt also remains unscathed, because we can (hypothetically) restore harmony by repairing the "damage" done. Guilt thus invites the moral community to forgive and trust us, since its very expression communicates concern for others' welfare; symbolically rectifies the "wrong," or soothes the victim's hurt feelings via our own emotional punishment (cf. Barrett, 1995; Baumeister, Stillwell, & Heatherton, 1994; Ferguson & Stegge, 1995; Ferguson, Stegge, & Damhuis, 1991; Frijda, Kuipers, & ter Schure, 1989; Hoffman, 1977; Izard, 1977; Kemper, 1978; Lewis, 1978; Lewis, 1992; Lindsay-Hartz, 1984; Lindsay-Hartz, De Rivera, & Mascolo, 1995; Olthof, 1996; Olthof, Bloemers, Deji, Ferguson, & Boom, 1998; Rimé, Mesquita, Philippot, & Boca, 1991; Scheff, 1988; Tangney, 1990, 1995; Thrane, 1979; Vangelisti & Sprague, 1998; Zahn-Waxler & Kochanska, 1990).

Expectations regarding gender differences in guilt and shame

Whether we should expect to find gender differences in either guilt or shame is a vexing question.[1] Many have contended and/or are not surprised by findings that females sometimes will report *more* guilt and shame than males (e.g., Brody, 1996). But, why should we expect to find *this* particular gender difference?

Gender-based roles and associated stereotypes

Gender roles and stereotypes are congruent with the expectation that women will express (if not also experience) both emotions. Women are supposed to be aware of their obligations and attachments to others, they are encouraged to be loving toward others, connected to them, and interpersonally sensitive (e.g., Hill & Lynch, 1983; Williams & Best, 1990). Women's greater communal orientation essentially makes it easier for them to see the self as unnecessarily disadvantaging another (the guilt-inducing condition). Gender roles and stereotypic expectations accord a central role to girls' loving identifications, making them particularly sensitive to the threat of 'loss of love' and increasing their dependency on others' good opinions (Lewis, 1971, 1978). Countless authors emphasize women's generally lower socially bestowed power and status (e.g., Brody & Hall, 1993; Fischer, 1993; Fischer & Jansz, 1995; Manstead & Fischer, 1996; Miller, 1995; Shields, 1991; Stapley & Haviland, 1989). Traditional feminine roles are associated with the least capacity for status, dominance, or agency (e.g., Harris & Schwab, 1990) and a lower status itself is considered less agentic (Conway, Pizzamiglio, & Mount, 1996). Women's sense of inferiority is additionally exacerbated by their continued exclusion from positions of economic power (e.g., Hochschild, 1983; Lutz, 1990). From most of these perspectives, women more than men may report (if not also experience) shame because of societally inculcated feelings of passivity, helpless-ness, and reliance on others for their own self-definition.

In contrast, general role-related expectations and stereotypes operate to undercut males' need to express (or experience) either guilt or shame. Males are generally stereotyped by peers, parents, and other adults as being more achievement-oriented, active, aggressive, autonomous, competitive, dominant, and stronger than females (e.g., Antill, 1987; Blank, 1993; Block, 1983; Hoffman, 1975; Williams & Best, 1990). Many men are likewise encouraged to compete successfully in the economic realm and are expected to adopt more agentic/provider roles (Bakan, 1966) that lead to their greater involvement in aggressive and competi-tive exchanges (Lewis, 1971, 1978). Disadvantaging others is therefore more societally accepted and even justified in men, making it easier for them to wield excess power, rationalize or minimize these displays, and thereby feel (let alone express) little guilt.[2] Men's greater status and power in relationships and the larger economic community effectively provide few reasons for them to be ashamed of possessing unwanted identities.

These general stereotypes and gender-related roles suggest that females more than males are expected to experience the specific emo-tions of guilt and shame, at least in Western society. Although certain results may appear contradictory (e.g., Fabes & Martin, 1991), these specific stereotypes are affirmed by two large samples of ours from Utah State University using one of the most popular instruments in this area – the TOSCA. In all, then, general stereotypes, gender roles, and specific stereotypes regarding guilt and shame suggest that the two sexes are actually treated in ways that encourage females to make greater guilt- and shame-relevant appraisals than males.

Socialization of gender-related appraisal differences

Angry, aggressive, disruptive behaviors. Many of the instruments measuring guilt and shame present participants with hypothetical sce-narios in which, among other behaviors, the protagonist engages in fairly disrespectful and sometimes downright relationally aggressive actions (e.g., the ASM, EST, SCAAI, TOSCA). Clearly, these actions dis-advantage others. If appraised as such, they should thus arouse consid-erable feelings of guilt. People might additionally feel ashamed about the same situations if they also represent threats to their identity. If more females than males are taught to see these behaviors as reflecting an "unfair disadvantage" or as inappropriate to their gender role identity, then females might end up feeling both guiltier and more ashamed than males. Certain studies in the social developmental literature suggest that females are taught to appraise situations in precisely these ways.

Socialization agents emphasize girls' responsibility and blameworthiness for others' well-being (cf. Eisenberg & Lennon, 1983; Strayer & Roberts, 1997; Zahn-Waxler & Robinson, 1995). Girls receive other-oriented or psychologically oriented inductions, which promote empathy and cultivate a stronger internal sense of right and wrong, much more frequently than boys (e.g., Hoffman 1975, 1977; Zahn-Waxler, 1993). In contrast, parents use power assertion and physical punishment more frequently with boys, which could promote a weaker internalized sense of social obligation and model behaviors supporting the externalization rather than internalization of blame (Hoffman, 1975, 1977). Not surprisingly, then, peers and adults more vigorously sanction misbehavior, anger, or negativism in girls compared to boys (cf. Brody, 1996; Fuchs & Thelen, 1988; Zahn-Waxler, 1995).

Failures. Since performance is a focus of many instruments designed to measure guilt and shame, we need to ask whether boys and girls differently appraise performance-related outcomes. Dweck and Leggett (1988) reviewed the voluminous literature showing that females are more prone than males to attribute failure to internal/global features (e.g., blaming their general low ability), although not all studies confirm this observation (cf. Eccles, Wigfield, & Schiefele, 1998). Boys, on the other hand, will attribute failure to specific internal factors (e.g., their low effort) or external factors (e.g., teacher attitudes, cf. Burgner & Hewstone, 1993; Deaux & Emswiller, 1974). If shame results from greater internal/global attributions for failure (e.g., Feiring, Tasaka, & Lewis, 1996), then we might easily expect females to experience greater shame than males. In addition, females might also feel guiltier than males for failing, because their greater communal orientation makes them keenly aware of how performance deficits dishonor those close to them.

But, why are there gender-related differences in failure appraisals? Michael Lewis and his colleagues show how adult socialization practices contribute to the different attributions that boys and girls offer regarding performance. Parents generally provide more negative feedback to girls than boys for their failures, whereas both teachers and parents lavish girls with less praise or acknowledgement for their successes (e.g., Alessandri & Lewis, 1993, 1996; Lewis, Alessandri, & Sullivan, 1992). Moreover, when adults criticize boys, their negative comments focus more on specific and non-intellectual aspects of their failures. In contrast, teachers' criticisms imply that girls are generally

lacking in competence or do not understand the work. Girls additionally receive emotional reactions from others that would reflect internal
attributions for failure (e.g., more disgust, contempt, and shaming emotional responses from their mothers), whereas mothers' greater use of
physical punishment with boys imply external or situationally specific
attributions for their misdeeds (Lewis, 1992).

In summary, diverse literatures suggest that socialization agents train
females much more so than males to appraise their performance failures
and interpersonal insensitivities in ways that promote feelings of guilt
and shame. The question is whether the evidence supports these expectations.

Gender-related differences in guilt and shame

One of our tasks was to review research that fairly unequivocally
addressed gender-related differences in the experience of guilt or shame
and in the situational antecedents and appraisals associated with both
emotions (cf. note 1). Unfortunately, researchers have not meticulously
examined these issues. There simply is no unassailable evidence regarding the extent to which men versus women differentially experience the
two emotions and little is also known about gender-related differences
in the situational antecedents of the two emotions. There is only indirect
evidence pertaining to gender-related appraisal differences. The only
additional evidence concerning appraisal derives from our own
research with adults who judged multiple aspects of appraisal for both
real-life and hypothetical incidents. Surprisingly, we found only one
meaningful difference between men's versus women's appraisals.
Women more often than men perceived people as intending to make
them feel guilty (cf., Ferguson, Ives, & Eyre, 1997) suggesting, perhaps,
that the emotion of guilt is subjectively experienced as more normative
for women and/or as more easily induced in them.

A second task was to summarize findings that directly bear on
gender-related differences in people's reports of guilt or shame as well
as actual behaviors that are thought to be associated with the two emotions. We were more successful in locating literature pertaining to these
questions.

Almost all of the procedures or instruments used to assess gender differences in this realm form aggregate scores by collapsing shame or
guilt responses across numerous items or trials. It is important to
remember that these totals are based on tremendously disparate procedures (cf. table 12.1). Two key differences involve the type of response
that participants provide and whether they rate hypothetical or true-to-
life incidents. For example, the TOSCA or SCAAI ask respondents to

Table 12.1. *Representative instruments used to assess guilt and/or shame in adult samples*

Title of instrument	Type of instrument and number of guilt/shame items	Sample item	Scale or rating
Self-Conscious Affect and Attribution Inventory (SCAAI; Tangney et al., 1988a, b)	Scenarios 13/13	"I'll find a way to make up for this." (guilt) "Why am I so selfish?" (shame)	Likelihood (5-point)
Test of Self-Conscious Affect (TOSCA; Tangney et al., 1989)	Scenarios 15/15	"I deserve to be reprimanded ..." (guilt) "I would feel incompetent ..." (shame)	Likelihood (5-point)
Emotion Story Test (EST, Brody, 1996)	Scenarios 48/48	Friend promises to pick up an important package, but forgets	Intensity (6-point)
Personal Feelings Questionnaire-2 (PFQ-2, Harder & Zalma, 1990)	Emotion words 6/10	Regret, remorse (guilt) Embarrassed, stupid (shame)	Frequency (5-point)
Adapted Shame and Guilt Scale (ASGS; Hoblitzelle, 1988)	Emotion words 16/14	Unscrupulous, delinquent (guilt) Mortified, abashed (shame)	True or characteristic (7-point)
Differential Emotions Scale (DES; Izard et al., 1974)	Emotion words 3/3	Repentant, guilty (guilt) Sheepish, bashful (shame, shyness)	Frequency (5-point)
Guilt Inventory (GI; Kugler & Jones, 1992)	Emotion statements 20 (state guilt) 10 (trait guilt)	"Guilt has been a part of my life ..." (trait) "Recently, I have done something I deeply regret." (state)	True or characteristic (5-point)
Internalized Shame Scale (ISS; Cook, 1987)	Emotion sentence 0/24	"Sometimes I feel no bigger than a pea." "I feel empty and unfulfilled."	Rating Frequency (5-point)
Mosher Forced-Choice Inventory (Mosher, 1968)	Forced-choice 79/0	When I tell a lie... A. it hurts B. I make it a good one	Chooses one of each pair

Table 12.1. (*cont.*)

Title of instrument	Type of instrument and number of Guilt/shame items	Sample item	Scale or rating
Affective Sentence Completion task (ASC; Ferguson et al., 1996)	Semi-projective 12 (guilt) 19 (shame) 14 (ambiguous)	"When I get caught . . ." (guilt) "I feel worthless . . ." (shame)	Complete sentence; choose emotion word that best describes feeling
Emotional Attributes Questionnaire (EAQ; Eyre & Ferguson, 1996)	Behavioral statements 77/61	"I make amends . . ." (guilt) ". . . I become quiet . . . subdued" (shame)	True or characteristic (7-point)
Triadic Inventory of Negative Self-Conscious Affect (TINSA; Chandler-Holtz, 1995)	Emotion and behavioral statements	". . . almost always apologize . . ." (guilt) ". . . wish I could disappear . . ." (shame)	True or characteristic (5-point)

Type of question asked

rate how *likely* they would be to act or feel in shame- and guilt-relevant ways in response to a large number of hypothetical failures and transgressions. Using more general descriptions of the types of antecedents represented in the likelihood measures (e.g., falling short of others' expectations, doing something one should not have), the EAQ and TINSA ask respondents to rate how *characteristic/true* shame- and guilt-relevant behaviors are of their friends (and/or themselves) when assessed in everyday situations or over the past year or more. There also are studies in which participants rate how *intensely* they feel or react in guilt- and shame-relevant ways in response to hypothetical incidents, real-life events, or no precipitating event. Other instruments such as the PFQ, GI, DES, and ISS are more frequency-based assessments, with participants rating *how often* or *how consistently* they actually have felt or acted in numerous shame- and/or guilt-keyed ways. Still others (e.g., the ASC) are more projective assessments. We will soon see that findings regarding gender-related differences in these emotions depend remarkably on the instrument or procedure employed. It should also be noted that conclusions are also limited by the primarily Western origin of many of the samples studied.

Shame

Observations of actual behavior

All of the published research that bears explicitly on gender differences in actual shame-related behaviors derives from research with children. Both 33- to 37-month-old and 4- to 5-year-old girls displayed more shame-relevant behaviors (e.g., lowered heads, collapsed bodies) after failure than did boys, especially on easy tasks (Alessandri & Lewis, 1996; Lewis, Alessandri, & Sullivan,1992). Barrett, Zahn-Waxler, and Cole (1993) also used a behavioral observation paradigm and found that more toddler-age girls were classified as Avoiders (thought to index facets of shame-related behavior) in response to having "broken" the experimenter's favorite toy.

Self- and other-reports about "behavior"

Peoples' beliefs about shame-relevant behaviors in adults can be culled from the self- and other-report versions of the EAQ and from self-reports on Chandler-Holtz's (1995) TINSA. In several college student samples of ours and Chandler-Holtz's, females judge shame-relevant behaviors from the EAQ and TINSA as being characteristic of themselves more than males do (Chandler-Holtz & Weinberger, 1996; Eyre,

1997). The EAQ other-report also revealed that shame behaviors are seen as slightly more characteristic of females than males.

Self-reports of likelihood (hypothetical incidents)

The most frequently used instruments in this area (the TOSCA and SCAAI) and its variants (e.g., the Adolescent Shame Measure, cf. Reimer, 1997) also yield the clearest evidence that female adults, older adolescents, and at times younger adolescents or children, rate themselves as likelier to experience shame-relevant reactions (e.g., Abell & Gecas, 1997; Bassen, Braveman, Pearlman, & Lamb, 1997; Ferguson & Crowley, 1997a; Haimowitz, 1996; Harder, 1995; Harder, Cutler, & Rockart, 1992; Lutwak & Ferrari, 1996; Pulakos, 1996; Tangney, 1990, 1994; Tangney et al., 1991).

Self-reports of intensity (hypothetical incidents)

With only one exception, we found no gender differences in the intensity of 5- to 12-year-old children's shame responses to hypothetical transgressions and failures for which the child is either undeniably or ambiguously responsible (Ferguson, Stegge, Miller, & Olsen, 1997, 1999). Moreover, although female relative to male students will offer higher intensity shame ratings after perpetrating a hypothetical transgression (breaking their mother's cherished vase) with varying degrees of responsibility, this effect was apparent only for immediate rather than delayed ratings (cf. Ferguson, Olthof, & Stegge, 1997). Four other studies also did not find robust gender differences in adults' ratings of shame intensity on the EST (Brody, 1993, 1996, 1997) or other procedures (Mills, Pedersen, & Grusec, 1989).

Self-reports of intensity (real-life incidents)

We asked a large number of college students to narrate instances from their own lives in which they perpetrated an untoward event either accidentally or with unjustifiable intent. Having recalled the incident, they rated how ashamed they felt immediately after the incident and several days later. Of the four gender comparisons that could have been statistically significant, we found only one: males actually reported feeling more intense shame than females immediately after narrating the incident.

Self-reports of experiential frequency

When we or other researchers use instruments that assess how often or how continuously people feel shame in their daily lives (such as the

ASGS, PFQ-2, ISS, or DES), gender-related differences are rarely found in clinical or nonclinical samples of Euro-American college students, older adults, and adolescents (e.g., Blavier & Glenn, 1995; Brody, 1997; Cook, 1996; Harder, 1995; Harder & Zalma, 1990; Izard, 1977; Lutwak & Ferrari, 1997; Tangney, 1990; Wright, O'Leary, & Balkin, 1989; cf. Harder & Lewis, 1987 for an exception). There is one exception: Izard (1977) and his colleagues consistently found that males score higher than females on the trait version of their shame/shyness factor using the Differential Emotions Scale.

In summary, actual observations of young children, adults' beliefs about shame-relevant behaviors, and methodologically solid assessments of adults' likelihood or intensity judgments of hypothetical scenarios generally show greater indications of shame in females than in males. However, few studies find gender-related differences in how frequently participants feel ashamed or in the intensity of shame following real-life incidents.

Guilt

Observations of actual behavior

The most methodologically sound observations of gender differences in guilt-relevant behaviors have been conducted with preschool-age children. Typically, although not always, these observations focus on how young boys or girls react after displaying or witnessing anger and/or overt aggression. In these assessments, girls relative to boys do appear to be more upset, they offer more reparative bids, and their restorative attempts are often accompanied by intense self-distress (e.g., Kochanska, 1991, 1993; Zahn-Waxler, Cole, & Barrett, 1991; see also Eagly & Steffen, 1986). However, using the "broken toy" paradigm, Barrett and her colleagues (1993) reported that more toddler-age boys than girls were classified as Amenders (guilt-related behaviors).

Self- and other-reports about "behavior"

Parental reports about children as young as 2 years affirm some of the actual behavioral results with boys and girls. Parents reported that girls display empathic behaviors, tend to apologize, and express concern about their relationships with parents more than do boys (Kochanska, 1993; Kochanska, Aksan, & Koenig, 1995; Kochanska, De Vet, Goldman, Murray, & Putnam, 1994). On the EAQ, college women judged guilt-relevant behaviors as much more characteristic of themselves than do college men; close friends of these respondents also rated these behaviors as more characteristic of women (Eyre & Ferguson, 1997). Interestingly, however, men judged guilt-relevant behaviors as more true of themselves than did women on Chandler-Holtz's (1995) TINSA.

Self-reports of likelihood (hypothetical incidents)

Numerous published studies and 5 of our new samples indicate that females spanning a wide age range consistently rate themselves as more likely to think or feel in guilt-relevant ways than males on measures like the TOSCA or SCAAI (e.g., Abell & Gecas, 1997; Bassen et al., 1997; Ferguson & Crowley, 1997a; Harder et al., 1992; Lutwak & Ferrari, 1996; Pulakos, 1996; Reimer, 1997; Tangney, 1990, 1994; Williams & Bybee, 1994).

Self-reports of intensity (hypothetical incidents)

Studies that assessed the intensity of people's reactions to hypothetical scenarios (e.g., Ferguson, Eyre, Stegge, Sorenson, & Everton 1997; Mills et al., 1989) found fewer gender differences. And, even these differences are fairly transient. For example, although females initially reacted with greater intensity guilt than males to various transgressions, the guilt that they reported one day later is greater for accidental transgressions only. Moreover, using a more diverse sample of hypothetical transgressions and failures, we find no evidence of gender-related differences in guilt intensity across a wide but relatively young age range (5- to 12-year-olds, Ferguson et al., 1997, 1999). Thompson and Hoffman (1980) actually found that 1st, 3rd, and 5th grade boys rated themselves as feeling greater intensity guilt than girls in response to hypothetical events (e.g., not helping another).

Self-reports of intensity (real-life incidents)

Findings are mixed regarding gender differences in guilt intensity in response to more real-life events. Some studies reported no significant gender-related differences in guilt intensity, or correlates of this construct, in response to real transgressions (e.g., Lake, Lane, & Harris, 1995). When we examined the intensity of our sample of college students' guilty feelings for accidental or unjustifiably intended events that they actually perpetrated, we found no gender-related differences in guilt intensity either immediately following the transgression or days later for accidentally harmful events. For the unjustifiably intended incidents, moreover, males actually reported feeling moderately more guilty than females at both time periods. However, Fischer (1993) argues that women respond with more guilt or anxiety than men when they have perpetrated an unjustified transgression. Consonant with these findings, women report greater guilty intensity than men when they actually "delivered" an electric shock to their victims (e.g., Buss & Brock, 1963) and younger girls anticipate feeling guiltier than boys when they aggress (e.g., Perry, Perry, & Rasmussen, 1986; Perry, Perry, & Weiss, 1989). Yet, when Wagner, Buck, and Winterbotham (1993) had male and female undergraduates watch slides of, for example, injurious or sexual events, men rated themselves (and were rated by outside observers) as experiencing more intense guilt feelings than did women.

Self-reports of intensity (other)

Some instruments are meant to assess individual differences in the intensity of guilty *affect*. Bybee and Zigler (1991) reported no evidence of gender-related differences in the intensity of guilty affect for 2nd, 5th, 8th, and 11th grade children who were asked, across many pairs, to choose which alternative of each pair is more like them (e.g., "When some kids do something wrong, they don't feel bothered by it very much" versus ". . . they feel worse than if they were sick"). However, Bybee (1998) cites other evidence suggesting that age-related increases in the intensity of guilty affect occur primarily for females.

Self-reports of experiential frequency

Various studies have examined gender differences in the reported frequency of guilt experiences using instruments such as the PFQ (original or revised) and the Guilt Inventory. In most cases, no significant gender differences are found (e.g., Boyle, 1989; Brody, 1996; Harder et al., 1992; Harder & Zalma, 1990; Izard, 1977; Kugler & Jones, 1992; Larsen & Diener, 1987; Lutwak & Ferrari, 1997; Quiles & Bybee, 1997; Wright et al., 1989; cf. Bybee, 1998), which we have replicated in our own samples using the PFQ-2, ASGS, and the GI. Gender differences on projective or sentence-completion indices of guilt frequency (e.g., Mosher's scales, 1968) also are minimal for themes related to hostility or morality con- science, although females more often selected guilt responses than males for certain sexuality-related themes, e.g., oral sex, having sex with a divorced person (see Heying, Korabik, & Munz, 1975; see also Stapley & Haviland, 1989). On a projective sentence completion task (the ASC), we find minimal differences in the number of times that men and women selected the term guilt to describe their reactions to sentence stems representing diverse failures and transgressions. Ferguson et al. (1999) likewise did not find gender-related differences in guilt frequency for 5- to 12-year-old children using the CIIDC projective measure (cf. Zahn-Waxler, Kochanska, Krupnick & Mayfield, 1988). There are exceptions that confirm females' tendency to report a greater incidence of guilt; however, we can find as many cases demonstrating the opposite result or no differences (cf. Binder, 1970; Harder & Lewis, 1987; Harder & Zalma, 1990; Heying et al., 1975; Hoffman 1975; Izard, 1977; Kochanska, 1991; Lewis, 1971; Newman, 1984).

In sum, the evidence pertaining to gender differences in guilt is mixed. It seems most fair to state that women see themselves as likelier to experience guilt than men for behaviors that clearly contradict feminine gender roles (e.g., anger, aggression, being inconsiderate of others). It is not fair, however, to conclude from the available literature that girls and women are universally more guilt-prone than their male counterparts. We found indications that men and boys feel guiltier than females about homosexuality, not helping, dishonesty, and perpetrating severe harms. These results align nicely with the kinds of situations that males describe more often than females when narrating autobiographical incidents of guilt (cf. Bybee, 1998; Williams & Bybee, 1994; Tangney, 1992). Moreover, we cannot simply ignore the studies finding no statistically significant differences – in particular those showing that gender differences in people's reports of how often they feel guilty are virtually nonexistent.

Recapitulation and conclusion

We first reviewed evidence supporting the traditional expectation that females report (if not also experience) guilt and shame more than do males. Starting in early childhood, females are taught more than males to be sensitive to others' feelings and outcomes. Females also fulfill – and therefore have the "opportunity" to violate – a multiplicity of roles that can lead them to disadvantage others. These differences, among many others, augment girls' and women's chances of perceiving that they have negatively impacted another, thereby enhancing their likelihood of feeling guilty or at least lowering the guilt induction threshold. Moreover, females' lower status and power frequently require them to manage situations by expressing certain emotions (e.g., guilt) and inhibiting others (e.g., anger or indifference). The evidence also suggested that certain behaviors (e.g., aggression) can be more threatening to females' identity. Given their greater interpersonal sensitivity and fear of negative evaluation by outsiders, such threats could facilitate both the experience and expression of extreme shame responses. Our subsequent review in fact often revealed greater indications of shame in females than in males. Gender differences in guilt were less universal, being most consistently found for likelihood judgments of hypothetical situations or certain behavioral equivalents. However, few studies reported gender differences in estimates of how intensely or how frequently people felt ashamed and guilty.

How do we explain this entire pattern of findings? Our explanation is based on the misleading nature of the gender differences reported in likelihood studies. These are deceptive because guilt and shame are highly correlated responses (e.g., Ferguson & Stegge, 1998). Guilt and shame are strongly linked for various reasons, including a shared basis in negative affectivity and in some of their situational antecedents. After all, if disadvantaging others (the primary source of guilt) is also an unwanted identity (the genesis of shame), then both responses are highly likely to co-occur. Practically all of the situations represented in the likelihood measures (e.g., TOSCA or SCAAI) represent transgressions or failures that impact other people. The person thus not only disadvantages others (the guilt-inducing condition), but also does so in ways that are especially threatening to a feminine identity (the shame-inducing condition). It is interesting that gender differences in guilt on these instruments virtually disappear when we remove the influence of shame (either statistically or by varying which incidents we examine). However, the gender differences in shame are robust no matter how we remove its association with guilt. Thus, a driving force behind gender differences in shame on the likelihood instruments involves females' beliefs that these events undermine their identity. Note that the same general explanation nicely accounts for gender differences observed on measures like the EAQ and TINSA and even in behavioral paradigms. In all of these, the focus is on behaviors having more worrisome implications for the integrity of female rather than male identities. All of these studies, too, find larger or more consistent gender differences for shame than guilt.

Essentially, then, we question the extent to which males' and females' identities are impacted equally by the types of situations involved (or implied) in these assessments. We also question whether uniquely male identity concerns are well represented in them. This observation is interesting in light of Ferguson and Crowley's (1997a) findings that shame-proneness scores on one likelihood measure (the SCAAI) were unrelated to males' defensive manoeuvres or gender-role orientation, suggesting that shame in response to *these* types of situations is simply not a central self-organizing feature for them. In contrast, many of the situations that are often used to assess shame bear on identity concerns central to many women, thereby possibly accounting for women's greater likelihood of expressing shame to them. Interestingly, Ferguson and Crowley (1997a) report that shame-proneness figures prominently in accounting for the variance in females' defensive styles (e.g., turning against the self) and gender-role orientations (e.g., passive-dependency). These links are remarkably consistent with the earlier depicted nature of women's shame experience, since their positive self-definition depends so profoundly on how successfully they maintain harmonious relationships.

Given this interpretation, we must entertain the possibility that males might actually be *more* prone to shame than females under certain circumstances. Recent research of ours bears this out. College men and women evaluated the original TOSCA scenarios, as well as new scenarios that we knew represented a greater unwanted identity for males than females (e.g., being physically weak, career-related failures, crying in front of others). Males responded with more shame than females to the situations depicting the negative male identities. In fact, the gender-reversal for shame in response to male unwanted identities was much greater than has been shown previously using procedures that prime mostly female unwanted identities. These results are not surprising given males' relatively greater sensitivity than females' to violations of gender-role standards (e.g., Levy & Fivush, 1993). They also convincingly demonstrate that previous research greatly underestimates males' proneness to shame.

The latter findings raise the question of whether males' guilt-proneness has been misjudged. Our tentative answer to this questions is "yes." Our male unwanted identity study, in fact, showed that males reported feeling guiltier than females when their unwanted identity also disadvantaged another (even after controlling for guilt's association with shame). Furthermore, males have often reported feeling as guilty as females for the events most widely studied in this area. Interestingly, moreover, males who reported higher levels of guilt about the more traditional incidents also endorsed the types of communal values that optimize concerns with disadvantaging others (cf. Ferguson & Crowley, 1997a). Males additionally reported feeling extremely guilty about disadvantaging others in particular ways (e.g., not helping others, damaging property, animal cruelty, and blatant aggressiveness) – events that are rarely represented in the most popular instruments in this area (e.g., the TOSCA). In all, then, the presence or absence of gender differences in either emotion is highly context dependent.

Our context-dependency argument and data partly explain failures to find gender differences in guilt or shame frequency, since these measures allow males and females to freely recall the *different* contexts in which they have felt either emotion. However, although context-dependency is part of the story, it certainly is not all of it. The absence of gender differences on frequency measures may additionally reflect the presence of gender differences in other domains. For various reasons (e.g., the severe repercussions that they suffer from the environment), women might actually avoid predicaments that would make them feel guilty or ashamed, thereby resulting in relatively low frequency reports. Conversely, men may have few pertinent experiences to report for other reasons, including their greater desensitization to negative events, the smaller likelihood of receiving negative consequences from the environment for their misdeeds or failures, and their greater tendencies to externalize blame. Note that this argument implies that women generally are more prone than men to experience the two emotions, but that frequency measures are not pure assessments of guilt- or shame-proneness, because of various confounding factors, including those related to gender. Both the context dependency and gender-as-moderator explanations deserve further empirical scrutiny.

In closing: we cannot conclude that women are generally more prone to both guilt and shame than men. We also know virtually nothing about the role that gender plays in facilitating or undermining the two emotional responses. Important foci for future research are whether gender, variables correlated with gender, or those cross-cutting gender operate to more chronically prime guilt- or shame-perspectives, to undermine them, or to deflect them across time and a wider variety of situations.

Acknowledgements

Portions of the research reported in this chapter were supported by the Women and Gender Research Institute of Utah State University. We thank Agneta Fischer and Tjeert Olthof for many helpful comments on an earlier draft. All inquiries, including those regarding sample characteristics and statistical results from our new studies, should be directed to the first author at the Department of Psychology, Utah State University, 2810 Old Main Hill, Logan, UT 84322–2810, USA, or via e-mail at uf734@cc.usu.edu. Heidi L. Eyre, previously at USU, is now at Simon Fraser University in Burnaby, British Columbia.

Notes

1. Statistical comparisons in this literature are typically between males and females as classified according to their biological sex, even though the differences are interpreted largely in terms of role-related characteristics associated with masculine and feminine gender. We use the terms "gender" and "gender-related" to refer to *interpretations* typically made by researchers when they find a sex difference in either emotion.
2. Lewis (1971, 1978) actually argued that men would manifest more guilt-prone orientations than women, because of their greater tendency to transgress. Research support for this assertion is minimal, however (e.g., Ferguson & Crowley, 1997a).

References

Abell, E., & Gecas, V. (1997). Guilt, shame, and family socialization. *Journal of Family Issues, 18*, 99–123.

Alessandri, S. M., & Lewis, M. (1993). Parental evaluation and its relation to shame and pride in young children. *Sex Roles, 29*, 335–343.

Alessandri, S. M., & Lewis, M. (1996). Differences in pride and shame in maltreated and nonmaltreated preschoolers. *Child Development, 67*, 1857–1869.

Antill, J. K. (1987). Parents' beliefs and values about sex roles, sex differences, and sexuality: Their sources and implications. In P. Shaver & C. Hendricks (Eds.), *Sex and gender* (Review of personality and social psychology, Vol. 7, pp. 294–328). Newbury Park, CA: Sage.

Bakan, D. (1966). *The duality of human existence*. Chicago, IL: Rand McNally.

Barrett, K. C. (1995). A functionalist approach to shame and guilt. In J. P. Tangney and K. W. Fischer (Eds.), *Self-conscious emotions: The psychology of shame, guilt, embarrassment, and pride* (pp. 25–63). New York, NY: Guilford Press.

Barrett, K. C., Zahn-Waxler, C., & Cole, P. M. (1993). Avoiders versus amenders – Implications for the investigation of guilt and shame during toddlerhood? *Cognition and Emotion, 7*, 481–505.

Bassen, C., Braveman, J., Pearlman, J., & Lamb, M. (1997). *Gender differences in normal adolescence: Guilt, reparation and shame*. Poster presented at the biennial meeting of the Society for Research in Child Development, Washington DC.

Baumeister, R. F., Stillwell, A. M., & Heatherton, T. F. (1994). Guilt: An interpersonal approach. *Psychological Bulletin, 115*, 243–267.

Binder, J. (1970). *The relative proneness to shame or guilt as a dimension of character style*. Unpublished dissertation, University of Michigan, Ann Arbor.

Blank, P. D. (Ed.) (1993). *Interpersonal expectations: Theory, research, and applications*. Paris: Cambridge University Press.

Blavier, D. C., & Glenn, E. (1995). The role of shame in perceptions of marital equity, intimacy, and competency. *American Journal of Family Therapy, 23*, 73–82.

Block, J. H. (1983). Differential premises arising from differential socialization of the sexes: Some conjectures. *Child Development, 54*, 1335–1354.

Boyle, G. J. (1989). Sex differences in reported mood states. *Personality and Individual Differences, 10*, 1179–1183.

Brody, L. R. (1993). On understanding gender differences in the expression of emotion. In S. L. Ablon, D. Brown, E. J. Khantzian, & J. E. Mack (Eds.), *Human feelings: Explorations in affect development and meaning* (pp. 87–121). Hillsdale, NJ: Analytic Press.

Brody, L. R. (1996). Gender, emotional expression, and parent-child boundaries. In R. D. Kavanaugh, B. Zimmerberg, & S. Fein (Eds.), *Emotion: Interdisciplinary perspectives* (pp. 139–170). Mahwah, NJ: Erlbaum.

Brody, L. R. (1997). Gender and emotion: Beyond stereotypes. *Journal of Social Issues, 53*, 369–394.

Brody, L. R., & Hall, J. A. (1993). Gender and emotion. In M. Lewis & J. M. Haviland (Eds.), *Handbook of emotions* (pp. 447–460). New York, NY: Guilford.

Burgner, D., & Hewstone, M. (1993). Young children's causal attributions for success and failure: "Self-enhancing" boys and "self-derogating" girls. *British Journal of Developmental Psychology, 11*, 125–129.

Buss, A. H., & Brock, T. C. (1963). Repression and guilt in relation to aggression. *Journal of Abnormal and Social Psychology, 66,* 345–350.

Bybee, J. (1998). The emergence of gender differences in guilt during adolescence. In J. Bybee (Ed.), *Guilt and children* (pp. 113–125). San Diego, CA: Academic Press.

Bybee, J., & Zigler, E. (1991). Self-image and guilt: A further test of the cognitive-developmental formulation. *Journal of Personality, 59,* 733–744.

Chandler-Holtz, D. M. (1995). *Differentiating shame, maladaptive guilt, and adaptive guilt: Development of the Triadic Inventory of Negative Self-Conscious Affect.* Unpublished master's thesis, Case Western Reserve University, Cleveland, OH.

Chandler-Holz, D. M. (1996). Triadic inventory of negative self-conscious affect. Unpublished instrument. Cleveland, OH: Case Western Reserve University.

Chandler-Holz, D. M., & Weinberger, D. A. (1996, August). *A new measure of shame, maladaptive guilt, and adaptive guilt.* Poster presented at the annual meeting of the American Psychological Association, Toronto, Ontario, Canada.

Conway, M., Pizzamiglio, M. T., & Mount, L. (1996). Status, communality, and agency: Implications for stereotypes of gender and other groups. *Journal of Personality and Social Psychology, 71,* 25–38.

Cook, D. R. (1987). Measuring shame: The Internalized Shame Scale. *Alcoholism Treatment Quarterly, 4,* 197–215.

Cook, D. R. (1996). Empirical studies of shame and guilt: The Internalized Shame Scale. In D. L. Nathanson (Ed.), *Knowing feeling: Affect, script, and psychotherapy* (pp. 132–165). New York, NY: Norton.

Deaux, K., & Emswiller, T. (1974). Explanations of successful performance on sex-linked tasks: What is skill for the male is luck for the female. *Journal of Personality and Social Psychology, 29,* 80–85.

Dweck, C. S., & Leggett, E. L. (1988). A social-cognitive approach to motivation and personality. *Psychological Review, 95,* 256–273.

Eagly, A. H., & Steffen, V. J. (1986). Gender and aggressive behavior: A meta-analytic review of the social psychological literature. *Psychological Bulletin, 100,* 309–330.

Eisenberg, N., & Lennon, R. (1983). Gender differences in empathy and related capacities. *Psychological Bulletin, 94,* 100–131.

Eccles, J.S., Wigfield, A., & Schiefele, U. (1998). Motivation to succeed. In N. Eisenberg (Ed.), *Handbook of Child Development: Social, emotional, and personality development* (Vol. 3, pp. 1017–1095).

Eyre, H. L. (1997). The Emotional Attributes Questionnaire: Self- and other-reports of guilt and shame. Unpublished honors thesis. Logan, UT: Utah State University.

Eyre, H. L., & Ferguson, T. J. (1996). Emotional Attributes Questionnaire. Unpublished instrument, Logan, UT: Utah State University.

Eyre, H. L., & Ferguson, T. J. (1997, May). *Do you see what I see? Self- and other-reports of guilt and shame.* Poster presented at the annual meeting of the American Psychological Society, Washington DC.

Fabes, R. A., & Martin, C. L. (1991). Gender and age stereotypes of emotionality. *Personality and Social Psychology Bulletin, 17,* 532–540.

Feiring, C., Tasaka, L., & Lewis, M. (1996). A process model for understanding adaptation to sexual abuse: The role of shame in defining stigmatization. *Child Abuse and Neglect, 20,* 767–782.

Ferguson, T. J., & Crowley, S. L. (1997a). Gender differences in the organization of guilt and shame. *Sex Roles, 37,* 19–44.

Ferguson, T. J., & Crowley, S. L. (1997b). Measure for measure: A multitrait-multimethod analysis of guilt and shame. *Journal of Personality Assessment, 69,* 425–441.

Ferguson, T. J., Eyre, H. L., Stegge, H., Sorenson, C., & Everton, R. (1997, April). *The distinct roles of shame and guilt in childhood psychopathology.* Poster presented at the biennial meeting of the Society for Research in Child Development, Washington DC.

Ferguson, T. J., Ives, D., & Eyre, H. L. (1997, April). *All is fair in love, but not war: The management of emotions in dyadic relationships.* Poster presented at the biennial meeting of the Society for Research in Child Development, Washington, DC.

Ferguson, T. J., Olthof, T., & Stegge, H. (1997). Temporal dynamics of guilt: Changes in the role of interpersonal and intrapsychic factors. *European Journal of Social Psychology, 27,* 659–673.

Ferguson, T. J., Sorenson, C., & Eyre, H. L. (1996). Affective Sentence Completion task. Unpublished instrument, Logan, UT: Utah State University.

Ferguson, T. J., & Stegge, H. (1995). Emotional states and traits in children: The case of guilt and shame. In J. P. Tangney and K. W. Fischer (Eds.), *Self-conscious emotions: The psychology of shame, guilt, embarrassment, and pride* (pp. 174–197). New York, NY: Guilford Press.

Ferguson, T. J., & Stegge, H. (1998). The measurement of guilt in children: A rose by any other name still has thorns. In J. Bybee (Ed.), *Guilt in children* (pp. 19–74). San Diego, CA: Academic Press.

Ferguson, T. J., Stegge, H., & Damhuis, I. (1990). Guilt and shame experiences in elementary school-age children. In P. J. D. Drenth, J. A. Sergeant, & R. J. Takens (Eds.), *European perspectives in psychology* (Vol. 1, pp. 195–218). New York, NY: Wiley.

Ferguson, T. J., Stegge, H., & Damhuis, I. (1991). Children's understanding of guilt and shame. *Child Development, 62,* 827–839.

Ferguson, T. J., Stegge, H., Miller, E. R. & Olsen, M. E. (1999). Guilt, shame, and symptoms in children. *Developmental Psychology, 35,* 347–357.

Fischer, A. H. (1993). Emotions and gender: A conceptual model of emotions in social interaction. In H. J. Stam, L. P. Mos, W. Thorngate, & B. Kaplan (Eds.), *Recent trends in theoretical psychology* (Vol. 3, pp. 325–331). New York, NY: Springer-Verlag.

Fischer, A.H., & Jansz, J. (1995). Reconciling emotions with Western personhood. *Journal for the Theory of Social Behaviour, 25,* 59–80.

Frijda, N., H., Kuipers, P., & ter Schure, E. (1989). Relations among emotion, appraisal, and emotional action readiness. *Journal of Personality and Social Psychology, 57,* 212–228.

Fuchs, D., & Thelen, M. H. (1988). Children's expected interpersonal consequences of communicating their affective state and reported likelihood of expression. *Child Development, 59,* 1314–1322.

Haimowitz, B. R. (1996). *The assessment of shame and guilt in elementary school children.* Unpublished dissertation, Medford, MA, Tufts University.

Harder, D. W. (1995). Shame and guilt assessment, and relationships of shame- and guilt-proneness to psychopathology. In J. P. Tangney & K. W. Fischer (Eds.), *Self-conscious emotions: The psychology of shame, guilt, embarrassment, and pride* (pp. 368–392). New York, NY: Guilford Press.

Harder, D. W., Cutler, L., & Rockart, L. (1992). Assessment of shame and guilt and their relationships to psychopathology. *Journal of Personality Assessment, 59,* 584–604.

Harder, D. W., & Lewis, S. J. (1987). The assessment of shame and guilt. In J. N. Butcher, & C. D. Spielberger (Eds.), *Advances in personality assessment* (Vol. 6, pp. 89–114). Hillsdale, NJ: Erlbaum.

Harder, D. W., & Zalma, A. (1990). Two promising shame and guilt scales: A construct validity comparison. *Journal of Personality Assessment, 55,* 729–745.

Harris, T. L., & Schwab, R. (1990). Sex-role orientation and personal adjustment. In J. W. Neuliep (Ed.), Handbook of replication research in the behavioral and social sciences. *Journal of Social Behavior and Personality, 5,* 473–479.

Heying, R. H., Korabik, K., & Munz, D. C. (1975). Sex differences in expected guilt reactions to hypothetical behaviors of sexual, hostile, and moral substance. *Perceptual and Motor Skills, 40,* 409–410.

Hill, J. P., & Lynch, M. E. (1983). The intensification of gender-related role expectations during early adolescence. In J. Brooks-Gunn & A. C. Peterson (Eds.), *Girls at puberty* (pp. 201–228). New York, NY: Plenum.

Hoblitzelle, W. (1988). *The measurement of shame and guilt and the role of shame in depression.* Unpublished doctoral dissertation, Yale University, New Haven, CT.

Hochschild, A. R. (1983). *The managed heart: Commercialization of human feeling.* Los Angeles, CA: University of California Press.

Hoffman, M. L. (1975). Sex differences in moral internalization and values. *Journal of Personality and Social Psychology, 32,* 720–729.

Hoffman, M. L. (1977). Moral internalization: Current theory and research. In L. Berkowitz (Ed.), *Advances in experimental social psychology* (Vol. 10, pp. 85–133). New York, NY: Academic Press.

Izard, C. E. (1977). *Human emotions.* New York, NY: Plenum Press.

Izard, C. E., Dougherty, F. E., Bloxom, B. M., & Kotsch, W. E. (1974). The Differential Emotions scale: *A method of measuring the subjective experience of discrete emotions.* Nashville, TN: Vanderbilt University.

Kemper, T. (1978). *A social interactional theory of emotions.* New York, NY: Wiley.

Kochanska, G. (1991). Socialization and temperament in the development of guilt and conscience. *Child Development, 62,* 1379–1392.

Kochanska, G. (1993). Toward a synthesis of parental socialization and child temperament in early development of conscience. *Child Development, 64,* 325–347.

Kochanska, G., Aksan, N., & Koenig, A. L. (1995). A longitudinal study of the roots of preschoolers' conscience: Committed compliance and emerging internalization. *Child Development, 66,* 1752– 1769.

Kochanska, G., DeVet, K., Goldman, M., Murray, K., & Putnam, S. (1994). Maternal reports of conscience development and temperament in young children. *Child Development, 65,* 852–868.

Kugler, K., & Jones, W. H. (1992). On conceptualizing and assessing guilt. *Journal of Personality and Social Psychology, 62,* 318–327.

Lake, N., Lane, S., & Harris, P. L. (1995). The expectation of guilt and resistance to temptation. *Early Development and Parenting, 4,* 63–73.

Larsen, R. J., & Diener, E. (1987). Affect intensity as an individual difference characteristic: A review. *Journal of Research in Personality, 21,* 1–39.

Levy, G. D., & Fivush, R. (1993). Scripts and gender: A new approach for examining gender-role development. *Developmental Review, 13,* 126–146.

Lewis, H. B. (1971). *Shame and guilt in neurosis.* New York: International Universities Press.

Lewis, H. B. (1978). Sex differences in superego mode as related to sex differences in psychiatric illness. *Social Science and Medicine, 12B,* 199–205.

Lewis, M. (1992). *Shame.* New York: The Free Press.

Lewis, M., Alessandri, S. M., & Sullivan, M. W. (1992). Differences in shame and pride as a function of children's gender and task difficulty. *Child Development, 63,* 630–638.

Lindsay-Hartz, J. (1984). Contrasting experiences of shame and guilt. *American Behavioral Scientist, 27,* 689–704.

Lindsay-Hartz, J., De Rivera, J., & Mascolo, M. F. (1995). Differentiating guilt and shame and their effects on motivations. In J. P. Tangney & K. W. Fisher (Eds.) *Self-conscious emotions: The psychology of shame, guilt, embarrassment, and pride* (pp. 274–300). New York, NY: Guilford Press.

Lutwak, N., & Ferrari, J. R. (1996). Moral affect and cognitive processes: Differentiating shame from guilt among men and women. *Personality and Individual Differences, 21,* 891–896.

Lutwak, N., & Ferrari, J. (1997). Shame-related social anxiety: Replicating a link with various social interaction measures. *Anxiety, Stress and Coping, 10,* 335–340.

Lutz, C. A. (1990). Engendered emotion: Gender, power, and the rhetoric of emotional control in American discourse. In C. A. Lutz & L. Abu-Lughod (Eds.), *Language and the politics of emotion* (pp. 69–91). Cambridge University Press.

Manstead, A. S. R., & Fischer, A. H. (1996, August). *Gender differences in communicating anger and sadness.* Paper presented at the International Society for Research on Emotion, Toronto, Canada.

Miller, R. S. (1995). On the nature of embarrassability: Shyness, social evaluation, and social skill. *Journal of Personality, 63,* 315–339.

Mills, R. S. L., Pedersen, J., & Grusec, J. E. (1989). Sex differences in reasoning and emotion about altruism. *Sex Roles, 20,* 603–621.

Mosher, D. L. (1968). Measurement of guilt in females by self-report inventories. *Journal of Consulting and Clinical Psychology, 32,* 690–695.

Olthof, T. (1996, August). *A developmental tasks analysis of guilt and shame.* Paper presented at the International Society for Research on Emotion, Toronto, Canada.

Olthof, T., Bloemers, E., Deij, M., Ferguson, T. J., & Boom, J. (1998). Illness-related elicitors of shame and guilt in children. Manuscript in preparation, Utrecht University and Utah State University.

Otterbacher, J. R., & Munz, D. C. (1973). State-trait measure of experiential guilt. *Journal of Consulting and Clinical Psychology, 40,* 115–121.

Newman, J. P. (1984). Sex differences in depressive symptoms. *Research in Community and Mental Health, 4,* 301–323.

Perry, D. G., Perry, L., & Rasmussen, P. (1986). Cognitive social learning mediators of aggression. *Child Development, 57,* 700–711.

Perry, D. G., Perry, L. C., & Weiss, R. J. (1989). Sex differences in the consequences that children anticipate for aggression. *Developmental Psychology, 25,* 312–319.

Pulakos, J. (1996). Family environment and shame: Is there a relationship? *Journal of Clinical Psychology, 52,* 617–623.

Quiles, Z., & Bybee, J. (1997). Chronic and predispositional guilt: Relations to mental health, prosocial behavior, and religiosity. *Journal of Personality Assessment, 69,* 104–126.

Reimer, M. S. (1997). *Fleeing from the self: Assessing shame and its implications in adolescent development.* Unpublished doctoral dissertation, Temple University, Philadelphia, PA.

Rimé, B., Mesquita, B., Philippot, P., & Boca, S. (1991). Beyond the emotional event: Six studies on the social sharing of emotions. *Cognition and Emotion, 5*, 435–465.

Scheff, T. J. (1988). Shame and conformity: The deference-emotion system. *American Sociological Review, 53*, 395–406.

Schimmack, U., & Diener, E. (1997). Affect intensity: Separating intensity and frequency in repeatedly measured affect. *Journal of Personality and Social Psychology, 73*, 1313–1329.

Shields, S. A. (1991). Gender in the psychology of emotion: A selective research review. In K. T. Strongman (Ed.), *International review of studies on emotion* (Vol. 1, pp. 227–245). New York, NY: Wiley.

Stapley, J. C., & Haviland, J. M. (1989). Beyond depression: Gender differences in normal adolescents' emotional experiences. *Sex Roles, 20*, 295–308.

Strayer, J., & Roberts, W. (1997). Facial and verbal measures of children's emotions and empathy. *International Journal of Behavioral Development, 20*, 627–649.

Tangney, J. P. (1990). Assessing individual differences in proneness to shame and guilt: Development of the Self-Conscious Affect and Attribution Inventory. *Journal of Personality and Social Psychology, 59*, 102–111.

Tangney, J. P. (1992). Situational determinants of shame and guilt in young adulthood. *Personality and Social Psychology Bulletin, 18*, 199–206.

Tangney, J. P. (1994). The mixed legacy of the superego: Adaptive and maladaptive aspects of shame and guilt. In J. M. Masling & R. F. Borenstein (Eds.), *Empirical perspectives on object relations theory* (pp. 1–28). Washington DC: American Psychological Association.

Tangney, J. P. (1995). Shame and guilt in interpersonal relationships. In J. P. Tangney and K. W. Fischer (Eds.), *Self-conscious emotions: The psychology of shame, guilt, embarrassment, and pride* (pp. 114–139). New York, NY: Guilford Press.

Tangney, J. P. (1996). Conceptual and methodological issues in the assessment of shame and guilt. *Behaviour Research and Therapy, 34*, 741–754.

Tangney, J. P., Burggraf, S. A., Hamme, H., & Domingos, B. (1988a). *The Self-Conscious Affect and Attribution Inventory (SCAAI).* Bryn Mawr College.

Tangney, J. P., Burggraf, S. A., Hamme, H., & Domingos, B. (1988b, March). *Assessing individual differences in proneness to shame and guilt: The Self-Conscious Affect and Attribution Inventory.* Poster presented at the meeting of the Eastern Psychological Association, Buffalo, NY.

Tangney, J. P., Wagner, P., Fletcher, C., & Gramzow, R. (1991, April). *Intergenerational continuities and discontinuities in proneness to shame and proneness to guilt.* Paper presented at the meeting of the Society for Research in Child Development, Seattle, WA.

Tangney, J. P., Wagner, P. E., & Gramzow, R. (1989). *The Test of Self-Conscious Affect.* Fairfax, VA: George Mason University.

Thompson, R. A., & Hoffman, M. (1980). Empathy and the development of guilt in children. *Developmental Psychology, 16*, 155–156.

Thrane, G. (1979). Shame. *Journal for the Theory of Social Behaviour, 9*, 139–166.

Vangelisti, A. L., & Sprague, R. J. (1998). Guilt and hurt: Similarities, distinctions, and conversation strategies. In P. A. Andersen & L. K. Guerrero

(Eds.), *Handbook of communication and emotion: Research, theory, applications, and contexts* (pp. 123–140). San Diego, CA: Academic Press.

Wagner, H. L., Buck, R., & Winterbotham, M. (1993). Communication of specific emotions: Gender differences in sending accuracy and communication measures. *Journal of Nonverbal Behavior, 17,* 29–53.

Williams, J. E., & Best, D. L. (1990). *Measuring sex stereotypes: A multination study (revised edition). Cross-cultural research and methodology series* (Vol. 6). Newbury Park, CA: Sage.

Williams, C., & Bybee, J. (1994). What do children feel guilty about? Developmental and gender differences. *Developmental Psychology, 30,* 617–623.

Wright, F., O'Leary, J., & Balkin, J. (1989). Shame, guilt, narcissism, and depression: Correlates and sex differences. *Psychoanalytic Psychology, 6,* 217–230.

Zahn-Waxler, C. (1993). Warriors and worriers: Gender and psychopathology. *Development and Psychopathology, 5,* 79–89.

Zahn-Waxler, C. (1995, April). *Higher order emotions, gender, adaptation, and psychopathology: A developmental perspective on empathy, guilt, and internalization of distress.* Paper presented at the Wisconsin Symposium on Emotion: Emotion and Psychopathology, Madison, WN.

Zahn-Waxler, C., Cole, P. M., & Barrett, K. C. (1991). Guilt and empathy: Sex differences and implications for the development of depression. In K.A. Dodge & J. Garber (Eds.), *The development of emotion regulation and dysregulation* (pp. 243–272). Cambridge University Press.

Zahn-Waxler, C., & Kochanska, G. (1990). The origins of guilt. In R. A. Thompson (Ed.), *Nebraska symposium on motivation: Vol. 36. Sociometric development* (pp. 183–258). Lincoln, NB: University of Nebraska Press.

Zahn-Waxler, C., Kochanska, G., Krupnick, J., & Mayfield, A. (1988). *Children's interpretations of interpersonal distress and conflict: Coding manual.* Laboratory of Developmental Psychology, National Institute of Mental Health.

Zahn-Waxler, C., & Robinson, J. (1995). Empathy and guilt: Early origins of feelings of responsibility. In J. P. Tangney and K. W. Fischer (Eds.), *Self-conscious emotions: The psychology of shame, guilt, embarrassment, and pride* (pp. 143–173). New York, NY: Guilford Press.

13. Sex differences in anxiety and depression: Empirical evidence and methodological questions

TRACEY E. MADDEN, LISA FELDMAN BARRETT, AND PAULA R. PIETROMONACO

The notion that women are more emotional than men is entrenched in our cultural beliefs and consistently supported by research on sex-linked stereotypes (e.g., Birnbaum, Nosanchuk & Croll, 1980; Fabes & Martin, 1991; Fischer, 1993b). Men and women typically report differences in their general emotional experience, such as overall emotional intensity or expressivity (Grossman & Wood, 1993; Johnson & Shulman, 1988), as well as in the experience and expression of specific emotions (Birnbaum et al., 1980; Fabes & Martin, 1991; Shields, 1984). This stereotype is particularly evident in the literature on anxiety and depression, the emotions which are the topic of interest in this chapter. In general, women are believed to be more susceptible to and more expressive of anxious and depressed feelings than are men. The closely related emotions, fear and sadness, are often described as prototypical female emotional responses and seem to be central to the emotion based stereotype of men and women (Fabes & Martin, 1991; Shields, 1984).

Anxiety and depression can be defined as emotional states or as clinical syndromes. Although a number of studies have focused on sex differences in the clinical syndromes (e.g., Kessler, McGonagle, Zhao, Nelson, Hughes, Eshelman, Wittchen, & Kendler, 1994; Nolen-Hoeksema, 1987, 1990; Robins & Regier, 1991; Weissman & Klerman, 1977, 1985), this chapter focuses on sex differences in anxiety and depression as emotional experiences. Therefore, it is not our intent to provide a comprehensive review of the clinical literature on anxiety and depression, but we will refer to the clinical literature when it is relevant for understanding sex differences in anxiety and depression as emotional states.

As an emotional phenomenon, anxiety is defined in terms of three components (Ohman, 1993): (1) a subjective experience consisting of an "ineffable and unpleasant feeling of foreboding," (2) perceptions of bodily responses (e.g., sweating, palpitations, shortness of breath), and

(3) behaviors associated with escape and avoidance. Anxiety is also defined as unresolved fear (Epstein, 1972), and the emotions of anxiety and fear are often treated collectively in reviews of the literature (e.g., Ohman, 1993). Similarly, the emotional phenomenon of depression is defined as a state of prolonged and ongoing sadness (Oatley & Jenkins, 1996; Stearns, 1993). As evidenced by these definitions, anxiety and fear are considered strongly related to one another, as are depression and sadness. If anything, the distinct emotion labels (anxiety versus fear; depression versus sadness) reflect differences in intensity and/or duration rather than fundamental distinctions in the nature of the emotions themselves.[1] As a result, we review relevant literature regarding fear and sadness when addressing sex differences in anxiety and depression. Moreover, throughout the chapter, we treat anxiety and fear, and depression and sadness, as interchangeable emotions.

Despite the popular belief that women are the more emotional sex, reviewers and researchers disagree as to whether there is empirical support for sex differences in emotional expression and experience (e.g., Brody & Hall, 1993; Fischer, 1993b; LaFrance & Banaji, 1992; Shields, 1991). The purpose of this chapter is to critically review a representative sample of the existing literature in an attempt to address this issue. We will pay especially attention to some methodological issues in relation to the current research.

Sex differences in the expression of anxiety and depression

Fear and sadness are the emotions that women express more than do men (Brody & Hall, 1993; Fischer, 1993b). Evidence suggests that women are more verbally and non-verbally expressive of fear than are men; they report expressing their fearful feelings with more intensity (Allen & Haccoun, 1976), more frequent facial expressions of fear (Kring & Gordon, 1998), and more crying and freezing when afraid (Wallbott, Ricci-Bitti, & Banninger-Huber, 1986). In addition, women have displayed greater reluctance than men to be close to a feared object such as a spider or a snake (Cornelius & Averill, 1983; Speltz & Bernstein, 1976).

Evidence also suggests that women express sadness to a greater extent than do men. Women, in comparison with men, express sadness with more intensity or more frequency (Allen & Haccoun, 1976; Balswick & Avertt, 1977; Dosser, Balswick, & Halverson, 1983), and report crying with greater frequency and intensity (Lombardo, Cretser, Lombardo, & Mathis, 1983; Oliver & Toner, 1990). Finally, women have reported a greater frequency of certain types of non-verbal expressions (e.g., facial expressions, Kring & Gordon, 1998), changes in voice quality and crying (Wallbott et al., 1986). Taken together, the empirical evidence supports the commonly held belief that women express anxious and depressed feelings more than do men.

Theories for understanding sex differences in emotional expression

A number of theories offer explanations for why women express more anxious and depressed feelings than do men. Although most of these explanations have not been tested empirically, they suggest several specific processes that will be important to examine in future investigations.

The role of stereotypes

Several theorists (Brody & Hall, 1993; Fischer, 1993b; LaFrance & Banaji, 1992; Shields, 1987, 1991) suggest that stereotypes contribute to sex differences in the expression of emotions such as fear and sadness. The essence of the prevailing stereotype is that women are more expressive than men of their fearful and sad feelings (e.g., Birnbaum & Croll, 1984; Fabes & Martin, 1991). This stereotype may give rise to two distinct effects. First, the stereotype may function as a cognitive structure (or schema) that leads perceivers to focus on stereotype-consistent information (Fiske & Taylor, 1991). Thus, perceivers may be more likely to notice women's expressions of fear and sadness, whereas similar expressions by men may go unnoticed. Any sex-linked disparity in people detecting fear and sadness expressions could lead to exaggerated estimates of stereotypic female expressivity and underestimates of non-stereotypic male expressivity. Furthermore, perceivers' expectations may lead women (or men) to respond in a manner consistent with the stereotype, thereby creating a self-fulfilling prophecy that provides further support for the stereotype. This cycle is particularly likely to occur for expressions of fear and sadness because these are the two emotions that are most representative of the female stereotype (Fabes & Martin, 1991; Shields, 1984).

Second, stereotypes provide the basis for socializing girls and boys about appropriate emotional behavior (for a thorough discussion of sex-based socialization practices, see Brody & Hall, 1993), and thus early differences in reinforcement histories may lead to later differences in the sex-linked expression of emotions such as fear and sadness. Girls are socialized to express their fear and sadness, whereas boys are not (Brody & Hall, 1993; see also Brody, this volume; Fivush & Buckner, this volume). A potent example of sex-based socialization practices regarding fear comes from a review of child-rearing manuals and children's literature covering the time period from 1850 to 1950 (Stearns &

Haggarty, 1991). Boys' expressions of fear, in particular, are depicted negatively in these books and parents are advised to discourage the expression of fear by their sons.

The connection between stereotypes and socialization practices provides a compelling explanation for how differences in expressions of anxiety and depression develop and are sustained. The theory suggests a proximal cause for the expressivity differences: stereotypes may play a role in producing sex-linked behaviors of expression, and those behaviors further reinforce the stereotypes. What the theory fails to explain, however, are the origins or functions of the stereotypes: why do the stereotypes exist and what purposes might they serve? If stereotypes play a role in producing sex-linked differences in anxiety and depression expressions, then we need to identify factors that might produce the stereotypes, as well as the functions served by stereotypic behaviors such as women's greater expression of anxiety and depression.

Stigmatization of women

At least one theorist (Lutz, 1990) argues that the emotional double-standard associated with the stereotype serves a function of preserving the social hierarchy. According to the emotional double-standard theory (Shields, 1987), women who express either fear or sadness are more likely than men to elicit an immediate positive response (presumably because the expression of these emotions is consistent with the female stereotype). At the same time, women's emotional expressions may produce less immediate, more subtle, and quite negative consequences for women (Lutz, 1990). According to Lutz, women's emotional expressions help to preserve a social hierarchy in which women (like their emotions) are viewed as irrational, chaotic, uncontrollable, and therefore dangerous. In contrast, men are associated with more valued processes such as rational, controlled thought. Furthermore, the presumption that men are more rational and less emotional than women may lead to perceptions that men are more justified than women when they do express their emotions (Shields, 1987; Shields & Koster, 1989). According to Lutz's theory, the belief that women are more emotional serves a larger social function of legitimizing women's subordinate rank in the power hierarchy. Expressions of fear and sadness, in particular, connote weakness, lack of control, and helplessness. As a result of the emotional double-standard, women who express fear and sadness may reap rewards in their immediate situation, but they may be stigmatized in the long run.

Social Role Theory

Another reason the sex-linked stereotypes regarding anxiety and depression might exist is that men and women actually behave differently as a result of differing demands placed on them by their distinct social roles in Western society (Eagly, 1987). Social role theorists (Eagly, 1987; Wood, Rhodes, & Whelan, 1989) propose that women's traditional domestic role emphasizes taking care of others and thus demands affiliative and relationally oriented behaviors. By contrast, men's traditional roles in the workplace elicit more agentic and instrumental behaviors (Eagly, 1987). Several theorists (Brody & Hall, 1993; Shields, 1987, 1991; cf. Fischer, 1993b) have suggested that sex-linked differences in social roles promote differences in the expression of emotions such as fear and sadness; affiliative tasks often require greater emotional expressivity than agentic tasks. According to this argument, expressions of emotions like fear and sadness facilitate a woman's ability to effectively meet her primary interpersonal goal, which is to care for and maintain her social relationships with others. In contrast, expressions of fear and sadness would be likely to inhibit a man's primary interpersonal goal of being instrumental and agentic.

Although this argument suggests that the stereotype has a "grain of truth" (i.e., reflects actual sex differences in fear and sadness expressions produced by social role demands), several questions exist about whether and how expressing sadness or fear might serve the demands of women's social roles. In general, emotional communications do tend to foster a feeling of intimacy (Laurenceau, Feldman Barrett, & Pietromonaco, 1998), thereby contributing to the maintenance of a relationship. According to a social role analysis, women's emotional expressions function to nurture their relationships and thus should be tied to giving help. The problem with this analysis is that women express more fear and sadness, and these particular emotions are likely to decrease help-giving and to increase help-seeking. Furthermore, expressions of fear and sadness may actually strain and deteriorate relationships rather than foster and maintain them (Feldman & Gotlib, 1993; Gotlib & Hammen, 1992). Specifically, it is not clear how the expressions of fear and sadness (as compared to any other emotions) would allow women to be more attuned to the needs and emotions of others. Another aspect of sex-based social roles, however, may provide a better explanation for both the stereotype and underlying behavioral differences in male and female expressions of anxiety and depression: relative levels of power and status associated with male and female roles (e.g., Fischer, 1993b).

The role of power

Men and women may differ in the expression of emotion because they typically differ in level of power; women are likely to hold positions of lower power and status than men. The emotions of fear and sadness are often described as expressions of "vulnerability, helplessness and powerlessness" (Fischer, 1993b, p. 312). Thus, women's expressions of these emotions may reflect that they have less power and less status (see Brody & Hall, 1993), making them more vulnerable to these feelings than men. In contrast, men express more anger than women, possibly because anger is associated with power and assertiveness (e.g., Fischer, 1993b). This theory assumes that emotional expressions serve to mark one's status or power in society, and is consistent with sociological theories in which all emotions are viewed as determined by relative levels of status and power in social interactions (e.g., Kemper, 1978). Furthermore, people in positions of power rely on stereotypes and notice stereotype-congruent behavior in assessing the behavior of persons of lower power (Goodwin, Gubin, Fiske, & Yzerbyt, 1998). Thus, power also may play a role in the application of stereotypes to judgments of emotional expression, leading observers to perceive more frequent fear and sadness in women's expressions than in men's.

From our perspective, the expressions of fear and sadness may convey not only powerlessness and lower social status as discussed above, but may also provide women with a way to be agentic in relationships without violating their social role. By expressing fear or sadness, women may elicit responses from others and this may allow them to enact an indirect form of interpersonal influence. More direct forms of influence are not always seen as socially appropriate for women, who are expected to be less agentic than men and more relationally oriented (Eagly, 1987). Thus, social role constraints may produce more creative and subtle means (e.g., the use of emotions) of interpersonal influence, allowing women to exert agency in their relationships in a way that is consistent with their relative levels of power and status.[2] This view suggests that expressions of fear and sadness might fulfill a different interpersonal function for women than they do for men.

In summary, empirical evidence supports the view that women express more anxiety and depression than do men. Stereotypes about the sexes and their emotions seem to play a role in both creating and sustaining sex differences in expression. In particular, the stereotype and related sex differences in expressions of anxiety and depression are apt to reflect women's positions of low power and status in society and/or their social role as relationship caretakers via communication styles and display rules.

Sex differences in the experience of anxiety and depression

Although women appear to express more anxiety and depression than do men, it is not clear whether they actually experience more frequent or more intense emotions. Studies incorporating reports of anxiety/fear and depression/sadness as either predictor or criterion variables have not produced consistent sex differences, although when differences appear they are typically in the stereotypic direction.[3] For example, some studies find that women report experiencing fear or anxiety more intensely or more often than do men (e.g., Alagna & Morokoff, 1986; Allen & Haccoun, 1976; Berenbaum, Fujita, & Pfennig, 1995; Dillon, Wolf, & Katz, 1985; Fischer, 1993a; Scherer, Wallbott, & Summerfield, 1986; Strube, Berry, Goza, & Fennimore, 1985), whereas others have failed to find significant sex differences (e.g., Gotlib & Meyer, 1986; Kring & Gordon, 1998; Nezu, Nezu, & Blissett, 1988; Pennebaker, Hughes, & O'Heeron, 1987; Philippot, 1993; Small, Gessner, & Ferguson, 1984; Sprecher & Sedikides, 1993; Stapley & Haviland, 1989).

A similar picture emerges for reports of both sadness and depression. Sometimes women report experiencing more frequent or more intense sadness and depression than do men (e.g., Alagna & Morokoff, 1986; Allen & Haccoun, 1976; Eisenberg, Fabes, Murphy, Karbon, Maszk, Smith, O'Boyle, & Suh, 1994; Fischer, 1993a; Grossman & Wood, 1993; Nolen-Hoeksema, 1987; Scherer et al., 1986; Sprecher & Sedikides, 1993; Strube et al., 1985), but some studies find no differences (e.g., Ganong & Coleman, 1984; Gotlib & Meyer, 1986; Kopper, 1993; Kring & Gordon, 1998; Larsen, Kasimatis, & Frey, 1992; Nezu et al., 1988; Nolen-Hoeksema & Morrow, 1993; Parrott, 1991; Philippot, 1993; Potts, Camp, & Coyne, 1989; Rothkopf & Blaney, 1991; Small, Gessner, & Ferguson, 1984; Watson & Clark, 1992).

Given the lack of consistent findings across studies, it is not surprising that review articles draw somewhat different conclusions regarding the status of sex differences in the experience of fear and sadness. Some reviewers (Brody & Hall, 1993; Fischer, 1993b) have concluded that women experience more intense fear and sadness than do men, whereas other reviewers (LaFrance & Banaji, 1992; Shields, 1991) have suggested that sex differences in fear and sadness occur primarily in specific contexts or in connection with the use of certain methodologies. Thus, although most theorists agree that sex differences arise in at least some contexts, explanations for these differences vary.

Theories for understanding sex differences in emotional experience

Cognitive appraisals

Many theories attempt to explain both the emotions and the clinical syndromes of anxiety and depression, but those focusing on cognitive appraisal are particularly relevant for understanding the processes that may link sex to the experience of emotion.[4] The basic premise of cognitive appraisal theories is that emotions are produced from a person's appraisal or interpretation of her or his environment (e.g., Frijda, 1986; Roseman, Antoniou & Jose, 1996; Smith & Ellsworth, 1985; Smith & Lazarus, 1993). Sadness, for example, is associated with a "belief that [an] unpleasant situation is controlled by impersonal circumstances and that nothing can be done to set it right" (Smith & Ellsworth, 1985, p. 834). The cognitive appraisals associated with this emotion are irrevocable loss, helplessness about the loss, and low perceived ability to control or act directly upon the situation (Roseman et al., 1996; Smith & Lazarus, 1993). Fear is "characterized by uncertainty about whether or not one will be able to escape or avoid an unpleasant outcome" (Smith & Ellsworth, 1985, p. 834). Cognitive appraisals associated with fear include danger or threat, uncertainty about the situation and about future outcomes, and a belief that another is in control of the situation (Roseman et al., 1996; Smith & Lazarus, 1993). Although little empirical evidence is available, some theorists believe that women are more prone than are men to the patterns of cognitive appraisal associated with these emotions, making women more susceptible to experiencing them (Brody & Hall, 1993; Fischer, 1993b). Similar to the emotion theories, several clinical theories focus on the role of negative cognitive schemas in producing feelings of anxiety or depression (e.g., Abramson, Seligman, & Teasdale, 1978; Beck, 1967). The theme of these theories is that anxiety and depression are associated with thoughts, perceptions, or behaviors reflecting helplessness, hopelessness and lack of control over outcomes of future events.

Given their relatively lower status and power, women may be more prone than men to judge themselves as lacking control over their circumstances and being helpless, which, in turn, may lead to thoughts of hopelessness about the future (Fischer, 1993b). Although these thoughts may accurately portray women's social position, they also may lead to increased susceptibility to anxiety and depression. An implicit assumption of many theories of depression is that beliefs of helplessness, hopelessness, or lack of control are irrational and, therefore, maladaptive. Within the larger social context, however, women's thoughts of helplessness or of lack of control may not be irrational.

Rather, they may reflect a reality of decreased social and economic power, either in everyday life or in the face of negative life events such as divorce or the loss of a job. Thus, women's vulnerability to anxiety and depression could be interpreted as a rational reaction to social and economic realities, rather than as maladaptive and psychopathological.

In addition to engaging in cognitive appraisal patterns associated with anxiety and depression, women also may be more prone than men to respond to depression in a way that prolongs and intensifies their depressed feelings (Nolen-Hoeksema, 1987, 1991, see also Fivush, this volume). According to the response style theory of depression, people who ruminate about being depressed, and who focus on symptoms, causes and the significance of their depression are likely to experience longer and more intense depressions. Women receive more advice to ruminate in stressful situations than do men (Ali & Toner, 1996) and women do, in fact, ruminate more on their sadness than do men (Conway et al., 1990; Nolen-Hoeksema, 1987).

In summary, women may experience more anxiety and depression because their position in the social hierarchy is associated with the cognitive appraisal patterns underlying these emotions. Because women on average hold positions of low status and low power, as a group they may have an increased propensity to make appraisals that they lack control or are helpless and hopeless about life events. Each of these appraisals is associated with experiencing anxiety and depression. Furthermore, a female tendency to ruminate on negative feelings may produce more prolonged and intensified experiences of depression by women.

Accessibility and memory

It is possible that sex differences observed in some studies reflect differences in the ability of men and women to access or recall particular aspects of their emotional experiences rather than actual differences in the experience of the emotions. The standard method for assessing sex differences relies heavily on memory; participants must answer global, retrospective questions about their emotional experiences by relying on their memory of past events (e.g., "I seldom feel sad or depressed"). Studies using this retrospective method typically find that men and women differ in their emotional experience. Stereotypic sex differences in the experience of emotion have not been found in diary studies in which participants answer brief, structured questions about their emotional experiences immediately following specific, everyday life events (Feldman Barrett & Morganstein, 1995; Feldman Barrett, Robin, Pietromonaco, & Eyssell, 1998). This methodology relies less on memory than do global, retrospective reports (Reis & Wheeler, 1991), and therefore may be less influenced by stereotypes, implicit beliefs, and differences in the accessibility of emotion knowledge. Interestingly, participants in these diary studies did respond in a stereotypic manner to global, retrospective measures (i.e., women report experiencing more anxiety and depression than do men), even when sex differences were not apparent in the immediate, context-specific measures. Furthermore, the discrepancy between the retrospective and concurrent ratings of fear and sadness is greater for women than for men. For both fear and sadness, the relationship between their memory-based and their concurrent ratings is stronger for men than for women (Feldman Barrett & Morganstein, 1995). Thus, the men appear to be more accurate in their memory-based ratings of sadness and fear than the women.

The reason for these sex differences is not clear. Although concurrent ratings are also self-report measures, they are made in real world settings, rich with context and cues for assessing one's feelings of anxiety and depression. They also are made concurrently with the emotional experience, without the necessity of retrieving, integrating, and aggregating memories. It may be that the presence of context and cues and the lack of reliance on memories produces concurrent ratings of experiences of anxiety and depression that are less influenced by emotion knowledge and by sex-based implicit beliefs and stereotypes about emotions. In contrast, the degree to which participants must rely on memory may influence whether women report experiencing more anxiety or depression than do men for at least two reasons: (1) men and women differ in their ability to remember previous emotional experiences (Feldman Barrett, Lane, Sechrest, & Schwartz, 1997), and (2) implicit beliefs and stereotypes about how men and women experience and express emotions may contribute more to memory-based judgments than to concurrent (and less memory-based) judgments (e.g., Fischer, 1993b; Shields, 1987, 1991).

Differences in memory for emotional experience

Women may remember experiencing greater emotion (e.g., anxiety and depression), because they are more likely than men to record and recall the details of their emotional experiences. Women are superior to men at identifying emotion from non-verbal cues (Brody & Hall, 1993), with the possible exception of decoding expressions of anger (Wagner et al., 1986). Women are better able to match emotion stimuli to emotion responses (Lane, Sechrest, Riedel, Weldon, Kaszniak, & Schwartz, 1996), and they display more complex knowledge of emotions than men, including a greater ability to differentiate among different emotions (Feldman Barrett et al., 1997). These sex-linked differences in emotion-related knowledge will likely influence responses on self-report measures, particularly those calling for the retrieval, summarizing and integration of emotion memories. Such global, retrospective self-report measures contain no immediate cues or context to assist a participant in assessing his or her emotions, and may require more reliance on emotion knowledge than measures answered concurrently with an emotional experience. Thus, women may report experiencing more emotion than do men because women are better able to access and recall their emotional experiences; however, in the immediate situation, men and women may not differ in the nature of their emotional experiences.

Reliance on implicit beliefs and stereotypes

People may also rely on implicitly held beliefs about their own emotional responses or on stereotypes about appropriate male and female emotional responses when answering global, memory-based questionnaires in a laboratory setting. The typical laboratory setting for psychological studies, by design, provides minimal cues to influence participants when they are completing psychological measures. Furthermore, retrospective self-report measures contain global items (e.g., "I seldom feel sad or depressed") that make no reference to specific or hypothetical situations and, therefore, provide little context within which to frame a response. As a result, participants must retrieve, integrate and aggregate their memories of specific events to produce global ratings of their experience; this reconstructive process is likely to be aided by implicitly held theories (for reviews see Fiske & Taylor, 1991; Greenwald & Banaji, 1995; Nisbett & Ross, 1980; Ross, 1989). As a result, women might reconstruct their memories in line with the societal belief that they are or should be emotional, whereas men's reconstructed memories might be tailored to fit the societal belief that they are or should be unemotional. Alternatively, study participants might minimize their cognitive efforts and respond to global, retrospective questions by invoking their stereotypes as a heuristic. Social observers frequently use sex-linked stereotypes to infer the emotional experiences of others (Birnbaum et al., 1980; Fabes & Martin, 1991; Grossman & Wood, 1993). People also appear to rely on such stereotypes in remembering their own past emotional experiences while in laboratory settings (Robinson, Johnson, & Shields, in press).

In order to be a viable hypothesis, the proposal that people rely on sex-based stereotypes in making global, retrospective ratings of their emotional experiences should be compared with other research on the use of stereotypes. In fact, the stereotype as heuristic explanation of sex differences in anxiety and depression is somewhat inconsistent with literature on the use of racial stereotypes (e.g., see review by Devine, 1995). According to this literature, people seem to rely less on racial stereotypes the more they engage in conscious, effortful processing of information. By contrast, the effortful processing required when making global, retrospective self-reports of anxiety and depression may actually foster reliance on sex stereotypes, according to both the theory and a recent study on sex stereotypes (Robinson et al., in press). Important differences in the methodologies used in these two lines of research may account for this discrepancy. It is also possible that differences in the contents and the targets of the stereotypes involved may account for the apparent inconsistency. Racial stereotypes generally are not considered acceptable in modern Western society. Therefore, people may be motivated to overcome socially unacceptable prejudices based on race and may achieve this goal through failing to rely on stereotypes when engaging in effortful processing of information. By contrast, people may be less motivated to overcome sex stereotypes regarding emotions, given that the socially desirable response is less clear for these stereotypes than it is for racial stereotypes. As a result, sex stereotypes may be regarded as both acceptable and accurate.

In summary, the evidence regarding sex differences in experiences of anxiety and depression is mixed. One possible explanation for sex difference findings comes from cognitive appraisal theories of anxiety and depression. According to these theories, anxiety and depression are associated with patterns of appraisals reflecting helplessness, hopelessness and lack of control. Because women are on average in positions of lower status and lower power in society, they may be more prone to making such appraisals, which would explain their increased susceptibility to feelings of anxiety and depression. Another possible explanation is that the findings actually reflect differences in the ability of men and women to access and recall their emotional experiences (while the experiences themselves may not significantly differ for the two sexes). Because the majority of studies use global, retrospective self-report questionnaires, they may be measuring stereotypes, implicit beliefs, and emotion knowledge rather than sex differences in the experience of anxiety and depression.

The role of culture

All of the sex difference findings reported in this chapter are from studies in Western cultures (primarily from North America). Cross-cultural differences are likely to play a central role in how women and men experience and express anxiety and depression, however. Culture may influence the definition of anxiety and depression, the context in which these emotions are experienced or expressed, or the meaning of their expression. To date, little empirical work has addressed these questions, and until it is conducted we cannot determine whether our knowledge regarding sex differences is culture-bound or not.

Nevertheless, considerable debate exists about whether culture influences the experience and expression of emotions. Some researchers and theorists referred to as "universalists" believe that "basic" emotions, including fear and sadness, are experienced and recognized universally by people across cultures (e.g., Ekman, 1992, 1994; Izard, 1994; Shaver, Wu, & Schwartz, 1992; cf. Russell, 1994). The universalist perspective might account for sex differences in *expressions* of fear and sadness in cultures where display rules vary with sex (e.g., like the Western emotional double standard for displays of fear and sadness previously discussed). But the universalist view does not provide any explanation for sex differences in *experiences* of fear and sadness, short of assuming or demonstrating that such differences are biologically based and found consistently across cultures.

Social constructionists have an alternative theory of the relationship between culture and emotions which may allow for the exploration of sex differences in anxiety and depression across cultures. The views regarding the role of culture range from believing that emotions are a complete product of culture, to more moderate views that distinct cultural patterns of emotions emerge from a limited range of universal emotions (e.g., Harré, 1986; Heelas, 1986; Lutz, 1988; Oatley, 1993; Oatley & Jenkins, 1996). Understanding the functions and social meanings of anxiety and depression may help to explain the appearance of sex differences. The social meanings of anxiety and depression are linked with concepts of helplessness and hopelessness in Western cultures, but they may not connote the same thing in other cultures (e.g., "tijituru-tijituru" is described as the closest counterpart to "sad" in Australian Aboriginal language of Pintupi, but it does not imply a "quiet resignation" of helplessness like the English term sad does; Wierzbicka, 1992). Moreover, in some societies, emotions that are central to the culture may not correspond exactly to Western emotional concepts. For example, in an anthropological study of people inhabiting the Pacific atoll of Ifaluk, Lutz (1988) observed that the emotion of "fago" links sadness with concepts of compassion and love and that "fago" cannot be adequately translated by any one of these three English emotion terms. "Fago" is felt when a loved one is in need. Similar to sadness, "fago" is experienced in connection with a loss, such as when a loved one dies or travels far away. In addition to these common eliciting conditions, "fago" and sadness also are associated with similar immediate behavioral patterns, such as crying, passively sitting, and losing one's appetite. However, the emotions also differ in fundamental ways. Importantly, "fago" does not imply loss of control as does sadness. In fact, quite to the contrary, "fago" is seen as empowering and as ultimately propelling to activity the one who experiences it. The loss and suffering associated with "fago" are those of another rather than of the self, and a desire to fulfill the needs of the other empower one to take action. If sex differences were found in the experience or expression of "fago" in Ifaluk, any explanation of such differences would need to take into account the distinct meaning of "fago" in that culture. Furthermore, if sex differences in anxiety and depression were revealed in other cultures, the reasons for such differences might be culturally bound.

The comparison of "fago" and sadness makes clear that emotions like anxiety and depression need to be decomposed to make meaningful cross-cultural comparisons of both the emotions and any sex difference findings relating to them. For example, one theory proposes that embedded in each emotion label is a narrative about the emotion, and this narrative must be parsed in different cultures to determine the existence of commonalities across cultures (Shweder, 1993; for a similar theory from a linguistic perspective, see also Wierzbicka, 1992, 1995).

Thus, the role that culture plays in the link between sex and anxiety or depression is far from clear. What emerges from the discussion of culture are more questions. More important than whether there are consistent sex differences in the experience and/or expression of anxiety and depression is whether these emotions mean the same thing or serve the same function across cultures. The act of comparing the constituent components (i.e., narrative slots) of anxiety and depression may shed light on the conditions under which sex differences might or might not occur.

Suggestions for future research

The purpose of the present chapter was twofold. First, we demonstrated that the answer to the question of whether there are sex differences in expressions and experiences of anxiety and depression is still far from clear. The most empirical support exists with respect to expression of these emotions, although the grounds for these differences remain to be determined. Some theorists believe that the existence of sex differences in the experience of emotion is an open question, because the methodology typically used to assess such differences actually measures other phenomena such as stereotypes, implicit beliefs, and emotion knowledge. Second, we identified several important methodological and substantive variables that may provide a context that amplifies or hides differences in anxiety and depression: power/status levels, appraisals of helplessness, potential bias in self-reports as well as observers´ reports.

Methodological improvements

Because of the problems inherent in the use of any single method in assessing sex differences, we believe that relying on multiple methods will yield more meaningful results. With a multi-method approach, for example, data-analysis could decompose the variance of sex difference judgements into analysis of variance-like components attributable to judgements by the self, judgements by others and their interaction and compare these components (e.g., Kenny's Social Relations Model of Interpersonal Perception, Kenny, 1994; Funder's Realistic Accuracy Model of Personality Judgements, Funder, 1995).

Combining observer ratings with self-report ratings is another example of achieving this multi-method approach (e.g., self and peer ratings from personality literature, Funder & Colvin, 1988; Kolar, Funder, & Colvin, 1996). As with self-report judgements, certain types of observer ratings may have less potential to be biased. One example of reducing bias involves having observers make judgments of expressions of anxiety and depression from transcripts of taped conversations (where the speakers' sexes are unknown to the observer). This method prevents an observer from relying on stereotypes and implicit beliefs invoked by the sex of the target whose emotions are being rated. Combining this method with more traditional self-reports may help to reveal where biases occur.

Sex-in-context

To the extent that environmental cues produce or inhibit sex difference findings in anxiety and depression, then such findings are highly contextualized. Viewed in another way, sometimes sex may have a psychological meaning (a stimulus value) such that it will affect a person's view of himself or herself or others' views of that person, and sometimes sex may not have such a stimulus value – it depends upon the context. Our second category contains recommendations for contextual variables that are apt to provide a more complete picture of the circumstances under which sex is associated with anxiety and depression. Throughout this chapter we refer to variables that may mediate or moderate the relationship between sex and anxiety and depression, such as the power and status levels of both the person experiencing or expressing anxiety or depression and the person(s) to whom the emotion is expressed; and the culturally derived functions, meanings and display rules surrounding anxiety and depression. None of these variables have been systematically tested for their impact on the relationship between sex and anxiety and depression and we believe that they must be. The paradigm to date seems to search for cross-situational consistency as evidence of a stable sex-linked difference in anxiety and depression. Instead, it will be important to look at whether the interaction between sex and any of these other variables manifests in predictable patterns of sex differences within similar contexts across time (e.g., behavior-in-context theory of personality, Mischel & Shoda, 1995)

Conclusion

Do women experience and/or express more anxiety and depression than men? The answer is not clear. If sex differences in anxiety and depression were robust, the findings would be more consistent than they are. Empirical evidence supports the idea that Western women express more anxiety and depression than do Western men, but we do not know why this relationship exists, or the boundary conditions of the relationship. Sex differences in the experience of anxiety and depression seem to be related, in part, to the way the questions are asked. Therefore, the underlying effect must be more clearly established or rejected. Our goal in this chapter was to lay the groundwork to begin searching for answers to some of these questions.

We end our chapter with this final observation. Although the question of whether sex differences exist in anxiety and depression is far from answered, the literature (including our own chapter) seems to be organized around searching for sex differences – as researchers, we try to explain when and why sex differences appear. This focus might reflect that, as part of the larger culture, our own stereotypes and implicit beliefs regarding men's versus women's emotions shape our understanding of the evidence.

Notes

1. In fact, when measured as emotional states, the distinctions between anxiety and fear, and between depression and sadness, are often arbitrary. For example, the Profile of Mood States (POMS; McNair, Lorr, & Droppleman, 1971) contains anxiety and depression subscales, whereas the Positive Affect Negative Affect Scale-Expanded (PANAS-X; Watson & Clark, 1994) contains fear and sadness subscales. Despite their different labels, the corresponding subscales from the POMS and the PANAS-X contain substantial overlap.
2. Many authors consider the use of emotions as an indirect means to influence others as dishonest or manipulative. An alternative explanation, however, is

that interpersonal influence through expressions of fear and sadness is adaptive for women, allowing them to be agentic within the confines of both their social role and their level of power in society.

3. The studies reviewed in this section should be considered a representative sample of those that incorporate specific emotions as either predictor or criterion variables. An exhaustive review of all of the findings pertaining to sex differences in emotional experience was not possible given the number of studies that test for differences between men and women when the theoretical focus is not concerned with sex differences in emotion.

4. In contrast to cognitive appraisal theories of emotion, other theories of emotion do not provide a viable explanation for why women may experience more anxiety and depression.

References

Abramson, L. Y., Seligman, M. E. P. & Teasdale, J. (1978). Learned helplessness in humans: Critique and reformulation. *Journal of Abnormal Psychology, 87,* 49–74.

Alagna, S. W., & Morokoff, P. J. (1986). Beginning medical school: Determinants of male and female emotional reactions. *Journal of Applied Social Psychology, 4,* 348–360.

Ali, A. & Toner, B. (1996). Gender differences in depressive response: The role of social support. *Sex Roles, 35,* 281–293.

Allen, J. G., & Haccoun, D. M. (1976). Sex differences in emotionality: A multidimensional approach. *Human Relations, 29,* 711–722.

Balswick, J. and Avertt, C. P. (1977). Differences in expressiveness: Gender interpersonal orientation, and perceived parental expressiveness as contributing factors. *Journal of Marriage and the Family, 39,* 121–127.

Beck, A. T. (1967). *Depression: Causes and treatment.* Philadelphia, PA: University of Pennsylvania Press.

Berenbaum, H., Fujita, F., & Pfennig, J. (1995). Consistency, specificity, and correlates of negative emotions. *Journal of Personality and Social Psychology, 68,* 342–352.

Birnbaum, D. W., & Croll, W. L. (1984). The etiology of children's stereotypes about sex differences in emotionality. *Sex Roles, 10,* 677–691.

Birnbaum, D. W., Nosanchuk, T. A., & Croll, W. L. (1980). Children's stereotypes about sex differences in emotionality. *Sex Roles, 6,* 435–443.

Brody, L. R. & Hall, J. A. (1993). Gender and emotion. In M. Lewis & J. M. Haviland (Eds.), *Handbook of emotions* (pp. 447–460). New York, NY: Guilford Press.

Conway, M., Giannopulos, C. & Stiefenhofer, K. (1990). Response styles to sadness are related to sex and sex-role orientation. *Sex Roles, 22,* 579–588.

Cornelius, R. R. and Averill, J. R. (1983). Sex differences in the fear of spiders. *Journal of Personality and Social Psychology, 45,* 377–383.

Devine, P. G. (1995). Prejudice and out-group perception. In A. Tesser (Ed.), *Advanced social psychology* (pp. 467–524). New York, NY: McGraw-Hill, Inc.

Dillon, K. M., Wolf, E., & Katz, H. (1985). Sex roles, gender, and fear. *The Journal of Psychology, 119,* 355–359.

Dosser, D. A., Balswick, J. O., & Halverson, C. F., Jr. (1983). Situational context of emotional expressiveness. *Journal of Counseling Psychology, 30,* 51–66.

Eagly, A. H. (1987). *Sex differences in social behavior: A social-role interpretation.* Hillsdale, NJ: Erlbaum.

Eisenberg, N., Fabes, R. A., Murphy, B., Karbon, M., Maszk, P., Smith, M., O'Boyle, C., & Suh, K. (1994). The relations of emotionality and regulation to dispositional and situational empathy-related responding. *Journal of Personality and Social Psychology, 66,* 776–797.

Ekman, P. (1992). An argument for basic emotions. *Cognition and Emotion, 6,* 169–200.

Ekman, P. (1994). Strong evidence for universals in facial expressions: A reply to Russell's mistaken critique. *Psychological Bulletin, 115,* 268–287.

Epstein, S. (1972). The nature of anxiety with emphasis upon its relationship to expectancy. In C. D. Spielberger (Ed.), *Anxiety: Current trends in theory and research* (Vol. 2). New York: Academic Press.

Fabes, R. A., & Martin, C. L. (1991). Gender and age stereotypes of emotionality. *Personality and Social Psychology Bulletin, 17,* 532–540.

Feldman, L. A., & Gotlib, I. H. (1993). Social dysfunction. In C. G. Costello (Ed.), *Symptoms of depression* (pp. 85–112). New York, NY: Wiley.

Feldman Barrett, L., Lane, R., Sechrest, L. & Schwartz, G. (1997). *Sex differences in emotional awareness.* Manuscript under review.

Feldman Barrett, L. & Morganstein, M. (1995, August). *Sex differences in the experience of emotion: Retrospective versus momentarv ratings.* Paper presented at the annual conference of the American Psychological Association, New York, NY.

Feldman Barrett, L., Robin, L., Pietromonaco, P. R. & Eyssell, K. M. (1998). Are women the 'more emotional' sex? Evidence from emotional experiences in social context. *Cognition and Emotion, 12,* 555–578.

Fischer, A. H. (1993a). *Deconstructing the stereotype of the emotional woman in five steps.* Poster presented at The International Society for Research in Emotion, Cambridge, UK.

Fischer, A. H. (1993b). Sex differences in emotionality: Fact or stereotype?. *Feminism & Psychology, 3,* 303–318.

Fiske, S. T. & Taylor, S. E. (1991). *Social Cognition* (2nd ed.). New York, NY: McGraw-Hill.

Frijda, N. H. (1986). *The emotions.* Cambridge University Press.

Funder, D. C. (1995). On the accuracy of personality judgment: A realistic approach. *Psychological Review, 102,* 652–670.

Funder, D. C., & Colvin, C. R. (1988). Friends and strangers: Acquaintenceship, agreement, and the accuracy of personality judgment. *Journal of Personality and Social Psychology, 55,* 149–158.

Ganong, L. H., & Coleman, M. (1984). Sex, sex roles, and familial love. *Journal of Genetic Psychology, 148,* 45–52.

Goodwin, S. A., Gubin, A., Fiske, S. T., & Yzerbyt, V. Y. (1998). Power biases impression formation: Stereotyping subordinates by default and by design. Manuscript under review.

Gotlib, I. H., & Hammen, C. L. (1992). *Psychological aspects of depression: Toward a cognitive-interpersonal integration.* West Sussex: Wiley.

Gotlib, I. H., & Lee, C. M. (1989). The social functioning of depressed patients: A longitudinal assessment. *Journal of Social and Clinical Psychology, 8,* 223–237.

Gotlib, I. H., & Meyer, J. P. (1986). Factor analysis of the Multiple Affect Adjective Check List: A separation of positive and negative affect. *Journal of Personality and Social Psychology, 50,* 1161–1165.

Greenwald, A. G., & Banaji, M. R. (1995). Implicit social cognition: Attitudes, self-esteem and stereotypes. *Psychological Review, 102,* 4–27.

Grossman, M., & Wood, W. (1993). Sex differences in intensity of emotional experience: A social role interpretation. *Journal of Personality and Social Psychology, 65,* 1010–1022.

Harré, R. (1986). The social constructionist viewpoint. In R. Harré (Ed.), *The social construction of emotions* (pp. 2–14). Oxford: Blackwell.

Heelas, P. (1986). Emotion talk across cultures. In R. Harré (Ed.), *The social construction of emotions* (pp. 234–266). Oxford: Blackwell.

Izard, C.E. (1994). Innate and universal facial expressions: Evidence from developmental and cross-cultural research. *Psychological Bulletin, 115,* 288–299.

Johnson, J. T., & Shulman, G. A. (1988). More alike than meets the eye: Perceived gender differences in subjective experience and its display. *Sex Roles, 19,* 67–80.

Kemper, T. D. (1978). *A social interactional theory of emotions.* New York, NY: Wiley-Interscience.

Kenny, D. A. (1994). *Interpersonal perception.* New York, NY: Guilford Press.

Kessler, R. C., McGonagle, K. A., Zhao, S, Nelson, C. P., Hughes, M., Eshelman, S., Wittchen, H. U., & Kendler, K. S. (1994). Lifetime and 12-month prevalence of DSMIII-R psychiatric disorders in the United States: Results from Comorbidity Survey. *Archives of General Psychiatry, 51,* 8–19.

Kolar, D. W., Funder, D. C., & Colvin, C. R. (1996). Comparing the accuracy of personality judgments by the self and knowledgeable others. *Journal of Personality, 64,* 311–337.

Kopper, B. A. (1993). Role of gender, sex role identity, and Type A behavior in anger expression and mental health functioning. *Journal of Counseling Psychology, 40,* 232–237.

Kring, A. M., & Gordon, A. H. (1998). Sex differences in emotion: Expression, experience and physiology. *Journal of Personality and Social Psychology, 74,* 686–703.

LaFrance, M. & Banaji, M. (1992). Toward a reconsideration of the gender-emotion relationship. In M. S. Clark (Ed.), *Review of personality and social psychology: Emotion and social behavior* (Vol. 14, pp. 178–202). Newbury Park, CA: Sage.

Lane, R., Sechrest, B., Reidel, R., Weldon, V., Kaszniak, A., & Schwartz, G. (1996). Impaired verbal and nonverbal emotion recognition in alexithymia. *Psychosomatic Medicine, 58,* 203–210.

Larsen, R. J., Kasimatis, M., & Frey, K. (1992). Facilitating the furrowed brow: An unobtrusive test of the facial feedback hypothesis applied to unpleasant emotion. *Cognition and Emotion, 6,* 321–338.

Laurenceau, J. P., Feldman Barrett, L., & Pietromonaco, P. R. (1998). Intimacy as a process: The importance of self-disclosure and responsiveness in interpersonal exchanges. *Journal of Personality and Social Psychology, 74,* 1238–1251.

Lombardo, W. K., Cretser, G. A., Lombardo, B., & Mathis, S. L. (1983). 'Fer cryin' out loud – There is a sex difference. *Sex Roles, 9,* 987–996.

Lutz, C. (1988). *Unnatural emotions.* University of Chicago Press.

Lutz, C. A. (1990). Engendered emotion: Gender, power and the rhetoric of emotional control in American discourse. In C. A. Lutz, L. Abu-Lughod (Eds.), *Language and the politics of emotion* (pp. 69–91). Cambridge University Press.

McNair, D. M., Lorr, M. & Droppleman, L. F. (1971). *EITS manual for the profile of mood states.* San Diego, CA: Educational and Industrial Testing Service.

Mischel, W. & Shoda, Y (1995). A cognitive-affective system theory of personality: Reconceptualizing situations, dispositions, dynamics and invariance in personality structure. *Psychological Review, 102,* 246–268.

Nezu, A. M., Nezu, C. M., & Blissett, S. E. (1988). Sense of humor as a moderator of the relationship between stressful events and psychological distress: A prospective analysis. *Journal of Personality and Social Psychology, 54,* 520–525.

Nisbett, R. E. & Ross, L. (1980). *Human inference: Strategies and shortcomings of social judgment.* Englewood Cliffs, NJ: Prentice-Hall.

Nolen-Hoeksema, S. (1987). Sex differences in unipolar depression: Evidence and theory. *Psychological Bulletin, 101,* 259–282.

Nolen-Hoeksema, S. (1990). *Sex differences in depression.* Stanford University Press.

Nolen-Hoeksema, S. (1991). Responses to depression and their effects on the duration of depressive episodes. *Journal of Abnormal Psychology, 100,* 569–582.

Nolen-Hoeksema, S., & Morrow, J. (1993). Effects of rumination and distraction on naturally occurring depressed mood. *Cognition and Emotion, 7,* 561–570.

Oatley, K. (1993). Social constructions in emotions. In M. Lewis & J. M. Haviland (Eds.), *Handbook of emotions* (pp. 341–352). New York, NY: Guilford Press.

Oatley, K., & Jenkins, J. M. (1996). *Understanding emotions.* Cambridge, MA: Blackwell Publishers.

Ohman, A. (1993). Fear and anxiety as emotional phenomena: Clinical phenomenology, evolutionary perspectives, and information-processing mechanisms. In M. Lewis & J. M. Haviland (Eds.), *Handbook of emotions* (pp. 511–536). New York, NY: Guilford Press.

Oliver, S. J., & Toner, B. B. (1990). The influence of gender role typing on the expression of depressive symptoms. *Sex Roles, 22,* 775–791.

Parrott, W. G. (1991). Mood induction and instructions to sustain moods: A test of the subject compliance hypothesis of mood congruent memory. *Cognition and Emotion, 5,* 41–52.

Pennebaker, J. W., Hughes, C., & O'Heeron, R. C. (1987). The psychophysiology of confession: Linking inhibitory and psychosomatic processes. *Journal of Personality and Social Psychology, 52,* 781–793.

Philippot, P. (1993). Inducing and assessing differentiated emotion-feeling states in the laboratory. *Cognition and Emotion, 7,* 171–193.

Potts, R., Camp, C., & Coyne, C. (1989). The relationship between naturally occurring dysphoric moods, elaborative encoding, and recall performance. *Cognition and Emotion, 3,* 197–205.

Reis, H. T. , & Wheeler, L. (1991). Studying social interaction with the Rochester Interaction Record. In M. P. Zanna (Ed.), *Advances in experimental social psychology* (Vol. 24, pp. 269–318). San Diego, CA: Academic Press.

Robin, L., Feldman Barrett, L., Pietromonaco, P. R., & Eysell, K. M. (1998). Sex differences in daily experience of emotions. Unpublished data.

Robins, L. N. & Regier, D. A. (1991). *Psychiatric disorders in America: The epidemiologic catchment area study.* New York, NY: Free Press.

Robinson, M. D., Johnson, J. T., & Shields, S. A. (in press). The gender heuristic and the database: Factors affecting the perception of gender-related differences in the experience and display of emotions. *Basic and Applied Social Psychology.*

Roseman, I. J., Antoniou, A. A., & Jose, P. E. (1996). Appraisal determinants of emotions: Constructing a more accurate and comprehensive theory. *Cognition and Emotion, 10*, 241–277.

Ross, M. (1989). Relation of implicit theories to the construction of personal histories. *Psychological Review, 96*, 341–357.

Rothkopf, J. S., & Blaney, P. H. (1991). Mood congruent memory: The role of affective focus and gender. *Cognition and Emotion, 5*, 53–64.

Russell, J. A. (1994). Is there universal recognition of emotion from facial expression? A review of cross-cultural studies. *Psychological Bulletin, 115*, 102–141.

Scherer, K. R., Wallbott, H. G., & Summerfield, A. B. (1986). *Experiencing emotion: A cross-cultural study.* Cambridge University Press.

Shaver, P. R., Wu, S., & Schwartz, J. C. (1992). Cross-cultural similarities and differences in emotion and its representation: A prototype approach. In M. S. Clark (Ed.), *Emotion* (Review of Personality and Social Psychology, Vol. 13, pp. 175–213). Newbury Park, CA: Sage.

Shields, S. A. (1984). Distinguishing between emotion and nonemotion: Judgments about experience. *Motivation and Emotion, 8*, 355–369.

Shields, S. A. (1987). Women, men and the dilemma of emotion. *Review of Personality and Social Psychology, 7*, 229–250.

Shields, S. A. (1991). Gender in the psychology of emotion: A selective review. In K. T. Strongman (Ed.), *International review of studies on emotion* (pp. 227–247). New York, NY: Wiley.

Shields, S. A., & Koster, B. A. (1989). Emotional stereotyping of parents in child rearing manuals, 1915–1980. *Social Psychology Quarterly, 52*, 44–55.

Shweder, R. A. (1993). The cultural psychology of the emotions. In M. Lewis & J. M. Haviland (Eds.), *Handbook of emotions* (pp. 417–434). New York, NY: Guilford Press.

Small, A., Gessner, T., & Ferguson, T. (1984). Sex role and dysphoric mood. *Sex Roles, 11*, 627–638.

Smith, C. A., & Ellsworth, P. C. (1985). Patterns of cognitive appraisal in emotion. *Journal of Personality and Social Psychology, 48*, 813–838.

Smith, C. A. & Lazarus, R. S. (1993). Appraisal components, core relational themes, and the emotions. *Cognition and Emotion, 7*, 233–269.

Speltz, M. L., & Bernstein, D. A. (1976). Sex differences in fearfulness: Verbal report, overt avoidance and demand characteristics. *Journal of Behaviour Therapy and Experimental Psychiatry, 7*, 117–122.

Sprecher, S., & Sedikides, C. (1993). Gender differences in perceptions of emotionality: The case of close heterosexual relationships. *Sex Roles, 28*, 511–530.

Stapley, J. C., & Haviland, J. M. (1989). Beyond depression: Gender differences in normal adolescents' emotional experiences. *Sex Roles, 20*, 295–308.

Stearns, C. Z. (1993). Sadness. In M. Lewis & J. M. Haviland (Eds.), *Handbook of emotions* (pp. 547–561). New York, NY: Guilford Press.

Stearns, P. N., & Haggarty, T. (1991). The role of fear: Transitions in emotional standards for children, 1850–1950. *The American Historical Review, 96*, 63–94.

Strube, M. J., Berry, J. M., Goza, B. K., & Fennimore, D. (1985). Type A behavior, age and psychological well-being. *Journal of Personality and Social Psychology, 49*, 203–218.

Wagner, H. L., MacDonald, C. J., & Manstead, A. S. R. (1986). Communication of individual emotions by spontaneous facial expressions. *Journal of Personality and Social Psychology, 50*, 737–743.

Wallbott, H. G., Ricci-Bitti, P. & Banninger-Huber, E. (1986). Non-verbal reactions to emotional experiences. In K. R. Scherer, H. G. Wallbott, & A. B. Summerfield (Eds.), *Experiencing emotion: A cross-cultural study* (pp. 98–116). Cambridge University Press.

Watson, D., & Clark, L. A. (1992). On traits and temperament: General and specific factors of emotional experience and their relation to the five factor model. *Journal of Personality, 60,* 441–476.

Watson, D., & Clark, L. A. (1994). *The PANAS-X: Manual for positive and negative affect schedule-expanded form.* University of Iowa.

Weissman, M. M., & Klerman, G. L. (1977). Gender and depression. *Trends in Neurosciences, 8,* 416–420.

Weissman, M. M., & Klerman, G. L. (1985). Sex differences in the epidemology of depression. *Archives of General Psychiatry, 34,* 98–111.

Wierzbicka, A. (1992). Talking about emotions: Semantics, culture, and cognition. *Cognition and Emotion. 6.* 285–319.

Wierzbicka, A. (1995). The relevance of language to the study of emotions. *Psychological Inquiry 6.* 248–252.

Wood, W., Rhodes, N., & Whelan, M. (1989). Sex differences in positive wellbeing: A consideration of emotional style and marital status. *Psychological Bulletin, 106,* 249–264.

PART IV

Epilogue

14. Gender and emotion: Notes from a grateful tourist

KAY DEAUX

The juxtaposition of gender and emotion creates a fascinating crucible for addressing a host of important questions. As the chapters in this volume show, these questions cover a range from biology to social construction; from internal experience to stereotypes and belief systems; from individual reactions to interactional scripts and societal norms. To some, the topic of gender and emotion might seem to define a relatively simple set of questions: for example, do women and men experience emotions differently, or do they express their emotions in different ways? Yet, as inevitably is the case when one tries to frame topics of gender in terms of easy "what are the sex differences" questions, simple formulations soon give way to more complicated, multilayered issues that demand attention.

Emotion, because it is such a complex area of study in its own right, offers a challenging partnership for students of gender. The study of emotion raises questions about the nature of the experience and the form of expression. Both gender and emotion require us to look beyond the individual to the context in which behavior occurs, and more broadly, to the norms and social representations that frame those contexts. Together, these two areas of study demand much of us. Simple, unitary process explanations do not go very far in elucidating the phenomena; complexity and multilevel analyses are imperative.

In recognizing this state, the editor and the authors of this volume should be applauded. Together, they offer a wealth of information and descriptions of many exciting and productive research programs. Much of this work was new to me, and it was a treat to have the opportunity to learn about all that has been going on at the interface of gender and emotion. Throughout the volume, many themes and issues are introduced, several of which I would like to pursue a little further here. These include the following: (1) beliefs about difference; (2) the nature of shared meaning and cultural construction; (3) the ubiquity of status; (4) the importance of context; and (5) the dynamics of social interaction. Finally, I will close with some ruminations on questions that, for me at least, represent future lines to be pursued.

Beliefs about difference

The associations between gender and emotions are ubiquitous. As Zammuner (this volume) observes, the dichotomy between emotionality and rationality is central to many analyses of gender, and indeed, emotionality is associated with femininity in most measures of both stereotypes and self-assessed masculinity and femininity. Similarly, Jansz (this volume) points to "restrictive emotionality" as a key aspect of masculine identity. Beyond the general term "emotionality," however, are a multitude of questions and distinctions that need to be confronted in order to understand both the beliefs and the realities of the gender-emotion linkage. Among the questions are the difference between the experience and the expression of emotion; among the distinctions are the specific types of emotion that are of concern.

Some years ago, LaFrance and Banaji (1992) concluded that differences between women and men are more apparent in emotional expression than in emotional experience (and further, that differences in expression are heavily dependent on certain contextual and methodological features). The weight of evidence presented in this volume bears out that conclusion. Sex differences in emotional expression are reported in terms of smiling (Hall, Carter, & Horgan, this volume; LaFrance & Hecht, this volume), facial and gestural expressiveness (Hall et al., this volume), the expression of positive emotions (Alexander & Wood, this volume), fear and sadness (Madden, Feldman Barrett, & Pietromonaco, this volume), depression (Fivush & Buckner, this volume), shame and guilt (Ferguson & Eyre, this volume), and in crying (Vingerhoets & Scheirs, this volume). At the same time, no differences in experienced emotion are found for fear, sadness, shame, guilt, or anger.

The expression-experience divide is best addressed by considering the kinds of constructions and socialization experiences that shape gender. There is ample evidence (see especially the chapters by Brody and by Fivush & Buckner, this volume) that the socialization of boys and girls differs in the emotional domain. Parents talk differently to girls and boys, they react differently to girls and boys, and girls and boys themselves anticipate different reactions for different types of emotional expression. As adults, these learned patterns continue to play out, although they are often made more intricate by subtle situational contingencies.

Once an association between gender and emotion is observed, or simply believed to be true, self-fulfilling prophecies can take over, affecting both what people notice and what inferences they make. As a consequence of these processes, gender and emotion will be more strongly linked than the reality would warrant. Even interpretations of one's own emotional experience are framed by more general beliefs about difference. Consider the study by Grossman and Wood (1993), which compared people's beliefs about sex differences in emotion with their own self-reports of emotion. To the extent that people believe that women are more emotional than men, they reported experiencing more extreme emotions (if they were women) and less extreme emotions (if they were men), in comparison to those less prone to believe in the gender difference.

Other cognitive processes can also exacerbate the perception of difference between women and men. The phenomenon of "shifting standards" is one example. As Biernat and her colleagues (Biernat & Manis, 1994; Biernat & Kobrynowicz, 1999) have shown, observers use different standards of comparison when judging women versus when judging men. In the case of aggression, for example, a woman is judged with reference to the range of aggressive behavior considered typical for women, while a man is judged relative to other men. As a consequence, a behavior that is moderately aggressive in an overall sense will be seen as highly aggressive for the woman but only average for a man. Further, because the woman's behavior is seen as more extreme, it will also be considered more diagnostic of her character than will the equivalent, but more neutrally rated, behavior by a man (Biernat & Manis, 1994). This same phenomenon of different standards can easily be applied to perceptions of emotional expression as well.

As this work suggests, beliefs about the link between gender and emotions can be influenced by the form in which a question is asked. This methodological warning applies to the domain of self-report as well. As Madden and her colleagues discuss, individuals asked to make retrospective self-reports of their emotion are often presented with very general questions such as "I seldom feel sad or depressed." Such phrasing presents at least two problems: first of all, the frame of reference (What is "seldom": once a day, once a week, once a year?) is rarely included with the question. Second, the task of summarizing some unspecified number and form of relevant events can make the self-reporter, much as the observer, more likely to be influenced by stereotypic beliefs. In this regard, it is interesting to note that Feldman Barrett and her colleagues have found no differences in self-reported experience of emotion when women and men did on-line diary recordings of emotional reactions, whereas they did find stereotypic sex differences in global, retrospective measures.

A similar distortion in the beliefs of observers could occur if there are selective biases in what situations come to mind when a global judgment is requested. If the exemplars of anger, for example, more frequently include fights on the ice hockey rink or rugby field than parent-child altercations, then beliefs about the gender-emotion link might reflect this biased information storage. To the extent that differences in emotional expression by women and men show situation specificity, then a selective initial coding could result in subsequent overgeneralized stereotypic beliefs.

In summary, considerable evidence is presented in this volume documenting differences in how and when women and men express emotion. The complexities of these patterns, often situationally-contingent, and the discrepancy between expression and experience, pose a fascinating set of questions dealing with the construction and interpretation of gendered emotions.

Shared meaning and cultural construction

Although much contemporary research on gender beliefs tends to conceptualize at the level of the individual, it is important to recognize that these beliefs are culturally shared constructions. Their power comes not from the individual, as a single information processor, but rather from the broad community support that they reflect. Communities or subcultures consensually share beliefs about a target group, communicate those beliefs among themselves, and act, often in concert, on the basis of those shared beliefs.

At the same time that we recognize that meanings are widely shared within a culture, we also need to be aware of the considerable variation that exists when one looks across cultures. On the one hand, a universalist view of emotion argues for the similarity of emotional experience across cultures. At the same time, it is widely recognized that the display rules for emotional expression can vary substantially between cultures. As Madden, Feldman Barrett, and Pietromonaco discuss in their chapter (this volume), the social meanings of various emotions such as anxiety and depression are not constant across cultures. Different connotations accompany the emotional labels, and they are applied to different circumstances. There are, it can be argued, different cultural narratives associated with emotional labels so that simple comparisons may be quite misleading (Shweder, 1993). On the one hand, these discontinuities argue for particular caution when one moves outside of a given cultural context. At the same time, the variations give us strong reason for making the effort to do comparative work that will extend our understanding of the complex construction of emotions and gender.

The embeddedness of gender stereotypes in a set of shared meanings and experiences, and indeed the elements of a narrative account of gender, emotion, and role, is illustrated in the work of Alexander and Wood (this volume). Working within the framework of Social Role Theory (Eagly, 1987), these authors argue that caretaking responsibilities are linked to the expression of positive emotions. Thus women, who more often assume the caretaking roles in a society, will in turn be more likely to express positive emotions. I might note that this explanation appears to assume that the caretaking experience is most likely to be positive, thus justifying the presumed link between caretaking and positive emotions. A series of negative experiences while caretaking would not so easily be linked to either the experience or the expression of positive emotions, despite the prescriptive stereotypes that might exist. At the same time, one can certainly agree that the normative expectations for caretaking – the prescriptive element of stereotypes – are for positive expression.

Alexander and Wood extended their analysis with a between-culture comparison of Pakistan and the United States. Here they found that although Pakistani women and men differ in their reported experience of emotion, there are no sex differences in the expression of love or joy. The same pattern was found when respondents were asked to estimate the cultural stereotype, suggesting that normative expectations are reflected in individual self-assessments.

This comparison between the US and Pakistan emphasizes the importance of looking at the issue of cultural construction more broadly. To date, the vast majority of the work in emotion and gender, like much social psychological work in general, has been based on data conducted primarily in North America and secondarily in Europe. An exception to this pattern, and one offering considerable potential for future investigations, is the international data bases to which Fischer and Manstead both refer and make use of. The ISEAR database, initiated by Klaus Scherer and his colleagues (Scherer, 1988; Scherer & Wallbott, 1994), includes 37 countries in 5 continents, and reports on questionnaire results for 7 different emotions. More targeted is Vingerhoets and Becht's (1996) project, which focuses on crying behavior among adults from samples in 30 different countries. With these data bases in hand, Fischer and Manstead were able to move to a cultural level of analysis, considering, for example, how gender differences in emotion may vary between countries with relatively high versus relatively low participation of women in economic life.

Their results were fascinating and, to the authors, somewhat surprising. In using a Gender Empowerment Measure (an index computed by the United Nations on the basis of the percentage of seats in parliament held by women, the percentage of administrators, managers, professional and technical workers who are female, and women's share of earned income in the country in question), they hypothesized that sex differences in reported emotion would be greater in societies with a low GEM than in societies with a high GEM. Instead, the opposite was found, whereby men and women were *more* similar in their emotional expression in cultures where women's economic participation was low. This is, in fact, the same pattern found by Alexander and Wood, that is, that sex differences in expressing the specific emotions of joy and love were greater in the more individualistic US than in the more collective Pakistan.

Alexander and Wood suggest that their findings could be expected, in that the specific emotions of love and joy would be socially desirable for both women and men in a collective culture that places high value on family, emotional interdependence, and mutual caring. Fischer and Manstead, however, need to account for a broader range of emotional expression, including anger, disgust, and fear, that seems less easily explained by an emphasis on intimacy and caring.

In offering an interpretation for their results, Fischer and Manstead consider the different constitutive and regulative rules (Levy, 1984) that might emerge in the two types of culture. Referring to the Markus and Kitayama (1991) analysis of interdependence, they note that collectivist cultures value interdependence between members and adjustment to others. In contrast, Fischer and Manstead suggest that individualistic cultures may need to develop task differentiation in order to maintain the social unit in the face of strong pressures toward independence. If this task differentiation is gender-linked, then sex differences in emotional expression would emerge. (The logic of this argument would seem to allow for other systematic patterns of difference, such as in ethnicity or social class, if designated groups were associated with different tasks and in turn with different emotional expression.)

Framing the analysis somewhat differently, one might speculate that the shared meanings and social constructions of collective societies imply, or indeed require, greater consensus among the members. To be part of a collective means that one must agree on common interpretations of group experience. In contrast, the potentially idiosyncratic definitions that characterize a more individualized society can be dysfunctional to the culture as a whole. To communicate regularly with others requires a common vocabulary – in this case, a common emotional vocabulary – which, even if used in a context that emphasizes division of labor in role assignment, nonetheless emphasizes the common base of the collective enterprise.

The ubiquity of status and power

Status and power emerge in many of the accounts in this volume as a factor to be reckoned with. Echoing lively debates in the literature on the causes of gender differences in nonverbal communication, the discussions in this volume attest to both the pervasiveness and to the complexity of the gender–status–power nexus. LaFrance and Hecht directly confront questions of power and status in their meta-analysis of smiling. Hall and her colleagues also consider status and power in their model of influences on smiling (although arriving at somewhat different conclusions). Madden et al. consider the ways in which status and power can affect anxiety and depression; Kring explores the association between expressions of anger and dominance; and Ferguson and Eyre speculate on the ways in which power and status differences between women and men might affect the expression, and the consequences of expression, of shame and guilt. Further, Social Role Theory and models that use expectation states theory (Berger, Rosenholtz, & Zelditch, 1980) make specific assumptions about status and gender, that in turn are used by Alexander and Wood to predict differential emotional display.

The ubiquity of status and power in the analysis of gender and emotion certainly indicates that many investigators have found these concepts helpful. Yet the data themselves are not always clear and suggest that we need to probe further. One issue that seems critical to me in this debate is the need to make a distinction between status and power. Power, as defined by Fiske and others, refers to "asymmetrical control over another person's outcomes" (1993, p. 623). In other words, if a person has power, he or she has the ability to control resources or the outcomes of another person. Status does not in itself confer power over another person or another group. Rather status refers to the evaluation that the person or group has, relative to other persons or groups that are being compared. With reference to groups, status hierarchy rankings are relatively stable. In the case of ethnicity in the US, for example, an ordering with Euro Americans at the top, followed by Asian Americans, and then Hispanics and African Americans (the latter two quite close with some recent shifts in ordering) is consistently reported (Sidanius & Pratto, 1999). Similarly, higher status for males than females in Western society is generally accepted, and indeed assumed by expectation states theory (Berger et al., 1980).

Although status and power can surely covary, they are not wholly interchangeable. One may have power over another person with no real difference in status. Consider the student guards and prisoners in the well-known Stanford prison experiment, for example, or prisoners of war and their captors in a more naturalistic setting, where status is essentially equivalent but power is quite discrepant. Similarly, it is possible to have status without any capability of directly influencing the outcomes of another (a student at a prestige university may have more status than one in a community college or technical school, but the former has no inherent ability to exert power over the latter). Further, there are some important differences in the way that we conceptualize status and power. Whereas status hierarchies tend to be relatively stable and slow to change, power has a more dynamic quality to it. From one situation to the next, the ability to control another's outcomes may change. This is not to deny that some of those who hold power may continue to do so over time and place; but it is to recognize the greater potential for changing dynamics and situational variation that power entails.

Why is this distinction between status and power, to the extent that it is valid, a potentially useful distinction for our analysis of gender and emotion? First, emotionality in general may be more strongly associated with status than with power. For example, evidence suggests that people see more emotion in the faces of people who are lower in status (women contrasted with men, and African Americans contrasted with Caucasians) than in the faces of people higher in status (Keltner, 1995). Similarly, emotionality in general is more associated with the female stereotype than with the male, with children as opposed to adults, and so on. It is not evident to me that the same association between emotionality and power exists, that is, that people who have more power are assumed to be less emotional than those who have less power. (Consider the images of crazed dictators, for example, as one example of high emotionality being associated with high rather than low power.)

A second reason for the distinction is the hunch that different emotions may be associated with the status dimension in contrast to the power dimension. This possibility calls to mind the distinction made by Fischer (1995) between "powerful" emotions, such as anger and disgust, and "powerless" emotions, such as sadness, anxiety, and despair. However, the difference that I am suggesting here is that power and status can be untwined, and that some emotions might have a stronger association with one rather than the other dimension. Anger, for example, might be more strongly linked to the display of power and the exertion of control than to status per se. More simple affective states, such as happiness or depression, could be more closely associated with the status dimension. Such statements at this point are quite speculative (such is the license of a commentator whose expertise lies somewhat outside the field of commentary!), but may be worth pursuing.

Apart from the question of differential patterns of emotional expression, the distinction between status and power has some cogency, I think, if we look at the work described in this volume. Perhaps it is seen most clearly in the work of LaFrance and Hecht on smiling. In proposing their theory of expressivity demand, these authors distinguish between gender expressivity norms and situational demands for expressivity. In effect, I believe, they are making a distinction between status and power. Meta-analytically considering the main effect of gender, LaFrance and Hecht find a moderately strong effect, showing that all else being equal, women smile more than men. Separately, they looked at the influence of power as established by experimental manipulations such as the ability to hire the partner or to praise or punish the partner. Although their analysis does not allow us to make a direct comparison of the variance accounted for by each dimension, as main effects, their conceptualization is consistent with a status–power distinction.

Hall and her colleagues also address the issue of smiling and gender, but the distinction between status and power is not so easily uncovered here. Although their model specifically defines status relative to others as a potential influence, their reporting of findings tends to merge status and power, such that the relative influence of one or the other cannot be determined. It is suggestive, however, that when they talk about "equating differences in status," they find strong gender differences. Perhaps in this instance it is power that is being equated, and the omnipresent status difference associated with gender is what is most strongly associated with smiling. Consistent with this speculation is the authors' report that manipulations of power are not associated with differences in smiling. Support for the association of positive emotions with status is also provided by Alexander and Wood, although these authors do not address the question of power as distinct from status.

Whereas smiling and general positivity might be more associated with status than power, it seems plausible that emotions such as anger have a closer link to the power dimension. Kring, for example, discusses findings that clearly relate anger expression to dominance and power, but she finds no clear evidence for a consistent gender (i.e., status) difference. How far this distinction can be pushed, and how many emotions might clearly line up on one dimension versus the other, is unknown at this point. In my view, however, it is a set of questions worth pursuing.

Given the possible independence of power and status, it seems unwise to overinterpret the link between gender and power. Assuming that power is inevitably linked to gender risks a kind of essentialist thinking that moves us very little from the earlier ways of thinking about gender. Power is, in my view, a much more dynamic process that needs to be interpreted in light of the particular situational dynamics.

To further document these dynamics, our research needs to look more carefully at situational variations in the gendered consequences of power, perhaps making more frequent use of designs that allow within-subject comparisons across a variety of situations that differ in their power relevance, as well as in content area.

The importance of context

Recommendations to take a more context-specific view are not limited to the investigation of status and power. As numerous chapters in this volume attest, context is critical to a full analysis of the link between gender and emotion. Recall just a few of the findings reported in previous chapters. In the case of anger, Kring shows that women report more anger in interpersonal contexts than do men, but show no difference in situations involving injustice to another. Fivush and Buckner detail the ways in which expressions of sadness, and particularly differences between women and men in such expressions, are dependent on context. Both Hall et al., and LaFrance and Hecht show the importance of situational moderators, such as the presence of others or the visibility of a camera, on smiling. Zammuner, in exploring lay theories about the nature of emotional experience, found that whether one observes sex differences "depends on what you look at".

These findings and interpretations are totally compatible with the "now you see it, now you don't" position that Brenda Major and I offered in our contextual model of gender (Deaux & Major, 1987). Proposing a model for a full range of sex differences in social behavior, we argued that simple main effects rarely capture the phenomena, and that interactions of gender and context are the rule. Further pushing the contextual analysis, Marianne LaFrance and I (Deaux & LaFrance, 1998) opened the lens to include more system and culture-based definitions of context.

Whereas many investigators recognize and point to the influence of context on both the expression and the experience of emotion, the conceptual status of context is, as Shields notes in her chapter, undertheorized. Many contextual variations have demonstrated influence on gender. Deaux and Major (1987), in their analysis, considered both characteristics of the other person in an interaction (e.g. gender beliefs, certainty of expectations), as well as situational moderators such as the saliency of gender cues. LaFrance and Hecht (this volume) include contextual factors such as the presence of an audience in their analysis of smiling behavior. Hall et al.'s model of the nonverbal communication of emotion includes other's expectations and audience characteristics (e.g. adults versus children) as potential moderators of gender effects.

Shields also notes that the presence of an audience typically has a strong effect on gendered expression.

Context effects are not limited to immediate situational variations, however, as Shields comments as well. Rather, a full contextual analysis needs to consider the broader social, cultural, and historical arena. From this perspective, one needs to think about gender and emotion as a domain of social representation (Moscovici, 1998), in which meanings are communicated and shared within cultures and may well differ substantially between cultures. Accounts of emotion and gender might also benefit from the kind of historical analyses that Stewart and her colleagues conduct (Stewart & Healy, 1989; Stewart & Ostrove, 1998). These investigators have considered how the historical period influences career and family orientation, identity development, and political involvement, as well as some personality dimensions. I can imagine a similar kind of analysis that would consider the prominence and variation of emotional display for women and men across time and place. Brody also suggests the value of this kind of analysis, pointing to the work of Cancian and Gordon (1988) as one example of normative changes. These authors found that the display rules of emotional expression for women, as represented in popular magazines, have changed over time, paralleling increasing autonomy of the female gender role. Other archival sources might be able to identify trends in actual experience and expression as well.

The dynamics of social interaction

Context emphasizes the forces that impinge upon actors, whether those forces be ones easily marked in the immediate context or more subtle and deeply embedded in the culture at large. Somewhat in contrast to this emphasis, but equally important to understanding the gender-emotion coupling, are the dynamics of ongoing social interactions. What do actors bring to an interaction? What are their goals? How are social interactions characterized or appraised? What functions do emotions serve in the exchange? These questions are all relevant and important to our understanding of gender and emotion.

Shields quotes Joseph Campos in describing the psychological study of emotion as one concerned with the relation of goals and strivings to emotions. From this perspective, emotions can act in the service of desired end states as well as immediate expression. Similarly, emotions can act as social signals that shape the course of interaction. Emotional expression thus becomes, at least in part, a choice (which could be nonconscious as well as conscious) to convey a particular message or to achieve some desired goal. Often these choices are made in recognition of the likely consequences, as defined by the norms or operating rules of the culture – norms that are not defined independently of gender. As just one example of such gendered norms, think of the work of Stoppard and Gunn Gruchy, described by Shields, showing that only women anticipate negative sanctions if they do not express positive emotions toward others. Further, as Brody describes, these contingencies are learned early.

Implicit understanding of the norms that exist can lead women and men to make different choices. Clark's work (again cited by Shields) shows that expressing sadness will result in attributions of neediness and lower likability, unless one is a woman expressing sadness to a man, in which case the negative consequences are minimized. In thinking about these issues, I was reminded of a chapter written many years ago by Edward Jones and Thane Pittman (1982), in which they identified a set of self-presentational strategies that people use to gain particular attributions from others. In describing supplication as one such strategy, they suggested that a person using this strategy was attempting to be seen as helpless, thereby arousing a sense of obligation in the other. As an illustration of the strategy, they invoked a "traditional female," who claims helplessness so that her equally traditional male partner will jump into the breach. Despite the stereotypical quality of the illustration, the authors noted that this strategy can be seen as a form of influence, getting things done that one wants done. Similarly, now nearly 20 years later, Madden and her colleagues suggest that expressions of fear and sadness may also serve agentic needs, eliciting responses from others and accomplishing an indirect form of social influence.

In another domain, I have suggested that one's choice and presentation of a social identity is based in part on the functions that identity can serve for the person (Deaux, Reid, Mizrahi, & Cotting, 1999). Thus an identity is not merely a cognitive category into which one fits (or is placed by others), but rather must be seen as a way in which an individual expresses herself and accomplishes desired goals (in the case of identity, these can range from self-understanding to social interaction to intergroup competition). Similarly, in the case of emotion, it seems that we can regard emotions as vehicles that a person chooses to facilitate the movement from one state to another. Extending the metaphor, these journeys are taken not in a vacuum but with an awareness of the terrain, or more concretely, the norms and expectations that the social system has established. Rather than viewing people as captives of their emotions, as some earlier literatures might suggest, this perspective presents the alternative (or at least supplemental) view of people as the directors of their emotional presentations, using them in conjunction with other forms of expression, to accomplish their goals.

Questions I still ponder

Having read all of the chapters in this volume, I know far more about emotions and the ways they intricately interweave with gender than I ever knew before. The questions are important, the findings are fascinating, and the promise for contribution to our understanding of human behavior is considerable. As I read these chapters, I found myself increasingly attuned to the display of emotions around me (and indeed, to my own emotional patterns) and often had new insight on the ongoing events. Yet, of course, not all of the questions have been answered or in some cases, even raised. Much work remains for those who study emotion and gender. Some of the areas in which questions still remain for me, 13 chapters later, are described below. Perhaps some of these questions can serve as a point of departure for future investigators in this field.

What are the variations on the interaction theme?

For the most part, studies of gender and emotion have focused either on the individual, comparing the average woman to the average man in terms of experience or expression, or on dyadic interaction – and in the latter case, primarily heterosexual dyads. Explorations of emotion and status, for example, typically use a male and a female, assuming that the latter has less status or power than the former. Typically as well, these dyads are undergraduate college students, mostly white and mostly middle-class.

What kinds of emotional patterns might we find if we broadened the lens of our inquiry? Do the emotional expressions and exchanges of gay and lesbian couples, where we might assume equal ascribed status between members of the dyad, differ from those of the heterosexual couple? What do we know about emotional expression in friends (either same sex or not) as compared to strangers? How do parents and children interact emotionally? How do adults interact with their older parents? In each of these domains, I can imagine studies that would carefully look at the communication of emotions between participants, ideally with an interactional frame of analysis that could look at sequences of exchange as well as single expressions.

I can also imagine moving the study of gender and emotion beyond the dyad, to interacting groups or even to crowds. How do ongoing groups, such as a soccer team, a fraternity or sorority, or a work group, establish norms or display rules for the expression of emotion? How are the rules applied and how are they enforced? Students of social cognition have begun to explore the ways in which shared cognitions develop and are communicated. Can we do the same for the emotional realm? And in documenting these learned patterns or display rules, can we hone in on the ways in which gender becomes part of the formula, so as to regulate the expression of anger, of sadness, or pride?

In all of these extensions, we need to go beyond the middle-class college student to gain a more representative view of emotional behavior. In this regard, it was interesting to note that LaFrance and Hecht found stronger sex differences in smiling among Euro Americans than among African Americans, and among college students compared to non-students. I was reminded here, too, of the classic work by LaFrance and Mayo (1976) on racial differences in gaze behavior. How many other forms of emotional expression might show class and ethnic variations?

How do we best deal with the biological aspects of emotion?

Few of the authors directly or extensively addressed the biological components of emotion and possible gender-linked patterns. One exception to this statement is the chapter by Vingerhoets and Scheirs, in which they consider possible biological bases for crying behavior. On the one hand, they find that there are no differences in crying behavior in children under 2 years of age (despite the activity and temperament differences that Brody cites). On the other hand, they suggest that the observed adult differences in crying could be biologically based – more specifically, related to hormones such as prolactin. Although the data to support the hypothesis are mixed at best, Vingerhoets and Scheirs argue in favor of continued empirical and theoretical work on biological bases. A few other authors note the possibilities for biological influences (e.g., Hall, Alexander and Wood, Fivush and Buckner), but for the most part they see a relatively minor role for biology in accounting for observed gender variations.

With the increasing popularity of functional magnetic resonance imaging (FMRI) techniques, there is the potential to learn a great deal more about the physical concomitants of emotions. It is possible, for example, that the distinction between the experience and the expression of emotion might be better understood by brain localization studies. Is the expression of emotion, in so far as it is regulated by display rules and norms, likely to involve cognitive as well as emotional areas of the brain? At the same time, such data will need to be interpreted with caution, particularly given the history of distortion and biased interpretation in studies of sex differences in the brain (Shields, 1975). Demonstrations of sex differences, if they are found in FMRI data, can not speak unequivocally to causality. Further, the kinds of contingencies that investigators have already documented, such as in task or context, will need to be systematically incorporated in the investigations. Too easily one can imagine the arbitrary use of single scenarios that are biased in themselves, with the result that the biological data could be misinterpreted to claim a physical reality for that which is a methodological confound.

How much complexity can our theories handle?

Often investigators focus their attention and their investigation on a single emotion (e.g. crying, smiling) or on a small set of related emotions (e.g. shame and guilt, anxiety and depression), with the reasonable goal of making the investigation of manageable size and complexity. Less frequently, investigators simultaneously consider the expression of multiple emotions (see Brody's chapter as an example of this strategy). One of the advantages of this volume is that it allows the reader to make comparisons across emotional domains, in some cases perhaps simulating a combined-emotion strategy. These combined, more complex views of emotion seem important to pursue. Often, I suspect, people do vacillate in their emotional experience, shifting between emotions and perhaps deciding upon which to express. Or, as one of the transcripts of Fivush and Buckner shows, an emotion like sadness can be transformed to happiness. Can we develop methods and models that can track these alternations and changes?

The functional basis of emotional expression might also be explored further. As some of the chapters suggest, men and women may react with different emotions to the same precipitating event. Conversely, different events can produce similar emotional reactions. These possible variations give additional weight to the recommendation by Stephanie Shields that we need to theorize context more directly. Additionally, they suggest the need to gain a greater understanding of how emotions shape as well as index the nature of events.

The multiplicity of emotional expression might well be accompanied by a multiplicity of methods. A wide variety of methods have been described in this volume, including observation of interactions, scenario responses, cross-cultural databases, diary studies, and physiological recording. This variation testifies to the creativity of investigators in this area, as well as to the complexity of the phenomena. Indeed, several of the authors specifically recommend that multiple methods be routinely used when exploring the connections between emotion and gender. With that recommendation in mind, I offer a few candidates for inclusion in the methodological tool boxes of future investigators. Relatively little archival work has been done, for example. The longitudinal study of child-rearing manuals, referred to earlier, is one valuable example of an archival approach. Many other media sources could be considered as possible archival sources as well, providing a means to bring an historical dimension into the interpretive frame. More qualitative assessments of emotional experience and expression might also enrich our understanding of the links between gender and emotion (see Denzin & Lincoln, 1994). Ethnographic approaches, for example, could provide opportunities for more cultural and subcultural extensions, extending the bounds of the more limited cultural picture we now have. Extended interviews allow the complexity of emotional expression as well as emotional stereotypes to emerge (Bloom, 1998). Discourse analysis would provide a richer database for analyzing the exchange and joint construction of emotional states, perhaps charting some of the alternations and changes that I noted above.

Gender and emotion is clearly an area replete with possibilities for creative work. From my outsider's perspective, I am impressed by how much of that work has been done and how sophisticated some of the analyses have become. We are long past the stage of simplistic questions, essentialist assumptions, and easy answers. The ground has been prepared, and many of the building blocks are on site. Where work remains is in developing the models that will put these blocks together, describing the processes that link component parts and gaining a better understanding of the constancies and variations across setting, time, and culture. Such an account, when fully constructed, will advance our understanding of both gender and emotion. I have great faith that the editor, the authors, and the readers of this volume will lead us to that next stage.

References

Berger, J., Rosenholtz, S. J., & Zelditch, M., Jr. (1980). Status organizing processes. *Annual Review of Sociology, 6*, 479–508.

Biernet, M., & Manis, M. (1994). Shifting standards and stereotype-based judgments. *Journal of Personality and Social Psychology, 66*, 5–20.

Biernet, M., & Kobrynowicz, D. (1999). A shifting standards perspective on the complexity of gender stereotypes and gender stereotyping. In W. B. Swann, Jr., J. H. Langlois, & L. A. Gilbert (Eds.), *Sexism and stereotypes in modern society* (pp. 75–106). Washington DC: American Psychological Association.

Bloom, L. R. (1998). *Under the sign of hope: Feminist methodology and narrative interpretation*. Albany, NY: State University of New York Press.

Cancian, F. M., & Gordon, S. L. (1988). Changing emotion norms in marriage: Love and anger in US women's magazines since 1900. *Gender & Society, 2*, 308–342.

Deaux, K., & LaFrance, M. (1998). Gender. In D. Gilbert, S. T. Fiske, & G. T. Lindzey (Eds.), *Handbook of social psychology*, 4th edn. (pp. 788–827). New York, NY: McGraw-Hill.

Deaux, K., & Major, B. (1987). Putting gender into context: An interactive model of gender-related behavior. *Psychological Review, 94*, 369–389.

Deaux, K., Reid, A., Mizrahi, K., & Cotting, D. (1999). Connecting the person to the social: The functions of social identification. In T. R. Tyler, R. M. Kramer, & O. P. John (Eds.), *The psychology of the social self* (pp. 91–113). Mahwah, NJ: Lawrence Erlbaum.

Denzin, N. K., & Lincoln, Y. S. (1994). *Handbook of qualitative research*. Thousand Oaks, CA: Sage.

Eagly, A. H. (1987). *Sex differences in social behavior: A social-role interpretation.* Hillsdale, NJ: Erlbaum.

Fischer, A. H. (1995, August). *Gender and emotions: The role of powerlessness.* Paper presented at the International Congress of Psychology, Montreal, Canada.

Fiske, S. T. (1993). Controlling other people: The impact of power on stereotyping. *American Psychologist, 48*, 621–628.

Grossman, M., & Wood, W. (1993). Sex differences in intensity of emotional experience: A social role interpretation. *Journal of Personality and Social Psychology, 65*, 1010–1022.

Jones, E. E., & Pittman, T. S. (1982). Toward a general theory of strategic self-presentation. In J. Suls (Ed.), *Psychological perspectives on the self, Vol. 1* (pp. 231–262). Hillsdale, NJ: Erlbaum.

Keltner, D. (1995). Signs of appeasement: Evidence for the distinct displays of embarrassment, amusement, and shame. *Journal of Personality and Social Psychology, 68*, 441–454.

La France, M., & Banaji, M. (1992). Toward a reconsideration of the gender-emotion relationship. In M. S. Clark (Ed.) *Emotion and social behavior* (pp. 178–201). Newbury Park, CA: Sage.

LaFrance, M., & Mayo, C. (1976). Racial differences in gaze behavior during conversations: Two systematic observational studies. *Journal of Personality and Social Psychology, 33*, 547–552.

Levy, R. I. (1984). Emotion, knowing, and culture. In R. A. Schweder & R. A. Levine (Eds.), *Culture theory: Issues on mind, self, and emotion*. Cambridge University Press.

Markus, H. R., & Kitayama (1991). Culture and the self: Implications for cognition, emotion and motivation. *Psychological Review, 98*, 224–253.

Moscovici, S. (1998). The history and actuality of social representations. In U. Flick (Ed.), *The psychology of the social* (pp. 209–247). Cambridge University Press.

Scherer, K. R. (Ed.) (1988). *Facets of emotion*. Hillsdale, NJ: Erlbaum.

Scherer, K. R., & Wallbott, H. G. (1994). Evidence for universality and cultural variation of differential emotion response patterning. *Journal of Personality and Social Psychology, 66*, 310–328

Shields, S. A. (1975). Functionalism, Darwinism, and the psychology of women: A study in social myth. *American Psychologist, 30*, 739–754.

Shweder, R. A. (1993). The cultural psychology of the emotions. In M. Lewis & J. M. Haviland (Eds.), *Handbook of emotions* (pp. 417–434). New York, NY: Guilford Press.

Sidanius, J., & Pratto, F. (1999). *Social dominance: An intergroup theory of social hierarchy and oppression*. New York, NY: Cambridge University Press.

Stewart, A. J., & Healy, J. M. Jr. (1989). Linking individual development and social changes. *American Psychologist, 44*, 30–42.

Stewart, A. J., & Ostrove, J. M. (1998). Women's personality in middle age: Gender, history, and midcourse corrections. *American Psychologist, 53,* 1185–1194.

Vingelhoets, A., & Becht, M. (1996). *The ISAC study: Some preliminary findings.* Paper presented at the International Study on Adult Crying Symposium, Tilburg, the Netherlands.

Indexes

AUTHOR INDEX

Studies in Emotion and Social Interaction

First Series
Editors: Paul Ekman and Klaus R. Scherer